D0843207

Enlightenment Orpheus

THE NEW
CULTURAL
HISTORY
OF MUSIC

SERIES EDITOR   **Jane F. Fulcher**

SERIES BOARD   Celia Applegate
Philip Bohlman
Kate van Orden
Michael P. Steinberg

Enlightenment Orpheus:
The Power of Music in Other Worlds
Vanessa Agnew

VANESSA
AGNEW

Enlightenment
Orpheus

The Power of Music

in Other Worlds

OXFORD
UNIVERSITY PRESS

2008

OXFORD
UNIVERSITY PRESS

Oxford University Press, Inc., publishes works that further
Oxford University's objective of excellence
in research, scholarship, and education.

Oxford   New York
Auckland   Cape Town   Dar es Salaam   Hong Kong   Karachi
Kuala Lumpur   Madrid   Melbourne   Mexico City   Nairobi
New Delhi   Shanghai   Taipei   Toronto

With offices in
Argentina   Austria   Brazil   Chile   Czech Republic   France   Greece
Guatemala   Hungary   Italy   Japan   Poland   Portugal   Singapore
South Korea   Switzerland   Thailand   Turkey   Ukraine   Vietnam

Published by Oxford University Press, Inc.
198 Madison Avenue, New York, New York 10016

www.oup.com

Oxford is a registered trademark of Oxford University Press

Publication of this book was supported by the Dragan Plamenac Publication
Endowment Fund of the American Musicological Society.

Library of Congress Cataloging-in-Publication Data
Agnew, Vanessa.
Enlightenment Orpheus : the power of music in other worlds / Vanessa Agnew.
   p. cm.
Includes bibliographical references.
ISBN 978-0-19-533666-5
1. Music—Germany—18th century—History and criticism.   2. Music—Germany—
18th century—Philosophy and aesthetics.   3. Burney, Charles, 1726–1814—
Travel—Germany.   4. Music and tourism—Germany.   I. Title.
ML275.3.A36 2008
780.943'09033—dc22   2007027106

9 8 7 6 5 4 3 2 1
Printed in the United States of America
on acid-free paper

For my parents, Patricia and Neville,
who love music and learning,
and for Kader and Sefa,
who sing in many languages.

ACKNOWLEDGMENTS

This book has received generous financial support from the Office of the Vice President for Research, the Rackham Graduate School, the Dean's Office of the School of Literature, Science, and Arts, and the Department of German, Dutch, and Scandinavian Studies at the University of Michigan, which supported my research leaves. A Caird Fellowship from the National Maritime Museum in Greenwich allowed me to conduct preliminary research, while postdoctoral fellowships from the Graduiertenkolleg Reiseliteratur und Kulturanthropologie at the Universität Paderborn and the Centre for Cross-cultural Research at the Australian National University provided forums for developing the project in its early stages. Additional research trips to Germany were funded by a Franklin Research Grant from the American Philosophical Society and a Richard H. Popkin Research Travel Award from the American Society for Eighteenth-century Studies. I would like to gratefully thank my host institutions, the Musikwissenschaftliches Seminar at Humboldt-Universität and the Forschungszentrum Europäische Aufklärung in Potsdam, and the Alexander von Humboldt Foundation for granting me the Dr. Theo and Waltraud Michael Research Fellowship in Musicology, which allowed me to spend a balmy spring in Berlin completing the revisions on the book.

I have been fortunate to have immensely kind and supportive colleagues at the University of Michigan, colleagues whose enthusiasm for interdisciplinarity provides an ongoing source of inspiration—Kerstin Barndt, Pascal Grosse, Julia Hell, Kader Konuk, Andy Markovits, Johannes von Moltke, Helmut Puff, Robin Queen, Scott Spector, George Steinmetz, and Silke Weineck. Steven Whiting, Amy K. Stillman, Naomi André, David

Porter, Vivasvan Soni, and members of the Eighteenth-century Studies Group offered valuable feedback and encouragement, while two departmental chairs, Geoff Eley and Fred Amrine, cultivated my diffuse interests and provided generous backing for the project. I am especially grateful to members of my writing group—Kerstin Barndt, Julia Hell, and Kader Konuk—who freely gave their ideas, time, and friendship. Their wisdom, tactful probing, and lively input have greatly improved this book and made for a rich and exciting intellectual life. I am indebted to them all.

For the support I received while researching and writing in Germany, Britain, and Australia I would like to thank Christian Kaden and Karsten Mackensen at Humboldt-Universität's Musikwissenschaftliches Seminar and Brunhilde Wehinger at the Forschungszentrum Europäische Aufklärung. Ernst-Eugen Schmidt, Thomas Betzwieser, Renate Schlesier, Gisela Ecker, Hartmut Steinecke, Annegret Laubenthal, Wilhelm Söhnge, Paul Turnbull, and Nigel Rigby also offered helpful suggestions at various stages of the research and writing. The staff at the Australian National Library, the Staatsbibliothek unter den Linden, and the Hatcher Library at the University of Michigan, in particular Beau Case, Marcy Toon, and Kathryn Beam, helped with numerous acquisition and permission requests. Philip Schwartzberg kindly made the map.

I have been inspired and encouraged by a wider community of scholars who have provided input at critical junctures in the life of the project. Jonathan Lamb, Iain McCalman, Harry Liebersohn, Philippe Despoix, Helmut Peitsch, Nicholas Thomas, Michael P. Steinberg, Richard Leppert, and Philip V. Bohlman graciously read and commented on sections of the manuscript; Celia Applegate, James Chandler, Simon During, John Noyes, Sanna Pederson, Alvaro Ribeiro, Peter Sabor, and Ian Woodfield also made suggestions that helped steer me in the right direction. I thank them for spurring me on and for the model provided by their own research and generous collegiality.

My thanks are due, too, to my hardworking copyeditor, Ellen McCarthy, and my research assistants—Cassandra Borges, Adam Brown, Susan Buettner, Tina Cocadiz, Ela Gezen, Seth Howes, Raji Mittal, Simon Walsh, and above all Ben Allen—who assisted, always under time pressure, with great resourcefulness, forbearance, and humor. The students in my undergraduate courses on *Die Zauberflöte* and *The Power of Music* and in my graduate seminars, *German Music and Its Others* and *Wunderkammer,* provided a testing ground for some of my ideas. Their questions and comments certainly helped make the book a better one.

My commissioning editor at Oxford University Press, Suzanne Ryan, assistant editor Lora Dunn, and series editor Jane Fulcher have been a pleasure to work with, and I thank them for their enthusiasm, as well as their efficiency. Oxford University Press readers offered helpful reports, which I would also like to gratefully acknowledge.

Chapter 2 is based on my article "Listening to Others: Eighteenth-Century Encounters in Polynesia and Their Reception in German Musical Thought," *Eighteenth-Century Studies* 41, no. 2 (2008): 165–88. I am grateful to the publishers for their permission to reprint this material.

John Addison, Sabine Boomers, Gülsen Güner, Anne Harris, Ovidius Kanu Lomi, Teresa Pinheiro, Özlem Konuk, the Konuk-Oluklu family, the McFinton family, the Perpich-Jones family, the Sickman-Garner family, my stepmother, Nancy, my siblings Rose, Emma, Jonno, and Dave, and, above all, my dear parents, Patricia and Neville, have in their own ways helped keep me and this book afloat. I thank them profoundly for their care. Their curiosity, sociability, and music making often reminded me why I wanted to write the book in the first place. My greatest debts are to Sefa, the darling child who champs at my knee, and Kader, who is kindness itself. She kept the family happy, the household running, and the ideas flowing. What I know about goodness and generosity, I learn from her.

CONTENTS

ILLUSTRATIONS

Enlightenment Orpheus

IT WAS 1772 and travel was the rage. Captain Cook was en route to the Pacific to look for the prized terra australis incognita, and James Bruce was returning from Africa, where he had bagged the source of the Nile. That summer Charles Burney, the central figure in this book (figure 0.1), was in Europe to do some exploring of his own. While most English tourists favored Italy and France, our music scholar headed for the German states, then said to be too little traveled even by Germans themselves.[1] He ventured south along the Rhine to Munich, via the Danube to Vienna, then by post chaise to Prague, Dresden, Leipzig, and Berlin. From there he turned west to Hamburg and Amsterdam, arriving at last in Calais to catch the packet back to Dover. Along the way he heard folk songs, hornpipes, and shanties; operas, symphonies, chorales, and chamber works—music that was surprisingly powerful and numbingly dull. Along the way he performed and he listened.

Burney (1726–1814) is often remembered as the father of talented offspring, two of whom appear in this book. His son James (1750–1821) became a rear admiral, and his daughter Fanny (later Madame d'Arblay, 1752–1840) was a novelist, whose best-known work, *Evelina,* made her famous in her own day.[2] But there are other ways of thinking about the paterfamilias. Until Burney set foot on the Continent, the image of German music in Britain had been shaped by people like C. F. Abel and J. C. Bach, and the many composers, performers, and impresarios who toured or took up residence in the well-paying capital. German musical life, on the other hand—its courts, theaters, concert rooms, and churches, its burgeoning publishing industry and increasingly important journalistic activity, its repositories of ancient manuscripts and instrument collections, to say nothing

FIGURE O.1. George
Dance (1741–1825),
Charles Burney (1794). By
permission of the National
Portrait Gallery, London.

of its plebian musical traditions—all remained beyond the ken of most Britons. Burney's central European journey was thus unusual. It opened a vista on regions that had previously remained shuttered and turned him into an important cultural interlocutor between Britain and the German states. Though he had ample detractors, supporters came to think of him as a Captain Cook of the Continent, a traveler harkening after new and uncharted sonic worlds (figure 0.2).[3]

Travelers had commented on exotic song and dance since Tacitus remarked on the Germans. Prior to Burney, however, the pursuit of musical knowledge was not in itself a motivation for travel.[4] His journeys, including an earlier one to France and Italy in 1770, pioneered a new genre, the specialized musical travelogue. With this came a related set of epistemological claims about the capacity of travel writing to convey knowledge about music. Conducting a sociological study of music before sociology, Burney ascribed indexical status to music by asking who and what music was for, what it did, and what this in turn signified about society at large.

This book focuses on two journeys that year: the first, Burney's tour through central Europe and the Netherlands to conduct research for his universal history of music; the second, Cook's state-sponsored voyage to the

FIGURE 0.2. James Barry (1741–1806), *The Thames, or the Triumph of Navigation* (1791). By permission of the National Portrait Gallery, London. Charles Burney, at a keyboard, looks over the left arm of the water nymph, while Captain Cook (below Father Thames's compass) and other naval heroes pull the chariot toward Asia, America, and Africa.

Pacific, where voyagers remarked on Polynesian music. These journeys were linked by a minor biographical detail—Burney's son James sailed with Cook. More importantly, the journeys were representative of the Enlightenment enthusiasm for travel, and each in its own way provided a litmus test for ideas about music. Confronted by unfamiliar vernaculars and new performance practices, the travelers were forced to examine long-standing assumptions about music. Was music's action universal or relative? What was its social purpose? How did it mediate between societies? And on what grounds could one form of music be called superior to another?

The late eighteenth- and early nineteenth-century reception of these travel findings coincided with decisive cultural changes in western Europe, particularly in the field of music. At the beginning of our period in the 1760s and 1770s, German instrumental music was still considered inferior to French and Italian vocal music; yet, by the 1810s or so, the German states were no longer terra incognita, and German music was being called the very apogee of human artistic achievement. The task of this book, then, is to investigate the relationship between Enlightenment travel and evolving musical thought. By examining the kinds of cultural and political investments in Anglo-German writings about music, I argue that the musical encounter was a critical site for working out some of the new aesthetic ideas. At the same time, the musical encounter was used to articulate national and imperial imaginaries at moments of domestic tension.[5]

We can think of the musical traveler as an heir to the Neoplatonist tradition that emphasized music's utilitarian character. Among the many properties attributed to music were regulating labor, demonstrating power and intimidating enemies, rousing ire and inspiring bravery, socializing and educating the young, treating disease, and civilizing the savage.[6] We find these ideas expressed in a range of textual and visual sources that included travel reports, journalistic criticism, music histories, medical treatises, paintings, and plays. Although they remain in the background of this book, such ideas were, of course, also taken up by eighteenth-century composers, including Telemann, Gluck, Benda, Mozart, and Haydn, who adapted the theme of Orpheus and the "wonder-working bards" for their operas, cantatas, and other musical works.[7] Orpheus stood at the head of the operatic tradition with Peri and Monteverdi and continued to be well represented in musical works throughout the eighteenth century.

It seems fitting to refer to the Enlightenment engagement with Neoplatonic thought as Orphic discourse, named for the classical hero whose music exerted irresistible effects on its listeners. It would be the task of Burney and other travelers to investigate utilitarian ideas about music—

arguably the most tenacious idea in the history of musical thought. We will find that these cross-cultural encounters forced a reevaluation of traditional assumptions about music's agency. Listeners were not necessarily charmed, swayed, or improved; sometimes they were indifferent or hostile. Sometimes, too, they ceased to be listeners and became performers instead. If such findings had implications for music aesthetics and the emergence of music historiography in the late eighteenth century, they also had implications for ethnomusicological thought. Orphic discourse constituted a kind of ethnographic yardstick that categorized and hierarchically ordered people according to their musical practices. At the same time, this book argues against the notion of an aesthetic break between the eighteenth and nineteenth centuries by showing that utilitarian ideas were adapted to the new purpose of promoting serious music. In the early nineteenth century, claims about music's wondrous power became a basis for leveraging certain kinds of music over others.

Reading Orpheus

My historical argument is complemented by a metalevel that operates outside of time. Here, the Orpheus myth functions as a frame through which to read musical action. This frame can be understood, first, as the Enlightenment's inherited episteme, the intellectual and cultural legacy of classical antiquity that was both advanced and interrogated by eighteenth-century music scholars. Second, it serves the contemporary reader as an archetypal story about music's utilitarian potential by acknowledging how music acts in the world.[8] Via Orpheus we will thus examine the utopian possibilities and dystopian warnings about music's capacity for either constituting or dissolving society.

Orpheus is a familiar myth, but, since it is central to this book and its interpretation important for my argument, it is worth rehearsing here. The story deals with the archmusician Orpheus, whose bride Eurydice dies on their wedding day after being bitten by a snake. The inconsolable Orpheus travels, as Ovid tells us, to the underworld, where Orpheus sings to the gods and entreats them to return his bride to the land of the living. The gods are unexpectedly moved by his powerful music and grant his wish on condition that he not look back at Eurydice while leading her out of the underworld. Orpheus violates this condition, only to see her slip irrevocably into the realm of the shades. His grief now redoubled, the musician returns to his home in Thrace, where he renounces women for adolescent boys.

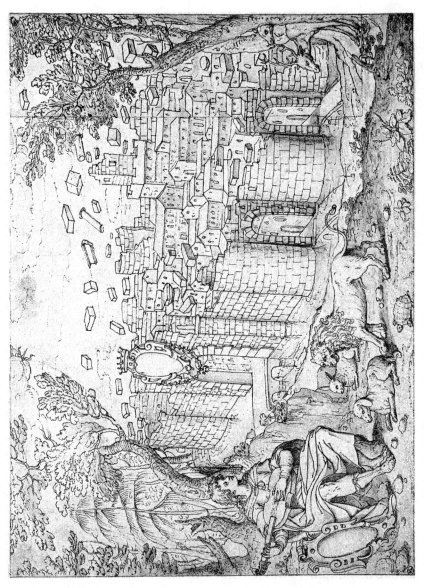

FIGURE 0.3. Anon., *Orphée charmant les animaux* (sixteenth century). Drawing, 27 × 36.3 cm. Photo: Madeleine Coursaget. Louvre, Paris, France. By permission of Réunion des Musées Nationaux/Art Resource, New York.

Still he sings, and his new listeners are the ones we remember him for—trees and plants, beasts, birds, rocks, and rivers that come to hear songs of mourning, regret, and forbearance (figure 0.3). Orpheus tunes the strings of his lyre as if to "temper them into a concord," evoking a "cosmic order, a pattern."[9] His musical idyll is interrupted, however, when, in the subsequent book of *Metamorphoses*, Ovid tells us that Orpheus is discovered by a group of Thracian women. Screaming, they swarm from the hillside to attack him. At first, his singing transfixes their spears and rocks. Then the women bang on their drums, blast their horns and flutes, and ululate riotously. His music loses force, for the frenzied women either do not listen or will not hear. Their missiles strike him, and they butcher the birds and animals. Then they set upon him, tearing his body to pieces. With this, the world grows silent, rivers weep, and the trees shed their leaves in grief. Orpheus's head, still singing, floats down the Hebrus with his lyre and washes up on the shores of Lesbos. At length, Orpheus is able to reenter the underworld to join Eurydice.[10]

Conclusion

Orpheus constituted a foundational, self-reflexive gesture for music scholarship in the late eighteenth century. This was articulated at the moment when music scholars were beginning to carve out their intellectual turf and to insist on their own specialist knowledge, as well as their prerogative to interpret music on behalf of the nonprofessional listener. With Orpheus as their emblem, scholars attempted to mediate a new place for serious music in relation to society as a whole. This attachment to reflexivity warrants the elevation of Orpheus to a hermeneutic paradigm for this book. As I contend, however, the Orpheus myth is also a discourse of alterity, a story about music's privileged responsibility vis-à-vis otherness. Orpheus's listeners—wild animals, trees, rocks, and savage women—exist outside the bounds of society, and his playing represents an effort to draw these listeners into the realm of the social.

We can thus see Orpheus as an ethical paradigm for one of our most pressing contemporary concerns: managing the boundaries of the societies in which we live. Instead of the right of blood or soil, criteria that are thought inherent to the subject, Orphic belonging is based on a form of social action. The mere act of listening—manifest as interest rather than pleasure—is what qualifies the listener for membership. In prioritizing the socially constitutive role of culture, Orpheus prompts us to ask how music can be used to manage this line between sociopolitical inclusion and exclusion. Within this perspective, musical agency is not just a discourse that was critically interrogated by the eighteenth-century traveler, then subsumed by aesthetic autonomy at the beginning of the nineteenth century. Orpheus was a prescription for action and a cautionary tale. The figure cautions us against the failure to listen and warns of destructive specular regimes. It urges attentiveness and presence as against noise, distraction, and deafness. It provides a lens through which to reevaluate questions about access and control over cultural representation, and it interrogates the locus of musical knowledge making.

Finally, this paradigm has at least one important implication for our understanding of modernity. Orpheus provides a mechanism whereby others can be proximated to hegemonic society through the medium of culture.[11] This model, it should be emphasized, describes more than just chains of cultural influence and appropriation, and it obviates the need to choose between the authentic and the hybrid, the pure and the mixed.[12] It offers instead a rigorous model of social inclusion, a model for the creation of a social group founded upon difference. Finally, because Orpheus acts on the margins of society, what is to be known about music—indeed what is to be known about society itself—must be investigated at that liminal edge.

CHAPTER ONE | Argonaut Orpheus

W E REMEMBER ORPHEUS as the heartbroken lover inventing music and poetry but forget his first love, travel. Before ever setting foot in the underworld, Orpheus was an Argonaut, a voyager to other worlds. His playing launched the *Argo* from the island of Lemnos; it saved the sailors from the Sirens and from rocks that imperiled the ship. In the end, it was our "tuneful Bard" who lulled the dragon so that Jason could steal the fleece.[1] Orpheus was also an Egypt traveler: There he was inducted into secret rites that he took back to Thrace, where they became known as the Dionysian mysteries (figure 1.1).[2] Finally, we come to the journey with which Orpheus is best associated, a descent into the underworld to reclaim his wife, Eurydice, dead on their wedding day from the bite of a snake. We hear him as he sings, slipping across the River Styx, past the three-headed dog, Cerberus, and through the realm of the shades to put his case before Hades and Persephone, the king and queen of the underworld (figure 1.2). Then comes his final important journey—the return to the land of the living and the fateful twist that denied him happiness.

Orpheus was always an artful traveler. Like travelers closer to our own time, he could claim to have gone farther than any man had gone before, seen things yet unseen, and returned with trophies unimagined. If all travelers have their tricks—their seven-league boots and antiscorbutic lemons—this was also true of our classical hero. It was his music that rendered travel possible by overcoming natural obstacles, negotiating forbidden boundaries, taming beasts, and persuading gods. His singing and lyre playing also made

FIGURE I.I. Orpheus Painter (fifth century BCE),
Orpheus among the Thracians. Red-figure krater from
Gela, ca. 450 BCE. Height 50.5 cm. Photo: Johannes
Laurentius. Antikensammlung, Staatliche Museen zu
Berlin. By permission of the Bildarchiv Preußischer
Kulturbesitz/Art Resource, New York.

possible what thence followed—power, knowledge, prizes won, and losses
recovered, or almost so. The relationship of music to travel was thus an
ontological one: Orpheus traveled with music and through it, for he went
where music enabled him to go.[3] Music's relationship to travel was also
epistemological: The musical journey produced knowledge about unfamiliar
places and peoples, whose playing, singing, listening, and silence would
suggest something about both their music and the strange new practitioners
themselves.

We can think of the Argonaut Orpheus, then, as a figure for reflecting on
later journeying and on the aesthetic, social, and political issues associated

FIGURE 1.2. François Perrier (1590–1650), *Orpheus before Pluto and Persephone.* Canvas, 54 × 70 cm. Photo: Erich Lessing. By permission of the Louvre/Art Resource, New York.

with Charles Burney's musical travel in the 1770s. Orpheus and Burney both
tell stories about travel's capacity to transform our understanding of music;
they show how music facilitated travel, structured the cross-cultural encounter, and shaped its interpretation. Beyond these simple resonances between the myth and its Enlightenment reanimation lie other parallels.
Burney and contemporaries like John Hawkins, Johann Nicolaus Forkel,
Christian Friedrich Daniel Schubart, and Padre Martini studied music in the
present with a view to writing its universal history. Theirs was a project that
hinged on determining the relationship between relativism and universality
and hence on making a synchronic (if piecemeal and often prejudicial) study
of the world's musical vernaculars.[4] Of course their historical project was also
a diachronic one and this brings me to the other important intersection
between Burney and Orpheus, the musicians who journeyed to retrieve the
past.[5] Historicizing music meant interrogating ancient claims about music
as ethos, and it meant comparing those claims with the way that music
worked in the present. Although classical conceptions of music as ethos
extended beyond the notion of musical utility found in the myth, Orpheus
has always been associated with this set of ideas. Taking the archmusician as
their emblem, eighteenth-century scholars wondered whether music could
still do the old things in the old ways. Could the sick be healed, savages
civilized, children better socialized, and whole nations advanced via improvements to their music? Those interested in broad anthropological
questions asked whether people could be compared and contrasted according
to their musical practices. If so, perhaps music could become an index for
categorizing people in ways that shed new light on the nature and development of human societies.

In subsequent chapters I return to eighteenth-century debates about
music and its impact on discrete types of listener, including the indigenous,
poor, and foreign. But here my concern is with eighteenth-century Britons
and Germans as the purveyors and interrogators of Orphic discourse and with
the role they played in developing ideas about music, travel, and national
belonging. Sometime between about the 1750s and the 1810s, the German
states would be transformed from a cultural terra incognita to Europe's
acknowledged "nation of music." The difficulty in understanding this shift
is, as Celia Applegate and Pamela Potter point out, compounded by the
difficulties in using the national paradigm in an age of cosmopolitan and
provincial identities.[6] While many scholars acknowledge this problem,
particularly with regard to the German states, the national framework still
tends to dominate our thinking.[7] Germany's rise to musical prominence is
explained, for example, in terms of the ascendance of German instrumental

music and the emergence of aesthetic autonomy, a set of ideas that gave new legitimacy to serious music, while the year 1800 is said to be the date that demarcates earlier functional conceptions of music from later ones that understood music on its own terms.[8] Implicitly, this narrative celebrates the triumph of German philosophical and aesthetic thought and marks the turning century as music's zero hour. Leaving aside for a moment the question of whether this shift was quite so neat, such explanations do succeed as an ex post facto justification for Germany's new cultural prominence in the nineteenth century. Yet they say neither how this shift occurred nor much about the professional, social, and political interests that impelled it. My wager is that, by focusing instead on the pan-European context and older cultural discourses like musical utility, we gain better insights into changing ideas about the value and purpose of music and about music as a means of managing the boundaries of gender, class, ethnicity, religion, and the state.

My intention is not to dismiss the significance of late eighteenth- and early nineteenth-century German cultural achievements but rather to argue against national isolation and monogenetic theories of aesthetic innovation in an age of self-conscious cosmopolitanism. When we examine the transnational context, it is clear that both Britons and Germans shared an interest in developing and promoting autochthonous forms of music making over and against France and Italy's long-standing dominance of the musical scene. The German states' cultural and political position within Europe created an impetus for change as German musicians sought to promote their music at home and abroad, and German writers looked beyond the German states for intellectual stimulus and recognition.[9] Britain was a natural focal point. Its global dominance and the strength of its intellectual institutions meant that it enjoyed unparalleled power and prestige, which lent a scholar like Burney special authority to map the German cultural and political scene.[10] We will find that the Enlightenment's musical mapping project contributed to the articulation of new national cultural imaginaries in Britain and the German states.[11]

Burney scholarship tends to emphasize the significance of his contribution to music historiography yet neglect his innovation, the musical travelogue. This bias toward historiography mirrors the general decline of scholarly travel writing: It is difficult today to think of the travel account other than as a genre whose entertainment value significantly outweighs its contribution to philosophical, historical, or political thought. In the 1770s, however, the hierarchy between history writing and travel writing was exactly inverted: Music history was still a new and untested intellectual enterprise, whereas travel writing was second in popularity only to the novel and was arguably the leading scientific genre. Yet it is also because travel writing had foundational significance to eighteenth-century music historiography and aesthetics that it warrants our attention. By attending to travel we come to understand the discursive underpinnings of musical thought and its social and political investments.

A Declaration of War

Our story begins with a letter written to Charles Burney in the summer of 1773 (figure 1.3). This yellowing document is not to be found where we would expect it to be—among the musician's manuscript papers in the Beinecke collection at Yale University, in the memoirs selectively compiled by Burney's daughter after the old man's death, or even in the scrupulously edited letters that have become a mainstay for researchers in the present.[12] Rather, the letter is housed in Hamburg, the city where it originated, together with other pieces of correspondence penned by a writer and teacher at the Hamburg Commercial Academy, Christoph Daniel Ebeling (1741–1817).

Although little is heard about Ebeling any more, during his own day he was well connected in intellectual and musical circles with acquaintances that included C. P. E. Bach, Friedrich Klopstock, Johann David Michaelis, Samuel Taylor Coleridge, and William Wordsworth.[13] He was also an important writer and cultural disseminator whose wide-ranging interests were channeled in writings on U.S. history, a ten-volume travel anthology, contributions to Friedrich Nicolai's *Allgemeine Deutsche Bibliothek* (1765–1796), and the coeditorship of a journal, *Unterhaltungen* (1766–1770).[14] Among his great passions was the cultivation of music. He published one of the earliest German music histories, "Versuch einer auserlesenen musikalischen Bibliothek" (1770), and, as the translator of Burney's first French and Italian tour, introduced German readers to a new way of studying and writing about music—the musical travelogue.[15] In the summer of 1773, when we pick up the story, he was all set to translate Burney's latest travel account dealing with the present state of German music.

However, examining Ebeling's letter in the Hamburg State and University Library, we understand why Burney's memoirist might have wished it had never been written. "Bella horrida bella et Tamesin multo spumantem sanguine cerno!"—"I see wars, terrible wars, and the Thames foaming with much blood!"—was the letter's opening salvo.[16] Having declared war on Britain, Ebeling went on to highlight each error and misjudgment in Burney's German travelogue. He pointed out that the Englishman had betrayed

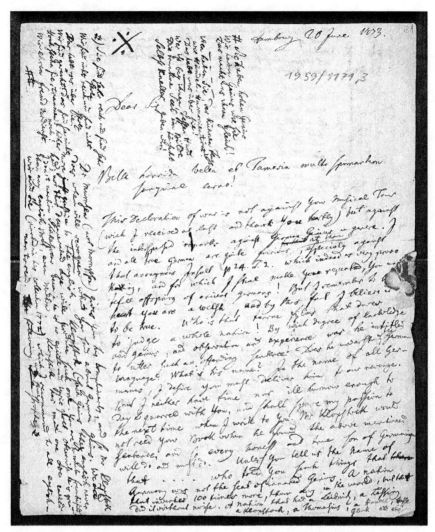

FIGURE 1.3. Christoph Daniel Ebeling's letter to Charles Burney, June 20, 1773. By permission of the Staats- und Universitätsbibliothek Hamburg.

his foreign friends when referring to their lack of genius, pedantic and labored music, impoverished literature, and ill-governed country. Burney's definition of Germany was also totally wrong: We are not "one people," he explained, for "History and Geography will acquaint You that we are composed of different clans or even little nations quite different from one another in dialects and customs, notwithstanding many of them have been altered by administration, mixture with foreigners, wars, migrations etc." Instead of talking about Germans as a whole, Ebeling thought Burney ought to have differentiated between Bavarians, Upper Saxons, Lower Saxons, and other kinds of Germans. Finally, Burney's political commentary missed the mark: Ebeling said that his observations were either well known, untrue, or too inflammatory for the censors in places like Prussia and Württemberg. The Hamburger conceded that the German states were not universally well governed, but, he said, "let even the [P]olish and the poor human fellow creatures in Eastindia tell the world who are the best men—the Germans who conquered Polonia, or the English who conquered Bengalia?" This was a reference to Friedrich II's political, administrative, and educational reforms in partitioned Poland, which Ebeling contrasted with the British East India Company's handling of a recent famine that had killed as much as a third of the Bengali population.[17] He ended his rant with a profession of fealty typical of the German eighteenth century: "I am of all Nations," he said, "but always a German when Germany is attacked."[18]

While we may be surprised by the degree of vitriol in this letter, Ebeling's uncertain cosmopolitanism was not out of the ordinary. Many of his contemporaries, including writer Oliver Goldsmith, made it clear that cosmopolitanism was never an easy condition of "world citizenship," which could be characterized by a sense of belonging to everywhere and nowhere: Goldsmith's *Traveller* is, in the end, a thoroughly national subject who returns home to ask why he ever "stray'd from pleasure and repose."[19] Immanuel Kant's essay *Zum ewigen Frieden* (On Perpetual Peace, 1795) similarly shows that cosmopolitanism was contingent upon firm local attachments: Visitors had to be hosted, yet they were also obliged to return home, making the cosmopolitan condition one of temporary sojourn rather than permanent mobility, exile, or migration.[20]

Contemporary scholars sometimes fall into the trap of overstating eighteenth-century cosmopolitanism's opposition to national affiliations and describe the philosophical position of thinkers like Voltaire, David Hume, Edward Gibbon, and William Robertson as one of "detachment" from national prejudice and commitment to a shared Europeanism.[21] My examples suggest, in contrast, that eighteenth-century cosmopolitanism was not opposed to regional or national chauvinism.[22] It embraced local and global affiliations, and both could be mobilized without necessarily offending each other. We can thus indulge in some speculative history and say that, had Ebeling responded directly to Kant, he would have argued that cosmopolitanism was not the precondition for lasting peace as Kant claimed. It was instead contingent upon an existing peace, and, when the chips were down, local allegiances had to prevail.

While Ebeling's admixture of cosmopolitanism and chauvinism could be seen as part of the late eighteenth-century Zeitgeist, his definition of Germanness is worth examining more closely. Ebeling balked at Burney's generalizations about Germany and insisted on a differentiation of Germans according to their respective imperial circles. At the same time, this citizen of an imperial free city turned Prussia into a metonymy for all of Germany. He might have contrasted British imperial abuses with Hamburg's press freedom, elected city assembly, and *Weltoffenheit*—its openness to the world. Instead, he sacrificed hometown achievements for some dubious gains.[23] Revising Polish administrative and legal codes, abolishing serfdom, and improving the educational system were reforms purchased at the cost of dividing Poland among Prussia, Austria, and Russia.[24] For the newly enlarged Prussia and, it would seem, for other German states, too, Britain's mishandling of its colonies was thus a means of leveraging the claim that eighteenth-century "Germany" was not just a colonial power; it was superior even to the great colonizer, Britain.[25] Ebeling's statements demonstrate, in other words, the nature of eighteenth-century political ambitions and the desire of many Germans to escape their provincial reputation and occupy a new place on the world stage.[26]

Striking is the ease with which music discourse was folded into this broader panoply of political concerns. As heirs to Romantic notions about aesthetic disinterest, today we tend to think of music as happily divorced from conflicts over identity, belonging, and state and imperial power. Music, we would like to think, is a universal language, the least instrumental and most harmonizing of the arts. Ebeling's attack on Burney shows, however, that music was debated with utmost gravity during the late eighteenth century and was increasingly important to German cultural and political life. His letter also shows how imperial discourse could become a bit player in a nationalized conflict over the status of music. This prompts us to investigate the extent to which music discourse was, even now—a good seventy-five years before Richard Wagner's belligerent musical nationalism—being marshaled in the service of German national and imperial ambitions.[27]

To understand what sparked Ebeling's "declaration of war" and the stakes in this Anglo-German relationship, we need to turn to Burney and Ebeling's earlier correspondence. In August 1771 Ebeling had issued the famous Englishman an invitation to visit Germany, saying he had read Burney's French and Italian travelogue and wished that his own nation would not be "entirely forgotten amongst the Italian, English and French Musicians." Germany, he added, had produced some first-rate musicians for export even to Italy, and it could boast "many considerable Genius's" whose vocal and instrumental music would be able to "rank amongst the best or at least amongst the good ones of any time and Nation." To prove the point, Ebeling appended his own abbreviated history of German music and offered to supply Burney with books. The classics of midcentury German musical writing were among the works Burney wanted to read—C. P. E. Bach's *Versuch über die wahre Art das Clavier zu spielen* (1753, 1762), Johann Mattheson's *Grundlage einer Ehrenpforte* (1740) and his translation of the first Handel biography (1761), Johann Adolph Scheibe's *Der critische Musikus* (1745), Friedrich Marpurg's *Historisch-kritische Beyträge zur Aufnahme der Musik* (1754–1778), and Johann Adam Hiller's *Wöchentliche Nachrichten und Anmerkungen die Musik betreffend* (1766–1770).[28] Entreating Burney to cross the sea, Ebeling assured his English colleague that he would find much of musical interest in the German states; Burney had only to see and hear for himself.[29]

Travelers and Hosts

It is axiomatic that cross-cultural misunderstandings provide a starting point for new insights. Anthropologists like Bronisław Malinowski and Claude Lévi-Strauss illustrate rather self-consciously that intellectual bumbling contributes to the researcher's knowledge. "Imagine yourself," says the author of *Argonauts of the Western Pacific,* "suddenly set down...alone on a tropical beach close to a native village."[30] With this act of sympathetic identification, the reader is to conjure up the first productive missteps taken by the anthropologist as he encounters his subject. Similarly, our cross-channel war of words between Burney and his German critics could be read as a case study in cultural misunderstanding and reflexive anthropological investigation. But it is also possible to see the dispute between Burney and the Germans as a story about the eighteenth-century's investments in travel and its capacity to contribute to collective imaginaries. The lessons to be learned in the collision of Anglo-German sensibilities must be gleaned not, so to speak, in the contact zone of Malinowski's tropical beach but in the archive. Occupying this metalevel allows us to see the traveler and the host as distinct entities and to thereby investigate their competing expectations of the journey. This collision of interests will show that music was *not* the sign of infallible or incontrovertible effects—of wondrous feats and triumphant victories. While the music of the Argonaut Orpheus might once have been transparent in meaning and force, in the eighteenth century travelers entered the modern age. From now on, the purpose of their journeys would be strictly contested, and music beset by problems of interpretation and value.

Interpreting Burney's journey depends, then, on whether we occupy the position of the traveler or the host. I do not mean to suggest that this "positionality" makes it impossible to describe what *really* happened when Burney trundled from one German court and town to the next listening to music: We will come to a stage-by-stage account of the journey later in the chapter. In this theoretical section, however, my interest is in the different stories that were told about musical travel and what these stories meant to their tellers.[31] By investigating the various meanings that were attached to the journey, we discover something about eighteenth-century traveling and what it stood for. Via the dual Anglo-German optic, we discover not only what musical travel could do but also what it was expected to do. And so, *pace* the scholars who see Burney's German problem (and conversely the Germans' Burney problem) as a case of "enflamed national sensibility," I see the Anglo-German dispute emerging from the burdens that were placed on music and mobility.[32] The antagonists' disagreement centered on the problem of competing cultural, social, and political agendas, for the traveling Burney did not hear what he had hoped to hear nor say what he had been expected to say. His traveling would thus highlight the political interestedness of music; it would show that the Germans' desire for greater musical recognition was incompatible with the kind of protosociological approach adopted by the traveling Englishman. Put another way, we could say that the aesthetic, critical, and historical views held by Burney and his interlocutors illustrate competing sets of interests and that musical thought during this period was coupled to the broader professional, cultural, and political purposes that it was intended to serve. Our definition of aesthetic history will be amended accordingly from a history of ideas with its own self-propelling logic to a project embedded in its social and political context and, to some extent, also constitutive of that context.

This then is a musical story told through travel and encounter. Scholars of the eighteenth-century encounter, as I am, think of travel writing as our bread and butter. Registered in these travel texts are the surprise, delight, incomprehension, illumination, revulsion, and indifference that convey the penalties and rewards of encountering other cultures. What we often lack, however, is a corpus of material that allows us to investigate both sides of the encounter equally: The traveler's voice dominates over subaltern ones, which remain less vividly preserved in material collections and the interstices of the travelogue. This imbalance has spawned an entire set of theoretical tools—from Greg Dening's and Anne Salmond's insistence on reconstructing both sides of a "double-sided history," to Bill Ashcroft, Gareth Griffiths, and Helen Tifflin's notion of "writing back," and Mary Louise Pratt's concept of "autoethnography."[33] In the case of Burney, however, we have a traveler's subject (Ebeling, among others), who literally does write back and does so volubly. The covalence of these voices allows for a more nuanced understanding of both Burney's journey and the stakes for his German hosts. At the same time, our case offers possibilities for theoretical generalization.

As I have suggested, we learn something about the encounter when we attend to the fact that journeys mean different things to travelers and hosts. Second, the bifurcated approach softens Edward Said's polemics about the (Western) traveler's discursive omnipotence.[34] By relativizing the traveler's position, we find that encounters were not necessarily adversarial: The traveled were sometimes complicit in, even advocates of, political projects structured by asymmetrical power relations.[35] Third, my approach recognizes a range of individual and collective interests and shows that these interests were not necessarily directly correlated to specific identity positions like ethnicity, social class, gender, or national affiliation. Instead, the journey turns out to be a site where alliances could be formed and conflicts articulated, a site of co-optation where traveler and traveled competed over the interpretation of the journey and over the broader uses to which such interpretations could be put. Finally, it shows that political interests at the micro- and macrolevels were not necessarily one and the same. The traveled sometimes pursued their own personal interests yet worked against collective ones. An example of this concerns indigenous participation in eighteenth-century British exploratory voyages. While these individuals were likely spurred by curiosity and personal ambition, inevitably they facilitated the very political projects—including missionization and colonial settlement—that spelled the radical transformation of their own societies.[36]

Eighteenth-century Anglo-German entanglements cannot, of course, be construed in the self-same terms. Still, my experiment involves transposing these postcolonial concepts to Europe to examine the ways in which discrete instances of cultural appropriation and transfer were implicated in larger-scale processes.[37] Rather than conceiving of intra-European travel in conventional terms—as an individual enterprise—we can think of it as having structural implications. Specifically, we can examine how and why Ebeling, the instigator of Burney's German journey, tried to recruit British intellectual resources for the making of what one could anachronistically call a German *Kulturnation* (cultural nation).[38] In a later chapter, this model allows us to examine how Burney's German adventures were also used to promote specific ideas of Englishness. And between these competing sets of German and British interests lay the journey itself. Investigating eighteenth-century music "in the field" was not the kind of exclusive enterprise it is today—the preserve of a select group of ethnomusicologists and anthropologists—nor was its addressee limited to the professional meeting and peer-reviewed journal. This was a project with national and transnational implications, and it was played out in the most public of arenas—not only in travelogues, journal reviews, letters, and parodies but also in theaters, concert rooms, and salons. With a correspondingly large and diverse range of people voicing their opinions, at stake were the professional interests of English and German music scholars, as well as the making and the reputation of nations and empires.

The Symbolic Capital of Travel

The Enlightenment was the great age of travel, and never before or since has it occupied so prominent a place in the European imagination. We can measure its significance by the quantity of published travel writing and by the sheer number of travelers (during the 1760s, there were, on average, as many as four thousand British travelers to the Continent each year).[39] However, we can also gauge the significance of travel by examining the careers of individual men. Journeying advanced working-class writers like Thomas Holcroft (1745–1809), son of a shoemaker and costermonger, whose livelihood improved after the publication of his *Travels from Hamburg through Westphalia, Holland, and the Netherlands* (1804).[40]

At the other end of the social spectrum was the grand tourist, whose visit to France and Italy was seen as a necessary culmination of the elite education process.[41] Writer James Boswell provides insights into the motivations for such travel. Following his own grand tour in 1764, Boswell drafted a letter saying that he had enjoyed the music in Mannheim but had been coolly received by the elector. Instead of being invited to dine, he had been forced to fraternize with "company that disgusted him." The slight must have been a deep one, for Boswell's letter (possibly addressed but not sent to the high chamberlain) concluded with the admonition for Britons to "shun the dominions of the Elector Palatine." In complaining about this troubled encounter, Boswell recognized that the relationship between the grand tourist and host was one of potential mutual benefit: Young noblemen "acquired polish in high company," while the ruler gained from having them "express their delight at his goodness." The expense involved in hosting was thus hopefully compensated by the traveler, who could praise the court abroad. Fostering a good reputation was all the more important when, as Boswell said, the court was so "very, very small" and thus had limited means of exhibiting its power.[42]

Others with an incentive to venture abroad were educated middle-class travelers like Charles Burney. Burney, it is sometimes said, would not have risen socially and financially had he relied solely on his abilities as a performer, composer, and harpsichord teacher to the rich and famous.[43] This is, of course, pure conjecture, yet it seems a reasonable assumption.[44] In the eighteenth century, being a professional musician carried a taint of the unrespectable that curtailed the individual's possibilities for social and even physical mobility. The musician's low status was marked on the body—boy singers were still sometimes castrated; musicians in service could not travel freely and were metaphorically, if not literally, kicked around (think of Mozart's ignominious handling by his Salzburg patron).[45] But rough and dismissive treatment made itself felt in psychic ways, too.[46] Covent Garden oboist William Parke remarked in his memoirs that musicians seeking employment were rarely dignified with the gentleman's presence. A steward or butler was sent instead to "haggle with them for a price, as they would for meat at the butcher's shambles."[47] While there were always exceptions to this base association of music with the muck and gore of the marketplace, the professional musician circa 1770 did not, as a rule, enter by the front door or share a place at the gentleman's table. As Mozart complained upon being seated near the cooks and the baker, the musician's station even among the servants was lower than he would have wished it to be.[48] Thus, while the general trend was toward increasing economic and creative independence, we should not underestimate the hard economic and social realities for the majority of late eighteenth-century musicians.

All the more remarkable then is Burney's ascent from metaphorical butcher's boy to consort of aristocrats and kings. As his biographer Roger Lonsdale has argued, Burney accomplished this rise thanks to his literary efforts.[49] Moreover, it was through his familiarity with famous travelers and his own travel credentials that Burney was able to first make his name as a writer. This connection between travel and literary and social recognition was spelled out by Thomas Nugent, author of one of the most used eighteenth-century guides to the grand tour: "Those who first distinguished themselves in the republic of letters," he said, "were all travelers, who owed their learning, name and reputation to different peregrinations."[50] Nugent was referring, of course, to the big names of antiquity, Homer and Herodotus, but by coupling travel with literary production and social mobility, he suggested a path to career advancement that even critics of travel could not really oppose.[51]

The Burney family understood this well: They traveled themselves, and their Queen's Square household hosted a steady stream of visitors. Consider, for instance, the weeks prior to Charles's departure for the Continent in early July 1772. Charles's son James left for a tour of the Pacific on the second

Cook voyage; with James on his way, the family welcomed into their home John Hawkesworth, commissioned by the Admiralty at Burney's instigation to produce the official account of Cook's previous voyage; next arrived William Hamilton, the British envoy to Naples and author of the first account of Vesuvius erupting; then came two Italian visitors, Giuseppe Baretti, who wrote travel accounts of Italy, France, Portugal, and Spain, and Abbé André Morellet, a visiting economist who had published a treatise on musical expression and imitation.[52] All these comings and goings suggest that travel must have been as popular a topic at the Burney dinner table as literature and music. More than this, travel offered a solution to the hardships of life as an independent musician and scholar during this period. Once Burney had earned his traveler's stripes, it was the publication of his travelogues and his history of music that opened the doors of London's smart houses—Sir Joshua Reynolds, Samuel Johnson and his circle, and ultimately the king himself.[53]

For a man like Burney, whose financial responsibilities weighed heavily until late in his life, such entrées were significant. They brought intellectual and social recognition, as well as material benefits that eventually included a position at court for his literary daughter Fanny.[54] Yet, there were also other ways of quantifying the value of travel to the traveler. Nugent, in his defense of the grand tour, had said that traveling was rewarded with a "high degree of reputation."[55] Johnson would invert this to say that the man who had *not* traveled was left with a sense of inferiority because he had not seen "what it is expected a man should see."[56] As Burney's experience bore out, however, what was a negative formulation for the (assumedly aristocratic) stay-at-home could be couched in positive terms for the middle-class traveler. The prestige of travel militated against the musician's low standing and gave middle-class individuals a degree of social mobility. To use Pierre Bourdieu's terminology, one could say that travel conferred symbolic capital—a reputation for competence and respectability that raised a person's social status.[57]

If travel made the man, in a sense it also made the nation. And it is this broader aspect of travel—largely neglected within Bourdieusian thought—that is of real concern for my argument.[58] During the eighteenth century, European states mounted large-scale expeditions that have come to be associated with names like Charles Marie de La Condamine, Louis Antoine de Bougainville, John Byron, Samuel Wallis, James Cook, and Alessandro Malaspina. The significance of these expeditions has typically been measured in terms of territorial and strategic gains, markets, natural resources, scientific findings, and the complex legacies of Europe's colonial past. Yet the value of travel extended beyond the collections now housed in the British

Museum, the Public Record Office, and the Bibliothèque nationale, for the return on travel also seemed to be nonmaterial. We see evidence of this in publications that claimed travel as the reigning national characteristic: Writers insisted that traveling was as English as roast beef; others said it was quintessentially European. Such claims suggest that the cultural and political work performed by the travel discourse operated within, as well as without the geographical and political bounds of the state: Travel positioned the individual within a domestic social hierarchy; it also positioned the nation relative to its neighbors and the rest of the world. Importantly, this positioning occurred on a scale of both economic and moral value.

Travel is still subject to hierarchical ordering. Tourists are compared unfavorably with backpackers and adventurers, while travelers generally attract stereotypes that play up their worst national features. During the eighteenth century, however, such typologies operated in converse fashion, with the scale tipping toward the positive pole in competition over the best, rather than the worst, sort of traveler. By competing over who possessed the most intrepid, knowledgeable, credible, and benign species of traveler, writers claimed to represent the world's leading travel nation. This was said about Britons—described in 1770 by an Italian resident in London as the world's "most active" people and as occupying the "head of mankind."[59] Perhaps this was to be expected of a country that sent ships to Antarctic waters on the chance they concealed a new continent. Yet curiously, such statements were also made about the German states, which sported notable travelers like Johann Reinhold and Georg Forster but mounted no large state-sponsored expeditions during this period.[60]

The inverse relationship between German travel's modest reality and its exaggerated claims can be traced in the work of Enlightenment writers. Occasionally, someone like Friedrich Nicolai conceded that Germans in fact traveled *less* than their European neighbors, but many others, including August Ludwig Schlözer, took the opposite tack. In his "Travel College" (*Reisecolleg*), a new course offered at Göttingen University in the winter semester of 1772, this pioneering statistician instructed his students that the Germans traveled "*more* often than perhaps any other people on earth" and that they could "count this reigning taste for travel...among [their] national characteristics."[61] That a pioneer of quantification played so loosely with the numbers might lead us to question the rigor of the statistical discipline. But it also raises some salient questions: What was at stake in occupying the pole position among Europe's traveling nations? And what was it about travel that promoted such hyperbole?

There has been comparatively little speculation about this discrepancy between reality and self-construction. However, one line of thought sees German travel discourse as a form of cultural compensation. German cultural and intellectual achievements, including travel, are said to have balanced out Germany's perceived lacks—a centralized nation-state, industrialization, and a large and durable empire. Hints of this argument were already circulating in the early nineteenth century, when Madame de Staël said that German pluralism came at the expense of its "political force" but at the gain of its "genius and imagination."[62] For Friedrich Ludwig Jahn, writing in 1810, this German "genius" was explicitly coupled with travel. Folk sayings like "He's as dumb as a nail in the wall" were supposed to confirm—albeit it in a backsy-forsy manner—the innate cleverness of the German and his ancient "travel drive."[63] This sort of argument has never really left us, notwithstanding rigorous critique by some contemporary historians and literary critics.[64] We find echoes of the compensation argument in contemporary scholarship, which ranks travel writers according to their expressions of relativism, humanism, and anticolonialism. German travelers and writers tend to come off well here. The German states' apparent lack of interest in "colonial adventure" becomes a way of emphasizing the disinterested, empathetic, and humanistic dimensions of travel while bracketing the larger sets of political interests within which such travel was in fact implicated.[65]

We may be justified in subsuming the discourse on travel under the rubric of German identity constitution when we consider that intense chauvinism was linked to German expansionism. By the same token, it is clear that there was always a strong ideological investment in promoting the notion of the "German wanderer" and playing up the superiority and disinterest of German cultural achievements.[66] In my view, these investments need to be disambiguated rather than taken at face value.[67] Moreover, the singularity/compensation argument implies a notion of German exceptionalism that is historically misleading. During the eighteenth century, it was not only Germans who participated in this competitive travel discourse: Western European states and elites generally were anxious to cast themselves as travelers and to emphasize the enlightened dimensions of their own forms of travel practice.

Understanding why they wanted to be hailed as Argonauts—Nugent's travelers of "high reputation"—calls for a word about the place of prestige within eighteenth-century philosophical thought.[68] By prestige (or "esteem," as it was often called), I mean a desire on the part of enlightened Europeans to think well of themselves and to have that high regard mirrored by others.[69] Whether it was Jean-Jacques Rousseau's *amour propre* or the more affirmative notions espoused by David Hume and Adam Smith, the desire for prestige was thought to motivate human action. Indeed, the very fabric of society was said to be tensioned by the ways in which the individual subject saw others and was, in turn, seen by them. Extending this principle to the realm of political economy, Smith argued that social approbation and wealth existed in reciprocal relationship: Since the rich were more highly regarded than the poor, the desire for approval became a powerful spur to the accumulation of wealth. In this way, Smith thought, individuals, like societies as a whole, benefited from the esteem of others.[70]

Prestige proposed a secular solution to the erosion of religiously sanctioned social and political hierarchies in the latter part of the eighteenth century. If we think of European states and elites as being engaged in a competition for high regard, with stakes that were individual, social, political, and economic, then the traveler occupied a privileged position in conferring or withholding some of that esteem. The individual traveler was simultaneously a beneficiary of travel's symbolic capital and an important stakeholder in this transnational competition. Bourdieu's insights are thus useful for understanding the ways in which individuals attempted to elevate their social position by invoking travel and its attendant gains. However, Germans, and indeed all Europeans, branded themselves as travelers not only because of travel's material associations. As I have already suggested, travel prestige was not confined to the internal boundaries of the nation-state (or, in the case of Germany, to a collection of states). By extending a Bourdieusian understanding of symbolic capital to the transnational context, we gain insights into how travel functioned across state borders. There were no obvious economic incentives underlying this transnational competition for status. Yet, in keeping with other forms of Enlightenment philosophy that exhibited a dual local/global character, individuals seemed capable of rising from their inherited position, just as nations were liable to rise or fall on some global barometer of value.[71] The traveler's journey was thus functionalized on behalf of local social and political interests, and, at the same time, it stood metonymically for the fate of the nation and/or the empire.

This helps explain why even those aggressive expeditionists, the Britons, cultivated their international reputation for travel. Britain was riding high after the Seven Years War, but, as I show in a later chapter, its global power belied domestic insecurities, particularly during the 1780s, when debates about national culture emerged in response to a range of political issues that threatened to transform British society. Cultivating a reputation for travel was, in other words, a way of stoking the home fires in response to domestic and international pressures. This also explains the motivations of those, like the Germans, whose literal claim on travel and its attendant capital was more tenuous. Transnationalizing the notion of symbolic capital thus demonstrates the problems with the German particularity argument—at least vis-à-vis the late eighteenth century. German travel discourse would become highly patriotic, even belligerent, and it would feed nationalist and colonialist projects during the Wilhelmine and Weimar periods. By the same token, the apparent continuity of the German travel discourse from the late eighteenth to the early twentieth centuries ought not to obscure the fact that the meaning and purpose of travel changed over time. This is to say, whatever jingoistic forms travel discourse later took, during the Enlightenment travel retained the outlook that was common to all Europeans. Playing the Argonaut meant being cosmopolitan, and being a "good" traveler—curious, perspicuous, benevolent, nonviolent, and commercial—meant exhibiting that prized set of ideas associated with enlightened liberal humanism. Styling oneself and one's compatriots as travelers was a proactive gesture—self-improving and of collective social and economic worth—and it meant taking the moral high road. As Burney found the day he stepped off the gangplank onto a foreign dock, to travel was to judge; it was to construct an image both of oneself and of others. And whatever Burney may have believed about the disinterestedness of his own project, eventually it would be brought home to him that musical travel was an act of contentious aesthetic and political adjudication.

The Traveler's Vantage

Traveling meant physical mobility, and with this mobility came the crossing of social, political, religious, and ethnic boundaries. This transgressive quality inclines us to think of the traveler as a lone individual, an outsider occupying a position of vulnerability within the host environment. Yet the traveler has always been an arbiter of difference. This helps to explain the special status of travel in the eighteenth century, for it was the traveler who held the ability to exercise a special set of judgments that tested and exposed the limits of the host's sociability. Travelers reported, for example, whether they were turned away, like Boswell at the Mannheim court, or welcomed and fittingly hosted; they determined whether the society was trade friendly like Tonga, which became known as the "Friendly Islands," or closed and protectionist like late eighteenth-century China, which acquired a correspondingly negative reputation.

In identifying travelers' privileges and obligations, I do not mean to follow Georg Simmel's insistence on the stranger's objectivity,[72] nor do I suggest with so-called standpoint theorists that travelers hold an automatic "epistemological advantage" by virtue of their outsider status.[73] Rather, my point is that the eighteenth-century traveler's vantage was itself privileged: Travel produced a specific form of knowledge making based on a common set of experiential and observational modes like eye witnessing and comparison. The traveler could compare the unfamiliar with the familiar, the strange with the yet stranger, and the past with the present. Many travel writers were conscious of this special status. For Burney, autopsy was a basis upon which to stress the superiority of his own observations—"pure" and "unadulterated" information was, he maintained, available only "at the source."[74]

Other travelers were more mindful of the burdens of comparison. In the account of her journey through Europe to Constantinople, Mary Wortley Montagu (1689–1762), for example, included among the traveler's "privileges" the liberty to fabricate, corroborate, witness, and, above all, compare cultures and interpret foreign customs. The English squire who never went farther than the farm gate could, Montagu thought, rest easy in the belief that local beer, golden pippins, and a rump of beef were the most delectable foods in the world. What the traveler possessed, on the other hand, was the spoiling knowledge of comparison—the superior delights of Greek wine, African fruits, Italian fig birds, and the brilliant sunlight of Constantinople.[75]

To travel was thus to compare, and this vantage was often literalized in spatial terms. We think of the mountain view in Caspar David Friedrich's painting *Wanderer Watching a Sea of Fog* (ca. 1818) as exemplifying the traveler's sovereign gaze: With his back to the viewer, the solitary traveler stands with one leg cocked in a posture of reflective contemplation as he looks at a mountain landscape shrouded in mist.[76] But whereas Friedrich's early nineteenth-century traveler has an interiorized gaze—the misty scene mirrors his psychological state—the eighteenth-century traveler operated in a less exalted mode. Enlightenment travel certainly emphasized subjective experience, as Laurence Sterne's sentimental travel writing shows, but the traveler's orientation was still a predominantly external one. Hazarding a generalization, I would say that, in contradistinction to nineteenth-century visual and literary conventions that sublated or fetishized difference and prioritized the viewer's emotional and mental worlds, eighteenth-century representational modes tended to uphold the polarity of cultural systems on which comparison was necessarily predicated. To the extent that eighteenth-century painters depicted travelers in their *voyages pictoresques,* travelers are shown as mediators, translators, and judges of foreign systems of meaning. Illustrations show them gesturing to new landscapes, peoples, and objects, and, as I show in greater detail later, these gestures demarcated what was exotic and unfamiliar. The traveler's task was to locate the traveled within an intelligible and useful system of value. This seems self-evident when we consider the ways in which European travelers described and tallied the non-European world and produced vast amounts of ethnological, physiognomic, cartographic, and visual data. However, travel was simultaneously a local activity with travelers like Giuseppe Baretti and Tobias Smollett criss-crossing the Continent, describing, comparing, and appraising its peoples and their cultural practices.[77] Domestic and intra-Continental forms of travel were obviously much more widespread than exploratory travel and, directly and indirectly, involved large numbers of ordinary people. Thus, it was not only the non-European world that was tabularized; European nations, too, were constructed in the eyes of their neighbors by the judgments and opinions expressed in travel accounts.

There was thus profit in being a traveler. As we will find in the following section, there was also profit in being traveled, something that Italy, a favorite destination for middle- and upper-class travelers, had enjoyed throughout the century. The German states, in contrast, were usually peripheral to the grand tour. Burney observed in regard to Vienna that the capital lay so far removed from England that travelers seldom visited and writers hardly reported on it.[78] Germans themselves identified this as a problem and emphasized that the German states would benefit from an increase in travel. Even decades later the problem persisted, and Goethe would ask polemically, "Germany, but where is it?"[79] In the 1770s many still thought of it as a terra incognita.[80]

Germany on the Umstroke

To many educated Germans, late eighteenth-century Britain occupied an almost mythical status. Intellectuals struggling against censorship and the constraints of patronage praised it as the land of manufacturing and commerce, thriving scholarly life, constitutional monarchy, and parliamentary institutions.[81] The orientation of northern cities like Hamburg, Hanover, Göttingen, Weimar, and Braunschweig was thus westward, and these "English outposts," as they have been called, served as important gateways for foreign ideas.[82] As traveler John Moore observed, however, this was also true of many smaller towns, where foreign correspondents, visiting scholars, translators, and publishers kept German readers supplied with the latest sentimental novels, plays, journalistic criticism, and music scholarship. Although Moore was not convinced that German readers necessarily gained an accurate picture of Britons through their reading of the English papers, he did note Germans' astonishment at the "acrimony and freedom" with which the English press dealt with people in positions of power.[83] This traffic in books, journals, and reviews, coupled with the reputation for free expression, ensured that Britain occupied a prominent place in the German intellectual imagination. Britain influenced the development of its scholarly and cultural institutions—particularly in the north German states—and contributed to a forum for voicing critical opinions, something we have come to think of as an emerging public sphere.[84]

The view from London was quite different. Despite the long Hanoverian reign and the ubiquity of Continental travel, the German states were not well known to most Britons, not even to outward-looking intellectuals like Burney. This is all the more striking given that Burney was one of Europe's foremost music researchers and his intellectual interests extended the length of Europe and beyond. More curious than most about musical diversity, he thought nothing of fetching to China or Russia for reports about exotic music and did not begrudge money, time, and health spent on a journey to Italy and France to collect his own research material. His substantial library included the latest, most authoritative accounts of not only western Europe but also Japan and China, central and southern Africa, and parts of Australia, the Pacific, and South America. His library also included a sampling of earlier, more fanciful works by writers like Johann Theodor de Bry, whose graphic depictions of the New World created a lasting impact on the European imagination.[85] Sources that dealt with the German states were, however, less well represented in Burney's library, and there is no evidence to suggest that he initially planned to tour that part of the Continent. He would never become a promoter of German contrapuntal music (not even after his German trip) and remained as committed to Italian vocal music as any Rousseauvian. As many scholars have observed, late eighteenth-century London was a musical mecca, and Burney perhaps felt that the best music could be heard right on his own doorstep: The Händels of the world seemed to come to England anyway, where they dropped their umlauts to became honorary Englishmen.[86]

To some extent, then, Burney's prejudices were those of his compatriots: Like the average educated Briton, he possessed little detailed knowledge of the German states or their cultural institutions.[87] For German musicians and publishers this was a source of obvious frustration. Referring pointedly to

Burney, C. P. E. Bach would complain in a letter to the music publisher Johann Gottlob Immanuel Breitkopf, for instance, that "in the whole of England there are perhaps only a couple of knowledgeable composers but they don't understand German, nor do they even want to." For both the composer and the music seller this meant a loss of professional and public recognition, as well as a loss of revenue.[88]

Power imbalances between centers and peripheries tend to skew the perspective toward the center, and, for the best part of the century, this state of affairs characterized the cross-channel relationship. Britain's global dominance meant that it exerted a potent gravitational pull, whereas Germany's tin-pot capitals must have seemed, at least to the educated and ambitious, like points of departure rather than alluring destinations. This is worth keeping in mind as a context for understanding the impediments to Burney's German journey. Italy and France were obvious destinations for a music scholar who wanted to gather information for a general history of music, just as they were obvious destinations for grand tourists: There was a well-beaten path that led south, at the end of which lay Europe's cultural storehouses. Traveling to the German states, in contrast, called for a degree of imaginative derring-do.

The imbalance suggests something about the German investment in Burney's journey, as it does about broader desires to newly envision the German states as the cultural and intellectual equal of the rest of western Europe. Yet it also serves as a corrective to contemporary historiography. In recent decades, the scholarly tendency has been to view the making of Europe's political and cultural institutions as either "imported" from the colonies or as the outcome of largely autochthonous economic, cultural, and political processes.[89] This polarization within contemporary scholarship means that the national context tends to have been overemphasized and pan-European relations deemphasized as contexts for understanding changes to eighteenth-century social and political life.[90] The study of intra-European travel shows, on the other hand, that, although we often locate the frontiers of European knowledge and understanding far from metropolitan centers—in the frozen reaches of Tierra del Fuego or coastal Tasmania—in fact there was much that remained hazy and ultimately productive right on Europe's own doorstep.

We can chart this in the cartographic conventions of the period. Early modern maps once included a space called the *umstroke,* an area on the edge of the map populated by vaguely located towns, beyond which lay sea creatures, ships, cornucopias, and cartouches.[91] Although, by Burney's day, mapmakers had renounced some of these flourishes in favor of greater sobriety, the umstroke was retained as a site of political or cultural imprecision and uncertainty. This makes it a useful figure for describing the hodgepodge of ducal principalities, free cities, bishoprics, and kingdoms that made up the German states during this period.[92] Although every brook and beck appeared on some scrupulously engraved maps, the German states still could not be satisfactorily imagined or totalized. We see this in the disagreement between Burney and Ebeling as they grappled with the question of how to refer to the German states. In response to Ebeling's accusation of geographical ignorance, Burney responded that he was thoroughly familiar with the German map, having learned about the "divisions" of the Holy Roman Empire as a schoolboy. Yet it was a question of perspective as to whether this space ought to be thought of as "Germany in general" (as Burney did) or as a discrete series of "circles" (as Ebeling preferred).[93] Whether highly detailed or sketchily drawn, it would seem that the map itself was not yet adequate to the ideological purpose—imagining national sovereignty and territorial coherence—that scholars like Thongchai Winichakul and Benedict Anderson have attributed to it.[94]

Travelogues of the period included relatively few maps: Illustrations and maps increased the marketability of books but also added to their expense, thereby absenting them from all but the most well-subscribed and authoritative travelogues. Their comparative scarcity thus makes them important for what they are able to tell us about the ways in which readers conceived of the German states. A map in *Travels through Germany, Bohemia, Hungary, Switzerland, Italy, and Lorraine* (1756–1757) provides one such example. First published in Hanover in 1740 by Johann Georg Keyssler (1693–1743), the work was popular among German readers—Mozart is said to have used it as a guide for his Italian journeys—and it quickly found its way into translation.[95] In Britain, it was read by Tobias Smollett, who said that Keyssler's laborious descriptions reminded him of the old adage that "the German genius lies more in the back than in the brain."[96] Samuel Johnson was more disposed to the work and compared it favorably with travel accounts by Richard Twiss, who wrote *Travels through Portugal and Spain in 1772 and 1773* (1775), and Richard Pococke, author of the important *Description of the East* (1743, 1745).[97] Keyssler's account was also probably read by Burney in preparation for his journey.

Burney would have found in Keyssler a wealth of information on antiquities, natural history, commerce, manufacturing, laws, customs, roads, and post stages. As the preface to the English edition claimed, this was a work devoid of "amorous intrigues, fictitious stories, and trivial observations," yet full of "lively descriptions, curious anecdotes, and ingenious remarks." In keeping with eighteenth-century travelogue conventions, entertainment was supposed to be reliably combined with instruction.[98] This promise of immediacy, utility, and accessibility was, however, belied by the message conveyed by the book's frontispiece, which depicted Keyssler's tour through central and southern Europe. The illustration, which I discuss in some detail, highlights the difficulties authors and illustrators faced in modeling travel, and it raises questions about travel writing's dependence on various forms of mediation and rhetorical legitimization. It will become clear that the traveler's great bugbear, the problem of credibility, was most acute when readers were confronted with the unfamiliar. Travel writers often attempted to overcome their credibility problem by insisting on the travelogue's reliability and usefulness. This rhetoric of utility had to do dual service. It was supposed, on the one hand, to erase the suspicion of mendacity that threatened all travelers' tales and, on the other, to establish the book's commodity value in a market already saturated with travel writing. The visual representation of Keyssler's journey seems to repeat this literary strategy. Using an accretion of rhetorical devices, the journey is visually modeled via a map, landscape, theatrical stage, and internal viewer.

Although Lorraine and northern Italy were well inscribed in the western European imagination, other legs of Keyssler's tour, like Bohemia, Hungary, and the north German states, were less so. This perhaps explains the cartographer's dependence on the visual rhetoric of the theater to convey information about the journey (figure 1.4). We see Mercury, the god of travel and commerce, holding a map juxtaposed against the topography that the map itself depicts—the onion-topped spires of what looks like a Bohemian hamlet, hilly landscapes, a river, forests, and, in the foreground, classical ruins evocative of the Italian leg of the journey. The map shows no state boundaries, only vaguely located regions and a welter of towns and rivers. Whereas cartographic conventions today prioritize place names in order of size and significance, this kind of ranking is largely absent in the Keyssler map. The wealth of geographical information makes the map difficult to read, and, to some extent, it is the surrounding apparatus—the ships that circle the Italian peninsula, the cartouche bearing the inscription "Keisler's [sic] Travels," and the classical references to the god Mercury and the ruins of antiquity—that confers authority on the image. It is, in other words, these forms of rhetorical staging that help legitimize the journey and ground it in its place.

The image is characterized by doubling—the repetition of map and landscape and the inclusion of a spectator, Mercury, who repeats the gaze of the external viewer. Such devices cast doubt on the author's and illustrator's

FIGURE 1.4. Johann Georg Keyssler (1693–1743), *Keisler's Travels*, frontispiece. By permission of the British Library.

capacity to effectively model the journey: What cannot reliably be conveyed once must be repeated and repeated in different forms—as map and topography, external and internal viewer, and the traveler's itinerary and mode of transportation. Further, the classical framing of the journey extends antiquity's imprimatur beyond its usual geographical scope. In Keyssler, it is not only the well-worn grand tour that retraces antique byways but also regions within central and eastern Europe. If the ruins of antiquity are supposed to hold historical lessons, the god of commerce and his ships tell a story about neglected mercantile possibilities. The illustrator establishes these regions as travel- and tradeworthy. At the same time, the illustrator deemphasizes the familiar grand tour and proposes an alternative route. This implies a new geographical understanding for Europe—a shift in perspective from a north-south axis to a transcontinental one that takes in the outer edges of the empire. It also lays claim to a particular form of historical under- standing in its superimposition of the Roman and Holy Roman empires. Continuity with classical antiquity—and the privilege this confers—will no longer be the exclusive preserve of Britain, France, or Italy; also the German states and parts of eastern Europe will now be able to stake their claim.

This kind of theatrical staging is not uncommon in visual representations of the period. We find a similar vocabulary used in Benjamin West's portrait, *Joseph Banks* (ca. 1773), a painting whose subject matter will become sig- nificant for our story when we come to the discussion of Europe's engagement with the Pacific in the following chapter. Comparing the Keyssler illustra- tion with West's history painting tells us something about visual codes in the late eighteenth century—the use of the observer in the landscape, for example, and the gaze and gesture as markers of ethnographic interpreta- tion.[99] The gesturing figure will prompt us to ask how the unfamiliar was apprehended—whether it could be apprehended on its own terms or whether ethnographic interpretation implied an erasure of difference.

West's history painting shows Captain Cook's first voyage naturalist framed by a classical column and a proscenium curtain raised to highlight the significance of the scene (figure 1.5).[100] The naturalist is surrounded by artifacts collected during the voyage, and, fixing the viewer's gaze, he points to the Polynesian garment that he is wearing. The act of pointing suggests that the artifacts can be made intelligible only through this intermediary figure and his meaning-making gesture. In *Keisler's Travels* we find a similar strategy at work. Like the gesturing naturalist, Mercury occupies a privileged position because he mediates between the external viewer and the topography on display. This mediation intensifies the experience of looking because the viewer looks and then looks again through the perspective of the figure in the frame. At the same time, the viewer is turned into an ethnographic voyeur because the subject matter is revealed but simultaneously withheld or con- cealed by the use of theatrical props. In *Keisler's Travels*, the winged Mercury has unfurled the map, but he hovers above the scene, poised to fly away, taking his map with him. For West's painting of Banks, it is the brocade

curtain that threatens to drop, thereby removing the scene from view. In
both examples, the scenes on display cannot be apprehended as objects of
direct appropriation but only as ones of exotic allure. Recalling the well-
known definition of the exotic as that which contains an element of the
forbidden, in the map and the museum, the unfamiliar is presented as a realm
"marked by frisson more than fear."[101] Looking, it would seem, is to be
understood as an act of desire, as well as transgression.

If this trope has come to be thought of as a colonialist one (as West's
painting suggests), the Keyssler illustration shows that the dividing line
between Europe and non-Europe, empire and nonempire, and indigenous
and foreign was not as distinct as we might imagine. While we may think of
the South Seas as a common site of eighteenth-century exoticization, more
surprising is the fact that central and eastern Europe were depicted using
similar theatrical conventions. The conformity of these conventions suggests

that the distance between different forms of alterity was not always so great: The allure of the strange—its exotic frisson—was also preserved within Europe itself. Examples like Keyssler's suggest that the German states fell into this category, to be regarded by Britons, at least, as an uncertain space and as western Europe's homegrown curiosity. Perhaps the German states still sported "anthropophagi and men whose heads grow below their shoulders," as one of Mary Wortley Montagu's correspondents hoped.[102] It would be the traveler's task to investigate this umstroke, where such Plinyesque phenomena seemed to lurk, and to negotiate that fine line between gratifying such desires and debunking them.[103]

Cultural Topographies

France and Italy were the main destinations for grand tourists during the eighteenth century, while those British visitors who made it to the German states tended to steer for the Catholic and princely south.[104] There were pragmatic reasons for this. For one thing, traveling in the German states was not easy. Whereas the average French or Italian citizen was accustomed to visitors and to hosting them well, Burney thought most Germans were "shy of strangers" and wished to be rid of them. Added to this were the difficulties posed by poor transportation and inadequate amenities, military checkpoints, where the traveler was detained and searched, and customs men who confiscated books and papers. Although Burney goes into more detail than most about the hardships of travel, such complaints were common enough that they came to stereotype German travel during this period.[105]

Would-be travelers might have recalled Tacitus, who alleged that the Germans must have originated in Germany because nobody would have chosen to move to a place so "rude in its surface, rigorous in its climate, [and] cheerless to the beholder and cultivator."[106] If this militated against moving to Germany, the prospect of boggy roads, inclement weather, and other grim discomforts seemed to discourage even native Germans from moving around. Our witness is one of Burney's contemporaries, Johann Kaspar Riesbeck (1754–1786). Riesbeck lamented the Germans' inadequate knowledge of their own homelands (further evidence that German travel was not as ubiquitous as was often claimed), and, disguising himself as a Frenchman to circumvent the censors, he set off to remedy this.[107] This undertaking was complicated not only by the many practical impediments to traveling. As Riesbeck pointed out in his 1783 account, Germany's political and confessional fragmentation gave rise to a degree of political, cultural, and religious pluralism that made generalization difficult. Getting to know Germany, he said, was incomparably more difficult than getting to know the rest of Europe. In other capital cities, one found the whole "nation in a nutshell."[108] Germany, on the other hand, was divided into numerous larger and smaller entities that differed in terms of governmental structure, religion, and culture. Music might later become a unifying force, but he thought that at this point a common language was the only thing linking the Germans.[109]

For Riesbeck, the German states resisted apprehension because of their cultural, religious, and political diversity. The difficulties of imagining Germany were, however, compounded by poor travel practice. Riesbeck thought that those who did travel were unsatisfactory observers. He, in contrast, promised his readers a more intimate acquaintance with the German peoples. Like Johann Gottfried Seume, who left Leipzig on foot in 1801 so as to see things up close, Riesbeck would not confine himself to fancy carriages and court visits like many a well-heeled traveler.[110] Instead, this self-described "scholarly traveler" and "world citizen" would go among the people and mix with all classes of society. Only thus, he insisted, could the "particularity" of the whole nation be penetrated.[111]

If there was personal gain in mounting such a venture, travelers like Riesbeck, Nicolai, and Seume also described their aims in utilitarian terms, as in the best tradition of Enlightenment travel writing.[112] While Seume's postrevolutionary notion of utility would be a socially critical one, for Nicolai and Riesbeck, writing several decades earlier, the politics of travel were more subterranean: The larger purpose of the journey was to forge the German states into a unified cultural ground.[113] Only at the end of his book did Riesbeck allow his chauvinism to emerge and the political dimensions of the project to become explicit. Dropping his French guise and detached stance, Riesbeck "cast a [retrospective] glance over the whole region."[114] Germany's salutary traits, he said, included its wealth in natural resources, geographical size (approximately one-fifth bigger than France), enlightened monarchs, juridical system, and national character.[115] Although Germany's political pluralism was detrimental to its "powers," Riesbeck, like de Staël, said that this had at least been conducive to its "inner cultivation." Where Germany's rulers had once competed over empty pomp, they now strove to improve their legal institutions, policing, education, industry, and commerce.[116]

Yet this happy account belied another agenda: If Germany were united under a single regent, Riesbeck went on, the empire would make much speedier cultural progress and would soon be able to dictate the rules for all of Europe.[117] At the time of writing, Germany was "despised by other peoples," he thought, because it could not "make its strengths felt."[118] However, by consolidating its resources—that is, becoming a maritime power, pursuing its own imperial aims (instead of facilitating those of other states), and cultivating a sense of national rather than regional pride—Germany could fulfill its true potential.[119] Then, Riesbeck concluded, all would know that the hardworking German was "the man for the world," capable of "cultivating himself anywhere and vanquishing all obstacles of nature."[120] Riesbeck concluded with an explicit statement of expansionism—"Which European Empire would then be able to measure itself against the Germans?" Furthermore, he compiled a reckoning of other nations' indebtedness: Poland, Hungry, Russia, and the English and Dutch colonies owed a debt of gratitude to the Germans; so did the leading European states, which could attribute part of their enlightenment to the Germans.[121]

It is against this background that we better understand the motivations underlying Ebeling's invitation to Burney to tour the German states and produce a musical travelogue that would help put German music on the map. We also understand Ebeling's angry response to the publication of Burney's German travelogue, the letter disavowing German cultural inferiority and proclaiming imperial superiority. As the examples of Ebeling and Riesbeck forcefully show, the desire to link Germans culturally was never disinterested, nor the idea of a cultural nation apolitical and compensatory. Culture was intended to do political work. Certainly, its politics were directed at the welfare of its own subjects, but the political arm of the cultural nation also extended beyond the boundaries of the state to intrude on other sovereign subjects. Culture, one could say, would be a foil for both nation and empire, and it is to the mechanics of this "cultural" program, and its specifically musical cast, that we now turn.

MUSICAL MAPPING

Even Burney's staunchest critics agreed that German music was too little known and that the traveler could serve a useful purpose by spreading its reputation. Yet any traveler seeking insights into the musical character of eighteenth-century Germany faced obstacles. Having decided to forego Naples, Rome, or Paris, the traveler contemplating Europe's umstroke was confronted with the problem of where to go. Today such a question would hardly arise. Austria and Germany have become synonymous with serious music, and composers like J. S. Bach, Haydn, Mozart, Beethoven, Brahms, and Wagner are canonized as at once uniquely German and universally significant.[122] Moreover, cities like Bonn, Leipzig, Bayreuth, Berlin, Prague,

Vienna, and Salzburg suggest their own kinds of musico-biographical itineraries, so that the tourist of today can, for example, retrace Mozart's career path from Getreidegasse 9 in Salzburg to Rauhensteingasse 8 in Vienna and cross Europe by luxury train in between.[123] The performance and reception of serious music have, in a sense, mapped the German-speaking countries culturally and geographically—much in the way Benedict Anderson thought that print culture contributed to the making of the nation in the nineteenth century.[124]

While this sort of musical mapping retains a national dimension, it is also currently promoted by institutions like the European Council as distinctly transnational in character.[125] "Mozart-Wege" (Mozart Ways), a project that maps Mozart's journeys, for example, has been conceived as one of Europe's designated "cultural routes," itineraries that are explicitly intended to demonstrate how the heritage of different countries is simultaneously a shared one (figure 1.6). According to project organizers, "following in the footsteps of Mozart" through ten host countries and seventy-five partner cities and regions—with opportunities for package tours and *Sound of Music* daytrips in between—will contribute to the effort to forge a common European identity based on values such as democracy, human rights, diversity, and cultural exchange.[126]

Yet this emphasis on travel as a signifier of "shared cultural heritage" and builder of bridges "across boundaries and centuries" elides an important point. Mozart's itinerancy—he is said to have spent one-third of his life on tour—was in fact the result of material conditions, cultural practices, and systems of patronage that were in many ways irreconcilable with the kinds of "values" now imputed to his journeys by the Mozart-Wege project and its sponsoring institution, the European Council. In other words, as an attempt to "authentically" reanimate something from the past, this reenactment rests on an empty promise. The way in which musical travel is construed here can be thought of as a reanimation of Orpheus: Musical travel is the magic medium that is supposed to overcome local differences. Eighteenth-century travel was, however, often a motion in the very direction of political and cultural particularism. Whatever the traveler's (sometimes considerable) contribution to collective human understanding and, for want of a better word, tolerance, the traveler was also co-opted in the service of emerging national and imperial endeavors that were largely antithetical to humanist ideals.

This co-optation was true of the German appropriation of Burney's travels, and it was true of British travel reception, too. Contrary to a strong reading of the Orpheus story, Burney's journey was never about music and

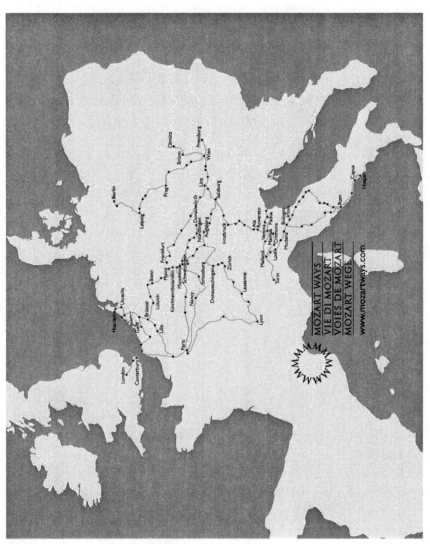

FIGURE 1.6. "Mozart's Journeys, 1762–1791," *Mozart-Wege.*

travel as forms of "universal language." For late eighteenth-century German music scholars, Burney's journey was conceived as an opportunity to promote German instrumental music over and against Italian vocal music and to forge the German states into something like a musical whole. For the English critics, on the other hand, the journey would provide an opportunity to delineate their own conservative form of national cultural imaginary. By examining the sheer interestedness of these enterprises, we are reminded of the limitations of reenactment as a form of historical understanding, as well as of the historically shifting valence of travel.

As we have seen, eighteenth-century Europe told a different story from the one presented by the Mozart-Wege. In the 1770s the German states still lacked something we might think of as a musical topography—an imaginative space in which musical communities were adequately linked by common musical idioms, touring performers, concert reviews, and various other discursive practices. The confessional divide between north and south constituted what was arguably the deepest rift between musical cultures, but "German music" was fractured in other ways, too—for example, by town and court rivalries and even by plain ignorance about the music being composed and performed in other parts of the country.[127] In Riesbeck's terms, the musical "nation in a nutshell" would not exist for another half century or so. We can thus see Ebeling's intellectual efforts as an attempt to address this problem. Mapping music through travel—and specifically through foreign travel—was envisioned as a means of creating a coherent picture of German music. This would serve the interests not only of musicians and audiences but also of Germans generally.

ITINERARIES

Ebeling was well informed about German cultural life. Yet, as his first letter to Burney makes clear, even the apparently simple act of compiling a musical itinerary was not easy. Berlin, Hamburg, and Vienna were obvious destinations, but what of the smaller musical centers?[128] The cultural promoter would have to consider where important music was being made and where the musical traveler should go to hear the best, most representative music being composed and performed. If there was a musical "route" of the kind imagined today, it was not evident from the career paths of Europe's itinerant musicians as they pendulated between sources of employment.

Neapolitan-born soprano Regina Mingotti (1722–1808) is a case in point. When Burney interviewed her in Germany in 1772, she told him that, prior to retiring to Munich, she had been attached to the court in Dresden but had also lived and worked in numerous other cities, including Naples, Prague, Madrid, Paris, and London.[129] This kind of peripatetic career was typical of elite musicians but, at the same time, singular in its specific trajectory.[130] In attempting to compile a list of important musical destinations, Ebeling could not, in other words, look to the examples of renowned musicians like Mingotti, let alone composers like Carl Friedrich Abel and Johann Christian Bach, who had made their names in London. If Ebeling was to propose a route that mapped the German musical centers, he would have to perform a new feat of intellectual labor and piece together whatever information was available.

Ebeling was aided in this enterprise by a Leipziger, Johann Adam Hiller (1728–1804). As a respected composer of comic operas and an important music journalist, Hiller had published a catalogue of musicians in the journal *Wöchentliche Nachrichten und Anmerkungen die Musik betreffend* (1768). This and Friedrich Wilhelm Marpurg's *Historisch-kritische Beyträge zur Aufnahme der Musik* (1754–1760) would have to serve as a Baedeker for musical travel in the German states. Such sources were not, however, without their limitations: Ebeling could personally vouch for only a few of Hiller's and Marpurg's recommendations; most had been reported secondhand, and not all of the information was up to date. Journals such as Hiller's had been helpful in disseminating information about domestic music and were recognized, even by nonmusicians, as potentially useful for the writing of music history.[131] Yet there could be no substitute for direct experience of local musical life. As Burney would observe once he had arrived on the Continent, one court did not know what the next was doing. German musical centers were, as he laconically put it, "so dazzled by their own splendor, as to be wholly blind to what is doing at the distance only of a day's journey among their neighbours."[132] This meant that, for all the cosmopolitanism of its elite musicians and the importance of journals and periodicals in disseminating information, discrete music communities still existed in a state of comparative isolation. What was needed was a musical traveler who could help forge a tighter professional network and investigate music as it was practiced on the ground.

Ebeling had warned Burney that Germany's musical centers were riven by petty jealousies and rivalries: "Every town and every band of musicians belonging to a little Prince think themselves intitled [*sic*] to a musical Monarchy, allowing no taste and no Genius to others," he complained. In pointing to the cultural implications of political fragmentation, Ebeling stressed that the pride, ignorance, and competitiveness of the German courts and cities were unconducive to musical life. At the same time, he was mindful of the difficulties involved in trying to remedy this state of affairs.

"All these humming bees will make much noise," he wrote to Burney about stating his musical opinions, "when I *appelle un chat un chat* [call a spade a spade]."[133] When we consider that musician and writer C. D. F. Schubart was jailed for ten years for offending the Duke of Württemberg, it becomes clear that scholars who demonstrated their partisanship risked consequences that were both aesthetic and political. One can assume, too, that there was every incentive to defer this task to the less politically entangled outsider. If the traveler was privileged to compare, as I have suggested, it was the foreign traveler's special prerogative to make the critical and aesthetic judgments that were too difficult or too sensitive to make at home. Yet as Burney would learn the day his travelogue hit the bookstands, sticking one's neck out came at a cost.

In addition to the obvious destinations like Vienna, Berlin, and Hamburg, Ebeling's itinerary included places like Mannheim, Baden, Stuttgart, Amsterdam, The Hague, Augsburg, Munich, Salzburg, Regensburg, Nuremberg, Bayreuth, Gotha, Weimar, Leipzig, Dresden, Potsdam, and Magdeburg. For each of these places, Ebeling suggested a few important contacts and musical venues—the opera in Stuttgart, for example, the expense of which had "ruined" the entire duchy; composers like Christoph Willibald Gluck and Joseph Haydn in Vienna; or Franz Benda and Johann Joachim Quantz in Berlin.[134] This was, by and large, the route that Burney followed. It was a tour as comprehensive as Cook's sweeps of the Pacific looking for the fabled continent, a tour designed to discover and make known every center of musical worth. If there were musical wonders yet to be found, strange claims to be tested, and daring observations to be made, such tasks would fall to the English traveler.

APODEMICS

Until the end of the century, travel instructions (or *apodemics,* as they were called) were crucial to any respectable traveler. This was true of the aristocrat's son embarking on a grand tour with a tutor and a set of recommendatory letters in his portmanteau; it applied to the middle-class traveler who wanted to "view the beautiful scenes" in England and Wales with the help of Thomas Gray's *Traveller's Companion;* and it was especially applicable to the state-sponsored expeditionist, who was issued with official instructions from the Admiralty and the Royal Society.[135]

In the apodemic, the traveler could expect to find practical tips on where to sleep, what to eat, where to change coaches, and how to avoid bandits. More importantly, though, this cross between *Lonely Planet* and fieldwork manual advised the traveler on what to do, see, and collect while away. For those visitors who could not afford a reputable cicerone to usher them around Europe's antiquity collections and curiosity cabinets, the apodemic was an indispensable companion: It provided the reassurance that they were traveling as they ought and seeing and doing what was socially (and professionally) expected of them. In general terms, this was also true of the state-sponsored voyager, for whom there was no haphazard traveling either. Official instructions stipulated the secret strategic and scientific aims of the expedition—the new territories that were to be claimed and the natural and ethnographic data to be collected. Such instructions established the intellectual and practical parameters of the expedition, as well as the political ones.[136] Further, formalized instructions allowed for comparison and categorization of new data, thereby making the accompanying "question catalogue" a cornerstone of early ethnographic and ethnomusicological inquiry. Above all, the apodemic systematized the traveler's experience.[137]

Consequently, nonmusical travelers had long since ceased to argue about *which* anthropological, geographical, or botanical data were worth documenting. Official expeditionary instructions spelled out the fact that, for example, voyagers needed to observe the "Genius, Temper, Disposition and Number" of indigenous peoples.[138] Similarly, private travelers made a habit of national typing and were routinely instructed on how to observe everything from manufacturing, agriculture, and commerce to national dress, art, architecture, and theater. Music's exclusion from this comprehensive list reflects the extent to which systematic musical inquiry occupied a blind spot in eighteenth-century intellectual life. Certainly, published travel accounts acted as a de facto model, and Burney's friendship with other travelers prepared him for his journey. However, if he and Ebeling shared the belief that German music needed mapping, the question of how to accomplish this hung in the air. In the 1770s there was no music-specific apodemic, and the lack of a tabularized approach to the study of music opened the way for the kind of acrimony exhibited by Ebeling and his German colleagues when they realized what Burney had made of their music.

The implicit assumption on Ebeling's part was that geography alone would be adequate to the task of documenting the current state of German music: Burney's route would map German music and, by extension, Germany itself. What Ebeling did not perhaps foresee was that an itinerary alone would not suffice. The lessons provided by a source like Keyssler's *Travels,* with its doublings and nervous mediations, might have hinted as much. Compared with culturally overdetermined spaces like France and Italy, the comparative unknownness of parts of Germany made the want of an apodemic all the more acute. I do not mean to suggest that apodemics and their resulting national typologies provided reliable, useful, or even comprehensive information. Such schemata tended to be predictably prejudicial, sometimes whimsical in their categorizations. (What value, one wonders, was there in associating nations with animals—"cat" [Turk or Greek], "horse" [English], "lion" [German]—or comparing where inhabitants would be most likely to die—"in bed" [Spanish], "at war" [French], "in the snow" [Russian], or, as in the case of the Germans, "in their cups"?[139]) We cannot necessarily conclude, in other words, that the apodemic added meaningfully to the sum total of human knowledge.

What is significant, however, is the fact that the apodemic offered a common frame of reference for all travelers. Its criteria structured the traveler's observations and allowed them to be corroborated or systematically refuted. Apodemics conferred authority not only on the travelers and their investigative projects but also on the objects of inquiry. And, thanks to the apodemic, the object of inquiry was assigned a place within a broad scheme of knowledge making. Yet, up until the late eighteenth century, that unruly object, music, had not been subject to the same regulatory disciplining. As Burney set off for the Continent, he had only a mud map of the German states and his own lights to follow. Without a shared set of musical instructions to guide his investigation—instructions that stipulated the mutually agreed-upon criteria by which to discriminate good music from bad—he would expose himself to an array of auditory experiences.[140]

The Journey

Burney arrived in Calais in the summer of 1772 ready to take up Ebeling's invitation to tour the Lowlands and central Europe and investigate music at the "source."[141] His first ports of call were cities in northern France and Belgium (figure 1.7). Here we already find the kind of investigative approach and range of interests that the musical traveler would pursue during the coming months. Besides going to a playhouse to see a company of strolling players performing a tragedy, he inspected the organ at the St. Omer cathedral (part of his ongoing and much lampooned fascination with organs and carillons); he went to hear military bands in Lille and Ghent (about which there will be more later) and attended a performance of one of Grétry's operas.[142] He kept up the hectic schedule in Antwerp, where he made time to hear church music (grumbling that the wind players were more out of tune than the London waits on winter nights), and announced that the primary

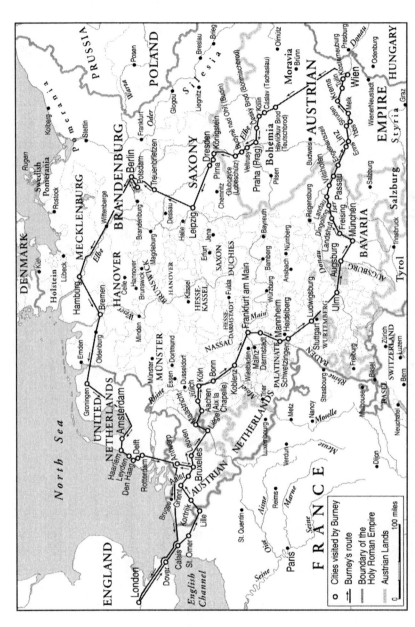

FIGURE 1.7. "Charles Burney's Journey through Central Europe and the Netherlands (1772)."

aim of the journey was to "meet with materials most important to the history of counter-point, or music in different parts."[143] This search necessitated a visit to the local Jesuit college and its library, where he posed his question to anyone who would listen: "Where and when did counter-point or modern harmony begin?" In France he had been sent north on this quest, but now he would be directed back to France. Frustrated by his inability to find, if not the very "first [compositions] that were made in counter-point," then at least some earlier examples, he pressed on to continue the search elsewhere.[144]

Arriving in Jülich en route to Cologne, Burney waited at a post house while the horses were changed, only to be entertained by two "vagabonds" who imitated the sounds of wind instruments and the "bellowing noise of the Romish priests." Burney was delighted by their imitation, although a bit alarmed by the parodying of priestly chanting in a Catholic town.[145] The fact that this anecdote found its way into the traveler's account tells us something about both Burney's eclectic interests and his investigative method. Besides going to operas and concerts and consulting with experts, he also attended to the pastimes and livelihoods of ordinary people. He commented on strolling musicians like the dulcimer player whose "musical genius" seemed at odds with his station and his instrument; elsewhere he listened to night watchmen, boatmen, and street criers, and he tipped so-called poor scholars singing for their supper.[146] Observations about this varied music making were all folded into a thickly textured account of the German soundscape.

While some musical observations were prompted by contingency, others were motivated by a desire to test long-standing assumptions about German musical life. The journey down the Rhine from Cologne to Koblenz provided one such opportunity, when, contrary to what he had always heard, he said he found no evidence of the German "passion for music." The street musicians in Frankfurt were tolerable, and a military band in Darmstadt was quite pleasing, but he thought that in the Rhineland there was less singing and playing than in other Catholic regions and little evidence of outstanding vocal or instrumental performers.[147] He left Hesse for the Palatinate and Württemberg, concluding with some remarks about the difficulties of traveling this stretch of the route. Besides extortionist postmasters and innkeepers, there were pestiferous beggars ("young, fat, robust, and fit for any labour") and "ugly" peasants. Drawing on a common travelogue convention that used the status and appearance of women as a yardstick for society as a whole, Burney remarked that, with their bare feet and ill-kempt hair, the women were particularly uncomely.[148] His frustration over the unavailability of informants and the difficulties in locating first-rate musicians also caused Burney to say that he sometimes wished a town crier could be employed to announce his arrival and inform the musical inhabitants about the nature of his search. As it was, he had to chase after musicians and archivists and constantly repeat his purpose, not always to a receptive audience. While he was generally loath to stereotype a whole people, he said that uncomprehending individuals could be considered "true Germans for slow apprehension and inactivity."[149]

In Mannheim, however, Burney would hear the best singing so far—a performance of *Zémire et Azor* (1771) by André-Ernest-Modeste Grétry. The Germans had now reached the point, he thought, where they could begin to cultivate their own opera, and it surprised him that they neither composed more operas in the vernacular language nor commissioned better translations.[150] But it was the Mannheim instrumental playing that really attracted his attention. The city had been home to the Bohemian Johann Stamitz (1717–1757), who pioneered modern orchestral playing, and Burney thought the orchestra deserved its reputation as one of the finest on the Continent. With its disciplined performers and first-rate soloists, he said memorably that the orchestra was "an army of generals, equally fit to plan a battle, as to fight it." Apart from the wind section, which was "naturally" out of tune, there was apparently "no imperfection in this band." Also worthy of remark were the public concerts: The elector held nightly performances at the palace and public concerts at the theater, to which there was free admission even for foreigners. In the summer, the elector's Schwetzingen residence seemed to be inhabited by a "colony of musicians": Every window and door emitted the sounds of musicians practicing their art, and Burney thought that the entire electorate had acquired a corresponding taste for music.[151]

Burney's next stops would be Stuttgart and the ducal residence in nearby Ludwigsburg. As it transpired, he was unable to hear the opera company, but he did gather information about the duke's huge theater and about recent compositions by Niccolo Jomelli (1714–1774) and Antonio Maria Gasparo Sacchini (1730–1786), composers he had met in Italy and greatly esteemed.[152] He noted that the duke maintained his stable of performers with a conservatory for indigent girls and boys who were trained from an early age in vocal and instrumental music. Also in residence were fifteen castrati and two Bolognese surgeons who were said to be "expert in this vocal manufacture." However, if Burney was pleased by the thriving musical life and (as we will see in the final chapter) intrigued by the idea of a conservatory, he was horrified by the duke's lopsided allocation of resources. Making a statement that would be excised from the German version of his travelogue, Burney noted that so great was the duke's expenditure on opera that the populace had complained to the Imperial Diet about the "ruin of the country." In consequence, there was supposed to be a new economizing that saw the performers reduced to half pay.[153] "The most shining parts of a German court," Burney observed, "are usually its *military,* its *music,* and its *hunt.*" But he believed this came at the cost of agriculture, commerce, and the "necessaries of life" and reduced the bulk of the populace to poverty. The Duke of Württemberg's enthusiasm for music was, he concluded, "as strong as that of the emperor Nero," making music "a vice, and hurtful to society; for that nation, of which half the subjects are stage-players, fiddlers, and soldiers, and the other half beggars, seems to be but ill-governed."[154] Such outspokenness would prompt Ebeling's outrage, to which Burney replied only half apologetically:

> If I have mentioned the Nakedness of the Land, & the wretchedness of the people, in some parts of my Tour, it was more to expose the Tyranny of the Government, & despotism of Princes, than to insult the people, whom I pitied with all my soul—a brave, honest & industrious race, by Nature, who are denied the common rights of humanity, to such a Degree, as to be rendered sour & unfeeling to others.[155]

Burney had less to complain about in Munich, where he heard a number of excellent musicians and found useful historical material. He met up with an acquaintance from London, the castrato Gaetano Guadagni, interviewed Mingotti, and was instructed (not always reliably) on Spanish, Polish, and German music by Louis Devisme (1720–1776), the British plenipotentiary to the Bavarian court. It was Devisme who supplied Burney's German travelogue with its most inflammatory and dismissive statement, namely that "If innate Genius exists, Germany is certainly not the seat of it, but it is that of perseverance and application."[156] The insertion caused significant offense and necessitated some serious backpedaling on Burney's part. He would later claim, not entirely convincingly, to have been the "retailer" rather than author of the remark.[157]

In Munich, Burney was also able to consult the elector's important library, which housed a significant quantity of early music; he visited the theater and saw the famous imperial collection. Also of interest was a Jesuit conservatory that Burney thought did in fact contribute to Germany's "great number of musicians" and its "national taste and passion for music." Evidence of this was to be heard in a fine "street concert" given by poor scholars outside his inn one night. Burney also received an audience with the music-loving electress dowager of Saxony and her brother the elector, who paid the traveler a cherished compliment in saying he was "the only modern historian who thought it necessary to travel, in order to gain information at the sources, without contenting [himself] with second-hand, and hear-say accounts."[158] Later they gave a concert, and Burney flattered the elector by referring to him as an outstanding *diletantti,* second only to Carl Friedrich Abel in the quality of his gamba playing.[159] Burney's habit of pandering to patrons while neglecting professionals did not go down well with either German or English critics. At the same time, it illustrates the kinds of social pressures felt by writers, who depended not only on the market for their livelihood but also to some extent on the good will of patrons.

Leaving Munich, Burney proceeded down the Isar and the Danube by raft. His account of the river journey belongs to a Twainian adventure, for it is here that the hardships of late eighteenth-century travel are impressed on the reader—a leaky cabin, lack of provisions, inadequate bedding, trouble with innkeepers and a recalcitrant servant, rapids and whirlpools, censors and customs men, and high prices. Nonetheless, there were also pleasures such as a musical traveler could truly appreciate. Floating downstream, Burney heard peasants singing for work and for pleasure; Bohemian "gypsies" who sang melodies with contrapuntal parts that reminded him of the *cantus firmus* singing of Italian pilgrims en route to Assisi; there were lovely songs and hymns sung in intricate four parts; and people who walked along the riverbanks singing, always together and always in harmony.[160] Making remarks that I discuss later on, Burney asked how these peasants could have developed the ability to sing polyphonically. Perhaps it had to do with the fact that this was a Catholic country and the peasants heard polyphonic singing in church. English peasants and urban laborers, he noted, did not share the same ability, and acquiring the skill took years of studious training.[161] As our traveler concluded this leg of the journey, he remarked that the voyage had added little to his knowledge of German music but much to his understanding of the people and the country. The river voyage had not afforded him sufficient time in port for collecting historical material and properly acquainting himself with "musical people." But, he added, "as to *national music,* perhaps the rude songs which I heard sung by the boors and watermen, gave me a more genuine idea of it, than is to be acquired from the corrupted, motley, and Italianized melody, to be heard in the capitals of this extensive country."[162]

The binary oppositions in this passage—musical peasants versus "musical people," "national music" versus "Italianized" (i.e., cosmopolitan) music, and "rude" music of the countryside versus "corrupted" music of the city—speak of the difficulties in defining something that could be called "German music" in the late eighteenth century. More than this, the passage gives us an insight into the nature of aesthetic evaluation during this period. Although charmed and intrigued by the skillful part singing he heard on the banks of the Danube, Burney drew a line between different registers of music making and the types of people who produced it. Aesthetic value, one could say, was not yet thought inherent to the artistic work. Rather, value was inexorably linked to the subject who produced the work and evaluating the one implied an evaluation of the other. If this meant staving off the preconditions for aesthetic autonomy, it also meant a step in the direction of the anthropological and sociological, for Burney affirmed the indexical value of functional music and the way in which it contributed to a picture of the people and their society.

Arriving in the Viennese capital occasioned some vivid impressions of urban life—the darkness cast on the narrow streets by tall buildings, the hawking of goods door to door, St. Stephen's Cathedral hung with Ottoman war trophies that gave the church the "appearance of an old wardrobe," visits to the theater to see Gotthold Ephraim Lessing's new tragedy, *Emilia Galotti* (of which the non-German speaker understood but little), bull bating and cock throwing, and the casual harmonizing of sentries and street singers.[163] In Vienna, as on the Danube, Burney was struck by the quality of this everyday music making. He reiterated his belief that "Physical causes operate but little . . . as to music. Nature," he added, "distributes her favours pretty equally to the inhabitants of Europe; but moral causes are frequently very powerful in their effects. And it seems as if *the national music of a country was good or bad in proportion to that of its church service.*"[164] The insight that it was possible to "form the ear of the inhabitants" by nurturing music explains Burney's later efforts to promote music in England. Yet the insight did not gibe with his repeated comments about the lack of quality music in the German states—a contradiction that German critics seized upon.

As in other cities, Burney's visit to Vienna was facilitated by letters of introduction and by personal contacts who escorted him about town and introduced him to prominent people. Joseph Haydn was out of town, and they would not meet until Haydn came to England in 1791.[165] Burney was, however, introduced to the poet and librettist Pietro Metastasio (1698–1782), whom he liked enormously and whose memoir he later wrote.[166] Compiling a picture of the local music scene, Burney identified the poet as belonging to one of two musical "sects" in the city. While Metastasio and Johann Adolf Hasse (1699–1783) were more traditional in their approach to opera and posited the equal importance of text and music, Burney thought their reformist rivals, Ranieri Calzabigi (1714–1795) and Christoph Willibald Gluck (1714–1787), emphasized theatrical effects, simple diction, and musical execution.[167] Burney claimed a bit disingenuously that he did not take sides in this rivalry because it was not the job of the "faithful historian" to "encourage exclusive approbation."[168] Yet he characterized Hasse (then one of Europe's most prolific and popular opera seria composers) as "superior to all other lyric composers," while for Gluck there was less effusive praise.[169]

At their meeting, Gluck played Burney excerpts from his operas *Alceste, Paride ed Elena,* and the still unnotated *Iphigénie en Aulide.* Burney praised the composer for his unparalleled talent for dramatic setting and theatrical effects but criticized him for adapting his music to suit the French. At the same time, Burney attributed Gluck's reforms to a "study of the English taste." Gluck had apparently observed that simplicity appealed most to English audiences and consequently had written arias for *Orfeo* that were as plain as English ballads.[170] Gluck, Burney concluded, was as much a poet as a musician but also an "excellent *painter*" (a "Michael Angelo of music" to Hasse's Raphael). By this he meant that Gluck's writing captured the meaning and emotion of the words, especially the boisterous, terrifying, and violent. Hasse's writing, in contrast, was thought to be more expressive of the graceful, elegant, and tender.[171]

During his two-week stay in Vienna there were visits to the imperial music library, which turned up interesting sources that dealt with early counterpoint, and meetings with Hasse and his wife, Faustina, whom Burney described as a fine singer and "living volume of musical history." He heard a recital by a little girl whose sensitive playing convinced him of the desirability of instructing children on the clavichord or piano rather than the harpsichord, which lacked comparable expressiveness.[172] There were numerous other meetings and concerts, including recitals given by a female composer, Marianne Martinez, and a performance given by a young prodigy of Georg Christoph Wagenseil.[173] After a series of reluctant farewells from the imperial capital, Burney finally turned northward.

Burney's lasting impression of the next phase of his journey was of the wretchedness of the traveling conditions.[174] However, he had heard that the Bohemians were the most musical people in Germany, even all of Europe, and, as we will find in a subsequent chapter, this was something he was eager to test, first in towns and cities like Havlíčkův Brod (whence Stamitz hailed), Jenitz, Cáslav, and Český Brod, then in Prague.[175] Burney noted that music was part of the general education system in this part of the world, and he concluded that it was "not nature, but cultivation, which makes music so generally understood by the Germans." To this observation, he appended Devisme's disparaging remarks about German industriousness and lack of genius, comments that had to be removed from the subsequent edition of the travelogue.[176]

Like Prague, Dresden had suffered heavy bombardment during the Seven Years War (1756–1763). Few of the city's old towers were left standing, and even a decade later the inhabitants were still recovering from the Prussian onslaught.[177] One of the few churches to survive intact was the Frauenkirche. Burney said that its almost three thousand–strong congregation singing in unison was one of the grandest choruses he had ever heard.[178] He also managed to hear some less inspiring music, including a Hasse symphony and a "soporific" burletta by Antonio Salieri. In contrast to Bohemia, where everyone learned to sing, here the people and even the aristocracy seemed too impoverished to pursue music. War, said Burney, had reduced this "Athens of modern times" to a "melancholy residence" that lacked impressive music, pleasure gardens, and other public diversions.[179] On the other hand, the compensations for visiting the city included meeting the elector and visiting the renowned imperial gallery. Since the large theater where Hasse had staged his operas was now closed, Burney had to content himself with repeat visits to the picture gallery and to churches to inspect the organs. Drawing on information supplied by the British envoy to Dresden, he also commented at some length on the origin of the *Singschüler,* poor scholars, and their contribution to the spread of Lutheranism in Saxony. Currently the singers performed on the street, were hired to perform for wealthy families, and sang on feast days and in church. He reported that the better among them were sent to the university, from which some graduated to become professional musicians.[180] Later editions of Burney's travelogue would take this opportunity to affirm the musicality of Protestant Germany.[181]

Leipzig to the north was similarly affected by the last war, and its once famous fair had been reduced, Burney said, to the size of that in an English market town. The city was nonetheless an important destination for anyone interested in music. Twenty years earlier it had been home to J. S. Bach and was still home to Europe's foremost music publishing house, run by Johann Gottlob Immanuel Breitkopf (1719–1794). Here it was possible to buy reasonably priced music, study tune indices, and see presses operating with newly developed musical type. Ebeling had also put Burney in touch with Hiller, the music critic, journal publisher, and pioneer of the German Singspiel.[182] Hiller conducted the Englishman around the city, first to an opera by Grétry, then to a rehearsal of one of his own works, which Burney thought pleasing but poorly performed, and finally on a tour of the city's many bookshops. Although Leipzig turned up no instrumental performers of real stature, Burney drew on the work of German music scholars to affirm J. S. Bach's great abilities as an organist.[183] The fact that Burney followed the Germans' lead and celebrated Bach more as a performer than composer reflects the troubled status of contrapuntal music during these decades. This would change only with the efforts of scholars like Johann Nicolaus Forkel and the beginnings of a Bach revival in the early nineteenth century.

Crossing the border into Brandenburg, Burney was again detained by customs officers, this time at bayonet point, and his baggage searched. It was not an auspicious start to the visit, but Burney said he was eager to go to Berlin, where there was a ruler known as much for his cultivation of the arts as for his militarism. Burney's conductor around the city was no less than Friedrich Nicolai (1733–1811), the important figure of the Berlin Enlightenment, who introduced him to some of the city's better-known composers and musicians. He met organist and court composer Johann Friedrich Agricola (1720–1774), the talented Benda brothers, and Gertrud Elisabeth Schmeling (later Mara, 1749–1833), whose expressive singing impressed Burney greatly.[184] He also heard His Majesty's sizeable orchestra (about fifty strong) and was introduced to its musicians and composers—Johann Joachim Quantz (1697–1773), the king's flute master and composer of an instruction manual and legion flute concerti; and Friedrich Wilhelm Marpurg (1718–1795), who was himself working on a history of music.

Burney's most memorable observations concerned Friedrich II and the impact of his artistic taste on the musical life of the city. The king's favorite opera composer was said to be Carl Heinrich Graun (1703/4–1759). Burney thought Graun had the right attitude toward harmony (it ought to "support melody not suffocate it"), and Graun had apparently been among the first to give up fugues and "laboured contrivances" for simple melody. However, Burney also thought Graun encapsulated all that was wrong with music in Berlin—namely, its failure to progress. "Though the world is rolling on, most of the Berlin musicians, defeating its motion, have long contrived to stand still."[185] Burney summed up the reasons for this musical stasis in an anecdote about the king, who, he said, always stood behind the *maestro di capelli* in order to perform "the part of director-general here, as much as of *generalissimo* in the field."[186]

Since the king usually resided in Potsdam, Burney was pleased to receive an invitation to the nearby garrison city, where his interrogation at the city gates seemed worthy of a city under siege.[187] Once admitted, Burney paid a visit to the Jacobite Scotsman, Lord Marischal (1692/3–1778), one of Friedrich II's chamberlains, who supplied Burney with a collection of national melodies and had his bagpiper perform for him in the garden. The two men discussed the whole gamut of topics interesting to a late eighteenth-century investigator of music, beginning with the obligatory comparison of national opera.[188] Marischal (drawing on Rousseau) said that testing the effects of opera on a Greek woman demonstrated the superiority of Italian opera; French opera, in contrast, was like the "hideous howlings of the Calmuc Tartars."[189] The same experiment performed on a Polynesian called Aotourou (Putaveri), brought to Paris by Louis Antoine de Bougainville in 1769, produced comparable results. Marischal claimed that, while he had been unable to test the effects of Italian opera on the islander because it was impossible to perform Italian opera properly in Paris, Aotourou thought French opera worthy only of parody.[190]

Burney would soon have his own Polynesian experiments to chew over— more about this in the next chapter—but Marischal's anecdotes about the effects of music on natives, the ill, and the homesick made a lasting impression.[191] They showed that aesthetic arguments could be made through recourse to a third party and that native reactions to music could be used to demonstrate what learned discussion could not necessarily prove. Second, music was the product of the culture that gave rise to it. Finally, music could be said to act on indigenous peoples in an irresistible, almost automatic fashion. These points would resurface later in Burney's thinking about the meaning and power of music.[192]

Burney's visit to Friedrich II's palace was an occasion to remark on the building's elegant design, the king's instrument collection, and the state of German instrument manufacture.[193] But it was a concert given by the king at Sanssouci that was of real interest to the traveler. While Burney talked to Benda and Quantz, the king could be overheard practicing the flute in another room; later the king gave a concert. Burney struck a diffident line when he said that Quantz and the two Grauns had been the king's favorite composers for the past forty years:

> If it may be true, as many assert, that music has declined and degenerated since that time . . . it is an indication of a sound judgment, and of great discernment, in his majesty to adhere thus firmly to the productions of a period which may be called the Augustan age of music; to stem the torrent of caprice and fashion with such unshaken constancy, is possessing a kind of *stet sol,* by which Apollo and his sons are prevented from running riot, or changing from good to bad, and from bad to worse.[194]

Burney was also diffident about the quality of Quantz's compositions and the flute teacher's definition of German music as a "mixed" (i.e., French and Italian) style. Burney said his compositions now sounded "old and common" but allowed that they may have been full of "novelty" when first composed. Every age since Plato had complained about the degeneracy of music, but,

ultimately, Burney said he sided with modern music and its greater orna-
mentation and expressivity: Too much simplicity could seem dry, rustic,
even vulgar.[195]

Burney returned to Berlin to hear more music and meet some of the city's
other better-known composers, performers, and music scholars. He was introduced to Johann Philipp Kirnberger (1721–1783), the composer and
scholar, and Johann Georg Sulzer (1719–1779), the leading aesthetician,
author, and editor of *Allgemeine Theorie der schönen Künste* (1771–1774), whom
Burney praised for his erudition and refined thinking.[196] Marpurg also took
him to see a music-transcribing machine that he was eager to compare with
reports he had read in the *Philosophical Transactions*.[197] This all made for a
stimulating and action-packed visit. Nevertheless, departing Berlin, Burney
said he was left rather disappointed for he did not share the king's taste in
music. Although there were musical "schisms" that demonstrated some diversity of taste and opinion, anyone who did not share the reigning taste—
Quantz, Graun, Agricola, or Hasse—was unlikely to prosper.

Burney's arrival in Hamburg was as easy as it had been difficult in
Potsdam. This reflected the difference, he said, between despotic German
states and free ones. Although the city was crowded and the streets were
narrow, Hamburg had an "air of cheerfulness, industry, plenty and liberty"
that was seldom seen elsewhere in Germany.[198] This had been the city of
Georg Philipp Telemann, composer of a polyglot opera called *Orpheus, oder die
wunderbare Beständigkeit der Liebe* (1726); it had been home to music scholar
Johann Mattheson and to Handel before he left for England, where he became
a competitor for the title of Orpheus.[199] More recently, of course, Hamburg
was home to Ebeling and Johann Joachim Christoph Bode (1730–1793),
who would be Ebeling's collaborator on the translations of Burney's travelogues and himself an important disseminator of English literature in German. Burney's purpose in Hamburg was the investigation of "purely German" music and musicians—not, as he said, Italian opera. To this end, he
went to inspect city organs, visited a well-stocked music purveyor to purchase sheet music, and attended various concerts, including one organized by
Ebeling and presided over by Carl Philipp Emanuel Bach (1714–1788).[200]
Burney learned that Bach had left the Prussian court for Hamburg, where he
was at greater liberty to compose his own music, music that Burney rather
admired.[201] Still Bach's sense of disgruntlement was palpable, and Burney
got the impression that this was "not a bright period for music" in the city-
state.[202]

By now in a hurry to get back to England, Burney passed through cities like Bremen and Groningen with minimal comment. In Amsterdam he

went to the synagogue because he said that every species of national music warranted attention and he wanted to compare it with music he had heard in synagogues elsewhere in Europe.[203] He was not flattering about the singing but conceded that he did not know what Jews themselves thought of the music. In referring to the congregation as letting out "a kind of cry, as a pack of hounds when a fox breaks cover," he said he meant to describe rather than censure Hebrew music. Making a statement typical of the Enlightenment effort to reconcile relative and universal values, Burney declared he would pronounce the music neither good nor bad, only unlike what Christians were accustomed to in church.[204]

With some passing remarks about Leyden, The Hague, Delft, and Rotterdam, Burney summed up the present state of German music and appended some information that had not hitherto found its way into the account. Among other things, this included a dismissive (albeit secondhand) appraisal of Mozart's musical precocity.[205] Burney conceded that he had not been able to visit all of the places (Brunswick, for example) that deserved his attention, but he stressed that he had covered virtually every capital on a journey of some two thousand miles.[206] Time had not allowed him to make a thorough study of the arts and sciences, but he noted that Austria and northern Germany had made greater progress in literature and the sciences than the southern states, the Rhine circle, and Westphalia, and, citing his Hamburg informant, he added a list of important writers, including Klopstock, Karsch, Wieland, and Lessing. Burney concluded that the fragmentation of Germany was detrimental to its music in part because of the rivalry between German princes, who set up "musical monarchies" and were jealous of one another. Italian musicians also tended to be given preferential treatment, and the best German musicians were to be found outside the country.

As we have seen, Burney's definition of music was not limited only to the serious and refined; it also included music making at its most informal and prosaic. His interest, moreover, lay in compiling an overall picture of German music. "German music" would thus be defined as contrapuntal music, as well as the music he heard while traveling in the German states. The music performed in Berlin would thus be considered representative ("more truly German than that of any other part of the empire") because it was composed by Germans (e.g., Graun, Agricola, or Hasse), even if in the Italian style.[207] Burney defended his views by appealing to his right as a critic to exercise his own judgment:

My intention was neither to write a panegyric, nor a satire, on the music of Germany, but to describe its effects on my own feelings. I set

out with a desire to be pleased; and if I have been sometimes dissat-
isfied, and my disappointment has produced censure, I hope it will not
draw upon me the charge of wanting either impartiality or candour.[208]

German musicians and scholars, in contrast, defined their music in more
affirmative terms and would not have objected to a panegyric. So began
Burney's problems with the Germans.

Reading Burney

Although contemporary scholars tend to reduce Burney's hostile reception to
national rivalry, in my view the reception paints a broader picture. As I have
argued, the Anglo-German encounter tells us something about the status of
eighteenth-century travel and the ways in which the musical traveler figured
in the constitution of national and imperial imaginaries. The political dispositions of Britain and the German states were, of course, inherently different, yet we find both Britons and Germans engaged in imbricated efforts
to construct new narratives that would promote specific class, professional,
and political interests. Linking Britain and the German states was the musical traveler, who brought them into closer proximity through personal
contact and the dissemination and exchange of culture. At the same time,
Britain and the German states were put on a collision course because of their
competing claims on the musical journey and on what that journey was
supposed to do and represent.

Burney had set out for the Continent with all the optimism of a British
empiricist schooled in travel writing. He was a reader of David Hume and
Baron d'Holbach and attached corresponding importance to observation as a
basis for understanding. In the spirit of the Argonaut Orpheus, he expected
musical knowledge to follow from observing music's uses and charting its
effects. The enemy of knowledge, in contrast, was baseless speculation and a
lack of firsthand experience of France, Italy, and the German states—it was
the music unheard and the manuscript sources unread. To the extent that he
had reservations about his approach, his doubts were likely to have concerned
his innovations to the travel genre. It is worth remembering that, in the
1770s, music scholarship still lacked a well-defined critical and historiographic apparatus, whereas travel writing was arguably the Enlightenment's
foremost scientific genre. Experimenting with travel and travel writing was
to challenge centuries of scientific thinkers; it was also to challenge the legion
tourists who had turned their hand to travel writing and thus felt qualified to

judge. By foregrounding music and producing a specialized travel account, Burney had done something new.

It should be said that Burney's innovation was not entirely unprecedented. We have an example of a specialized travelogue in the work of one of Burney's own family members, his brother-in-law Arthur Young, whose *Six weeks tour, through the southern counties of England and Wales* (1768) focused on the state of British agriculture, manufacturing, and rural life.[209] It is difficult to know whether Burney was directly influenced by his in-law, but it seems possible that Young set an idea in motion. The imperative for firsthand observation, useful knowledge, and the benefits of comparison were among the lessons he offered. In his *farmer's letters* (1767), for example, Young compared English agricultural practices with European and Chinese methods: Whereas China was "thoroughly cultivated," it was a regrettable fact that vast tracts of English land still went unimproved.[210] Thus, Young called for travelers to tour the globe and profit from the systematic study of its agriculture. Since grand tourists neglected this as an object of study, and no travel book had yet adopted the kind of plan he had in mind, Young compiled an apodemic for his "attentive traveller."[211] The ideal traveler ought, he said, to possess physical vigor, a "pliancy of disposition," perspicuity, thoughtfulness, and attentiveness, a vast knowledge of languages, and a scholarly yet practical understanding of agriculture, husbandry, and botany. Since the traveler would need to possess wealth sufficient to embark on such an undertaking, public investment in the "plan" could help bring it to fruition. The result, Young proclaimed, would be "the most useful book of travels that ever appeared in the world!"[212]

Although Young had created a model for the specialized travelogue, Burney never tired of emphasizing the fact that musical travel was what he described as a "quixotic" enterprise: Travelers had long reported on music in their letters, but no one had explicitly set out to redefine the travelogue for musical purposes.[213] On the whole, the British reception was positive: Nice things were said about the German travelogue by David Garrick and Oliver Goldsmith, among others.[214] Burney's innovation did, however, raise flags for some critics, who stumbled over the novelty of foregrounding music.[215] A piece in the *Monthly Review* (1773), for instance, stressed not only that Burney's German endeavor was full of "novelty, variety, and [an] abundance of agreeable and excellent matter" but also that it was a "new and almost unbeaten track of enquiry." The anonymous reviewer (actually Burney's friend William Bewley) said that, in light of this, he was "embarrassed where to make a stand."[216] Others, like Samuel Johnson, were less circumspect and described Burney's French and Italian tour as too much about "fiddles and fiddle strings." The dictionary maker was better satisfied with Burney's German travelogue and is said to have used it as the model for his own tour of Scotland, one of the century's highly influential books of travel.[217] Nevertheless, Johnson could not refrain from describing his predecessor in unflattering terms such as "that clever dog Burney" and complained about his tedious preoccupation with German carillons and organs.[218]

The fact that British critics could not agree on the appropriate balance among musical, social, and political phenomena suggests that Burney's experiment with the travel genre was one of the impediments to unanimous approbation. At the same time, their critique hinted at unresolved questions about the proper place of music within British society: Did music and music scholarship warrant the kind of elevation on which Burney and other music professionals were insisting? Such concerns signal the changing position of music within aesthetics, where music had always been subordinate to the other arts, but they also signal changes within society as a whole. When we recall the misuse of musicians, described at the beginning of the chapter, and compare this with their future status, the change can be more properly described as a revolution. By the early nineteenth century, musicians would no longer need to fight for the recognition of music per se: A concert-going public endorsed serious music, and music would become a defining criterion of the national character—particularly in the case of Germany. Other questions would be raised about the proper identity of domestic musical culture. Some critics seized on Burney's musical catholicity (meant in both senses of the word) as an excuse to agitate for music that was more "Heart of Oak" than Italian recitative. If Burney had set out for the Continent at an opportune moment in British history—a moment of maximal interest and enthusiasm for scientific travel and cultural relativism—the following decades would be a tipping point that directed the British gaze inward.

Let us cross the English Channel, then, to take stock of some of the German responses. Ebeling's angry letter provided the first spark in Burney's trouble with the Germans, but it was Hamburg-based publisher and translator Johann Joachim Christoph Bode who turned the smolder into a bonfire. During the preceding decade, Bode had published a significant quantity of English literature, including works such as Laurence Sterne's *Tristram Shandy* (1759–1767) and *A Sentimental Journey through France and Italy* (1768).[219] This familiarity with British literature seems to have emboldened Bode, who thought that Burney could be negatively contrasted with the model of travel writing that British authors had themselves perfected and popularized. Bode tried first to mobilize a group of readers who would identify Burney's errors; then he solicited essays from scholars living in various cities on Burney's route. Bode planned to publish these essays as a kind of counternarrative to Burney's own, but the announcement of a rival translation in Leipzig accelerated his need to publish and left insufficient time to bring this critical material together.[220]

Still, Bode seemed to relish the task of critiquing Burney's work himself: He highlighted factual errors, interjected sarcastic comments, and cut whatever he thought superfluous or offensive to readers and censors.[221] Gone were descriptions of places and sights (like the impressive Ludwigsburg orrery and the Dresden picture gallery) that were apparently familiar to German readers;[222] so, too, was material of an explicitly political nature, including Burney's remarks about Württemberg's impoverished subjects and Potsdam's resemblance to a city under siege.[223] At the same time, Bode augmented the text with many extraneous remarks (he mentioned, for example, the worthiness of erecting a statue to a dead general) and was quick to defend composers like Graun and other members of the Berlin circle, whom Burney had described as derivative and out of date. Bode also inserted anecdotes about personal acquaintances, including an encomium to violinist and composer Franz Benda (whom Bode hoped would read the book) and Johann Mattheson, whose extensive musical writings Bode considered "very useful."[224] While most of Burney's musical observations were left intact ("In musical matters the translator wanted to let Dr. Burney say in the text what appear[ed] in the original"), Bode supplemented these observations with editorial comments that consistently questioned and mocked the Englishman's views.[225]

For all of this heavy editorializing, Bode included some interesting observations about German musical life. In response to Burney's remarks about royal composer and flute teacher Quantz, Bode made a minor concession when he explained why German music was not uniformly high in quality. He pointed out that in many places *Stadtmusikanten* had the exclusive right to play at public events and that these musicians had to master a great number of instruments. This, he said, "held back many a musical genius from achieving excellence on a [single] instrument."[226] Although Bode disagreed with Burney about the status of old music (Burney, remember, was a modernist), Bode's purpose was less to espouse a well-developed aesthetic position than to defend German musicians against Burney's preferences and oversights. Bode excused the harshness of his own critique by saying that he wanted to forewarn the reader about Burney's forthcoming general history; the reader also needed to be made aware of the fact that in Burney's travelogue "judgment had been passed on an entire nation about an art that had supplied all other nations with the most admirable masters and this judgment had been uttered using four words [patience, profundity, prolixity, and pedantry] as cavalierly as if a young gentleman were to judge his tailor for making an outfit he didn't like." Burney, he concluded, was not a bad person, just susceptible to "national prejudice and evil circumstances."[227] This critique, which ranged from attacks on the Englishman's character to assaults on his judgment, erudition, and investigative method, would, as we will see, have a significant impact on the reception that followed.

Up until the Bode publications, German music journals had excerpted letters and travelogues that dealt only with music, but hereafter a number of German scholars would emulate Burney's model. Music journalist, composer, and musical traveler Johann Friedrich Reichardt published four volumes of musical travel writing in the form of "intimate letters," with the last work appearing in 1810. Carl Friedrich Cramer's *Magazin der Musik* (1786) published several announcements for his work and informed readers that the *Musikalische Reisen in England, Frankreich, und Deutschland* (Musical Travels in England, France, and Germany) was about to go to press and would be available in time for Michaelmas of the following year. Making a claim that could have been lifted directly from Burney, *Magazin der Musik* stated that the work would provide an account of the present state of music in all of the countries the author had visited and contain a "true presentation of all curiosities that [the author] had seen and heard himself." As if to disavow any unfortunate comparisons with unnamed earlier musical travelers, the new account was going to provide the "most faithful description" of all.[228] Johann Nicolaus Forkel was another who enticed the German reading public with the promise of a superior musical travelogue, this one supposedly to appear in time for the Leipzig Easter book fair. Forkel's travelogue has never been found and is now presumed not to have actually been written.[229] However, the fact that both Reichardt and Forkel felt bound to contribute to the genre, even while lambasting its best-known practitioner, testifies to the abiding significance of travel writing and to the fact that no other genre had yet arisen to decisively take its place.

Such promises of exclusivity and superior musical travel writing tell us something about German objections to Burney's methodological approach. A work that takes this as its express challenge is Reichardt's earlier travel piece, *Briefe eines aufmerksamen Reisenden, die Musik betreffend* (Letters of an Attentive Traveler, concerning Music, 1774). It is less bellicose than Ebeling's fiery letter and not as sarcastic as Bode's editorializing, but it is all the more devastating for its point-by-point critique, and, as the most analytic treatment of Burney's German travelogue, it warrants our attention.[230] Reichardt was troubled by the problem of Burney's contradictions, and it was this anomaly that framed his piece. He began by setting out the personal and intellectual criteria that he deemed necessary in the musical traveler. Like Arthur Young, from whom we heard earlier, Reichardt stressed that the ideal traveler ought to possess "fine feeling" and perspicuity, personal experience, thorough knowledge of the art, and rigorous schooling in the works of the masters. This schooling, he said, had only to be modified by impartiality and openness to new experiences. Further, the traveler ought to travel specifically in order to listen (not just to look) and to listen only to the best. Above all, the traveler needed to keep his goal foremost in mind and sacrifice everything to this intellectual purpose. Finally, the traveler had to be able to convey his impressions in a clear, considered, and appealing way.[231]

Where Reichardt thought the Englishman had most erred was in his capacity for discrimination. Reichardt said that the traveler asked everyone he encountered—"whether partisan, ignoramus, or troublemaker"—for an opinion. If someone came along holding a different opinion, that person too was questioned and the response dutifully noted. Reichardt thus attributed the inconsistencies in Burney's work to the fact that he had simply given his own name to all views.[232] This error was predicated on an inability to appraise informants accurately and choose the one most qualified to express an opinion. Reichardt considered this shortcoming tantamount to being spoiled by the French and Italians and becoming "too little an Englishman."[233] It was refined criticism on the German's part, for, by describing Burney as insufficiently English, Reichardt managed to target the cultural hegemony of France and Italy and, at the same time, oppugn the intellectual and economic liberties that caused late eighteenth-century Britain to be labeled a free and happy isle. Having routed Britain, France, and Italy with a single remark, it was not necessary to spell out the implication that German scholars could do better, if not politically and economically, then at least culturally.

Reichardt backed up his point by stressing that Burney had fraternized with "bad people," whom he defined as those who were unknowledgeable and lacking in moral probity. While the talented had to be studied in the minutest detail, the inexperienced and untalented warranted no attention whatsoever.[234] Yet, he added, only if informants exhibited "good character" and were free of "envy and partisanship" should their opinions be noted; otherwise the traveler ran the risk of mistaking falsities for "true knowledge." The perspicuity of an observant traveler thus rested on both appropriately judging works of art and judiciously choosing informants. According to Reichardt, Burney's inability to "read the soul" correctly had left him open to error and deception. Finally, the Berlin critic spelled out the consequences of

Burney's poor adjudication: "Almost an entire public has been hoodwinked," he said.[235] Even if we excuse Reichardt's rhetorical flourishes, his statement intimates the scope of the German investment in Burney's undertaking. For Reichardt, the Englishman's failure to compile an accurate and salutary account of the present state of German music was an affront to the truth, but, by cornering public opinion and conveying erroneous information, Burney had also thrown the Germans' own musico-political agenda into jeopardy.

Equally critical was Johann Nicolaus Forkel. As the prospective author of his own universal history of music, the *Allgemeine Geschichte der Musik* (1788–1801), Forkel was moved to ask whether it was possible to expect anything of value from a music history written by an author who consistently associated with the wrong kinds of people:

> We thus ask, for example, what is to be expected from a universal history of music, whose author, in selecting his material, is capable of finding ordinary itinerant musicians or even so-called *Schenkenvirtuosen* (beer fiddlers) so important that he often tells us about them for entire pages, evaluating their taste, their execution, their pieces, and everything about them in the exactest detail? Is this any different from an art historian taking into serious consideration the skill of the whitewasher or common housepainter and trying to draw conclusions from this about the state of art in a country?[236]

Forkel was witty but not entirely fair. Burney had indeed listened to diverse kinds of music and questioned its practitioners no matter what their occupation or social standing: the music of buskers, peasants, and aristocratic amateurs no less than that of professional musicians had all been of interest. But there was an element of hyperbole in Forkel's suggestion that that much-maligned species of musician, the beer fiddler, had dictated the Englishman's views on music. As I pointed out earlier, Burney may have stereotyped and criticized German music, but he was not given to the sorts of category confusion implied in Forkel's critique: Peasants singing on the banks of the Danube and orchestral playing in Mannheim both contributed to a general picture of German music making, but Burney never equated one with the other. Forkel's insistence on professional expertise and his sensitivity to the distinctions of social class—something English travelers often observed about Germans—thus mark an important difference between the German critics and their English counterpart.[237]

What might have been construed as Burney's democratic approach to scholarly investigation was seen by the likes of Forkel as a flagrant disregard, even disdain, for scholarly expertise and for serious music itself. Burney's other indiscretion was to refer to music as nothing but a pleasant diversion and to subordinate his scholarly activity—the history of music—to weightier matters.[238] Such understatement was anathema to scholars like Reichardt and Forkel, whose efforts to develop scholarly practices, institutions, and standards and to delineate their own spheres of expertise were all undermined by Burney's approach. Where Burney seemed aleatoric, they demanded focused attention (hence the title of Reichardt's counter-travelogue); where Burney was catholic in his approach, they insisted on exclusivity; where he entertained the opinions of the amateur and the peasant, they called for the authority of the professional scholar, composer, or performer.

By seizing on the problem of the informant and the resulting confusion between false and "true knowledge," Reichardt and Forkel drew on a familiar critique. As we see in the case of Samuel Johnson's *Journey to the Western Islands of Scotland* (1775)—a work said to have been modeled on Burney's own—late eighteenth-century travel writing was under increasing suspicion as a reliable basis for knowledge making.[239] When Johnson's travelogue appeared in print, it was criticized both for its English bias and its investigative mode. A critic complained, for instance, about Johnson's tendency to question informants indiscriminately and did so in terms very similar to those employed by Reichardt and Forkel:

> [Johnson] might, for instance, question one of his *brogue-makers* concerning some nice point of antiquity, to which the poor fellow could make but a very imperfect answer. The next *taylor* he met might vary, in some circumstances, from the former; and a third person, not better informed than either of them, might differ a little from both. What then? Is there any thing surprising or uncommon in all this? Or can such a variation in the accounts of illiterate mechanics justify the Doctor's general inference, "that there can be no reliance upon Highland narration?"[240]

Perhaps, as Mary Poovey argues, the experience of traveling caused Johnson to question the epistemological status of travel writing and, indeed, to doubt the value of all systematic knowledge projects.[241] Burney, in contrast, did not seem to share the same concerns about "illiterate mechanics" and the unreliability of native "narrators." To be sure, he complained about unknowledgeable informants like the "ignorant cleric" in Antwerp who sent him chasing after his tail in search of the origins of harmony, and he complained about those who failed to give his historical project due attention.[242] Unlike Johnson, Reichardt, and Forkel, however, Burney did not conceive of the traveler's informant as part of a broader epistemological problem.[243] The poor scholar and strolling player—the equivalents of Johnson's "illiterate mechanics"—could be questioned because they possessed their own forms of musical expertise and because Burney trusted his ear to discern what he would have thought of as a kind of musical veracity—a lyrical melody, pleasing harmony, and faithful performance. For him, musical truth resided in an opera by Hasse, but it also lodged in, say, the affecting performance of the dulcimer player in Maastricht or the fine street concert in Munich.[244] Although these musicians belonged to different social classes and their music to distinct categories, Burney found them all pleasantly diverting. Burney's critics, on the other hand, were not prepared to subordinate them under a single aesthetic heading or even under the label of "German music."

These differences of opinion could still be debated today. What is interesting, however, is that Burney's musical judgment was critiqued according to a set of criteria that belonged to the epistemological analysis of travel rather than what we would think of now as musicology. When Reichardt and Forkel pointed out Burney's contradictions, they stressed his shortcomings as an ideal traveler. The nub of their critique was that truth and comprehensiveness could not be founded on haphazard investigation and unsound sources. Musical investigation needed to be guided by an overarching aesthetic principle. Underscoring this epistemology of music were of course some occult assumptions that were never spelled out. We can draw a conclusion from this that explains both subsequent aesthetic developments and the decline of the musical travelogue after the turn of the century: Interrogating travel experience as an epistemological ground highlighted the need for a newly articulated set of aesthetic criteria. Musical knowledge would gradually cease to be thought of as the sum of what music did and instead come to be defined as something inherent to the work itself.

In his own musical travel writing, Reichardt later fell victim to the same difficulties as Burney and produced what has been described as a travelogue fraught with contradictions. It has been argued that these contradictions arose because of the genre itself and because of the political and ideological constellation that existed at the time the account was written.[245] The French Revolution, Inge Stephan argues, caused insecurity about ideological positions and categories of judgment and perception.[246] We can, I believe, extend similar concessions to Burney. If he traveled during the eye of the storm—that settled period between the Seven Years War, the loss of the American colonies, and the outbreak of the French Revolution—his moment of revolutionary tumult was a cultural one. The problem was how to liberate the pleasure and interest of the ear from assumptions about disparate categories of music and how to free judgments about music from judgments about its producers. Once serious music had been established as having meaning and value inherent in the work, it could be reclaimed (and celebrated) as German.

Conclusion

Ebeling had insisted in 1773 that he was "of all nations" and that the German states amounted to "Germany" only when viewed from afar, but at the end of the century the regional-national tension was still operative. We see this in comments made by the outspoken musician and scholar Christian Friedrich Daniel Schubart (1739–1791), whom Burney had met when passing through Ludwigsburg.[247] Schubart complained in his memoirs that he had arranged for Burney to hear a concert of music that was *ächt deutsch*—dances, chorales, fiddle tunes, and other "national songs." Yet what Burney seemed to hear was just a "bough chopped off the great *welsch* [i.e., Italian] stem and transplanted onto Swabian soil." This reference to "welsch" was a play on Burney's Italophilia and his Celtic origins, but the word was also an invective for sodomite that cast aspersions on the Englishman's sexuality (about which more in chapter 3).[248] By heaping such disapprobation, Schubart implied that Burney had heard only what he wanted to hear and been deaf to the music that really counted.

Such remarks remind us that "German music" was even now an oppositional category rather than an affirmative one and that music scholars, critics, and travelers had not yet succeeded in stitching a whole cloth out of Germany's diverse fabrics. The English traveler had run afoul of scholars like Ebeling and Schubart because he had failed to adequately promote German music; he had overlooked regional and national specificities, confused the musical import with the domestic article, and given neither its proper due. One could label this national pride.[249] Yet, in my view, there is something reductive, even ahistorical, about thinking of Burney's German reception only in these terms. Critics like Ebeling, Reichardt, Forkel, and Schubart were certainly wounded in their "Germanness," but this was not necessarily the same as "national pride." The critics' responses show precisely that national musical culture was an aspiration rather than a fact of life in the last decades of the century. Burney had been invited to tour the German states in the hopes that his musical travels would be the making of Germany's musical reputation. In his privileged role as traveler, Burney was to compare German music with its French and Italian counterparts—music he was well qualified to judge because of his earlier journey to France and Italy. On the strength of the comparison, he was supposed to discover the superiority of German music to the rest of Europe and to Germans themselves. This was of course especially true of German instrumental music, but it was hoped that Burney would spread the good word about its vocal music, too.

At the same time, Burney's musical travels were supposed to forge some coherence out of the diversity of German musical life, to accomplish what journals and letters had imperfectly done so far—create a contiguous musical topography. Burney's critics did not spell out the fact that mapping German music would be akin to forging a unified *Kulturnation* out of a political "perplexity."[250] Yet, as I have shown, there was a widespread desire on the part of travel propagandists like Nicolai, Riesbeck, Schlözer, and Seume to increase domestic knowledge about the German states and, by extension, to stage Germany for its European neighbors. Other states had capital cities, Riesbeck would say, but Germany lacked a city to which "all the people contributed a single tone." Only greater knowledge of Germany and a sense of collective identity would allow Germany to realize its cultural and political potential.[251]

Traveling was at the center of the enterprise to distill and export Germany's "essence," and musical travel was part of this broader Enlightenment project. When Ebeling and his colleagues set about organizing and promoting Burney's travels, they shared an implicit understanding about three things: what travel could accomplish on behalf of a common set of cultural practices and collective identity; what music could do on behalf of the "nation"; and what the outsider could do that they could not do themselves. Burney would confirm some of these assumptions. He commented in minute ways about many aspects of German social, cultural, and political life, so that his travelogue is still thought of as one of the most intimate and instructive sources on late eighteenth-century music. He also created a whole picture of German music for his own domestic audience. But, as we by now know, his journey was not able to gratify the Germans' need to have their music promoted and figuratively amalgamated by an outsider. The failure to adequately perform this cultural labor, indeed to subvert its very project by casting aspersions on the quality of German music and questioning the German capacity for innovation (or "genius," as it was called), would make enemies of Burney and his German critics.

Additionally, the reception makes clear that the Anglo-German brouhaha stemmed from methodological and aesthetic differences. Britons and Germans functionalized Burney's journey, competed over its symbolic capital, and claimed the right to inscribe their own respective national and imperial narratives, but they also disagreed—at least on paper—about the purpose of music and the nature of musical knowledge making. Disagreement centered on whether music was first and foremost utilitarian and musical knowledge historical and sociological. Alternatively, was music essentially autonomous and musical knowledge hence aesthetic? Burney inclined to the former: Coming from a tradition of enlightened empiricism and shaped by the conventions of eighteenth-century travel writing, he saw music as an index of social and political progress. Examining the present state of music indicated something about the level of musical development, as well as about the society that produced and supported such music. Historical and ethnological comparisons readily followed.

Within Burney's conception, the Orpheus myth thus figured as a story about music's uses in society. The German critics, on the other hand, were inclined to disagree with Burney's contextualized approach, looking upon music discourse (especially wondrous Orphic claims) as a paean to music. If music could be said to tame beasts, facilitate travel, charm gods, or cure ailments, this was a way of emphasizing the significance of music and, by extension, a way of promoting the importance of music professionals. It was not, on the other hand, an accurate descriptor of music itself. We can say, then, that Orphic discourse constituted the intellectual paradigm for the subsequent development of ethnomusicological and music sociological approaches: It was a story that framed music as something to be used instrumentally within society but whence could also be read something about society itself. In the hands of German scholars, in contrast, Orphic discourse would become the hyperbolic element within the rhetoric of aesthetic autonomy, which emerged around the turn of the century: It provided the metaphysical grounding upon which the musical work's self-sufficiency was said to be predicated. What becomes then of our confident Argonaut, whose music cuts through the waves? The celebrated companion of Jason, whose music charms and conquers? We will not find this Orpheus again in the remainder of the book. Our later figures of Orpheus will be riven, fearful, nostalgic, mournful: From now on, music will be a cipher for the split between being and knowing, the sign, one might say, of loss.

CHAPTER TWO | Music's Empire

O NE HAS TO marvel at the way Orpheus dispatched with his enemies. With a simple song and a strum of the lute he dealt with sirens, dragons, beasts, and three-headed dogs. Until the last desperate battle, when no music was strong enough to save him, his adversaries always bent to his musical will. Music was not just a soothing, pacifying, and ameliorating force; it was also humiliating, violent, even murderous.

Perhaps Burney meant to test this coupling of music and might when he headed for Potsdam to pursue one of Rousseau's claims about military music.[1] Prussia had won a series of aggressive territorial wars that established it as Europe's new power broker, and with this came a reputation for the best military music on the Continent. Burney entered the parade ground expecting to find the band well drilled and the musicians hard at work. But he would be as disappointed by the king's "Marsch in Es" (I am guessing this was the piece) as he had been by some of the military bands in the Netherlands and France.[2] Where were the fortifying effects and the quickened pulse one expected from a march? The dash of sound that sent infantrymen over the ramparts, urged young apprentices to enlist, and made old veterans sit taller in their seats? Reflecting on this later, Burney would be reminded that the ancient Tyrrhenians had been humane enough to whip their slaves to the strains of the flute because this eased the pain and so lessened the punishment. But, Potsdam was no Etruria: At the Prussian court the flute was the rod of punishment itself. Burney remarked naughtily in his *General History,* "It seems, by the lightness of the music...that the Prussian soldiers are scourged to the sound of instruments at present." The music historian departed, disappointed by what he had seen and heard of German music generally and also increasingly skeptical about what he called "the empire of music over the passions."[3]

There was, however, one realm where agential music retained something of its ancient potency. To revisit this discursive space, we must leave Potsdam for the Berlin neighborhood of Dahlem and purchase a ticket to the Ethnology Museum. The museum's modernist façade gives no clues to the venerable collection of ethnographica assembled two hundred years earlier. In the South Seas Hall, visitors marvel at the Polynesians' seafaring ships with their vast outriggers and magnificent pandanus-mat sails; they are intrigued by navigational charts made of sticks and shells and riveted by the assembly of shrunken heads with eyes staring and mouths fixed in constant exclamation like depictions of wonder that Descartes called "the sudden surprise of the soul."[4] Visitors can also study musical instruments collected in the Pacific in the 1770s by Captain Cook and his German naturalists, Johann Reinhold Forster and Georg Forster. Arrayed in the dim display cases are nose flutes, panpipes, conch trumpets, and drums. They are tacit now, but their music once enlivened the dance steps of Tongan women who greeted a handful of voyagers on a spring day in 1773; their music also augmented the fury of Maori men as they gathered on a beach.

Burney knew these instruments, or ones very like them. They had been exchanged for cloth and nails, stored in a naturalist's trunk, and shipped around the world, where they were swapped again for social prestige, professional favors, and academic advancement.[5] While most eighteenth-century scholars had to make do with organological references in travelogues, literary reviews, music journals, and treatises, Burney was lucky enough to handle such instruments in his own drawing room; he also received music reports from traveling friends and acquaintances.[6] Such material perhaps persuaded him that one needed to look further afield if one wanted to fathom music's power: In remote places like Tahiti, Jehol (Chengde), or Batavia (Jakarta) music's effects could be tested and its purpose properly interrogated; there scholars could find clues to the origins of music, the relation between past and present, simple and complex, and performer and listener.[7] The thought must have crossed his mind that, although music's empire may have been teetering at home, possibly it still had life on the margins.

In a moment of intellectual convergence, such sentiments struck a chord with Burney's German critics. The odd military buff still believed that the "Grenadier March" had won the Seven Years War, but a greater number of scholars were beginning to think that music no longer acted on domestic listeners as it had in the olden days: Simple tunes did not call nations to arms, temper violent passions, improve civic responsibility, or foster couth behavior among fellow citizens.[8] Friedrich Wilhelm Marpurg, one of Germany's leading midcentury critics, went so far as to question whether music had ever been capable of acting thus on its listeners. He suggested in *Historisch-kritische Beyträge zur Aufnahme der Musik* (1756) that Amphion and Orpheus had probably just tricked their audiences into believing in music's wondrous properties.[9] The author of an anonymous article in *Gelehrte Beyträge zu den Braunschweigischen Anzeigen* (1773) arrived at a similar conclusion, claiming that the classical stories about music were fanciful because they flew in the face of all current experience.[10]

Like Burney, these German critics took a contradictory approach to the question of music's agential powers. They were skeptical about antique claims and subjected them to new intellectual scrutiny. At the same time, they upheld Neoplatonist ideas when it came to discussions of the non-European world.[11] Aestheticians like Johann Georg Sulzer and Carl Ludwig Junker, anonymous journalists, and other commentators on music thought that here the old maxim *artes emollient mores* still ought to apply: The passions of savages could be tempered, the seeds of virtue sown, and the power of music evidenced through its effects on the "raw" and "unpolished."[12] Johann Gottfried Herder made this claim quite explicit by saying that, if one wanted to know Orpheus, one had only to look to the "war feasts and war songs, and singing leaders of the North Americans."[13] For these scholars, not only would music bring the benefits of Enlightenment to those who needed it most, but its good agency would also confirm, even bolster, the social, moral, and political value of serious music at a time when its powers seemed rather doubtful.[14]

The reason music commentators looked farther afield is not hard to find. Europe had always been permeable to the outside world, but the mid- to late eighteenth century saw a significant rise in exploratory travel, including state-funded expeditions that reported on music.[15] The confrontation with unexpected, sometimes inexplicable, cultural practices—Fuegians who shivered in subzero temperatures while making no efforts to dry or warm themselves; Tahitians who practiced infanticide; or Maori who were suspected of cannibalism—troubled metropolitan systems of belief.[16] As we will find in this chapter, music likewise brought surprises. New sonic worlds strained expectations about musical sophistication and progress and probed beliefs about what music could do. For the first time, Orphic discourse would be systematically put to the test.

The use of music in cross-cultural encounters tells us something about the nature of music and the ways in which we position ourselves in relation to others. These were also the lessons for eighteenth-century commentators. Sitting at home, trying to make sense of the new information imparted from afar, metropolitans would be forced to compare the promises of the ancient agential discourse with the changing social and political dynamics wrought by the use of music in foreign encounters. The greatest challenge to their thinking arose, I will argue, not because of European music's effects (or lack thereof) on non-Europeans but because of non-European music's unanticipated, sometimes undesired effects on themselves. This gave rise to fresh concerns about music as a violent and uncontrollable force, concerns that found voice in Enlightenment and later writings on music. Where commentators might once have stressed the pacifying, ameliorative effects of music, they now cited travel stories about bellicose Iroquois intimidating their enemies with songs before scalping them.[17] In other words, European confidence in their own form of "aesthetic technology" seems to have been shaken by the encounter.[18] Instead of Europeans playing the commanding performer, they were cast in the new role of vulnerable listener. It was brought home to them in visceral ways that Odysseus managed to resist the Sirens' song only by blocking his sailors' ears with wax and binding himself to the mast (figure 2.1). They recalled the mythic story of Orpheus dismembered when Thracians countered his singing with a raucous ululation of their own;[19] they were plagued, one might say, by the reminder of what could happen when others began to sing.

We can trace this challenge to musical thought by examining an exemplary case of cross-cultural exchange and its reception in later German writings on music. James Cook's second voyage to the Pacific (1772–1775) was motivated by both national commercial interests—the attempt to find new markets for British commodities—and cosmopolitan scientific ones. Since Ptolemy, scholars had speculated that the northern hemisphere was counterbalanced by a yet undiscovered southern continent—terra australis incognita—and Cook's voyage was to provide the disappointing answer to this ancient geographical problem. He also collected an immense amount of botanical, zoological, and anthropological data that fundamentally changed the European perception of the globe.

Music was likewise the object of scientific study. While seafarers had always remarked in passing on indigenous music, interest in music assumed a more formal dimension during the second Cook voyage. The Admiralty fitted out Cook's two ships with musician marines, and the voyagers were given new occasion to comment on the musical exchanges that occurred in foreign waters. This resulted in the first real documentation of Polynesian music—instrument collections, a few transcriptions, and reports

FIGURE 2.1. Python Painter (fourth century BCE), "Ulysses and the Sirens." Bell krater from Paestum. Height 37.8 cm. Photo: Johannes Laurentius. Antiken-sammlung, Staatliche Museen zu Berlin. By permission of the Bildarchiv Preußischer Kulturbesitz/Art Resource, New York.

about indigenous performances. While these observations cannot be compared with the fully fledged music ethnographies produced in the mid-nineteenth century (nor even with those of some of their eighteenth-century French counterparts), they provided the most extensive accounts of Polynesian music to date. Forster senior had been the intended author of the official voyage account—a potentially lucrative and important commission—but an altercation with the Admiralty meant that the task devolved to Cook.[20]

The younger Forster produced his own counternarrative, a highly readable and informative philosophical account that contained information about music and dance. These reports by the voyage naturalists, together with other voyage travelogues, circulated widely, especially in German-speaking regions, where the Forsters' activities were followed with immense interest. This handful of musical observations acquired a disproportionate significance in the later reception: Although the voyagers' remarks were comparatively few and superficial, they were repeatedly cited and commented upon by subsequent music scholars. Certainly, this was due to the European interest in Polynesian culture. However, it also had to do with the fact that Polynesian culture changed with the coming of Europeans. Early twentieth-century ethnologists like Victor Segalan perceived the voyagers' observations to have preserved the last vestiges of a musical culture that was lost after the arrival of missionaries, the prohibition of indigenous cultural practices, and the introduction of hymn singing, musical notation, and Western musical instruments.[21] We do not need to share this belief in fatal contact and salvage ethnology to recognize why it is then that a few bars of song and some scattered remarks about part singing came to assume the status they did in later music criticism and historiography.

As we will see, the voyage findings raised aesthetic and historiographical problems for music scholars. These encounters were also an important test case for ideas about musical agency because of the position Polynesia occupied within a broader intellectual discourse. Unlike the disparaged Aborigines and Patagonians, who were assigned the lowest rung on the civilization ladder, eighteenth-century Polynesians occupied a more elevated position: They were associated with the origins of culture and, in effect, seen as "living ancestors" of classical society. Scholars seemed to expect the introduction of European music to advance them, just as it might retard the descent of the Chinese, who were thought to be slipping down the ladder. The fact that music did not realize these aims would open an epistemological window. Commentators would have to explain why their own music acted, or failed to act, in the ways that it did.

———

While it has long been recognized that ethnomusicological thought arose in conjunction with European travel and exploration, the impact of the encounter has received less critical attention.[22] This is partly attributable to disciplinary biases that deemphasize music as a form of exchange, as well as to the cleft in music scholarship that discourages imbricated avenues of inquiry.[23] Eighteenth-century ethnomusicological thought has, for example, tended to be seen as the preserve of historical ethnomusicologists and anthropologists, and musical exoticism and music aesthetics as the home turf of musicologists and music philosophers. Only relatively recently have postcolonial theory and cultural studies contributed to a rapprochement between these long-divided fields—a trend that is reflected in the work of scholars such as David Gramit, Philip V. Bohlman, Desmond Harmondshalgh, Georgina Born, and Gary Tomlinson, who variously argue that the engagement with the non-European world played a role in the making of Western music scholarship and various forms of musical identity.[24]

A further bias springs from the nature of the primary material itself. Eighteenth-century German ethnomusicological commentary tends to be overshadowed by the work of French scholars like Jean-Benjamin de Laborde (1734–1794), Joseph Amiot (1718–1793), and Charles Fonton (1725–?), whose ready access to source material gave them a different type of investment in foreign musical vernaculars.[25] On the other side of the Rhine, the ethnomusicological project was still in its infancy: Only during the Wilhelminian period would Germany be in a position to mount the types of missionary and scientific undertakings that had long contributed to scholarly knowledge in France and Britain.[26] Nonetheless, the historian of music passing through late eighteenth-century Hamburg, Braunschweig, Gotha, Leipzig, Berlin, or Hanover would have found evidence in published travelogues and journals of a growing interest in the comparative study of musical difference. Surveying the roughly thirty-three hundred music-related articles published during this period in north and central German journals reveals that some two percent of the articles dealt with non-Western musical themes. This may seem like a trivial quantity. Yet if we consider the fact that articles devoted to topics like military music and polyphony were even fewer in number, then two percent seems like a respectable portion of the musical pie.[27] To this figure we could add the other literary and philosophical genres, including plays, poems, histories, and travelogues, that also thematized non-Western music.

This body of work, like the travel writing on which it was often based, has been largely neglected by contemporary scholars. To the extent that it has been examined at all, scholars have tended to see the corpus mostly in terms of its inadequacy.[28] This is not without some justification. Reference to non-Western music in eighteenth-century scholarship was often fleeting, prejudicial, and undifferentiated; inevitably it was buried within ethnographic observation and narratives of travel, and rarely, if ever, did it conform to present disciplinary standards of objectivity and comprehensiveness. For some historians of the discipline, this has obstructed the task of locating the origins of ethnomusicology in the eighteenth and early nineteenth centuries.[29] I stress, however, that music history, aesthetics, criticism, and the ethnomusicological were intertwined realms of inquiry in the eighteenth century, a fact that is reflected in Enlightenment scholars' heavy dependence on the travelogue as an investigative genre. For this reason alone, I think it is worth revisiting this body of work and setting it like a missing tessera into the larger picture of Enlightenment cultural thought. Eighteenth-century ethnomusicological commentary may tell us regrettably little about non-Western musical cultures of the past. On the other hand, it tells us a great deal about how professional, cultural, and national identities were constituted through musical encounters and the responses to these encounters.

At this decisive juncture in the history of musical thought, the Orpheus story underwent a shift in emphasis. Savage, juvenile, animal, and inanimate listeners had once contributed to music's raison d'être—music was said to have drawn them into an enchanted circle where the distinctions between selves and others were overcome in the act of collective listening.[30] Now music's harmonizing force seemed in question, for music could also divide. When the ships returned to Europe with strange tales of voyagers embarrassed by vulgar songs, audiences held captive by prolonged musical displays, and beach landings repulsed by aggressive dances, scholars would have to rethink their ideas about Orpheus.[31] They may have lamented the end of music's empire in Europe, but for the non-European world there would be no end to music's dominion. In the view of many metropolitan commentators, non-Europeans would not achieve real aesthetic or subjective independence, and the empire of effects would survive in Western thought as a mode for apprehending others and inscribing their radical difference.

Listening to Others

Enlightenment scholars were heirs to a long tradition that associated music with foreign travel and conquest. We see early examples of this in Hans Holbein the Younger's painting *The Ambassadors* (1533), most famous for its anamorphic skull teetering on the floor. Arranged on an oriental carpet are a lute, a wooden flute in its case, and a musical score, together with a set of calipers, a book of mathematical formulae, a collection of scientific instruments, and a globe with Africa prominently displayed. These objects represent the tools of the ambassadorial trade—the ambassadors' literal and symbolic offerings to their hosts and Europe's gifts of science and the arts to new worlds. But they also point to another set of meanings. In addition to the visually encrypted skull, we see that the lute has a broken string and that the flute is disassembled in its case—all early modern allegories for *vanitas*.[32] Music, one might say, puts the ambassadors' command of the world into larger perspective by reminding the viewer of the insignificance and impermanence of worldly endeavors.

More than a century later, another Dutch painter, Pieter de Ring (1615–1660), arranged a similar collection of objects for his *Still Life with Musical Instruments* (1650). A violin, a recorder, and a book of music are positioned below a globe that is rotated to show Mexico. In the center is a large, well-inscribed notebook with a drawing of a young man blowing bubbles, which, like the set of dice in the painting, speak of earthly transience and the brevity of life (figure 2.2). Like Holbein, de Ring includes the trappings of scholarly labor and foreign travel—an exotic shell, a pearl necklace, gold coins, a quill, and an ink pot. Richard Leppert argues in relation to such paintings that, as symbols of wealth and cultural achievement, these objects celebrate social status and consumption. Because musical instruments fall into the same category, they can be seen as a celebration of music. Yet, the instruments are simultaneously a reminder of *vanitas,* and this reminder in effect indicts music.[33]

Although early modern allegory insists on this double meaning for music, my assumption is that the coupling of music and travel told a different story for later viewers. For the eighteenth century, the juxtaposition of musical instruments, ethnographica, maps, and weapons seems to hint at music's capacity for a literal apprehension and an appropriation of the world itself. Enlightenment music scholars saw music as a medium of travel and diplomacy and as a means of furthering their own interests. In a 1747 report about the music of the "Juda Africans" (probably Ethiopians), for instance, Lorenz Mizler commended European settlers for successfully introducing many improvements to Ethiopia. On the other hand, he was critical of the fact that the settlers had not yet introduced Western musical instruments and persuaded Ethiopians to forego "barbaric concerts that wrenched even the toughest ears." Once the Africans were successfully converted to Western music, he said, all manner of positive change would follow because progress in music was inevitably linked to progress in the other sciences.[34]

The belief that music could order, improve, and cultivate non-Europeans was predicated on certain assumptions about not only music, of course, but also the nature of non-Europeans. Popular journals like *Der Wißbegierige* (1784) reported, for example, that Gold Coast Africans started dancing the moment they heard an instrument played.[35] Scholarly publications likewise spread the idea that the native was innately receptive—a listener awaiting the benefits of introduced music. One of Forkel's *Musikalisch-kritische Bibliothek* (1778) articles claimed, for instance, that because of their torpid character the Japanese, Chinese, Siamese, and Indians stirred themselves to work only if they heard sharp sounds. The author hardly needed to spell out the colonialist applications of using sound to control the labor of so-called recalcitrant Asians.[36] Besides being thought of as naturally receptive to sound, non-Europeans were typically considered closer to nature than contemporary Europeans, and even as their "living ancestors." This geographical-temporal slippage meant that non-Europeans could be used as a laboratory for the study

FIGURE 2.2. Pieter de Ring (1615–1660), *Still Life with Musical Instruments* (1650). Oil on canvas, 105.6 × 81.7 cm. Photo: Joerg P. Anders. Gemäldegalerie, Staatliche Museen zu Berlin. By permission of the Bildarchiv Preußischer Kulturbesitz/Art Resource, New York.

of both present and past social, economic, political, and cultural development. Because there was a presumed conformity between climatic conditions, physiognomy, and social structures, music was thought to be a useful ethnographic yardstick: Simple music indicated simpler people, while simple people produced simpler music. An article published in *Gelehrte Beyträge* (1773) claimed, for example, that, just as children produced basic noises, the "Hottentots" were content with a rudimentary three-note ho! ho! ho!, which, according to the anonymous author, was as gratifying to them as opera to an expert or a beer fiddler to a village gathering.[37] This kind of relativism (to each his own kind of music) was turned into an explanation for the native's apparent inability to adjudicate. At the same time, it reinforced the need to introduce a higher, more improving level of musical culture. Commentators implied that advancing non-Europeans could be accomplished via the agency of more sophisticated European music.

No one who reviewed these kinds of sources would have gained an impartial or a detailed understanding of any specific musical vernacular. Yet arguably this was never the point of such commentary. In contradistinction to the handful of Enlightenment scholars like Amiot and Fonton, who focused on a single musical tradition and achieved a degree of nuanced understanding, German commentators were more concerned with studying music's general uses in native ceremonies, games, and work. This emphasis on utility made the cross-cultural encounter all the more important for a stocktaking of music's agential powers. Scholars would have to account for the sometime ineffectiveness of European music versus the unexpected results of native music making, and they would have to rethink themselves as listeners and not only performers. As a result, the notion that music promoted only domestic interests—that it was a tool confidently manipulated by Europeans alone—was one that would now come into question.

The Performative Use of Music

Although eighteenth-century travelers were schooled in a classical discourse that emphasized music's detriments, as well as its benefits, travelers often learned the hard way that music was an instrument of power and that it had the capacity to cut both ways. The second Kamchatka expedition (1733–1743) conducted by Vitus Bering under the auspices of the Russian Academy of Sciences provided one such lesson. The expeditionary results were initially suppressed by the Russian crown on strategic and economic grounds, but they finally found an audience in the 1770s and 1780s, when naturalist Peter Simon Pallas (1741–1811) was assigned the task of publishing the scientific data.[38] It was Pallas who really put Kamchatka on the German map, and thanks to his efforts we find a surge of popular and scholarly interest in the ethnography of the region. As journal articles and other sources indicate, this interest extended to indigenous music.

Drawing on firsthand accounts, Pallas reported that music was used in the Kamchatkans' elaborate hospitality rituals. When strangers came to visit from other islands, he said, the women approached singing and dancing, while the men followed beating small drums. Guests were then treated to a sumptuous meal and entertained with more music until the evening's festivities were brought to a happy close.[39] However, a less rosy picture of native hospitality emerges when one compares Pallas's redaction with the travelogue written by one of the expedition's naturalists several decades earlier. Bering's naturalist, Georg Wilhelm Steller (1709–1746), reported that the Itelmen were indeed highly musical and treated newcomers to impromptu songs composed and performed by local women.[40] Yet Steller's travelogue shows that Pallas and others elided an important point about Itelmen music and the way in which it was used in the encounter: The Itelmen songs were not harmless expressions of hospitality, as Pallas had suggested, but topical, sexual satires.[41] Instead of entertaining the expedition participants, the singers mocked them, singling out the cook and the naturalists for particular critique. "If I were the student [the naturalist, Stepan Krasheninnikov]," sang the Itelmen, "I would describe all the young girls / If I were the student, I would describe the fish *uranoscopum*..." A footnote explained that the fish was known locally by the "vulgar word for female genitals." Steller's travelogue also included song transcriptions that provided further evidence of what he referred to as the "shamelessly sexually explicit" character of their music (figure 2.3).

From Steller's travelogue we learn that the Itelmen were not overtly hostile to the expeditionists: They neither drove the visitors away by attacking them openly nor denied them hospitality. The Itelmen's satirical songs, however, had a sharp edge, for during this party the guests were mocked in song. The fact that this mockery was passed over in later redactions of Steller's travelogue is instructive. On the one hand, we can attribute the elision to concerns about the sexual content of the Itelmen's lyrics: Journals like *Die Akademie der Grazien* and *Gelehrte Beyträge zu den Braunschweigischen Anzeigen* would have been unable to publish anything nearly so prurient. But sex was not the only topic potentially offensive to middle-class German readers. What was true for other eighteenth-century scientific expeditions was true for this one as well, namely, the legitimacy of the undertaking hinged to some extent on the staging of indigenous cooperation. The Itelmen's musical mockery meant a withholding of cooperation, and, with German naturalists well represented in the venture, Pallas was probably reluctant to cast the expedition in a poor light.[42]

FIGURE 2.3. "Itelmen Air," in Georg Wilhelm Steller (1709–1746), *Steller's History of Kamchatka,* 252. Reproduced from the Rasmuson Library Rare Books Collection, University of Alaska, Fairbanks.

We can think of this episode in the Orphic terms envisioned by Plato or Saxo Grammaticus and thus follow Burney and his contemporaries when they claimed that music continued to exert its strange power in the non-European world. Within the context of cross-cultural encounters, music was indeed used to do nonmusical things. The Russians were known to be an unwelcome presence in the region, and it seems reasonable to assume that the Itelmen developed this form of mocking encounter practice as a response to unwanted visitors—an act of resistance that avoided overt hostility yet showed the limits of their own hospitality. To what extent the gesture altered power relations or helped set territorial boundaries is difficult to say: The travelogues do not tell us whether the naturalists collected fewer artifacts, abandoned their ethnological work, or cut short their stay because of their double-edged musical reception. Yet what is clear is that the Itelmen's barbed songs pricked European sensibilities because of the songs' capacity to censure and humiliate the visitors.

We have taken this Kamchatkan detour because the episode provides a condensed account of the cross-cultural musical encounter and its treatment in late eighteenth-century journalistic criticism. The thesis put forth here and in the later sections on Polynesia is that aesthetic and historiographic ideas were tensioned by exploratory travel and cross-cultural exchange. Understanding what music did and how it was interpreted calls, however, for more detailed theoretical explication.

In one of the pioneering studies on music and voyaging, Ian Woodfield uses the concept of "musical diplomacy" to describe the role music played in Elizabethan exploration. Woodfield shows that, because music was a sign of sociopolitical status, mariners were able to use musical performances as a means of negotiating power relations between delegated authorities.[43] The diplomacy concept helps us understand the utilitarian character of these musical exchanges and their representative nature, but it does not really capture their double-sidedness. Music, we know, was performed by both Europeans and indigenous peoples, and it is wrong to assume that both transacting parties necessarily used it to the same ends or the same effect. This means that we need to develop a way of thinking about music that accounts for its independent use by each transactor, a concept that allows for possible changes in subject position when performers become listeners and listeners performers.

Following the work of John Austin, Greg Dening, and Tia DeNora, I propose that we think of music's use in the encounter in terms of the "performative."[44] We can reformulate the linguists' question "How can saying something make it so?" as a musical one to ask how music does things and how it "gets into action."[45] For our purposes, this musical doing encompasses a whole range of actions: It initiates contact and expresses hospitality; stems aggression but also initiates it; controls time, regulates labor, imposes dynamic levels on audiences; curtails physical movement; and marks territorial possession, to list but a few. We know that music achieved these things, yet explaining how and why is more difficult. The cross-cultural encounter will be a testing ground where eighteenth-century commentators have to ask whether music has its own agency. They will wonder, as we do, whether music's capacity to act is attributable to human physiology or to some contextual element. Should music, they will ask, be counted as a universal or a particular?

For Austin, the speech act is bound by its context and relies on a common interpretive framework if it is to take effect. In Austin's famous example (the "I do" that is uttered at a wedding ceremony), the binding words have performative force only if the transacting parties are qualified to speak the words and share a sense of the words' meaning and import.[46] We are inclined to think of musical performances in similar terms and to assume that listeners and performers needed to share a musical vernacular before music could do its work. This seems like a reasonable assumption because we tend to think of culture and identity in the kind of relativistic terms that predispose us to contextual (or "culturalist") understandings of the performative. Following this line of thought, there can be no signification that is not the product of its own culture and no meaning making that is independent of a specific interpretive framework. The question arises, then, as to how consensus is achieved about the meaning (and hence effects) of musical performances. If music did something in eighteenth-century cross-cultural encounters—if it created or reinforced power hierarchies, managed the listener's use of time, intimidated and subordinated its listeners—then we must investigate on what grounds it did so. Couched another way, we must ask why European sailors were cowed by a Maori *haka* and Tahitians, as far as we know, charmed by the bagpipes?

The problem of cross-cultural hermeneutics is certainly not exclusive to music. Scholars have long been troubled by the problem that mutual unintelligibility poses to the transfer of knowledge, culture, and power. In writing about the sixteenth-century encounters between Aztecs and Spanish conquistadors, Tzvetan Todorov asks, for instance, how a handful of men could have effectively conquered a continent. He does not propose the type of materialist answers—environment, weapons, and disease—made popular by Jared Diamond in his work on the fates of human societies.[47] Todorov's answer lies rather within the realm of communication and mental outlook, when he suggests that it was in part thanks to a translator, La Malinche, that Hernando Cortés was able to decipher and master Moctezuma's signs. It was this element of cultural mediation, together with Cortés's historical consciousness—his belief in linear time and historical change—that allowed the Spanish to dominate a society that remained bound by cyclical thinking. Using an argument similar in contour to Marshall Sahlins's insights into Cook's encounter with the Hawaiians, Todorov argues that the Aztecs were constrained by existing patterns of interpretation.[48]

We gain other insights into the question of cross-cultural semiotics from Greg Dening's work on the theatricality of the encounter. Dening suggests that voyagers' and islanders' capacity to understand one another's unfamiliar words, signs, and songs had something to do with the larger framing of these performative events. His specific example concerns the appropriation of territory through a speech act. While the linguistic content of the speech act was not literally intelligible to indigenous peoples, the props that augmented possession ceremonies—the firing of cannon, presentation of medals, flying of the flag, and speechifying—were part of an unmistakable theater of power.[49]

Here we can draw parallels for our understanding of the use and interpretation of music in the encounter. Voyagers targeted their musical selections at indigenous peoples in an attempt to breach the hermeneutic gap; indigenous peoples may have done the same. However, since the latter remains largely a matter of conjecture, we can only confidently report on gestures like the Royal Society guidelines for navigators, an apodemic that stipulated that alarming trumpet pieces and drum tattoos be substituted with soft and gentle airs since the latter were more likely to appeal to native listeners.[50] The use of bagpipes and pentatonic melodies characteristic of Highland music was also part of the attempt to promote cross-cultural understanding. Many non-European cultures were known to use "primitive" five-note scales, and Scottish music was thus regarded as a kind of bridge that might appeal to those who were thought to share the same "rudimentary" level of musical development. The implication was that, by speaking to non-Europeans in their own "musical language," cross-cultural musical communication might be promoted.[51]

We can conclude that the construction of meaning was contingent, arising from the interplay between musical attributes and contextual ones. We find that the performative character of music depended not only (or not necessarily) on specific attributes in the music itself but on the broader context of the cross-cultural encounter. These exchanges of music tended to be staged events rather than casual, everyday affairs.[52] The extramusical "frame" included specific kinds of performance practice that conveyed interpretive clues as to how the unfamiliar music was to be heard and received. Among these were, for example, people in authority commanding music to be played, certain instruments and musical genres being reserved for important audiences and special occasions, the choice of music relative to the event, and the incorporation of music into other festivities.

Finally, music acts performed by Europeans on behalf of indigenous peoples had not only local listeners but also remote ones. The music act can be compared in this regard with linguistic utterances. We know, for example, that the European speech acts that were used when appropriating territory were performed more for a metropolitan public than a local indigenous one.[53] This means we ought perhaps to rethink the audience for the music acts that eighteenth-century European voyagers performed in the Pacific and elsewhere. In the immediacy of the encounter, musical events were staged on behalf of indigenous peoples, but these acts also resonated farther afield. While local listeners were often indifferent to what they heard, there were metropolitan audiences with an ear tuned to the Highland pipers in New Zealand's Dusky Bay (Aotearoa's Tamatea). We will find that what troubled these audiences most was the prospect of another singing and the unsettling effects on themselves.

Having laid out the ways in which I think performativity is helpful for analyzing the use of music in cross-cultural encounters, I would also like to set some limits. The examples I discuss in this chapter indicate that music operated in ways that run parallel to linguistic speech acts, yet also tangentially. Within eighteenth-century cross-cultural encounters, musical performances were capable of doing things. At the same time, music sometimes acted independently of a shared or improvised cultural context that predetermined its meanings. On occasion, performances had unexpected outcomes when music acted on listeners and performers in ways they did not necessarily anticipate or desire and later found difficult to understand or rationalize. The use of music in these encounters thus illuminates some of the ways in which language and music are different, and different not only because of their varied capacities for expressing concrete thought and abstract ideas. In contrast to language, which is inevitably bound by convention for its use and interpretation, music, to some extent, resists the culturalist model. This is not to suggest that music is a universal language, mutually intelligible to all who perform and listen to it: The examples I discuss here do not sustain such a view. Rather, I contend that, because music has its own form of agency, it sometimes has the ability to surprise and disrupt our sense of ourselves and to trouble the boundaries we place on cultural difference.

Orpheus in Other Worlds

Burney returned from the Continent with a jaded view of German music and his main research question unanswered. His European tours had been partly conceived as a quest for the origins of harmony or polyphony (the terms were often used interchangeably in the eighteenth century to refer to either parallel or independently moving parts). Yet despite Burney's assiduous looking, evidence about the origins of polyphony remained as elusive as the Grail itself.[54] As the trunks of books, manuscripts, and research notes were lugged up the stairs to his Queen's Square study, the task of writing must have seemed impossibly daunting. A second travelogue was waiting to be written, and looming ahead was his magnum opus, the general history of music. Burney got down to work on the German travelogue, all the while sifting and sorting what he knew about the history of music. However, in July 1774 our music investigator paused to welcome home his sailor son James, who was returning from a voyage around the world with Captains Cook and Furneaux.[55] In bounded the newly appointed lieutenant with rare trophies—Polynesian tunes he could play on the piano, transcriptions, instruments, and stories about fabulous performances on antipodean beaches.[56] James also returned with some unexpected musical observations; for the historian struggling to order the stages of musical progress, these findings were like something out of left field.[57]

Half of London society gathered to hear from the returning voyagers, but James's most avid listener must have been his father.[58] The elder Burney had a vested interest in the voyage not only because of a family share in the enterprise and his own hunger for musical curiosities but also because he had always cultivated the study and practice of music where he could. This included his friendship with John Montagu (1718–1792), fourth Earl of Sandwich. Sandwich was at this time First Lord of the Admiralty (1771–1782), a great music enthusiast and theater habitué who came to share the Burneys' interest in non-European music.[59] (The elder Burney would later send Sandwich reports supplied by his offspring that dealt with their impressions of Polynesian music [figure 2.4].[60]) This close connection with naval circles suggests that, if Sandwich and the other Admiralty lords had not already thought to send musician marines on Cook's second voyage, then Burney may have swayed the decision to do so.[61] The day James arrived home, Burney was understandably eager to find out what had become of the Admiralty order.

But whatever Charles Burney's role, the story of Europe's engagement with Polynesian music antedates the work of this energetic family. We know there was singing and dancing on Cook's first voyage, just as there had been on earlier English, French, and Dutch exploratory voyages.[62] The National Maritime Museum's *Endeavour* replica shows a doll-sized model of Cook's first voyage fiddler, listed as marine drummer Thomas Rossiter in the navy's muster books at the public record office in Kew.[63] These records indicate that

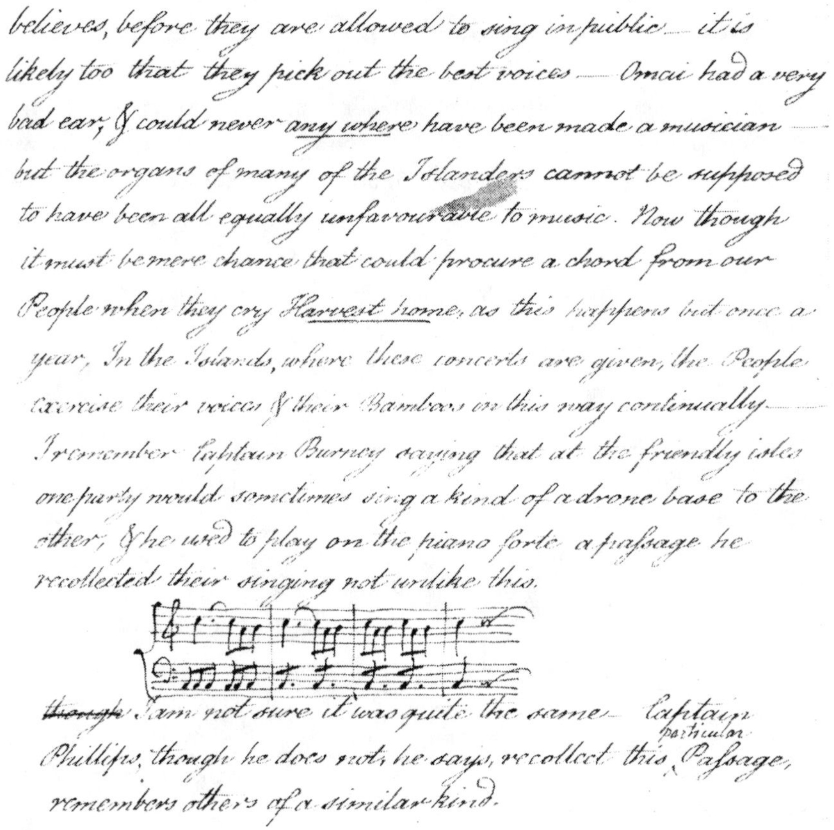

believes, before they are allowed to sing in public — it is
likely too that they pick out the best voices — Omai had a very
bad ear; & could never any where have been made a musician —
but the organs of many of the Islanders cannot be supposed
to have been all equally unfavourable to music. Now though
it must be mere chance that could procure a chord from our
People when they cry Harvest home, as this happens but once a
year, In the Islands, where these concerts are given, the People
exercise their voices & their Bamboos in this way continually —
I remember Captain Burney saying that at the friendly isles
one party would sometimes sing a kind of a drone base to the
other; & he used to play on the piano forte a passage he
recollected their singing not unlike this.

though I am not sure it was quite the same — Captain
Phillips, though he does not, he says, recollect this particular Passage,
remembers others of a similar kind.

FIGURE 2.4. "Friendly Isles Song." As recollected by Susanna Phillips in a letter
to her father, Charles Burney. "Letter to Lord Sandwich with enclosure, 11 February
1784," in *Papers of John Montagu Sandwich, 1771–1784*, MS 7218, item 32. By
permission of the National Library of Australia.

the fiddler's presence aboard ship was nothing out of the ordinary. The navy
disallowed shantying because ships had to be worked quietly, but fiddlers
nonetheless played while the men turned the capstan; there were also rec-
reational opportunities for music making at sea, and some captains hired
their own personal bands of musicians.[64] In the 1770s, however, the Admiralty specifically ordered musician marines recruited, trained, and dispatched on the ships now "bound for discoveries."[65] Although the Admiralty
evidently thought that musical expertise could be as easily acquired as the
medals and trinkets it ordered from its Birmingham manufacturer, getting
the musicians aboard Cook's ships took some doing. Shortly before departure, a drummer and violinist was ordered to "perfect himself" on the fife;

then two bagpipers were seconded from another ship and taken out to the Nore as the ships awaited the order to sail.[66]

The Admiralty did not spell out its motivations for dispatching these musicians: Orders were issued for immediate implementation rather than the benefit of future researchers. It is clear, however, that the Admiralty was not principally concerned with using music to maintain morale when the ships crossed the Line and hit the Doldrums. The training and seconding of musicians, as well as the Admiralty's choice of musical instruments, all point to another purpose—the musicians' potential role in promoting cross-cultural encounters. Mariners depended on the goodwill of local people for trade, provisioning, useful geographical and ethnographic information, companionship, and sex. The Admiralty, like the lowliest cook's mate, knew that a hostile reception could jeopardize a voyage, and if music were capable of deferring hostility, smoothing the voyagers' reception, speeding their passage, and preparing the way for future trading relations, then so much the better.

Underlying this conception of music is something Marshal Sahlins calls a "starting mechanism," an act that initiates new social relations and what I referred to earlier as the performative use of music.[67] By adhering to the Royal Society's tips for sea captains and playing gentle airs instead of frightening trumpets, perhaps the encountered could be induced to respond in kind. If that were so, then music might be to the cross-cultural encounter what John Harrison's invention of a reliable watch would be to the problem of longitude—a solution to one of the more dangerous and uncontrollable aspects of voyaging. With his musician marines ordered aboard, Cook was issued with the usual ethnographic mandate: His instructions solicited basic information about native peoples.[68] There was nothing specifically related to music in this secret document. However, the mere presence of musicians on the ship meant that the possibilities for musical observation increased considerably. For *Resolution* naturalists Johann Reinhold Forster and Georg Forster, whose ethnographic interests were wide ranging, the musical exchanges would provide new insights into Pacific peoples. It is largely through the latter's efforts that Polynesian music first entered the Western scholarly imagination, and it is to this that we now turn.

Musical Encounters in the South Seas

Cook's initial musical encounters did not scuttle ancient theories about the power of music but did not exactly confirm them either. His first listeners were a retiring group of Maori (likely the Ngati Mamoe of Tamatea) seen standing on the rocky shore in Dusky Sound. The group was unimpressed by the voyagers' offer of handkerchiefs and sheets of paper, but when Cook later ordered the bagpipes, fife, and drum to be played, the group grew less reticent. They seemed to like the beating of the drum the best and "entered with great familiarity into conversation with such of the officers and Seamen as went to them." Even so, they could not be induced to board the ship.[69]

In Tahiti, things were more auspicious for the music makers. The voyagers anchored at Aitepeha Harbor (Vaitepiha Bay on the Taiarapu peninsula) in August 1773 in order to provision the ship with fresh greens, water, and meat, for which they exchanged ironware and other commodities. It was the end of the antipodean winter; the trees and plants had stopped producing, and there would be no new livestock for many months. The islanders' desire for ironware thus had to be balanced against the threat that the voyagers posed to the local food supply. Within a few days, the Tahitians stopped offering hogs for trade, precipitating Cook's decision to move on and look for meat elsewhere. For the islanders, however, there were incentives in persuading the Europeans to stay, and they duly turned over another pair of hogs. Cook's departure was delayed, and for the moment, at least, both Tahitian and European interests seemed to have been met.

However, this direct exchange of things—or balanced reciprocity—left no surplus of goodwill. As I have argued elsewhere, such immediate, equivalent requital was seldom adequate when it came to fostering cross-cultural relations: Happy encounters hinged on a meeting of mutual interests and then some.[70] It was, namely, when things were given for "free," or over and above the direct exchange of goods, that goodwill was generated.[71] For this, Cook sometimes resorted to music, ordering the men to dance and sing and the Highland marine to play the bagpipes. Forster reported that the piper's "uncouth music, though almost insufferable to our ears, delighted the [Tahitian] king and his subjects to a degree which we could hardly have imagined possible. The distrust which we perceived in his looks at our first interview was now worn off." Forster and the assistant naturalist, Anders Sparrman, shared the view that, had they remained there long enough, the islanders' standoffishness would have been replaced by "an unreserved confidence."[72] The high-ranking Tu was said to have been particularly enthusiastic about the bagpipe music, and he presented the piper with a large piece of *tapa* cloth after the performance.[73] On the strength of this, Cook ordered further bagpipe demonstrations, as well as country dances and hornpipes, at ceremonial visits elsewhere on the island.[74]

This use of music within the context of trade, hospitality, and ceremonial visits confirmed what was already known from practical experience: Music was a useful means of promoting friendly interactions and was thus invaluable to voyagers, who hoped for a hospitable welcome when they returned in the future. In some instances, music was also able to achieve more than other kinds of gift giving. Nails, hatchets, red baize, paper, beads, and the other baubles that made up the ships' store of tradable goods were generally well received—sometimes greedily or by stealth—but they did not necessarily produce the kind of "feel-good" factor that voyagers associated with classical and biblical stories. Forster believed that the pipes had an effect on Tahitians that was "similar to that of David's harp, whose harmonious sounds soothed the atrabilarious [sic] temper of Saul."[75] Also on Huahine, the islanders were apparently delighted by the bagpipes and "required it to be constantly played."[76] With ill humor thus transmuted, the voyagers found themselves capitalizing on the islanders' amenability and furthering their own material interests.

Although the performative use of music provided a context for ethno-musicological reflection, the voyagers' observations were often burdened by the weight of stereotype.[77] Forster's friend and fellow naturalist Thomas Pennant tells us something about the nature of these prejudicial associations. The bagpipes, said Pennant, were the loudest and most ear splitting of any wind instrument. They roused Highland listeners, sounded the alarm, and rounded up people for battle, making the instrument eminently "suited to the genius of this warlike people." Besides being warlike, Pennant thought the Highlanders indolent, hospitable, proud, vengeful, polite, and super-stitious.[78] James Macpherson's *Ossian* was another important source for views taken up in late eighteenth-century German criticism, where the wild simplicity and potency of Scottish melodies were compared with the wondrous effects of ancient music.[79] More than a quarter of a century later, an article that discussed the *Bergschotten* in Friedrich Rochlitz's *Allgemeine Musikalische Zeitung* (1800) would offer a no more differentiated view of music's effects on the Highlanders' naturally bellicose, patriotic, and passionate character.[80]

For the Enlightenment scholars who fueled this discourse it was thus unsurprising, even expected, that "primitive" people would respond enthusiastically to bagpipe music.[81] The Tahitians' delight simply reinforced the Highland stereotypes that had been transported from Europe's edges to its antipode. Certain characteristics of Tahitian music compounded the problem: Like some Highland music, it had a narrow tonal range; it was also monophonic and repetitive.[82] Other features of the music did not have a corollary in the Gaelic periphery and struck metropolitans as correspondingly odd. The nose flute (*vivo*), for example, attracted much attention for its method of playing (figure 2.5). While the Tongan panpipes (*mimiha*) seemed to conspire with the image of Polynesia as a classical idyll, stories about Apollo's mistreatment of Midas served as a reminder of the price of poor musical judgment.[83] Whether music historians and critics doubted their own capacity for independent musical judgment and, metaphorically speaking, feared a set of ass's ears, I do not know. The fact remains that they proved unwilling to dignify the Polynesian panpipe: Burney, for example, would take the new discovery of the panpipes as an indication only that the instrument was "natural to every people emerging from barbarism."[84] The combined picture of Polynesian music was then of a rudimentary level of musical development that corresponded to the island's respective socio-economic, political, and cultural standing. The Tahitians' rung on the civi-lization ladder might be higher than that of their Pacific neighbors, but Tahitian responses to the "uncouth" bagpipes and Tahitian music itself seemed to indicate that musical tastes were utterly relative.[85]

It is worth remembering, however, that cross-cultural encounters are always double-sided, and on another set of Polynesian islands the voyagers would be confronted with experiences that challenged the supremacy of the performing Orpheus. In October 1773 a hundred or more Tongans gathered to welcome Cook's men, singing a song that Forster described as "exceed-ingly simple" but with a "very pleasant effect, and . . . highly musical when compared to the Taheitian [*sic*] songs." What most appealed to the naturalist was the sweet, mellow tone of the women's voices and the way they kept time by snapping their thumbs and forefingers while holding their other fingers elegantly aloft. Forster went on to say that the Tongan singers were joined by others, who repeated the melody until the whole group sang in chorus.[86] Until this moment, no Pacific visitor had thought to transcribe Pacific music, or, more likely, they had never been trained or instructed to do so. In the seafaring Lieutenant Burney, however, Forster found a uniquely qualified assistant, musically literate and sensitized by his famous father to exhibit an interest in musical curiosities.[87] Forster acknowledged the debt to James in his travelogue by saying he was grateful to this "very ingenious Gentleman" for notating a melody so he could include it as a "specimen" in his narrative. The voyagers observed that these rather slowly sung four notes were "sung in the minor key" and "varied" without going lower than A or higher than E (figure 2.6).[88]

The Tahitians had bored the voyagers with the monotony of their music (the nose flute was said to produce a mere "drowsy hum").[89] In Tonga, how-ever, the music surprised them. The voyagers noted with amazement that

FIGURE 2.5. F. Bartolozzi after Giovanni Battista Cipriani (1727–1785), *A View of the Inside of a House in the Island of Ulietea*, in Hawkesworth, *Account of the Voyages*, vol. 2, plate 7, fp. 265. By permission of the University of Michigan Special Collections.

FIGURE 2.6. Georg Forster, "Tongan welcome song, sung 'in parts,'" in Forster (1754–1794), *Voyage round the World,* vol. 1, 233. Reproduced courtesy of the University of Hawaii Press.

Tongan singing contravened two key tenets of European musical thought—Europe's grip on invention and the nature of musical progress. Contravening what every educated Northerner knew and believed about the exclusive Westernness of polyphony, the voyagers found that Tongan singing was not in fact monophonic but sometimes sung "in parts."[90] In New Zealand, further surprises were in store. The voyagers found Maori singing and dance unexpectedly affecting. Even if the *haka* was hard to interpret—sometimes it seemed to be a gesture of furious welcome, other times a prelude to attack—they thought that the "war dance" was perfectly suited to its purposes.[91] This, too, was the voyagers' verdict about the Maori "mourning song." All who heard the "dirge" sung for Tupaia, a man who had previously accompanied Cook and died meanwhile in Batavia, were struck by how moving it was (figure 2.7). Forster took it as an occasion to affirm both the superiority of Maori music and their common humanity:

> The taste for music of the New Zeelanders, and their superiority in this respect to other nations in the South Seas, are to me stronger proofs, in favour of the heart, than all the idle eloquence of philosophers in their cabinets can invalidate. They have violent passions, but it would be absurd to assert that these only lead them to inhuman excesses.[92]

What surprised the voyagers most of all, however, was the discovery that Maori also sang in parts (figure 2.8). Cook's observers noted a song they sang in thirds—a simple, not unpleasing phrase that was repeated many times over:

> We frequently heard him [Peeterré] and the rest of the natives singing on shore, and were sometimes favoured with a song when they visited us on board. Their music is far superior in variety to that of the Society and Friendly Islands; and if any nation of the South Sea comes in competition with them in this respect, I should apprehend it to be that of Tanna. . . . [James Burney] assured me that there appeared to be some display of genius in the New Zeeland tunes, which soared very

A - ghee   mat - te   a - whay   Tu - pa - ya

FIGURE 2.7. Georg Forster, "New Zealand dirge," in Forster, *Voyage round the World,* vol. 2, 616. Reproduced courtesy of the University of Hawaii Press.

far above the wretched humming of the Taheitians, or even the four notes of the people at the Friendly Islands. Of this tune they continue to sing the two first bars till the words of their song are at an end, and then they close with the last. Sometimes they also sing an under-part, which is a third lower, except the two last notes, which are unisons.[93]

The observation was doubly perplexing, first because to European minds polyphony was never supposed to exist much south of the Tropic of Cancer, and here was part singing nearer to the Tropic of Capricorn, and second because Maori were thought less sophisticated than other, "cleverer" Polynesians like Tahitians, who only sang and played in unison.[94]

In actual fact, naturalist Joseph Banks had reported Polynesian part singing ("the women sing prettily enough in parts") as early as 1769 and remarked on flutes that could be tuned with a slide made from a rolled leaf.[95] Such observations were initially scarcely noticed by a European public that was preoccupied with the first titillating reports about erotic lyrics and lewd South Sea dances.[96] Until the late 1770s and early 1780s, one could say that polyphony thus remained the exclusively European phenomenon that Rousseau had insisted was a marker of Northerners' hypercivilization:

> Every people of the earth have a music and a melody, [but]...the Europeans alone have a harmony of concords...when we reflect that the world has subsisted so many ages, and that among all the nations,

FIGURE 2.8. Georg Forster, "New Zealand tune sung in thirds," in Forster, *Voyage round the World,* vol. 2, 615. Reproduced courtesy of the University of Hawaii Press.

who have cultivated the fine arts, no one has ever known this harmony; that no animal, no bird, no being whatever in nature, produces any other concord than that of unison, nor other music than that of melody.[97]

Only with Georg Forster's observations and James Burney's transcriptions would this view start to be reexamined. The latter's transcriptions produced some tangible evidence of non-European part singing that metropolitan scholars could disseminate and discuss, while the former conceived of Polynesian polyphony as a theoretical issue with both musical and extramusical implications.[98] As the two men saw it, the problem that extended beyond the narrow preserve of music scholars to the broad-ranging interests of philosophers, historians, geographers, and social theorists was this: First, Tongans and Maori were simple people with unaccountably complex music; second, their music was surprisingly affecting.[99] As we will find when we come to look at the scholarly reception, the encounter had turned up evidence that destabilized a number of intellectual edifices, including the hierarchical ordering of uncultivated peoples and Europe as the true home of invention. Above all, the identity of the archmusician Orpheus, originator of all music, had been implicitly called into question. Orpheus was no longer a performer with his audience neatly arrayed before him, but a listener captive to wild, violent, and uncontrollable sounds. Recalling the Thracians and the disastrous consequences of their music making, music scholars found that the implications were, at the very least, disturbing.

Perhaps the Admiralty had not considered the consequences of performers being turned into listeners when it dispatched musician marines to the Pacific. At any rate, it was left to the voyagers to discover what the organizers had failed to foresee: The seamen were themselves subject to unexpected, often unwanted, forms of indigenous musical agency. One of the most striking examples of this occurred on Cook's return visit to Polynesia, when indigenous music was repeatedly construed as threatening and its effects difficult to contain. Anxieties about non-European music were expressed in reports about the tedium of the natives' ceremonies and the voyagers' enforced attention to music they found incomprehensible and dull.[100] The voyagers found their time managed by the islanders' concerts and their mobility thus curtailed. Yet there was also a more frightening intersection of indigenous music and the exercise of power.

Unlike the ballads and theater pieces that the sailors heard at home, cross-cultural performances did not deal thematically with the problem of power. Here, power relations were negotiated by the actual performances themselves. We see this at work during Cook's 1777 visit to Lifuka in the Ha'apai Group in Tonga during his third and final voyage (figures 2.9 and 2.10). A Tongan chief, Finau, had requested to see the marines being drilled. This display of military maneuvers was trumped by a native exhibition so magnificent and strange that the commander said he was at a loss to describe it.[101] The documents tell, however, of more than a hundred men, ranged in neat lines and moving and acting "as one man." They carried small wooden paddles that they flourished with powerful finesse to the accompaniment of drumbeats and a huge chorus of singers. By all accounts, the performance was vastly impressive, and, according to Cook, the voyagers agreed it would have met with "universal applause" on a European stage.[102]

Yet this "applause" caused a shift in the balance of power that had been struck between the visitors and their hosts. The islanders' polished performance had trumped the voyagers' modest display. Cook said that it had, in fact, so exceeded any attempt he had made to entertain them that they now "seemed to pique themselves in the superiority they had over [the voyagers]." Cook seemed to recognize that reciprocating with his own grand performance would not be possible because of the Tongans' musical preferences: "Not one of our musical instruments except the drum, did they hold in the least esteem, and even the Drum they did not think superior to their own; as to the French horns they very seldom would attend to them at all either here or at any of the other islands."[103] For the voyagers, this was a dangerous turn of events, and, in an effort to gain the upper hand, Cook resorted to a visual spectacle. He hoped that putting on a fireworks display would impress them. After dark, the rockets and crackers were duly lit, and this seemed to please and astonish the islanders "beyond measure." "The scale," said Cook, was now turned "in our favour."[104]

The Europeans believed they had gained control, when in fact this was just the opening salvo in an exchange that saw both sides upping the ante in an effort to establish superiority. The Tongans responded with another performance of instrumental music and singing, then a succession of elaborate dances and boxing matches, as well as a pantomimic dance that parodied the fireworks and brought guffaws from the crowd. The events lasted many hours and involved vast numbers of performers, and the precision, scale, and strange beauty of it dazzled the Europeans.[105] At the same time, doubts arose in the minds of the seamen: Were the performances a sign of island hospitality or islander superiority; were they intended to honor the voyagers or humiliate them?[106] Marine corporal John Ledyard was among the observers who saw the performances for what they were—a musical and dance contest with strategic dimensions:

FIGURE 2.9. John Webber (1751–1793), *A night dance by men at Hapaee*, in Cook, *Voyage to the Pacific Ocean*, vol. 4, plate 10. By permission of the University of Michigan Special Collections. Europeans are depicted as the audience for a non-European performance.

FIGURE 2.10. John Webber, *A night dance by women at Hapaee*, in Cook, *Voyage to the Pacific Ocean*, vol. 4, plate 11. By permission of the University of Michigan Special Collections.

These exhibitions on the part of the natives were considered by us in a kind of dubious light for though they evidently entertained us, we were not certain they were solely intended for that purpose, and if they happened to be numerous on any of those occasions we had always the guard under arms. However we never let them know by any superfluity of parade or other means that we were jealous of their numbers or their boldness and skill, though we certainly were, and prudence demanded it. Our only defence was certainly our imaginary greatness.[107]

There is ambiguity in Ledyard's neat coinage, for the meaning shifts depending on where one places the emphasis. The voyagers certainly imagined themselves greater than the islanders, but Ledyard also pointed to their efforts to control the semiotics of the encounter. The word "imaginary" is thus also used in the sense of the symbolic. Ledyard was ultimately persuaded that the voyagers' own display, their scientific instruments, and their prediction of an eclipse allowed them to control this symbolic dimension. Yet a note of deep insecurity remained in his and others' reports. In retrospect it is clear that this insecurity was well founded: The voyagers were highly vulnerable in this contest over the "imaginary" and came close to losing everything. Decades later it came to light that the performative contest had almost ended with the slaughter of the Europeans on the beach.[108]

Metropolitan readers quickly recognized that a lot was riding on the power struggles taking place in remote corners of the Pacific. As if to point to the precariousness of the larger project itself, journalists stressed the islanders' numerical strength and the voyagers' comparative vulnerability. A 1777 report in *Hannoverisches Magazin,* for instance, stressed that only goodwill had prevented the Pacific Islanders from exploiting the visitors' weakness and turning the Europeans into slaves.[109] A later report similarly emphasized the need for the voyagers to dominate this theater of power by subjecting native audiences to displays of superior "European ingenuity."[110] It was not only the well-being of a handful of sailors that hung in the balance. With the hardship of individual voyagers reported against the broader political backdrop of the revolt in the American colonies and slave unrest in Haiti, incidents like the cannibalization of a boat crew in New Zealand and Cook's murder in Hawaii provided vivid object lessons in native resistance. This made the performative use of music not just a simple accessory to power but also a potent and contested instrument of domination in European struggles with colonial and prospective colonial subjects. The fact that the German states did not have formal commercial or territorial stakes in the exploration of the Pacific and were not directly affected by the encounter did not diminish Germans' concern over the nexus of music and power. If anything, German music scholars took such questions all the more seriously as they attempted to carve out their own spheres of cultural influence.

It was thus the task of the German reception to negotiate the problem of Orpheus's unstable identity and his transformation from commanding performer to vulnerable listener. We will find that metropolitan commentators tried to contain this threat by questioning the veracity of travelers' reports and stressing the need for expert knowledge—a measure on the one hand of the increasing professionalization of music scholarship but of the defensiveness of its scholars on the other. In the face of contravening evidence, music scholars denied the cultural commonalities between selves and others and insisted on the radical alterity of non-European music. Above all, Orpheus had to soften, civilize, and improve; only at his own mortal risk could he stop and listen to the sounds emanating from the mouths of cannibals and savage women.

Containing Music's Threat

The level of Enlightenment interest in the musical encounter is reflected in the fact that Polynesian music began to vie with more salacious topics like sex, cannibalism, infanticide, and thievery in the metropolitan reception of the Pacific voyages. In the quarter century following the return of James Burney's ship *Adventure* in 1774, the number of publications on the subject grew. Readers showed tremendous interest in Polynesia, and, in the German reception alone, Polynesian music was referenced in scholarly review journals and moral weeklies like the *Hannoverisches Magazin* (1777, 1783), *Gelehrte Beyträge zu den Braunschweigischen Anzeigen* (1785), *Neue Bibliothek der schönen Wissenschaften* (1788), and *Deutsche Monatsschrift* (1794). It also found its way into scholarly music journals, bibliographies, histories, and encyclopedias by some prominent writers, including Johann Nicolaus Forkel (1778, 1792), Friedrich Arnold Klockenbring (1787), and Heinrich Christoph Koch (1795, 1802).

Enlightenment interest in Polynesian music was disproportionate in relation to the remoteness of the islands, scholars' lack of immediate contact with Pacific Islanders, and Europeans' (especially Germans') limited material investment in the region. This reinforces the general point that a disjunction existed between Europeans' material and imaginative investments in places like Polynesia. The expansion of missionary activities and settler colonies in the Pacific during the nineteenth century would change all of this, but for the time being the Enlightenment discussion of Polynesian music points to these musical encounters as an intellectual thorn in the side of philosophers, naturalists, and above all scholars of music: In many ways, Polynesia troubled Europe's idea of itself.

More than a decade after the publication of Cook's second voyage travelogues, Friedrich Arnold Klockenbring, the chancellery secretary in Hanover, addressed himself to Forster's dual problems—the simple people with unsimple music and its effects on the listener. Klockenbring is likely to have been the anonymous redactor of an earlier contribution to the *Hannoverisches Magazin* (1777),[111] for there, as in his essay "Etwas über die Musik in den neuerlich entdeckten Südländern" (Something about the Music in the Recently Discovered Southern Lands), he pointed out a discrepancy: "Although the New Zealanders are far tougher, more warlike, and fiercer in their passions than the inhabitants of islands located closer to the equator in milder latitudes, their music exceeds that of Tahiti and Anamoka in terms of its complexity and gentle tonality."[112] The chancellery secretary framed the implicit question within the context of an as yet inchoate ethnomusicological project, lamented the fact that travel writers had hitherto neglected music, and called for special attention to be devoted to its study in the future. A lot was at stake in this project, he stressed, because music was the human race's oldest and most universal art form. It acted profoundly on primitive peoples and was more closely linked to human beings' physical and moral condition the closer they were to the state of nature.[113]

In agitating for increased scholarly attention to non-European music, Klockenbring outlined the minimum requirements for sound ethnomusicological inquiry. Paramount was the need for well-trained observers, a need that was all the more acute if the music under observation was radically different from that at home. Simply knowing how to "handle" various instruments and being able to read musical notation was insufficient. Also needed, he said, was technical expertise in composition and some philosophical and historical knowledge of the art. Klockenbring conceded the difficulty in finding such uniquely qualified observers. This kind of training, along with all the other specialized skills required for participation in major scientific expeditions, was extremely rare when combined in a single individual.[114] With backhanded finesse, Klockenbring pointed out that Forster was a self-acknowledged musical layman whose highly interesting observations would have been more interesting still had he been better equipped to observe and evaluate what he saw and heard.[115]

Turning to Forster's problem, Klockenbring posed New Zealand as the ideal testing ground for sociopolitical and cultural theories because the islands were geographically remote and had only recently been discovered.[116] For these reasons, he believed, Maori music was unlikely to have been tainted by fatal contact with foreign music. If scholars were interested in music at its earliest stages of development, then this was the place to look, for here was music prior to its corruption and artificiality, music as it still existed in the state of nature. By comparing musical systems—the artificial and the natural, the proximate and the geographically distant, and the present with the temporally remote—scholars could better understand this most interesting of arts. Klockenbring reminded the reader that the ancient Greeks and Romans, like the contemporary Greeks, Persians, Chinese, and Asian Turks, had once used a different intervallic system and that the present European intervallic system was mathematically imprecise. If Westerners had not been schooled in their own tonality from childhood on, they would find even their own music highly disagreeable.

At first glance, this intervention appears to be a striking example of late eighteenth-century historical and cultural relativism that endorsed non-European music and fueled the debate about the origins of the Western diatonic scale. Klockenbring added that, if the Forster-Burney observations were correct, then they would prove that the modern intervallic system (and hence the entire basis of Western music) corresponded to its "natural" antipodean counterpart.[117] What a miracle it would be, he said with an ironic tone, if New Zealand could deliver a sample of national music that came "directly from the hands of nature" without having "yet entered the hands of art," a sample whose intervallic system corresponded with the one introduced into Europe after the ancient Greek modes fell out of favor and also with the one published in Forster's travelogue.[118]

This musical marvel quickly collapsed under Klockenbring's withering critique, for, as he himself pointed out, miracles had little place in enlightened thought. If the present Western musical system were to be brought into line with the non-European one, then this could occur only on the basis of far more rigorous scholarship. The claims about Maori music had, on the other hand, been made on the basis of poor observation. Forster had virtually admitted as much when he acknowledged he was no music expert and had asked a friend (James Burney) to take musical dictation. Klockenbring conceded that there were difficulties in notating a piece of music so tonally different from European music. Unfortunately, Forster's friend had not been equal to the task: In the Maori "dirge" the melody's rhythm did not match the scanning of the lyrics, and the final measure was not in 4⁄4 time.[119] More importantly, how could the Maori have a scale that was so "Western," when even the "far more cultivated and refined Tahitians" had nothing of the sort?[120]

Even while insisting on the impoverished state of ethnomusicological reporting and the fallaciousness of the so-called evidence, Klockenbring had found a way to subordinate Maori to Tahitian music and Polynesian to Western music. Improvements to ethnomusicological reporting left a slim possibility that these hierarchies might be reversed in the future. However, the driving message of Klockenbring's text was another one. By insisting on the fallaciousness of the voyagers' observations and denying the specificity (and complexity) of indigenous music, he created an intractable split between European and Polynesian listeners: "Just as our music is incomprehensible, cumbrous, and without any affect to them, so too is theirs to us."[121] The rationale for Klockenbring's argument was neither a musical nor an experiential one. Tahitian music, he said, was in the same state of infancy as the islanders generally, and their proximity to nature meant that it was not possible for their singing to make a pleasant impression on Europeans. After all, he added, Europeans could no more enjoy Tahitian music than "drown their modicum of knowledge in the Lethe or swap their many needs for Tahitian frugality." Nor was Tahitian music capable of leaving a physical impression on the listener because the European ear was no longer sensitized to such minute tonal distinctions. Compared with the highly impressionable Tahitian, the enlightened European had become half blind and deaf.[122]

Klockenbring's cultural-physiological argument flew in the face of the voyage findings, which had shown, if anything, that music on both sides of the encounter could be mutually pleasing and highly affective. However, Klockenbring's next sally would come like a *tierce de Picardie* at the end of the piece to reverse its minor tone. He argued that, since Tahitians were at a developmental stage comparable to that of ancient Greeks, their destiny would be a similar, if speedier, one. Instead of Tahitians being indifferent to European music, as he had previously claimed, Klockenbring now suggested that the Scottish bagpiper might have already brought about a revolution in Tahitian music. This view was shared by Friedrich II's philosopher, Cornelius de Pauw, who likewise thought that Cook's bagpiper possessed the ability to "ravish the minds of savages," to "conduct them at will," and to throw them "into inconceivable extasies." De Pauw, however, took the argument one step further by arguing that such music ushered in "a fixed mode of life among a race of men, who from their cradle had never quitted the bosom of thick forests, nor ceased to wander like wild beasts from one solitude to another."[123] For de Pauw, Cook's musical experiments had confirmed the wondrous power of music in classical times. More importantly, it had shown music's utility in the present and its benefit for the future progress of native societies.

Klockenbring concluded with the sour note of a civilization critique. The bagpiper's musical upheaval would not necessarily enhance the Tahitians' general well-being, he said, because the visiting ships had introduced thousands of additional needs that the islanders could have done without.[124] Echoing Forster's sometime anti-encounter position, Klockenbring suggested that, although music revolutionized and improved native society, it could not entirely compensate for civilization's ills—the prostitution, venereal disease, materialism, and thievery—that inevitably accompanied the arrival of the Europeans.

There was nothing unusual in hinting at the fatal taint of Europe. Forster had called for the connection between Europeans and Polynesians to be severed before the "corruption of manners" reached "that innocent race of men living in ignorance and simplicity," while Diderot had enjoined the wretched Tahitians to weep for the arrival of the "wicked and grasping men" who enslaved and catechized indigenous societies.[125] An earlier redaction of the Cook and Forster travelogues published in *Hannoverisches Magazin* (1777), and likely also by Klockenbring, had used equally strong language. The author said that when Europeans discovered an island in the South Seas they inaugurated an unhappy epoch, albeit one that Providence ordained (figure 2.11).[126]

This kind of flip-flopping did not, however, sit well with one of Klockenbring's contemporaries. An anonymous review of his essay published in *Neue Bibliothek der schönen Wissenschaften* (1788) challenged Klockenbring for bending Forster's findings to suit his own ends. For, said the reviewer, it did not follow that the voyagers' observations about New Zealanders were any less wrong than their remarks about Tahitians. If anything, Forster's pleasure in Maori music would have made it superior to Tahitian music, rendering Maori more, not less, civilized than they had been claimed to be. Klockenbring had undermined his own argument by insisting on the very opposite.[127] In making this point, the critic showed that Klockenbring had collapsed the voyagers' evidence about two distinct island groups in order to perpetuate conventional views about Tahitian superiority and deny the efficacy of Maori music. In "Etwas über die Musik in den neuerlich entdeckten Südländern," Klockenbring had resolved the Forsterian problems only by sidestepping them. The anonymous reviewer, on the other hand, was content to leave the Orphic threat unresolved: Indigenous music might well be affecting, and its people not so simple after all.

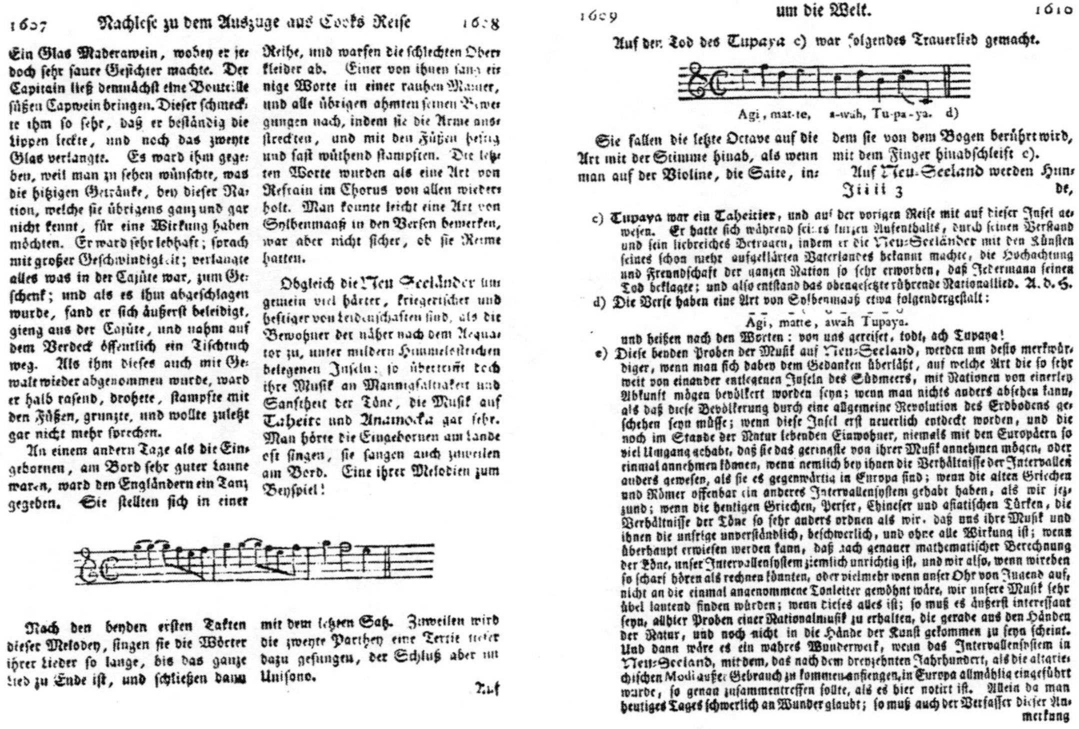

1607 Nachlese zu dem Auszuge aus Cooks Reise 1608

Ein Glas Maderawein, wobey er jedoch sehr saure Gesichter machte. Der Capitain ließ demnächst eine Bouteille süßen Capwein bringen. Dieser schmeckte ihm so sehr, daß er beständig die Lippen leckte, und noch das zweyte Glas verlangte. Es ward ihm gegeben, weil man zu sehen wünschte, was die hitzigen Getränke, bey dieser Nation, welche sie übrigens ganz und gar nicht kennt, für eine Wirkung haben möchten. Er ward sehr lebhaft; sprach mit großer Geschwindigkeit; verlangte alles was in der Cajüte war, zum Geschenk; und als es ihm abgeschlagen wurde, fand er sich äußerst beleidigt, gieng aus der Cajüte, und nahm auf dem Verdeck öffentlich ein Tischtuch weg. Als ihm dieses auch mit Gewalt wieder abgenommen wurde, ward er halb rasend, drohete, stampfte mit den Füßen, grunzte, und wollte zuletzt gar nicht mehr sprechen.

An einem andern Tage als die Eingebornen, am Bord sehr guter Laune waren, ward den Engländern ein Tanz gegeben. Sie stellten sich in einer Reihe, und warfen die schlechten Oberkleider ab. Einer von ihnen sang einige Worte in einer rauhen Manier, und alle übrigen ahmten seinen Bewegungen nach, indem sie die Arme ausstreckten, und mit den Füßen heftig und fast wüthend stampften. Die letzten Worte wurden als eine Art von Refrain im Chorus von allen wiederholt. Man konnte leicht eine Art von Sylbenmaaß in den Versen bemerken, war aber nicht sicher, ob sie Reime hatten.

Obgleich die Neu Seeländer ungemein viel härter, kriegerischer und heftiger von Leidenschaften sind, als die Bewohner der näher nach dem Aequator zu, unter mildern Himmelsstrichen belegenen Inseln; so übertrift doch ihre Musik an Mannigfaltigkeit und Sanftheit der Töne, die Musik auf Taheite und Anamocka gar sehr. Man hörte die Eingebornen am Lande oft singen, sie sangen auch zuweilen am Bord. Eine ihrer Melodien zum Beyspiel!

Nach den beyden ersten Takten dieser Melodey, singen sie die Wörter ihrer Lieder so lange, bis das ganze Lied zu Ende ist, und schließen dann mit dem letzten Satz. Zuweilen wird die zweyte Parthey eine Terzie tiefer dazu gesungen, der Schluß aber im Unisono.

Auf

1609 um die Welt. 1610

Auf den Tod des Tupaya c) war folgendes Trauerlied gemacht.

Agi, mat-te, a-wah, Tu-pa-ya. d)

Sie fallen die letzte Octave auf die Art mit der Stimme hinab, als wenn man auf der Violine, die Saite, indem sie von dem Bogen berührt wird, mit dem Finger hinabschleift e).

Auf Neu-Seeland werden Hunde,

Iiiii 3

c) Tupaya war ein Taheitier, und auf der vorigen Reise mit auf dieser Insel gewesen. Er hatte sich während seines kurzen Aufenthalts, durch seinen Verstand und sein liebreiches Betragen, indem er die Neu-Seeländer mit den Künsten seines schon mehr aufgeklärten Vaterlandes bekannt machte, die Hochachtung und Freundschaft der ganzen Nation so sehr erworben, daß Jedermann seinen Tod beklagte; und also entstand das obengesetzte rührende Nationallied. A. d. H.

d) Die Verse haben eine Art von Sylbenmaaß etwa folgendergestalt:

Agi, matte, awah Tupaya.

und heißen nach den Worten: von uns gereiset, todt, ach Tupaya!

e) Diese beyden Proben der Musik auf Neu-Seeland, werden um desto merkwürdiger, wenn man sich dabey dem Gedanken überläßt, auf welche Art die so sehr weit von einander entlegenen Inseln des Südmeers, mit Nationen von einerley Abkunft mögen bevölkert worden seyn; wenn man nichts anders absehen kann, als daß diese Bevölkerung durch eine allgemeine Revolution des Erdbodens geschehen seyn müsse; wenn diese Insel erst neuerlich entdeckt worden, und die noch im Stande der Natur lebenden Einwohner, niemals mit den Europäern so viel Umgang gehabt, daß sie das geringste von ihrer Musik annehmen mögen, oder einmal annehmen können, wenn nemlich bey ihnen die Verhältnisse der Intervallen anders gewesen, als sie es gegenwärtig in Europa sind; wenn die alten Griechen und Römer offenbar ein anderes Intervallensystem gehabt haben, als wir jetzund; wenn die heutigen Griechen, Perser, Chineser und asiatischen Türken, die Verhältnisse der Töne so sehr anders ordnen als wir, daß uns ihre Musik und ihnen die unsrige unverständlich, beschwerlich, und ohne alle Wirkung ist; wenn überhaupt erwiesen werden kann, daß nach genauer mathematischer Berechnung der Töne, unser Intervallensystem ziemlich unrichtig ist, und wir also, wenn wir eben so scharf hören als rechnen könnten, oder vielmehr wenn unser Ohr von Jugend auf, nicht an die einmal angenommene Tonleiter gewöhnt wäre, wir unsere Musik sehr übel lautend finden würden; wenn dieses alles ist; so muß es äußerst interessant seyn, allhier Proben einer Nationalmusik zu erhalten, die gerade aus den Händen der Natur, und noch nicht in die Hände der Kunst gekommen zu seyn scheint. Und dann wäre es ein wahres Wunderwerk, wenn das Intervallensystem in Neu-Seeland, mit dem, das nach dem dreyzehnten Jahrhundert, als die altgriechischen Modi außer Gebrauch zu kommen anfiengen, in Europa allmählig eingeführt wurde, so genau zusammentreffen sollte, als es hier notirt ist. Allein da man heutiges Tages schwerlich an Wunder glaubt; so muß auch der Verfasser dieser Anmerkung

FIGURE 2.11. [Friedrich Arnold Klockenbring], "Nachlese zu dem Auszuge aus Cooks Reise um die Welt," *Hannoverisches Magazin* 15, no. 101, column 1610. By permission of the Staatsbibliothek zu Berlin, Preußischer Kulturbesitz.

For a scholar like Johann Nicolaus Forkel, who was interested primarily in Western music history, the particularity of Polynesian cultures was of no real concern. In Forkel's redaction of a *Monthly Review* piece by "B." on Georg Forster's travel account, Forkel referred to Polynesians as islanders who lived "around the South Pole," cleaved the Tongan archipelago to New Zealand, and relocated both to nearby Tahiti.[128] The havoc he wrought on the Pacific map serves as a reminder of the limits of geographical knowledge and the flexibility of the imagination in the late eighteenth century. Cook's geographical goose chase had put an end to the search for the imagined southern continent, terra australis incognita, but Europe's elites still gained only a hazy grasp of world geography. As a better-informed contributor to *Hannoverisches Magazin* pointed out, the armchair traveler moved quickly on paper, and even enlightened readers were inclined to confuse New Holland (Australia) with New Zealand and reduce the vast sweep of the Pacific to the short distance between Kassel and Braunschweig.[129] On the other hand, we see that this leveling of geographical and musical specificity paid dividends for those music commentators who were otherwise unable to resolve their own theoretical contradictions. Like Klockenbring and de Pauw, Forkel collapsed Forster's distinctions to combine the musical attributes of Tonga, New Zealand, and Tahiti and forge a pan-Polynesian sound.

To begin with, Forkel acknowledged the surprising findings in New Zealand by pointing out that "It must seem strange that harmony, or polyphonic music, which, as we now generally believe and for good reason, was not even known to the inventive and refined Greeks, should have been found [to exist] with certain barbarians living in complete isolation from the rest of the world."[130] Forkel published the transcriptions as "specimens" of this refinement and inventiveness and hence as evidentiary proof of "South Pole" polyphony. Yet he also introduced a critical note that raised methodological objections to the voyagers' observations. Adding the second voice to the transcription, Forkel corrected what he insisted was an error. "The second voice in the last bar," he said, "was probably taken down incorrectly and ought to [end with a third]."

For Forkel, reason, and crucially *not* firsthand hearing, dictated that the transcription had to end with a third rather than in unison. He pointed out that Maori "counterpoint" was just a sequence of mixed major and minor thirds but that this was still a sign of musical refinement, all the more so considering that it was just the "product of a bunch of hungry and miserable cannibals" (figure 2.12).[131] Following the original reviewer, Forkel also called into question Forster's assertion that the Maori use of glissando in the "dirge" was affecting. It might have come across that way to those who first heard it, he said, but to "our ears" it bespoke something else. It was a genuine *Grazie* (embellishment), and such "musical refinement" had only recently been introduced in Europe—whether for good or ill.[132]

Reasoning thus, Forkel revealed himself to be a convinced travel skeptic, disdainful of ear- and eyewitness testimony and doubtful about the traveler's veracity. Like Klockenbring, whose work he knew, Forkel pointed to the inadequacies of ethnomusicological observation without, however, going so far as to outline a program for improving such musical knowledge making. Privileging reason over sensory experience, he stressed that the junior Forster and Burney's observations had to be erroneous because they were counter-rational. He said that he was able to posit a more sensible alternative for non-European music because all music was subject to a universal logic. True musical knowledge thus had to be the prerogative of the reasoning *Kenner* (expert), not the amateur who lacked sufficient knowledge of how music worked. Such methodological precepts led the music historian to conclude that, because the Polynesians were "living ancestors" of the ancient Greeks, the Maori could not reasonably have invented something that had not already been invented in antiquity. Furthermore, musical embellishment could not be a sign of affecting Maori music because it did not signify as much in present-day Europe (indeed, the implication was that such embellishment was rather too affecting to be tasteful). Europe was thus preserved as the sole wellspring of musical innovation and aesthetic adjudication—with polyphony invented in the past and the interpretation of effects deferred to the future.

FIGURE 2.12. "Neu-Seeländische Contrapunkt," in [Johann Nicolaus Forkel], "Etwas von der Musik," *Musikalisch-kritische Bibliothek,* vol. 2, 318. Reproduced courtesy of the University of Michigan Music Library.

Of all the late Enlightenment music scholars with an interest in historiography, it was Heinrich Christoph Koch who seized on the centrality of Polynesian music to this project. A contribution titled "Kurzer Abriß der Geschichte der Tonkunst bey den Völkern der Vorzeit" (Brief Outline of the History of the Tonal Arts in Prehistoric Peoples), which appeared in his short-lived music periodical, *Journal der Tonkunst* (1795), set out the guiding principles. A history of music, said Koch, must encompass the nature of music, the occasions for its use, the nature of musical instruments, its outstanding contributors, and the lessons that one might learn for the future progress of the art.[133]

Like Klockenbring and Forkel, Koch pointed to the inadequacies of existing ethnomusicological observation and the need for expert observers. For example, he would have wanted to know more about the nature of Polynesian musical intervals and the use of rhythm because this would have provided clues to the development of human culture.[134] Atypically, however, Koch endorsed travel writing as an epistemological genre and offered the travelogue in compensation for what he conceded was the highly speculative character of his prehistory of music. Those of his readers, he said, who did not find the necessary proofs in antiquity or were skeptical about the ancients' marvelous claims only had to turn to the reports of scholars who had traveled among the yet uncultivated peoples and described the state of their music.[135] Chief among these was Georg Forster, whom Koch explicitly and repeatedly identified as German—as if this quality were in itself a sign of Forster's superior perspicuity and erudition.[136]

Like most of his contemporaries, including Burney and Forkel, Koch identified the ancient Egyptians, Hebrews, Greeks, and Romans as key historical players because of their singular contributions to the development of music.[137] Polynesia's place in this universal history, on the other hand, was not a substantive one. Although Forster's comments on Tahitian and Tongan music were included in Koch's historical sketch, no reference was made to antipodean part singing. Instead, the historian took Forster's observations as confirmation that a group of people still existed who used a narrow tonal range in an imperfect way.[138] Koch would return to Forster's travelogue when he came to compile the entry on the syrinx or panpipe for his *Musikalisches Lexikon* (1802). It was pointed out that the instrument was invented by Pan (but notably not the Polynesians) but had also been found more recently among peoples who had not yet progressed to a high level of cultivation.[139] As "living ancestors," the Polynesians represented merely the opportunity to study the origins of music in the present.

Conclusion

Georg Forster and James Burney brought home news that music in the Pacific was unexpectedly complex and affective. Perhaps naively we expect such observations to have elevated European views on Polynesian culture and even left its shine on non-European peoples generally. In fact this was not the case. Although autoptic German travel formed the conceit for Koch's prehistory of music, the travel enthusiast skipped over Forster's most significant observation—Maori part singing—so as to preserve the logic of a sequential, universal progress in music. Forkel had intended to cover the whole world in his *Allgemeine Geschichte der Musik* but never got around to doing so. The best we are left with are references to non-Western music in Forkel's music bibliography and some stray comments in the universal history. His dismissive view of eye- and earwitness testimony and commitment to the Westernness of musical invention meant that he too played down the voyagers' findings.

We expect more from Charles Burney: He was actively engaged in the search for non-Western sources, tackled musical agency, and hunted for the origins of harmony. His vast network of foreign correspondents, to say nothing of his own family members, kept our music investigator supplied with transcriptions, musical instruments, and firsthand accounts of other musical vernaculars. He learned about Polynesian music from those who knew most about it: the Ra'iatean Islander Mai and voyagers like his son James and son-in-law, Molesworth Phillips. His daughter Susanna had specifically told him that, according to her husband, Tongans sang "in Chorus, & not only produced octaves to each other, according to their different species of voice, but fell on concords such as were not disagreeable to the Ear."[140] He had also written to Molesworth Phillips himself to inquire whether "this method of singing in parts, as it is called, was peculiar to any one place or Island in the South seas" or whether Phillips could recall having heard it elsewhere. To this Phillips replied that he had heard it only in Tonga.[141] Such statements confirmed the existence of part singing in Tonga; others proved its existence in New Zealand.

Yet for all this, Polynesian music did not ultimately warrant a chapter in the *General History of Music,* which remained, like Forkel's project, too ambitious in scope to be completed in a single lifetime. At best, non-Western music featured as part of Burney's historical conception and explained how the West had arrived at its current state of development. Yet, when it came to Polynesia, there was a breakdown in the logic of looking to the geographically remote present in order to reconstruct one's own historical past. The voyagers had not discovered counterpoint—defined as independently moving parts—but they had found harmony. Yet even subequatorial harmony had to be refuted or at least played down because historians like Burney knew that the ancient Greeks, Romans, and Chinese had not developed it.[142] In other words, Polynesian music was not *dissimilar* enough to serve as a convincing analogue of Western musical origins because it had, so to speak, progressed too far. Eighteenth-century historical method depended on using present evidence as a means of modeling the past, and such a method could not comfortably accommodate this anomaly.

There was just the occasional dissenter like an anonymous contributor to the *Monthly Review* who did not believe that scholarly method ought to obstruct firsthand observation. This reviewer of articles published by Joshua Steele in the *Philosophical Transactions* complained that the tunes Steele had composed for the *vivo* (nose flute) should not be passed off as authentic "specimens" of Tahitian music. "We violently suspect . . . ," fumed the reviewer, "that these tunes would scarce be recognized, as just specimens of his country music, by Omiah [Mai, the Polynesian visitor to London]; from whom we think our Author might have derived more knowledge of this subject, by only listening to one of his songs, than by thus learnedly conjecturing what, and how, his countrymen sing, or may possibly sing, *a priori.*"[143] In keeping with the kinds of arguments made by Forster, this reviewer stressed that firsthand observation, an inductive method, and indigenous informants were the appropriate way to arrive at the truth about Polynesian music. For a greater majority of musical commentators, however, the converse was true. When experience strained the ancient myths, it was experience that tended to give way.

And so Burney prevaricated on the subject of Polynesian polyphony. In his communications with Lord Sandwich, who had solicited additional information for the official account of Cook's final voyage, Burney did not insist on the fact of Polynesian polyphony, and the coauthor of that account, Captain King, would be made to refute the evidence of his own (and everyone else's) ears.[144] It would be "a rash judgment," concluded Sandwich in a footnote to Cook and King's published account, "to venture to affirm that they [Polynesians] did or did not understand counterpoint: and therefore I fear that this curious matter must be considered as still remaining undecided."[145] As Sandwich's rough draft to this note shows, however, the matter was not undecided at all and his strikeouts betray the problem:

It would be a rash decision judgment to affirm that they did not or did understand counterpoint ~~tho' the mode by which they attained that know-ledge does not agree with our comprehension. It is therefore to be feared that this matter must still remain an object for the matter therefore must remain undecided till it is cleared up by future navigators and musicians of more curiosity and accuracy than those who heard these musical performances.~~ & therefore I fear this matter must still be considered as remaining undecided.[146]

These elisions show that it was not possible to officially confirm the existence of Polynesian polyphony because Sandwich could not understand how "a people semi barbarous should naturally arrive at any perfection in that art."[147] The problem of comprehension was, in other words, posed not by the music itself but by a contradiction between the nature of the people and their level of culture, as well as by an explanatory gap that could be elided but not filled. Years earlier Forster had said that it must be left to the "connoisseurs in music [to] acquit or condemn the New Zealanders," and by implication also Tongans and Tahitians.[148] Metropolitan authority and scholarly method were these connoisseurs, and their judgment had indeed fallen.

Close to a century after the Pacific encounters, Polynesian music had still not been given its due by most historians of music. Eduard Hanslick, one of the first university-appointed professors of music and a pioneering aesthetician argued that rhythm was the only "musically primordial element in nature" and was the first element to "awaken" and "develop" in the child and the savage. By way of example, Hanslick contrasted the Tyrolean peasant, seemingly untouched by art but capable of producing "artful" music, with the Polynesian: "When the South Sea Islanders clap rhythmically with metal pieces and wooden sticks while emitting an unintelligible howl," he said, "then that is natural music for the very reason that it is no music."[149] Three decades later, the influential music historian August Wilhelm Ambros was more willing to concede, although not without caveats, that the Polynesians were capable of music. It is "interesting," he wrote, "to encounter this powerful element of the tonal arts [polyphony] already even here." Polyphony was, he added, "an oddity, because, as if in a dream, natural peoples found something that remained hidden from the entire antique world—and also from the Christian one until into the 10th century—harmonic singing: even if only the first seeds thereof."[150]

According to Ambros, there were two distinct paths to musical progress. The first was via revelation: Polyphony was part of a divine order whose secrets were gradually and systematically disclosed to the West. The second was via a more circuitous route, in which the germ of musical progress was stumbled upon by accident. Whereas the former was the preserve of "cultural peoples," the latter belonged to "natural" ones.[151] Ambros's use of "already even" shows that, for European commentators, polyphony in the Pacific was anomalous; it was essentially out of time and out of place. As Rousseau had hinted more than a hundred years earlier, polyphony might be a "barbarous" invention, but it should not be left to barbarians to invent it.[152]

One explanation for this intractability lies, I believe, in what voyagers and subsequent commentators noted about the performative use of music. Rather than classical ideas about musical agency being refuted in the encounter, they were often confirmed. Just as promised, music was capable of eliciting some of the sociopolitical and moral effects of yore: It could indeed be used to militarize, pacify, subordinate, and make friends or enemies. At the ends of the earth, though, music was shown to act both ways, in effect confirming the murderous pendant to the Orpheus myth that no one liked to recall: Voyagers could amuse islanders with bagpipe concerts, but islanders could also entertain, humiliate, and terrify voyagers with songs and dances of their own. Like Odysseus, the voyagers had been offered the irresistible— pleasure and knowledge through the medium of music: "Come near, much-praised Odysseus," said the Sirens, "Bring your ship in, so you may listen to our voice. No one ever yet sped past this place . . . before he listened to the honey-toned voice from our mouths, and then he went off delighted and knowing more things."[153] Perhaps metropolitan commentators had learned their classical stories too well to succumb to such temptations of knowledge, for they were mindful of the divine warnings. Rather than pay for enchanted listening with a pile of bones and rotting corpses on the Sirens' isle, metaphorically speaking, they would prefer to tie themselves to the mast and deafen those around them.[154] They would stay impervious to the wild and dangerous sounds and turn the Europeans' "deafness" into the marker of cultivation and superiority.

A second explanation for this intractability lies in the nature of musical epistemology during the Enlightenment. The preeminent German music historian, Forkel, had had to argue the impossible to resolve Forster's difficulty over the simple people with complex music, all the while turning a deaf ear to the obvious fix. The fact that Forkel did not simply revise his ideas about climate and sociopolitical development or amend his beliefs about musical progress tells us something about not only his own intellectual limitations but also those of the period generally. The Enlightenment was strongly committed to the belief that societies progressed through stages of development and that criteria like culture, climate, geographical location, physiognomy, and sociopolitical development were indexed to one another. Crucially, this stadial indexing presumed that societies progressed stepwise, with indices like culture, climate, and physiognomy moving synchronously. The theory could not accommodate hyperdevelopment in one area and retardation in another: As one criterion rose or fell on the ladder, so must the others in concert. Thus, polyphony, associated with a more advanced stage of development, ought to have either improved its native listeners or designated their already elevated state. The fact that it did neither caused an embarrassment to the system.

The voyagers had observed several other phenomena that contraindicated the theory of stadial indexing. Tahitian infanticide, prostitution, and cannibalism, for instance, all challenged the tidy correspondence between various indices. On the whole, however, metropolitan commentators tended to emphasize only those criteria that supported the theory of stages: Maori, for example, were labeled too bellicose and harsh in their treatment of women and not sufficiently mercantile, socially refined, or politically advanced.[155] Maori and Tongan music were contained within this intellectual strongbox but so, ironically, were scholarly ideas about music in general. Theories about progress in music—including musical "monogenesis" (the notion that musical practices originated in a single place whence they spread), the inherent sophistication of harmonic music, the superiority of string over wind instruments, and the diatonic over pentatonic scale—all became more rather than less entrenched within the Western discourse. In particular, they came to characterize early twentieth-century German comparative musicology.[156]

It would be tempting to see this rigidity as indicative of the conservatism and ingrained prejudices of eighteenth-century (and later) music scholarship. In fact, I think it demonstrates the extent to which music scholarship, including music historiography and ethnomusicology, was a child of Enlightenment philosophical and politico-economic thought. In much of the musicological reception, the travelogue (and hence the traveler's aural experience) was subordinated to an inflexible explanatory system. Klockenbring's anonymous reviewer thus took a lonely step when he sided with the earwitness and conceded the possibility that non-European music could be both affective and innovative. Most scholars adopted a position closer to that of Klockenbring, Koch, and Forkel, who thought that the shrieking of Egyptians was as unappealing to Europeans as European music was to Turks and Arabs.[157] Rather than risking the vulnerability of the listening Orpheus and sacrificing his exclusive grip on invention, scholars returned to

FIGURE 2.13. Ferraresischer Meister, *The Death of Orpheus* (ca. 1480). Hamburger Kunsthalle, Hamburg. By permission of the Bildarchiv Preußischer Kulturbesitz/Art Resource, New York.

Boethius's sixth-century dictum that only "rough people like rough music" so as to deny the possibility of a musical rapprochement between others.[158]

Burney seemed to share this view.[159] Invoking the child's preference for rattles and drums over refined melodies and learned polyphony, he argued that simple music was more affective because people in a state of nature were less discerning and more impressionable than choosy, cultivated ones.[160] Burney, avowedly not historicist, would use the argument about musical effects as ammunition in the debate between ancient and modern music. Those, he said, who insisted on music's wondrous properties were prejudiced against the present because they continued to see it as inferior until such time when it would be able to elicit the same effects as the "wonder-working bards."[161]

Nineteenth-century scholars pushed this to more sinister nationalist and racialist conclusions. Selectively reading earlier travel sources, Christian Friedrich Michaelis claimed that Europeans did not like the "ugly" music of Negroes and Hottentots, nor did Negroes and Hottentots like Europeans' music. He said the same was true of Chinese and South Asians.[162] Friedrich Rochlitz, the great man of nineteenth-century musical letters, supplied the punch line. Receptivity was not a marker of music's ancient power; it sprang instead from innate differences between the cultivated and the uncultivated, who were capable of responding only sensually.[163] Thus, the hierarchy was inverted to claim a new superiority for European music on the grounds of its very lack of affect. This shift shows that the Enlightenment was a keystone between the Baroque view of music as a symbol of power, and itself instrumental, and the nineteenth-century aestheticization of music, which construed music as a legitimization for the exercise of power. Mediating these changing ideas about what music could do (and hence what it was for) was the encounter with the non-Western world, where musical agency came to be retained as its defining characteristic.

Orpheus's song had once held the power to unite performer and listener, forge a collective response, and thereby minimize the difference between subjects. By the beginning of the modern age, however, a cautionary reading of the ancient tale had become common. Hospitality on foreign shores was more or less at an end, and in its place came the phantom of Orpheus's severed head washing up on the beach (figure 2.13). Fictional appropriations of South Seas travelogues tell the story about a fatal taint in reverse: Voyagers would not be greeted by manna, waving palm fronds, and islanders dancing and singing at the water's edge. Rotten fish and stinking seal oil, thievery, scalping, cannibalism, and the native cautioning them to stay away would be their welcome.[164] The lovely dream of hospitality and shared music making had been replaced by a self-imposed injunction to resist the other's song.

| Anti-Orpheus

HERE IS NO laughter in Orpheus's story, no lighthearted music. If there was hilarity among the sailors on the *Argo*—uproarious sea songs that mocked the captain and made fun of the voyage—we do not hear it, for the classical sources are silent on the subject. It is unlikely that there was laughter among the shades in the underworld, and certainly there was none on the Aegean shore where Orpheus was slaughtered and his head cast into the sea. Yet even before his last desperate murmurings, Orpheus's music was never a cheerful affair. Ovid tells us most about the character of his lyre playing and songs: The music, says the Roman author, was about "how things go in the world"; it was music full of the "pity of things and the secret of how to bear it."[1] The traveler's music, it seems, was to be transmitted to us from antiquity not as an expression of pleasure or joy but as a somber outpouring, a response to fear, violence, loss, and grief.

The Enlightenment thought of itself as a risible age.[2] Its platitudes about ushering in the happiness of the many may not have held true, but humor, wit, and irony were among its acknowledged accomplishments. It hardly need surprise us, then, that many eighteenth-century writers, critics, and composers did not feel bound by the gloomy character of the Orpheus myth. If, as classical authors had suggested, the power of music gave voice to life's tragedies, in the hands of a sizeable number of eighteenth-century cultural producers, its themes could also be transformed into playfulness, critique, and mocking laughter. Gluck would compose a surprisingly cheerful and spirited melody for the lament "Che farò senza Euridice," which earned *Orfeo ed Euridice* (1762) the approval of contemporaries like Burney but criticism from more literal-minded nineteenth-century critics like Eduard Hanslick, who used the aria as leverage in his argument against aesthetic expression. The laughter here came from the apparent discrepancy between the meaning of Calzabigi's words and the character of Gluck's tune (figure 3.1).[3] In *Die Zauberflöte* (1791), Mozart would also get a laugh. This chirpy adaptation of Orphic ideas was not without gravitas or sinister aspects—the misuse of the Moor Monastatos and his misuse of Pamina, for example—but Papageno's antics reminded audiences that music could be funny. Listening to Papageno and Monastatos sing "Hu, hu" as the characters mistook one another for the devil, audiences could laugh through music, as well as at it, and take pleasure in the very consonance of the music and its meaning (figure 3.2).

In examining the cultural and political work that eighteenth-century Orphic discourse was enlisted to do, this study has emphasized its protean character. I have shown how travel and musical mapping were co-opted for the making of a German cultural imaginary and how music professionals tried to advance their own interests by highlighting music's wondrous properties, even as other scholars debunked the literal truth of such assertions. The second chapter showed how music commentators negotiated the threat of music's instrumentality by arguing that scholars deemphasized structural similarities between European and Polynesian musical vernaculars in order to preserve a narrative about the historical progress of music, the exclusivity of European genius, and the autonomy of the European listener. These various permutations of the discourse all engaged with the idea that music acted on

FIGURE 3.1. Christoph Willibald von Gluck (1714–1787), "Che farò senza Euridice," *Orfeo ed Euridice* (1762).

FIGURE 3.2. Wolfgang Amadeus Mozart (1756–1791), "Hu, hu!" *Die Zauberflöte* (1791).

listeners in the irresistible, often fraught ways handed down from classical antiquity.

In this chapter, however, we turn to a strand of aesthetic thought whose surface character was entirely different. Within this "anti-Orphic" discourse, music's utility would be conceived of as a source of laughter, mockery, and social critique. We see this parodying of music in works such as Bonnell Thornton's "paean" to music, "An Ode on Saint Cæcilia's Day" (1749); articles in Christopher Smart's journal *The Midwife* (1750) and pieces in his variety show *Mrs. Midnight's Oratory* (performed at the Haymarket in the 1750s); Charles Churchill's poem *Gotham* (1764); Andrew Marvel's "Essay upon the Unfortunate Charms and Power of Music" (1770); John Bicknell's spoof on Burney, *Musical Travels thro' England* (1774); Paul Jodrell's farce *A Widow and No Widow* (1779); satires on Italian opera like the anonymous *Remarkable Trial of the Queen of Quavers* (1780?); and George Colman and Samuel Arnold's opera *The Enraged Musician* (1789), based on William Hogarth's print of the same name. While anti-Orphic discourse was clearly a pan-European phenomenon, the focus here is on its specifically British cast. The parodying of music seems to have been particularly widespread and highly developed in late eighteenth-century Britain, and this raises questions about the broader function of the discourse.[4] If, as I have argued, the figure of Argonaut Orpheus was mobilized for the constitution of various kinds of professional, social, national, and imperial identities, what then was the purpose of mocking musical utility and the musical traveler?

The few to have written on burlesquing music stress its scholarly neglect.[5] Given the ubiquity of the anti-Orphic discourse, this neglect perhaps warrants some explanation. First, research on eighteenth-century culture has tended to concentrate on discrete genres such as the novel, play, or ballad. Such research has been enormously important in establishing the relationship between literary forms and the constitution of class and gender positions, but less often has it taken a thematic and hence pan-generic approach to the question of identity constitution. Yet, we have good reason to see the parodying of music in late eighteenth-century literary, critical, and visual forms as a related corpus—for the reason that neither cultural producers nor their middle-class and aristocratic consumers were particularly sensitive to generic distinctions. To the contrary, playwrights mocked travel writers, novelists squibbed scholars, painters ironized classical models and contemporary theater pieces, and the shared target of their fulmination was music and those who insisted on its grave, metonymic status.

Second, in intellectual historical terms, the anti-Orphic discourse (to the extent that it has been studied at all) has tended to be regarded as somehow anomalous. Samuel Johnson, for example, was said to be interested in just about everything but was, according to his friend James Boswell, "very insensible to the power of musick." This disdain for music tends to be taken as a sign of personal curmudgeonliness, when in fact Johnson may also have been saying something incisive about music in relation to his times.[6] Third, the musical trend in Britain was an affirmative one: Music had long been thought of as inferior to the other arts and musicians as socially subordinate, but, by the turn of the century, the music profession was gaining both intellectual credibility and social respectability. In short, music's fortunes were on the rise. In consequence, the story that has been handed down to us is one that follows a celebratory trajectory, as though the late eighteenth century were a kind of curtain raiser for the nineteenth century's prioritization of music.[7]

The potency of this story and its teleological character make it all the more important to investigate another version of the narrative. Rather than stressing music's ever-compounding value, we can reinstate the polyphonic character of late eighteenth-century musical thought and ask why parodying musical utility was an important counterdiscourse at this time. My approach to the question presumes that specific cultural, social, and political impulses manifest themselves variously in any given period. It further presumes that the same problematic is simultaneously exhibited in a range of media and tackled from discrete class and gender positions. In taking this approach, I follow the example of James Thompson, who argues, for instance, that two distinct cultural forms emerged in response to the eighteenth-century crisis over value—political economy and the novel. Thompson points out that contemporary scholars typically treat them as exclusive discourses with their own separate constituencies, those of economic men and domestic women. He counters, however, that political economy and the novel should in fact be understood as dialectically related because both forms dealt in complementary, even mutually dependent, ways with the problem of differentiating nominal from intrinsic value.[8]

There is indeed a payoff in taking this kind of pan-generic approach. First, it questions the isomorphism between genre and social class, gender, or nation, a view that dominates much contemporary scholarship on the eighteenth century. Second, it opens us to the possibility that, in British society circa 1775, specific forms of cultural expression articulated shared interests, cross-class alliances, and transnational influences. This contributes to a more nuanced picture of the ways in which, say, elites guarded their privilege by allying themselves with the poor under the banner of social welfare. We also gain insights into how members of the middle class were torn between the emancipatory aims of the period and economic constraints; between their professional ambitions and traditional forms of social and political curtailment. Moreover, we learn something about how the idea of a national musical culture was carved out via xenophobia and specific constructions of gender and the male body.

Music's parodic discourse can be shown to have charted and advanced some of these complex interests. At the same time, the parodic discourse raises questions about the social spaces where these interests collided. Orpheus and anti-Orpheus met, for example, on the Haymarket: On one corner was His Majesty's Theatre in the Haymarket (the so-called King's Theatre), the London home of Italian opera and social exclusivity; opposite was the Little Theatre in the Haymarket (also called the Theatre Royal or the Haymarket Theatre), which staged "world-upside-down" burlesques, plays, and English operas and poked fun at high society.[9] The juxtaposition of these theaters and their overlapping audiences tell us something about how these discourses worked against one another to advance discrete interests, as well as in tandem to preserve the status quo.[10] We can also look to the taverns and inns where journals like the *Gentleman's Magazine* and the *London Magazine* were read and discussed in mixed company; the well-to-do homes where aristocratic amateurs were forced into uneasy proximity with professional musicians like Charles Burney and Felice de Giardini; charitable institutions like the Foundling Hospital, which became a flashpoint for competing views of music; and the concert rooms, where aristocratic patronage collided with the dictates of the market.[11] Finally, we might think of the traveler's journey as a mobile site of contestation, where new aural experiences turned once stable and familiar sonic regimes upside down.[12] The parodic discourse certainly gave such spaces vim, but it was also thanks to these spaces—characterized by unlicensed social mixing, unfamiliarity, novelty, even danger—that music could become a barbed and reflexive discourse.

In thinking through the kinds of ideological work performed by the parodying of musical utility, I draw on notions of transgressive space, abjection, and the carnivalesque. In particular, I owe a debt to Peter Stallybrass and Alon White's observations that four symbolic realms—cultural forms, the human body, geographical space, and social formation—are constructed according to interconnected, mutually dependent hierarchies of high and low and that transgression within any one of these symbolic realms has important ramifications for the others. Whatever is "socially peripheral," they argue, "becomes symbolically central."[13] Their insight lends weight to the notion of culture as a site for potential political action and rejuvenation. By the same token, Stallybrass and White take issue with Bakhtin's utopianism and his embrace of the emancipatory potential within the carnivalesque. As they and critics like Terry Eagleton point out, "world-upside-down" forms were often licensed by official culture and may in fact have served the very interests they seemed to oppose.[14]

The question of symbolic inversion has particular salience for the present study. Late eighteenth-century musical parodies typically reversed the polarities of high and low in order to provoke a laugh. Moreover, commenting reflexively on orders of musical signification meant commenting on hierarchies that were external to music itself—for example, the social inferiority of musicians or the shifting economics of musical performance. It is my sense that the reordering of aesthetic hierarchies in the musical parody also constituted an attempt to reorder social and political hierarchies. At the same time, parodists' treatment of "low" cultural forms (e.g., folk songs and peasant instruments) must be acknowledged as a form of middle-class appropriation; we must also recognize that this element of citation or mediation necessarily complicated the cultural and political work that the genre performed. Further, the architecture of anti-Orphic discourse was more intricate than the straightforward symbolic inversion discussed by theorists like Stallybrass, White, and Babcock, who emphasize that culture is always structured in relation to its inverse.[15] We will find that, instead of simply reducing the high and elevating the low, music parodies typically resorted to a form of triangulation—for example, a third term like non-Western music—in order to destabilize existing hierarchies of value.[16] One of the tasks of this chapter, then, is to investigate the purpose of this fulcrum and, in so doing, shed light on eighteenth-century musical exoticism, whose location within Western aesthetic hierarchies has not been particularly well understood. The discussion thus departs from the long-standing preoccupation with musical borrowing and the question of authenticity and focuses instead on the kinds of uses to which musical borrowing could be put.[17]

It has often been observed that the margins are a critical site for the constitution of various forms of identity.[18] Yet this study departs from Stallybrass and White in terms of where it situates those margins. While they point to geographical space as one of the four linked symbolic realms, their analysis remains strictly within the geographical bounds of the nation-state. My study of anti-Orphic discourse suggests something different. I show that the project of imagining an English national musical culture occurred to considerable degree in what we might think of as transnational space. Certainly, the margins were located internally—at the juncture between young and old, healthy and sick, male and female, hetero- and homosexual, human and animal, urban and provincial, aristocrat and middle class, and middle class and plebian. However, the margins were also located externally—between England and the Celtic periphery, Britain and Italy, France or the German states, Britain and its overseas colonies, and, one might even say, Germany and its imaginary colonies. This put travelers and their engagement with musical alterity at the center of the frame because, traditionally, it was travelers who had transgressed these liminal spaces and mediated their representation within. Increasingly, however, travelers themselves came under suspicion. Anti-Orphic discourse would draw attention to the constitutive potential of the margins but at the same time question the traveler's right to exert symbolic authority over the margins.

Traveling Music

By the 1770s and 1780s, travel and music had become easy targets for literary wags. The return of seafarers and intrepid pedestrians like James Cook, James Boswell, Samuel Johnson, Samuel Sharp, and James Bruce established music as the new object of interest. A decade or so earlier there had been talk about exotic curios, but now the buzz was about the songs and musical instruments that one could see and hear in places as mutually remote as Polynesia and Scotland, Italy and Abyssinia. To be sure, this commentary on music reflects a serious (and growing) interest in music ethnography: Writers, naturalists, and philosophers were making the first systematic efforts to come to terms with the diversity of the world's musical offerings.

Coterminous with this, however, was a good deal of skepticism on the part of the lay public about this latest peregrine preoccupation. In many of the travel parodies published during the last decades of the century, music is the butt of the joke—it demonstrates the very excess of the traveler's curiosity, his fascination with oddities, and his propensity for exaggeration and confabulation. In fine, it is the parody of music that cast suspicion on travel. Laughing at the exotic cacophony, the reader and theatergoer are presented with a rudimentary lesson in musical taste: Domestic music is transposed to Aberdeen or Tahiti, where it is given a good drubbing. At the same time, audiences learn that travel is an unstable epistemological mode insofar as reports about improbable musical vernaculars set a limit on the credibility of travelers and the reliability of their knowledge.

We see this at work in a parody like John Wolcot's, written under the pseudonym Peter Pindar, where island music is said to "beggar . . . all the music of the spheres" and the travelogue is described as "A book like Mandeville's, that yields delight, And puts poor probability to flight."[19] We also see it in Paul Jodrell's farce, *A Widow and No Widow,* which opened at the Haymarket in July 1779.[20] As in Wolcot's parody, Jodrell's main character is based on the doughty James Bruce (1730–1794), whose journey through North Africa to find the source of the Blue Nile attracted considerable public and scholarly attention. As an autodidact and antiquarian, Bruce was genuinely interested in music—he collaborated with Burney on the Egyptian section of the *General History of Music*—and the Burney family thought him entertaining. (Fanny referred to him as "Man-Mountain" because of his unusual height.[21]) However, doubt about his observations on the ancient harp and his penchant for self-dramatization also earned him another punning nickname, "the Abyssinian lyre." Disdain grew, and he became the object of fun in this as well as several other parodies.[22] In *A Widow and No Widow* Jodrell has a thinly disguised Bruce (Macfable, speaking in mock brogue) discourse on music with a character called the Doctor, along with a Mrs. Sharp:

DOCTOR: What part of the world has been principally the object of your attention?

MACFABLE: Parts, Doctor, quite unknown. I had no ambition to see an Italian senger [*sic*], or an opera-girl; so did na' care to gang where every body had been before me—

DOCT. And did you find much amusement in these unknown countries?—I suppose the inhabitants of them are all savages.

MACF. Yes, yes; a kind of savages.

DOCT. Quite unacquainted with everything?

MACF. O, no; vara clever and agreeable.

MRS. SHARP. Clever!—what, savages clever!—How!

MACF. O they have a damn'd deal of wet; and are remarkable for invention.

DOCT. So indeed, it seems. [Aside.]—Invention! What kind of invention?

MACF. O, they have a variety of inventions—in music—particularly, I think.

DOCT. Music!—What, the bagpipe, I suppose?

MACF. Yes, they are enchanted with the sound; and I had a fine opportunity of indulging my taste there.[23]

The dialogue goes on in this vein, its one-liners and asides no doubt funnier to audiences in 1779 than to readers in the present. This gap tells us something, much in the way that the "funniness" of eighteenth-century cat torture is suggestive to a cultural historian like Robert Darnton. Our inability to get the eighteenth-century joke highlights what Darnton describes as an experiential gap between the then and the now: "When you realize that you are not getting something—a joke, a proverb, a ceremony—that is particularly meaningful to the natives, you can see where to grasp a foreign system of meaning in order to unravel it."[24] This gap reminds us that the Haymarket's diverse theatergoers—not just a select group of musically literate intellectuals—were familiar with Jodrell's rich allusions. Further, the fact that theatergoers could, as James Beattie put it in his *Essay on Laughter and Ludicrous Composition* (1778), perceive the relationship between "the copy and its archetype," provides a good indication of the class and gender dispersion of the travel discourse.[25] To wit, the playwright pokes fun at geography and travel (the source of the Nile, terra australis incognita, and the Northwest Passage were among the great prizes of eighteenth-century cartography); he mocks the kind of cultural relativism that deems the savage clever; he invokes the practice of performing bagpipes for native peoples (as we have seen in the previous chapter); and he plays on the tediousness of Italy as a travel destination. This is all crowned with frequent references to the mendacity of travelers.

In what is perhaps the most topical dialogue in the play, the character Macfable describes a remarkable discovery he has made on his journey. By boring holes in their tongues, says Macfable, the savages achieve a form of music that is at once vocal and instrumental, something no less wonderful than "the weevow, the invention they brought from Otaheite." For, he adds, "did not they sail round the world, to investigate the airt [*sic*] of snuffling a tune thro' their noses." With a gesture that we will find repeated in other parodies, Macfable promises to banish castrati from the European stage and restore manly vigor to the opera thanks to this discovery.[26] Clearly, theater audiences did not need reminding that the "weevow" referred to the Tahitian nose flute (*vivo*) collected by Cook during his late voyages nor that travelers like Burney had traveled the length of Italy commenting on the soon-to-be-obsolete practice of castrating singers.

A few years later playwright John O'Keeffe (1747–1833) and composer William Shield (bap. 1748/9–1829) would draw on a similar set of references for their pantomime *Omai, or, a Trip round the World* (1785). As in Jodrell's play, South Seas travel, exotic music, and unfamiliar musical instruments were set to make another exciting appearance on the London stage—with one important difference. O'Keeffe and Shield's central character was based not on the figure of the European traveler but on Mai, a Pacific Islander who had been brought to London under the auspices of the second Cook voyage some years earlier. Capitalizing on the considerable public interest in Mai's visit and in the Pacific generally, the playwright and composer drew on the expertise of voyage artist John Webber and designer Jacques Philippe de Loutherbourg to significantly increase the work's production values.[27] The resulting costume designs closely mimicked some of the articles of clothing collected by Cook in Polynesia and the Pacific Northwest. A character called the Chief Mourner of Otahaite, for example, was clad in a costume that bore strong resemblance to the mourning dress that had been acquired in Tahiti and attracted extensive interest in London (figure 3.3).[28]

We can contrast this emphasis on visual similitude with Shield's music, which aimed for a mixture of familiarity and foreignness, yet also took greater liberties with the musical source material. In a 1786 review, the pantomime was billed as using the "vernacular airs of Otaheite"—Tahiti standing metonymically for all of Polynesia.[29] One such "vernacular" song, "Chorus of Villagers of the friendly Islands" (figure 3.4), attempted to evoke a distinctly Polynesian flavor by using a dotted rhythm and a flattened, descending leading note. The song was also accompanied by actual Tongan instruments like "naffas" (*nafa*, a slit drum that was used to accompany the *me'elaufola* dance and was described by Cook in 1784 as being several feet long, twice as wide as a man, and played with two thick sticks) and "pagges" (*pagge*, a wooden, paddle-shaped instrument also reported to have been used in dancing) (figure 3.5).[30] Other songs in the pantomime were punctuated with blasts of the conch trumpet. Whatever its pretensions to authenticity, however, the composer did not limit himself to the elements that scholars already associated with Polynesian music—homophony (rather than poly-

FIGURE 3.3. Philippe Jacques de Loutherbourg (1740–1812), *Chief mourner Otahaite* (1785), watercolor, 31.4 × 18.9 cm. By permission of the National Library of Australia.

phony), a narrow tonal range (rather than the wider range heard in Vanuatu), repetitive melodic and rhythmic patterns, and vocal portamento (or what the *Philosophical Transactions* referred to as a "wholly *enharmonic* slubbering and sliding").[31]

Even when European composers were familiar with non-Western musical elements (for example, a rhythmic pattern like the Ottoman *usul*), they did not always incorporate them into their compositions but instead preferred elements like percussion instruments and repeated thirds that were more easily adaptable.[32] During the eighteenth century, musical borrowing was thus generally limited to musical elements that were markedly exotic but with a loose Western corollary. For the majority of Shield's public, on the other hand, South Seas music was a complete unknown. This lack of an exotic aural referent explains why the pantomime music exhibited less ethnographic fidelity than the costumes. It was enough to use conventional Western tonality and draw on disparate musical idioms and styles to create a pastiche out of Irish tunes, sea shanties, recitatives, arias, choruses, and minstrelsy. The reality effect, to use Roland Barthes's phrase, was generated by the

FIGURE 3.4. William Shield (1748/49–1829), "Chorus of the Villagers of the Friendly Islands," *Omai, or, a Trip round the World* (1785).

occasional exotic instrument like the conch trumpet and the drum, extra-musical elements like Tahitian words (*mahee* for bread, for example), and references in the song lyrics to plantains, yams, and hogs.[33]

Londoners appreciated the new South Seas feel of *Omai*'s music. At the same time, its exotic specificity was undermined by a form of indiscriminate alterity in which musical idioms, geographical spaces, and class positions were interchanged and allied in complicated ways. Perhaps the most striking example of this is "In de big Canoe," an Irish tune sung in minstrel style by a character called the Otaheitian Traveller (figure 3.6). With the song's mix of Irish, North American, and Polynesian references, one could be forgiven for seeing it as an act of wish fulfillment that collapsed past, present, and prospective colonies into a seamless, imperial whole. But besides highlighting colonial peripheries, the pantomime emphasized the metropolis's liminal spaces: Songs by Polynesian characters were interspersed with songs sung by, for example, sailors, swindlers, barrow pushers, street hawkers, and a Jewish usurer. What was one to make of this conglomeration of domestic and exotic alterity that seemed to give new voice to what were usually marginalized positions?[34]

A closer look at the pantomime shows that its heroes are Omai and the apotheosized Captain Cook, while its villain is Don Struttolando, a Spaniard. At first glance, Struttolando seems like an odd choice for a scoundrel. Most of the other characters in the pantomime have historical corollaries, but Struttolando seems to lack a real-life counterpart. In fact, this axis of good and evil mirrored the geopolitical realities of the 1760s, 1770s, and 1780s, when the French and the Spanish were contesting British claims on Tahiti.[35] The Spanish, in particular, were demonized as Europe's "bad" voyagers and

TOMBEAU DE PANGAI

« Hifo » (Tonga Tabou)

FIGURE 3.5. Hippolyte Vanderburch, *Tombeau de Pangai a Hifo, Tonga Tabou* (Paris): Tastu, [1833] ([Paris]: Lith. A. Bes), one print: lithograph, hand col., 21.2 × 33 cm. By permission of the National Library of Australia.

FIGURE 3.6. William Shield, "In de big canoe," *Omai, or, a Trip round the World* (1785).

blamed by Britons for their violent encounter practices and the spread of venereal disease.[36] The territorial squabble that was being played out on a Tahitian beach by a succession of European voyagers competing to mark the island as their own would, in other words, receive its definitive inscription in the pantomime. The Briton Samuel Wallis's claim on Tahiti was challenged by the Spanish, then defended by Cook, who erected a new inscription, "Georgius Tertius Rex," on the island.[37] The pantomime took this battle back to the metropolis: By aligning Omai with Cook—the prospective co-lonial subject with the representative of empire—the Spanish claim on the island was effectively erased. Moreover, into the mouths of the Polynesians would be placed a triumphal expression of fealty to the British Crown: With a blast of the conch, the Tahitian chiefly characters Oberea (based on Purea), Otoo (Tu, Pomare I), and Oedidee (Hedeedee) entreat their fellow islanders to hail their new king (figure 3.7). The scene acquired unexpected pathos and added political meaning when, during the 1780s, George III seemed to go mad with a bout of porphyria and began commanding metropolitan dem-onstrations of loyalty.

In O'Keeffe and Shield's pantomime, "race" forms an allegiance with empire against nation and class (Spain and the aristocracy) in a crisscrossing of identity positions.[38] This insight sheds some light on the potential lim-itations of our analytic categories. Whereas the "low" is often understood to be the underprivileged term within social, economic, and racial hierarchies and seen as a category with critical—even emancipatory—potential, here the contrary seems to be true. The pantomime overturns accepted orders of

FIGURE 3.7. William Shield, "Trio," *Omai, or, a Trip round the World* (1785).

value by giving agency to working people and non-Europeans and by creating a space for "low" culture in one of London's middlebrow theaters. However, the kind of ideological work performed by this reprioritization is far from straightforward. *Omai* does not ultimately privilege the world-upside-down position so much as circumnavigate it. In some sense, foregrounding the "low" becomes merely a way of valorizing empire.

Parodying the traveler acquires an added level of complexity, for, in the hands of Shield and O'Keeffe, the fad for travel appears to have radiated from Europe to the utmost edges of the earth. The native's journey to the metropolis is, as the pantomime's subtitle suggests, a voyage that has come full circle in order to comment self-reflexively on its point of departure.[39] It is at once a celebration of imperial might, a critique of the European traveler's ethnographic interests, a laugh at the expense of Polynesian peoples and cultures, and, like ethnography in reverse, a peep at England through the fresh eyes and ears of the "native." The ambiguity that arises from this tangle of perspectives certainly added to the appeal of the work because *Omai* had a bit of something for everyone. On the other hand, it also undermined the pantomime's critical potential by in effect preserving existing aesthetic regimes and inscribing imperial hierarchies.

By the time Jodrell's play opened at the Haymarket and O'Keeffe and Shield's pantomime at Covent Garden, this sort of drollery and cultural double entendre was part of the London vocabulary. Travel and music, as the song lyric says, now went together like a horse and carriage. As I emphasized in the first chapter, scholars were setting out to explore the world's oceans and investigate agriculture, commerce, and manufacture; others went specifically to study its music. At the same time, the first men of travel—including Cook, Bruce, and Burney—had begun to strain the public's credulity with reports about improbable instruments and rarified practices—trilling castrati and natives who blew flutes with their noses and leapt with joy at the sound of the Highland pipes. For audiences at home, music had become the funny part of travel. And in the summer of 1774, travel was about to become the funny part of music.

Music Education and the National Good

Burney was not in a laughing mood that year. The cause of his ill humor was a work of real animus called *Musical Travels thro' England, by Joel Collier, Organist* (1774). As arguably the greatest music lobbyist of his day, Burney was modest in his intellectual assertions but far reaching in his professional and social ambitions. And in the author John Bicknell he found an energetic and outspoken adversary. Cloaked behind the pseudonym Joel Collier, Bicknell questioned many basic assumptions about music's agency and purpose. Traditional claims that music could pacify, soothe, or heal; that it could civilize or antagonize; and that it could improve society's morals and educate its young were all now under contention. Anti-Orpheus had entered the bear pit to battle with Burney over the status of music, and the ensuing "book fight," to use one of Fanny's terms, would engross the public for years to come.

In order to trace the genesis of Bicknell's parody and the long battle it sparked, we must look first to Burney's activities earlier that summer, when he and an Italian violinist and impresario by the name of Felice de Giardini (1716–1796) turned their attention to a venerable London institution, the Foundling Hospital.[40] The hospital was already famous for its annual performances of Handel's *Messiah,* but Burney and Giardini envisioned a new charter that would raise music's profile. Instead of just maintaining exposed and deserted children as it had since its founding by an act of Parliament in 1740, the hospital would be turned into a hatchery for young musicians. Burney described how, after ruling out various other possible venues, he finally chose this particular institution: "A House, a Chapel, a number of Children to choose out of, a want of Musical Exhibitions & employment for Orphans, from the time they quit the nurse, till they are 21—all this makes that Hospital the properest place for our establishment."[41] The conservatory would be the first such institution in the country and, it was hoped, would resuscitate English music through a rigorous program of publicly-sponsored music education.[42] However, the ambitious plan was not to be. The board met on July 20, 1774, to pass the proposal, but at the next meeting, on August 3, the plan was rescinded. The orphans of Guilford Street were sent back to their knitting and gardening without having seen the inside of a piano lid. Burney's vision for a London conservatory would not be realized until 1822.[43]

The fact that the conservatory met with staunch opposition is perhaps understandable. The Foundling Hospital was, after all, a flagship for the humane and socially progressive ideals of the period, and it had the support of some of the country's most influential citizens, who did not like to see their philanthropic efforts subverted by a pair of upstart musicians. Moreover, the proper use of charitable monies and abuses of public trust—"pilfering from the poor," as one journalist put it—were matters of general civic concern. Public attention had recently been drawn to the misappropriation of funds at another hospital, where the committee was charged with "pilfering from the poor and spending more on their pleasures than on the necessary business of the trust."[44] Still, even after the conservatory plan had been rejected, objections were revived in one form or another for almost four decades. Long after Burney had shelved his idea, the plan for a music school was still being parodied, and Burney and Giardini continued to be lampooned, directly and indirectly, in print and on the stage.

Why their plan should have occupied such a disproportionate place in the literary-musical imagination thus requires some explanation. We are prompted to ask how music came to be regarded as part of the national weal and orphans its likely vehicles, as well as why the civic function of music in the 1770s and 1780s warranted such attention from writers like John Bicknell and so much interest from his readers. We will find that the plan was not unprecedented. Seventeenth-century Venetian and Neapolitan orphanages were known for their cultivation of music—Vivaldi famously held a position at one such institution—and, in England, the idea for a music school had already been suggested a decade or so earlier.[45] But we will also find that some of the answers lie in things seen and heard firsthand, and so we must turn to the Continent to track Burney's experiences there listening to rehearsals, concerts, and the stray sounds of musicians performing on the street.

Burney, we know, set off for Europe with the aim of learning about Continental music and researching his *General History of Music.* However, his larger aim then, as later, was promoting the cause of English music, and it was while crisscrossing Europe that he got an idea that could be imported back home. First in Italy, where he visited a Venetian conservatory described as a "kind of Foundling Hospital for natural children," then in the German states, he was struck by the training young musicians received.[46] He came to attribute the generally high level of musicianship to childhood education, church singing, and institutional instruction. Today, in an age when children are fast-tracked through early development programs, it seems obvious that such an approach might both promote a high level of general musical literacy and, at the same time, produce a handful of outstanding composers and performers. Yet to Burney's contemporaries, the nature and origins of intellectual and creative excellence were still intractable problems. Philosophers and natural historians were uncertain whether excellence—sometimes coded as "genius"—was the product of cultivation or whether its origins lay in natural causes, divine providence, and the coincidence of geography and a temperate climate.[47] In a point that has been lost in the controversy over Burney's dismissive remarks about the state of German music, Burney was cautious about deterministic arguments. At least in terms of Europeans, he thought that cultural practices could not be reduced to a single causal factor or the individual easily conflated with the group. "I could never suppose effects without a cause," he noted in his travelogue, because "nature, though often partial to individuals, in her distribution of genius and talents, is never so to a whole people":

> Climate contributes greatly to the forming of customs and manners; and, it is, I believe, certain, that those who inhabit hot climates, are more delighted with music than those of cold ones; perhaps, from the auditory nerves being more irritable in the one than in the other; but I could, by no means, account for climate operating more in favour of music upon the Bohemians, than on their neighbours, the Saxons and Moravians.[48]

While conceding ground to the Buffonians, who correlated progress to geographic and climatic factors, Burney, like many travelers of his generation, was forced to acknowledge the increasingly obvious point that similar climates sometimes produced different results and different climates similar results. Empirical observations like these obstructed conventional explanations of social, cultural, and political attainment and the theory that societies moved through fixed stages of development. This is perhaps one reason why we find observers looking to other contexts. They studied musical prodigies like William Crotch (later the first director of the Royal Academy of Music), whom Burney investigated on behalf of the Royal Society in an effort to distinguish the "strange" from the "common" in the young "bard Lilliputian."[49] Observers also sought evidence further afield—among agricultural workers and the urban poor in Continental Europe and, as we have seen in the previous chapter, among non-European peoples in the southern hemisphere. Whereas climate and geography had once sufficed as critical determinants for explaining musical difference, now the palette was more colorful: The young, poor, uneducated, savage, and sick were scrutinized as well. And, importantly, their musical accomplishments would come to be regarded not only as evidentiary but also as potentially prescriptive for the understanding and possible transformation of music making at home.

Burney outlined some preliminary ideas for a music school and shared the plan with Giardini.[50] The Italian conservatories had been his first inspiration, but his commitment to the cause of music pedagogy was redoubled, thanks to what he observed on the eastern edges of the Holy Roman Empire, at the Jesuit music school in Munich, and among the *Singschüler* in Dresden.[51] In the summer of 1772 he set out specifically to investigate musicality in Bohemia—reputed by travelers like Thomas Nugent, the great propagandist for the Grand Tour, to be the most musical region in Germany, if not all of Europe.[52] The Bohemian origins of renowned composers like Gluck seemed to confirm Nugent's opinion.[53] Yet not content with such stereotypes when matters could be investigated firsthand, Burney turned to local music. He noted the singing of workers in towns like Teutschbrod (Havlíčkův Brod), birthplace of Stamitz, who had relocated to Mannheim to invent modern orchestral playing.[54] Burney also listened to the band of musicians that gathered outside his inn, and he climbed to Prague's hilltop cathedral in the hope of hearing Germany's finest organist dazzle his congregation.[55]

Notwithstanding the political and economic ravages that had seen a twelfth of the region's population succumb to famine a year or two earlier, the performances that Burney heard between the Danube and the Elbe suggested that Bohemian musicality was due in no small part to their forward-looking education system: Children, both male and female, learned music just as they learned to read and write. "These schools," said Burney, "clearly prove that it is not from a partiality in *nature* that Bohemia abounds so much with musicians; for *cultivation* contributes greatly toward rendering the love and knowledge of music general in this country." He added that the Bohemians were superior musicians because they were trained to play instruments and because musical and textual literacy were regarded as an essential part of "common education."[56] In other words, a high general standard of education produced a musical populace, but, importantly, it also seemed to foster the abilities of the talented few.

Perhaps because he was something of a self-made man and a follower of the pedagogically minded Rousseau, Burney was sympathetic to the idea that talent was not simply innate; it could also be nurtured. Comparing two child prodigies—Crotch and Mozart—Burney concluded that, although both were exceptionally talented, Crotch had been "left to nature," whereas Mozart had "been nursed in good music." The results were clear, and there were lessons to be learned from this.[57] The presence of Continental musicians in Britain also contributed to an awareness of the importance and high standard of musical training abroad.[58] Finally, Burney learned something about music as a form of social practice from the street musicians, agricultural laborers, and conservatory students he encountered on the Continent, where music making seemed better integrated into daily life.

Burney's musical tastes may not have been radically altered by the performances he heard in Munich, Hamburg, Berlin, or even Vienna: He returned, just as he had set out, predisposed to an Italianate style. Yet his travels in Italy and the German states provided evidence of a distinctive model for music education, and they confirmed the profound significance of music to communal life. With proper training, he concluded, English musicians could likewise be better cultivated and the cultural life of his own nation elevated to a standard commensurate with its political and economic hegemony. I must thus disagree with Kerry Grant's conclusion that the Continental travels made little difference to Burney's perception of music.[59] Each chapter devoted to the history of German music in Burney's magnum opus would open by reiterating the same point, namely that Germans were among the "most successful cultivators" of music. The German states had long incorporated music into their system of general education: Music was offered at "almost all the common schools of every city, town, and village" throughout the Holy Roman Empire, and no children "gifted with genius" were denied the opportunity to cultivate their talent. "Cultivation" was neither a pejorative term, nor was it antithetical to "genius."[60] The experience of traveling and listening seemed to persuade Burney that a nation's greatness was pegged to its music and that this was to be measured in terms of not only outstanding composers and performers but also the man on the street. It was music's anthropological moment.

Thus we return to the subject of the Foundling Hospital to find Burney plotting about the welfare of the orphans in Guilford Street and concocting a plan to reverse the fortunes of English musical life. If he got his way, England would have its own institution for fostering indigenous talent, and the country would no longer need to import musicians to the detriment of the nation's international reputation.[61] "We [English] love good singing," said

Burney later, "but will not be at the trouble or expence of establishing a school where our natives might be taught; which a little resembles the conduct of those men of pleasure, who, not having time or patience to *make love,* seek it where it can be purchased *ready made.*"[62] The point was taken up by Fanny in her memoirs of her father. A music school would, she said, "save English talent from the mortification, and the British purse from the depredations, of seeking a constant annual supply of genius and merit from foreign shores."[63] The newly organized Foundling Hospital, renamed the Public Music School with Burney himself and Giardini at the helm, would spearhead the effort.

There is an element of jingoism in the kind of thinking that turned the Foundling Hospital into a flashpoint for debates about national culture. But, and this is more to my point, the controversy also circled around music's meaning and agency and the difficulties involved in determining music's proper place in society. When evaluating the plan presented to them in the summer of 1774, the board of governors and directors was asked to consider the prosaic reasons for transforming the hospital: Burney and Giardini argued in their proposal, for example, that trained orphans would soon be able to pay for their own upkeep by offering public concerts and performing services like teaching, copying music, and repairing instruments.[64] The board was also presented, moreover, with a set of arguments that operated at a macroeconomic level. Britain, claimed Burney, had become dependent on what he described as "the productions and performances of Strangers."[65] Music consumed a generous portion of the private as well as public coffers, and it was disgraceful that the world's most commercial nation was suffering from a kind of musical trade deficit:

> Now an Establishment for the cultivation of Musical Talents among our own Natives, would not only save the National Honour, but the National [*sic*] Wealth; & thus be of use to us as a Commercial People on the side of Public Oeconomy. This must appear to every one who considers the immense Sums that are annually paid to the Foreign Performers at Operas, & other public as well as private, Musical Performances.[66]

To reinforce the point, Burney added that Continental musicians were staging the country's most expensive performances, but their wages were being "carried *out* of the Kingdom." It would be so much better, he suggested, if the money could instead be "thrown into the Hands of our indigent Natives, and by that means remain circulating in the Kingdom," where it could do the nation some good.[67]

Whether Burney's musical protectionism embraces any literal truth is difficult to gauge. England's public institutions and private houses were indeed well stocked with imported singers, instrumentalists, and teachers (German musicians gained visibility during the 1770s), but it is doubtful that they had quite as deleterious an effect on the broader economic climate as Burney wanted to imply. Certainly, an Italian like Guiseppe Baretti was infuriated by the assertion that Italian musicians were getting rich on the backs of English citizens. In 1769 he claimed that, in ten years of watching opera at the Haymarket, he had seen all of the Italian performers return home very poor, despite what were alleged to be "enormous salaries" and "prodigious benefits."[68]

What cannot be overlooked, on the other hand, is the fact that Burney was giving voice to a not uncommon view that the country was overrun with Italian performers, in particular castrati, and that these foreign musicians were corrosive to English culture, society, and masculinity.[69] Dating from the early decades of the century, English critics like Joseph Addison and Richard Steele had already complained about the English predilection for Italian music. William Hogarth likewise played on the disenchantment with foreign performers in his well-known engraving, *The Enraged Musician* (1741), while another engraving attributed to him shows vain and monstrous castrati with chests swelled like pouter pigeons—figures of looming, tottering masculinity who dwarf the female soprano (figure 3.8).[70]

Such sentiments were articulated as outright xenophobia by later parodists like Andrew Marvel in a *London Museum* article dating from 1770:

> O! hapless England; thou who gavest laws to the world, declareth this *italick* madness. Will not the soft transporting voice of our beauteous countrywomen captivate the soul, without raking amongst the nerveless sons of Italy for eunuchs! . . . Shall the first personages amongst us, allow such cat-gut enchanters to possess, and receive at their hands double the pay of an Admiral or a General! Shall the highest of our highest nobles devote their time to private consorts and strum a guitar, instead of firing at the sound of a cannon![71]

In terms similar to the ones Burney employed a few years later, these parodists (and serious commentators, too) complained that Italian musicians were being paid disproportionately large salaries and draining the country of money.[72] Certainly, this applied only to a handful of opera stars, but it was a *primo uomo* like Luigi Marchesi, who earned fifteen hundred pounds in a single season, that provoked indignation. With most other singers earning a salary of a few hundred pounds or less, Marchesi seemed to encapsulate everything

FARINELLI, CUZZONI, AND SENESINO.

FIGURE 3.8. William Hogarth (1697–1764); J. Barlow, *Farinelli, Cuzzoni, and Senesino (and Berenstadt)* (1798), performing Handel's *Flavio* at the King's Theatre. By permission of the Museum of London.

that was wrong with a system that held local musicians in low social esteem yet paid the best foreign musicians unthinkable sums of money.[73]

There was no resolving these contradictions of value in Burney's and Giardini's address to the board. Within a few short decades, musical absolutism would enter the philosophical and aesthetic discourse, and music would come to be regarded not merely as a means to a social, moral, or political end but as an end in itself. At this moment, however, the arguments of the philosophical tradition that privileged aesthetic autonomy were not yet at Burney's disposal. When he attempted to elevate music from its lowly position to one of collective significance, he did not anticipate E. T. A. Hoffmann, Arthur Schopenhauer, or their metaphysical imprimatur. Rather, the arguments upon which Burney could draw were essentially Platonist: Music was worthy of being promoted because of what it could do for the moral education of the individual and, by implication, for the state.[74] Strictly utilitarian in his vocabulary, our new Orpheus thus stressed music's indispensability to the church, army, and ruler and its benefits to the poor, young, and uneducated.

At a hastily convened meeting, the hospital board (stacked with music enthusiasts like Sandwich, antiquarian and naturalist Daines Barrington, and the governor, Sir Charles Whitworth) was initially persuaded by Burney's rhetoric. Then, just as quickly, the board changed its mind when it met in full a second time. Whether more aggressive and politically astute lobbying on the part of Burney and his supporters could have avoided such prevarication is impossible to know. Technically, the plan was overturned because it contravened the hospital charter, which had been established by an act of Parliament, but its failure was also attributed to opposition from "a small cabal."[75] Judging by the board's "discursive and perplexing" discussions of the proposal, however, as well as by the subsequent literary uproar, it is clear that Burney's arguments were not sufficiently persuasive because they were marred by a flaw.[76] The "Sketch for a Plan" had forged an uneasy alliance between two ill-matched views of music. On the one hand, it created a Dryden-like paean to music's functional utility, and, on the other, it argued for music's commodity status and hence its autonomy.[77] The question the board members debated that summer, as to whether music was either a luxury or a necessity, had been answered with Burney's unsatisfactory insistence upon the necessity of luxury. For a board member like Thomas Day and his socially minded friend John Bicknell, the possibility that the Foundling Hospital might be reduced from one of the century's great social experiments to a moral and political oxymoron was thus something they intended to vigorously oppose.[78] Burney would soon feel their invective.

Musical Travels

This then was the climate in which publisher George Kearsley brought a new book onto the market. Late in the summer of 1774 the *Public Advertiser* announced the appearance of *Musical Travels thro' England* by a Mr. Collier.[79] To some of Burney's friends, including amateur musicians like the Earl of Sandwich and Thomas Twining, the advertisement looked enticing. They were enthusiastic about the prospect of a domestic complement to Burney's travels, a work that promised an account of the "true state of the musical improvement and progression" in the British Isles. Everyone had been awaiting a travelogue such as this, and the unwitting Sandwich even asked Burney whether he had read the book.[80] Just a glance at its octavo pages, however, was enough to change their minds. Like the *Supplement au voyage de Bougainville* by Denis Diderot, the new travelogue was a trenchant social and political satire full of daring innuendo and risqué humor. Readers found that

Burney and Giardini's plans for the Foundling Hospital, travelers generally, even Sandwich himself, were prime objects of ridicule. For a man like Sandwich, the attack was perhaps little out of the ordinary: His personal and political indiscretions had accustomed him to censure.[81] Conflict was also no stranger to the cantankerous Giardini: He had been involved in a legal dispute about the management of the 1764 opera season at the King's Theatre and had already been the subject of a mock panegyric ten years before Bicknell put pen to paper.[82] However, for the more private Burney, a man whose professional fortunes and deepest passions were staked to music, the parody cut frighteningly close to the bone.

Like many an eighteenth-century parodist, the author of *Musical Travels thro' England* had taken pains to conceal his identity by publishing this and other works (including articles in German journals) under the same pseudonym.[83] Assiduous efforts to identify the author were unsuccessful, and Burney was said to have spent two hundred pounds buying up copies of the book in an attempt to keep it off the market—to no avail.[84] *Musical Travels* would eventually see six editions in print (the final 1818 edition possibly authored by someone else) and sell even better for its obscure parentage.

The many different editions of *Musical Travels* make it difficult to settle on a definitive version. Nevertheless, I focus here on the fifth edition, published in 1785. The text is a composite of earlier editions, and its amendments reflect both the intervening critical reception of the work and important topical developments like the abolition movement and the American War of Independence.[85] The parody has been attributed to various men of letters, including violist George Veal, abolitionist Thomas Day, hack author Alexander Bicknell, and the writer on hunting Peter Beckford. However, thanks to investigative work in the 1970s by Burney's biographer Roger Lonsdale, there is now agreement that Joel Collier was in fact John Bicknell (1746?–1787), a lawyer and writer with a commitment to social causes, an amateur interest in music criticism, and an active dislike of Charles Burney and his idea for a public school of music.[86]

As Bicknell accurately sensed, the literary market was ripe for laughter, especially when it came at the expense of musical travelers and their odd preoccupations. Playwright Jodrell had said in *A Widow and No Widow* that it was now time for the traveler to pay, and, in Bicknell's parody, pay he certainly would.[87] At the reasonable price of one shilling, the work sold well, went through many editions, and was reviewed in a number of major journals. Almost unanimously, reviewers criticized the author's gutter humor— he "descends too low"—but this did not stop journals like the *London Magazine* from titillating readers with lengthy excerpts.[88] To the defense came old friends like Thomas Twining, who tried to reassure Burney that a person's merit was only confirmed when he had *also* received "the inverted praise" of a detractor.[89] William Bewley, a contributor to the *Monthly Review*, also stepped up to accuse the author of "f—ting in the face of his audience" and using "nasty or obscene" humor to parody Burney's journals.[90] *Musical Travels* was indeed rough on Burney, but on balance reviewers (and certainly the general public) thought it highly entertaining, and there is some indication that Burney's and Bicknell's travelogues were read as companion pieces.[91] The public would not have overlooked the fact that Bicknell had a serious axe to grind.

Dedicating *Musical Travels* to the governors of the Foundling Hospital, Bicknell had found a way to retaliate against what he and the uncompromising Thomas Day seemed to feel was a misuse of public resources. But the book was more than just a one-time response to a poorly executed plan; it dealt explicitly with the idea that music served a moral, social, and political purpose. By praising where he meant to criticize and advocating where he meant to disavow, Bicknell questioned the high priority attached to music by supporters of the proposed music school and, by extension, music advocates generally:

> It might prove of more national utility to breed these adopted children of the public, to Husbandry, and Navigation . . . than to convert one of the noblest of our public charities into a nursery for the supply of musical performers at our theatres, gardens, and hops. But this is a vulgar prejudice. The improvement of the fine arts ought to be the first object of public attention in an age of luxury, peace, and plenty, like the present. When we have rivaled the Italians in music, it will be time enough to think of our Navy, and our Agriculture.[92]

The narrator adds drolly that, thanks to poor management, the American colonies have been lost along with the conservatory.[93] Bicknell, of course, supported the American War of Independence as vigorously as he opposed a public music school, but, stretching Burney's argument, the author joked that the fate of music was that of the empire.

From the global we move to the cosmic, for *Musical Travels* continues with a jab at Burney's astronomical interests (an earlier Burney publication dealt with Halley's comet).[94] In an advertisement announcing a spurious publication, "An Enquiry into the Present State of the Music of the Spheres," the protagonist complains that critics have compared his "celestial orchestra" with the philosopher's stone and the perpetual motion machine. He assures readers, however, of the sufficiency of his data and the accuracy of his observations. By rigorously studying the sound of thunder as a basso continuo for "all heaven's harmonies," he promises to compute the motions of the planets as easily as counting out a country dance.[95]

Here we find a clear indication of Bicknell's objections to the metaphysical understanding of music. Burney is construed as an heir to Plato and Pythagoras, who believed that the cosmos was ordered according to the same numerical proportions that govern musical harmonies and as an heir to the medieval and Baroque Neoplatonists, who believed a correlation existed between *musica mundana* and *musica humana* (i.e., between celestial and earthly harmony).[96] According to his parodist, Burney has unreasonably promised to "tune" the world and restore it to order by promoting the cause of music. Bicknell parries this with an attack on the limits of music as an explanatory system, implying that music cannot explain the motions of the planets any more than it can elucidate or dictate human and natural laws. Music scholars, he suggests, might insist on empiricism and the evidence of their ears, but, in fact, their explanations operate merely by metaphor and analogy.[97] By pointing this out, Bicknell undermined the integrity of late eighteenth-century music scholarship by questioning both its methodology and its metaphysical pretensions. As a system of knowledge, music had been declared dead. Bicknell's next step would be to interrogate the agency of music itself and hence to question its fundamental social and political utility.

I examine this in three sections that deal with *Musical Travels*—"Musical Margins," "Curative Music and the Critique of Scientism," and "The Castrato, or, Orpheus Dismembered." The first focuses on a topography of the peripheral to consider Bicknell's handling of binary oppositions like the self/other, high/low, English/German, and professional/amateur. One would expect Collier's topsy-turvy world to reclaim the abject and make the low high. In fact, we will find that Bicknell is far from consistent. The subordinate category is mobilized differently depending on Bicknell's discrete agendas, and, in the case of the professional/amateur dichotomy, neither category is privileged. I argue that Bicknell's ambivalence about Orphic discourse leads to a fracturing of musical agency in the parody, which curtails music's political efficaciousness but enhances its aesthetic significance. The second section, "Curative Music and the Critique of Scientism," discusses Bicknell's humorous handling of the curative tarantella and *Katzenklavier* (cat clavichord) and shows how the parody makes a larger point about the limitations of musical knowledge making. Bicknell puts scientism under suspicion, that is, the belief that scientific methods could also be applied to a field like music scholarship. The final section returns to the question of national culture to look at how middlebrow Englishness was constituted.

Social class, nation, empire, body, and sexuality collide in debates over Italian opera and the status of the castrato. I show that the castrato becomes a repository for fears about the threat to the domestic and imperial body.

MUSICAL MARGINS

Orphic discourse always occupies the margins. As I have pointed out in earlier chapters, Orpheus often performs for those who exist outside the signifying realm, and it is only thanks to his irresistible playing that the young, female, savage, or animal may enter the domain of the social. When Orpheus sings, new order prevails—birds, beasts, and trees gather around, the inanimate becomes animate, the uncouth couth. This tells us something important about the interrelationship between culture and society, for, although neither Ovid nor Virgil explicitly addresses this point, it is instructive that Orpheus does not play for those we would expect to attend him—his wife, Eurydice, the wedding guests, or his friends. Rather, it is the otherworldly and abject who listen, they who both mark the bounds of society and show the extent to which those bounds are permeable. Further, Orpheus's music holds the possibility for mediating that crossing. Those who cannot hear his song remain excluded from sociable intercourse and pose a mortal threat to the integrity of both the collective and the individual body. (Orpheus, we recall, will be killed and dismembered by Thracian women, whose cacophonous singing drowns out his own music.) Put another way, from Ovid on, adherents of Orphic discourse have recognized that agency can be measured only if something is at stake. The ultimate test of culture's capacity to promote or retard communal interests—to extend and preserve bonds of sociability and civility—is not located within society itself but at its untamed and natural edges, where the host culture has no real home.

I argued earlier not only that *Musical Travels* was a response to the Foundling Hospital controversy but also that we may consider it an important interrogation of late eighteenth-century ideas about the efficacy, value, and meaning of music. Unsurprisingly, then, Bicknell takes his reader to the marginal sites, where he shows that music exerts some critical agency. Via a topographic displacement from the center to the provincial margins Bicknell explores a series of binary oppositions between self and other, high and low, and professional and amateur. Thus we find Joel Collier, Burney's doppelgänger, setting out to find England's most memorable musical phenomena, not, as we might expect from an account of the present state of English music, in the nation's capital—in opera venues like the Haymarket, Covent Garden, and Drury Lane, pleasure gardens like Vauxhall and Ranelagh, or concert rooms like Hanover Square. Rather, Collier ventures to England's industrial centers (Lincoln, Sheffield, Wolverhampton, and Birmingham); its major port cities (Bristol and Liverpool); market towns like Beverley; and border towns like Chester and Carlisle.

Bicknell's emphasis on the provinces is not entirely out of place. The late eighteenth-century's emerging concert system was an essentially urban phenomenon: It was the major cities that developed purpose-built venues for public music making. However, the fashion for concert going also extended to the provinces, where musicians made use of town halls, inns, theaters, and assembly rooms, and even relatively small towns soon began to sport music clubs, subscription series, and festivals.[98] Bicknell provides few details about these provincial towns and cities—references to cathedral spires in York or the clamor of Birmingham's factories convey only the vaguest sense of local specificity. Collectively, however, Bicknell's provincial towns figure as a site for the unruly aping of the metropolis. And it is here, at the empire's edges and commercial junctions, that Orphic assumptions about music are put to the test.

Our first port of call is Liverpool. In the 1770s the city was the world's busiest harbor: It monopolized roughly a quarter of the global trade and saw as many as a hundred slave ships arriving each year. Bicknell seizes on this fact to reiterate the antislavery sentiments he had expressed in *The Dying Negro* (1773), an influential poem cowritten with Thomas Day. In keeping with Liverpool's liminal character and the trafficking of goods, peoples, and ideas, the city figures as a site of cultural collision. Bicknell has his protagonist meet the captain of a former slave ship, Mr. Cable, who has since "quitted that inhuman employment" in favor of a life of music.[99] Collier plays his cello for the rugged sea captain, needlessly congratulating himself on his capacity to disarm and soften "rough dispositions" with music. Mr. Cable has in fact slept through the entire concert, but he awakes to give a performance on the *gom-gom,* a stringed instrument that he simultaneously blows and bows, while stamping and hollering "ho! ho!" (The reference is to a Khoikhoi *gora,* or mouth-resonated musical bow, described by travelers to the Southern African Cape.[100]) We gather that the captain learned to play the instrument during his voyages to the coast of Africa, where, by his own account, he became so proficient that the king of Benin offered to make him prime minister. "Did [Collier] not prefer it," inquired the captain, "to an over-grown fiddle, and all the Italian whimsies, and tweedle-dums, that people played upon in these days?"[101] Collier responds that, although it might be suitable for seafarers, this "horrid discord" sounds barbarous to cultivated ears. Wouldn't a caprice be nicer instead?

And so, like Phoebus and Pan, the sea captain and the musical traveler engage in a contest over good and bad music. When Collier cannot be convinced of the superiority of African music, he is deemed to have lost the contest and must accept his Midas punishment: He is keelhauled under an Indian canoe while the captain stands on the banks of his horse pond and plays a "war-like measure" on the gom-gom.[102] This is harsh treatment, to be sure. Still, the sea captain's whimsical performance reminds the reader that he, not Collier, has learned moral and musical discernment: He has renounced the slave trade and retired to a treehouse to play his odd instrument.

The Liverpool episode is reminiscent of Burney's musical encounters in London, Paris, and Potsdam, where he made a study of Polynesian, Chinese, and African musical instruments and interrogated foreign visitors about non-European vernaculars. It also invokes the cross-cultural encounters taking place on remote beaches and in colonial outposts, encounters that served as a constant reminder to metropolitan readers about the surprising diversity of social and cultural mores. Bicknell seems to suggest that, in his rigid indifference to non-Western music, Collier has insisted on a form of aesthetic absolutism that unquestioningly privileges serious music (coded as an Italian cello caprice). Bicknell does not go so far as to advocate an aesthetic alternative, but he gestures toward the growing relativism in musical taste. In this permutation of the Orpheus story, the locus of true society is not to be found on the decks of a Liverpudlian slave ship or in the fine concert rooms financed by slave profits but thirty feet off the ground in a treehouse. The sea captain and his appropriated music humorously attempt to convert Collier to a higher ethical, aesthetic, and political purpose. Yet the very improbability of the arboreal scene and Collier's indifference to the captain's music reflect the utopianism of this project. Music's political agency has strict limitations because, although the gom-gom performance offers the possibility for cross-cultural rapprochement, its refusal means that no new order can be enacted. In other words, music is not the irresistible medium of classical myth—neither in the mouth of Orpheus nor in the mouths of the Thracians. The song that hopes to bridge the divide between inclusion and exclusion, society and barbarity can in fact be resisted. With this comes a denial of music's socializing potential. Bicknell makes this point as if to echo the political conjuncture of his day, which saw the first steps toward abolition taken by writers like Granville Sharp, Thomas Day, and Bicknell himself, though British slavery would continue for at least another generation.[103]

Bicknell's gesture toward aesthetic relativism did not have quite so difficult a passage. As we now know, consumers were eager to expand their cultural palettes by sampling foreign ideas, customs, and things. At the same time, Bicknell's move signals the complicated status of non-Western music within late eighteenth-century musical debates. For Burney, non-Western music was the object of independent ethnomusicological interest; for the lay listener, it was the object of potential amusement and ridicule; and for Bicknell, it was a lever that could be used to destabilize an aesthetic regime. In *Musical Travels,* the Liverpudlian's gom-gom is supposed to seem ridiculous, and its productions sound crude. What eighteenth-century reader would not have laughed at a string instrument that was simultaneously bowed and blown and then heaped scorn on a listener who preferred gom-gom scraping to the mellifluous cello? However—and this is the crucial point—when the gom-gom is compared with foreign imports like an Italian caprice or, as elsewhere, with opera seria, then the latter loses ground. No matter how ugly, funny, or improbable, the gom-gom is still preferable to this hyperrefined art form with its stodgy recitatives, ridiculous castrato arias, and contorted plots. Bicknell's foregrounding of non-Western music over Italian opera recalls Jodrell's handling of the Tahitian nose flute in *A Widow and No Widow,* discussed earlier. Like the gom-gom, the vivo will restore the sexual order that has been thrown off kilter by castrato singing. Serious European music is, in other words, subject to a radical reprioritization thanks to the introduction of a third term, non-Western music, which acts like a fulcrum, seesawing existing aesthetic values, dethroning opera seria, and opening the space for a yet unstipulated musical alternative. Elsewhere in the parodic travelogue we will find "low" instruments and popular music taking this pivotal position.

We can thus think of Collier's provincial itinerary as a gesture of decentering. Bicknell dispatches his protagonist to the margins in order to investigate English musical life. Avoiding London's theaters and concert rooms, Collier travels from factory city to slave port and listens to the kinds of low instruments that would normally have escaped the notice of scholars of serious music—Jew's harps, cleavers, bagpipes, barrel organs, drums, comb and brown paper, reed whistles, and ram's horns. This theme was clearly intended to burlesque Burney's catholic tastes and his refusal to categorically exclude any type of music on the grounds that it did not conform to his own (or others') aesthetic preconceptions. Yet the low instruments in *Musical Travels* would have had special meaning even to those of Bicknell's readers who had not read Burney and mused over his fascination with peasant instruments.

During the early modern period, instruments like these were used in a social practice called "skimmington" or "rough music." (There are many regional variants on the term; on the Continent it was called *Katzenmusik* or charivari.[104]) This was a form of noisy protest against individuals who had violated communal norms—typically those that dealt with sexuality, gender, and marriage. Most often the target of invective was a man who had been cuckolded or beaten by his wife.[105] The practice involved riding the offending pair (or their effigies) around on a horse or a staff (hence the expression "to ride skimmington") to the accompaniment of a jeering procession making mock music on cacophonous instruments. The purpose of rough music, E. P. Thompson points out, was to mete out communal justice, and it did so by adopting symbols of authority like the solemn procession and the emblem.[106] Music's occasional function was, in other words, transformed from a sign of the ruler's power to a sign of the people's. Their raucous music conferred shame, humiliation, and public disapprobation on its listeners with the aim of either expelling them from the community or coercing them to adhere to social norms. The fact that "henpecked" husbands were targeted for abuse shows that the practice was intended to reinforce traditional gender roles. Although it was the man who was forced to ride skimmington, the object of the practice was, in some crucial sense, women who defied the patriarchal order. Thus, far from seeking to overturn existing social or political hierarchies, rough music in fact seemed to confirm them.[107]

By the mid-eighteenth century, writers had begun to appropriate elements of rough music for parodic ends and to marry the practice with another custom, the celebration of music on November 22, Saint Cecilia's Day. Thought of as a kind of female Orpheus, Cecilia was celebrated in Restoration England as the embodiment of divine order: Music was praised for its salutary effects on human behavior and its analogous relation to the Newtonian universe.[108] Thus, we find writers like Christopher Smart (1722–1771) and Bonnell Thornton (1724–1768), under the pseudonym Fustian Sackbut, writing paeans to music in the tradition of Dryden and Handel, but with a "rough" twist.[109] In typically parodic form, Thornton inverts conventional aesthetic values in his "Ode on Saint Cæcilia's Day" (1749): Instruments like the violin and harpsichord become "mean" and "vile," while rough music instruments like the bagpipes, marrowbones, and cleaver are called "exalted."[110] The work is constructed like an Orphic parody, but the rough musical effects remain the conventional ones we know from legend: Rivers change course, and rocks and trees begin to dance.

By comparison, Bicknell's handling of these traditions is less straightforward. Instead of the simple inversion of aesthetic values that we find in Thornton's parody, in *Musical Travels* Burney's interest in the "low" is turned against him.[111] Bicknell finds a way to jeer the music scholar by using the very rough music that Burney himself attempted to privilege. Burney's ethnographic gaze is, in other words, censured by the object of its own interest: popular instruments, peasant life, and the music of ordinary folk. However, Burney is jeered in another sense, too. As I discuss in greater detail later in this chapter, Burney's interest in castrato singing is parodied in *Musical Travels* as an ongoing preoccupation with adultery, sex, genitalia, and castration. We can say, then, that the rough music that censures Collier during the course of his travels is perforce a censuring of Burney, for Collier's social and sexual transgressions are mapped to Burney's aesthetic ones.

Bicknell elaborates some of these themes in his treatment of folk song. During his travels, Collier listens to popular ballads like the Irish "Lilli-bulero" and the Scottish "Chevy Chase." In imitation of Burney, Rousseau, and Herder, who all collected so-called national tunes, Collier is shown "enriching his collection" with these songs and advancing a theory about musical diffusion.[112] (A boy heard singing "Yankee Doodle," for example, is thought to prove that Worcester was once inhabited by Americans.) These sorts of references must have added to the appeal of *Musical Travels* because readers, irrespective of their social class, would have remembered the familiar songs as those of childhood, sung by nurses, washerwomen, and scullery maids.[113] Others would have heard their explicitly political overtones, that is, Bicknell's revolutionary and abolitionist sympathies. Yet others, espe-cially the better educated among Bicknell's readers, would have recognized the inclusion of folk songs as a pointed cultural critique and a nod toward the reigning European enthusiasm for folk music. Thus, just as non-Western music is used as a foil for aesthetic reprioritization in Bicknell's work, pop-ular music—a kind of other within—also serves to unsettle existing hierar-chies. Ballads and peasant instruments become the authentic, indigenous counterpoint to imported, aristocratic musical culture, *as well as* a means of parodying the current fad for folk music.

As I have suggested, Bicknell's spatial and aesthetic decentering was informed in several ways by his literary progenitor. Traveling through the German states, Burney was constantly confronted by the fact that there was no "there" there; as a result, the travelogue meanders through duchy, mo-narchy, free city, and rural backwater in search of its object. Vienna is, of course, a high point—it was, after all, the capital of the empire and home to Burney's heroes, Metastasio and Hasse. However, Vienna did not yet possess the centripetal force of a London or a Paris, and so Burney's musical itinerary is, of necessity, a trip with no single telos. Recall from the first chapter that his first order of business was to rout out the German musicians and create a musical topography of the German states where none had existed before. Bicknell adapts this feature of Burney's travelogue for his own ends, in effect superimposing the German states onto England: Whole sections from the *German Tour* are quoted verbatim (Bicknell even gives page references), and characters like Friedrich II pop up in English provincial towns.

We can read the overlayering of German, English, and Italian references in many ways. Certainly we can see in Bicknell's palimpsest a hint of anti-royalist sentiment—a Britain Germanified by the Hanoverian line—and a rekindling of old fears that Britain was being deprived of its sovereign status, for Hanover was said to have "robbed [it] of the benefit of being an is-land."[114] At the same time, there is an implicit critique of German political and cultural fragmentation. The parodist's optic is, after all, a stereoscopic one that simultaneously brings the English and the German into clearer focus. But Bicknell's topographic confection may also be understood as an aesthetic intervention. Whereas his inclusion of non-Western music and folk instruments played on the binaries of self and other, high and low, here Bicknell's object is the professionalizing of music. Traveling around the provinces, Collier locates little, if any, serious music worth listening to. Everywhere he encounters dilettante musicians—a poke at the musi-cal pretensions of two well-heeled amateurs and Burney confidantes, the timpani-playing Earl of Sandwich and the flute-toting King of Prussia. In Lincoln, for example, Collier meets Mr. Dilettanti, a castrato and "illustrious timeist," who eats, defecates, and performs "conjugal endearments" with metronomic regularity. Moreover, Mr. Dilettanti concertizes on a Jew's harp, the "twing, twang, twong" of which sends its listeners into paroxysms.[115] Collier's picaresque adventure turns up no music of greater sophistication than this.

Thus Bicknell references Burney's quest for musical excellence, a quest that was frequently accused of having bypassed musicians and composers of real note. Bicknell suggests that, by traveling off the beaten track, Burney listened in all the wrong places. In making this point, Bicknell was play-ing on Laurence Sterne's *Tristram Shandy,* with its account of fiddling on the page—"Ptr . . r . . r . . ing—twing—twang—prut—trut"—and the listeners "with good ears," who consider this fine music.[116] He was also in fact allying himself with German critics like Ebeling, Reichardt, and Forkel, who charged Burney with favoring the opinions of beer fiddlers and buskers over professional musicians.[117] According to these critics, such lack of discern-ment was at odds with the obligations of the music scholar and critic, whose first responsibility was to preserve the distinction between the *Liebhaber* and the *Kenner* (the amateur enthusiast and the expert). Recall, too, that such critique highlighted the problematic relationship between the musical fact and the aesthetic judgment. Burney's mistake (and hence Collier's) would be to attach undue significance to the opinions and performances of lay musicians. Bicknell seemed to suggest that music and music criticism were now serious business, commanding all the rigor and exclusivity of the trained professional. This was a hypocritical position for an author who was himself merely an amateur critic of music. Nor did it jibe with Bicknell's reprioritization of aesthetic values, specifically his privileging of popular music and his condemnation of rarified genres like opera seria. Such contradictions, however, are never disentangled in *Musical Travels,* and on this basis we must conclude that, rather than espousing a coherent aesthetic position, Bicknell reacted opportunistically to a range of cultural, social, and political irritants.[118]

At some level then we can agree with William Wordsworth and with Burney's defenders about the plagiaristic character of parody.[119] *Musical Travels was* a knee-jerk response to Burney's travelogues, at once contradictory, derivative, and more reactive than aesthetically proactive. On the other hand, Bicknell took a consistent position on the question of musical agency, and here lies some of *Musical Travels'* value to the present-day reader. From Bicknell's handling of the theme, we learn how Burney's contemporaries read him (the German critics, after all, echoed Bicknell's sentiments). We also learn about the status of Orphic discourse in the last decades of the century: The parody shows that Burney's German travelogue was seen as an encyclical on music's effective powers and only secondarily as a work that provided insights into emerging instrumental aesthetics, the "German" style, or, as Burney thought of it himself, a fact-finding exercise about Germany for the *General History.* In Bicknell's view, Burney's travels were a drawn-out meditation on what music could do.

CURATIVE MUSIC AND THE CRITIQUE OF SCIENTISM

Setting out to spoof the agential discourse, Bicknell treats the reader to a crash course in Neoplatonist ideas, with each way station in the protagonist's journey treating a particular aspect of music's powers. So, for example, whereas the archmusician could command only birds and animals, the musician in *Musical Travels* is able to summon footmen bringing ale, cold beef, and mustard.[120] Collier can do great things with music, but he is also hypersensitive to its effects—irrespective of whether that music is the march from a Handel oratorio like *Saul* (1739), the sound of martial instruments like the bagpipes, or a simple nursery rhyme like "Hey, Diddle Diddle."[121] Conquering enemies, conjuring food, and cows jumping over the moon are all within music's fantastic ambit.

Burney took a cautious approach to musical agency. He believed that music acted on the listener's emotions and likely had some psychological benefit, particularly to those suffering from depressive disorders. On the other hand, music's effects on fever, bone fractures, the plague, epilepsy, and tarantism (the ailment said to arise from the bite of a tarantula) received little credence.[122] Bicknell nonetheless turns Burney into a proponent of musical healing. Thus, Collier encounters a man with a broken leg that no surgeon has been able to mend. Hoping to remedy the leg like Odysseus his wound, Collier plays and sings some rowdy drinking songs. Our musical medicine man has to concede defeat: His playing stanches the flow of blood but cannot knit the bones. Here Burney is invoked as a distinct character and the embodiment of Orpheus's powers. Only the miraculous powers of a "Dr. Burney or Lord S. [Sandwich] and his kettledrum," says Collier, could have cured the scorbutic patient.[123]

We also find Collier heading to Sheffield to investigate the present state of music in that city, where he encounters a girl who has been bitten by a tarantula. With a "trut turrut, phub, phub, bush!" his bassoon sets her dancing, and, when thrown a coin, she strips off her clothing and dances "like a Heinel" (a popular ballerina of the day). This, says Collier with a wink, drives off the evil spirit, and the girl is cured of her affliction that very night.[124] This episode reflects the strain of Enlightenment thought that queried the medical use of music for the treatment of ailments like tarantism.[125] In Bicknell, musical exchange becomes a thin metaphor for prostitution, and tarantism is construed as fraud. Music in the parody, like desire in the eighteenth-century novel and autobiography, is supposed to generate social intercourse. In fact, Bicknell makes clear that neither desire nor music making is adequate to its task. The sociosexual relations that a figure like Casanova enacts on the basis of (asserted) mutual attraction are in fact lubricated by the exactest bookkeeping: Casanova pays his way into bed.[126] In Bicknell's parody we see something similar at play. Whereas the proponents of Orphic discourse insisted on music's socially constitutive powers, Bicknell shows that it is money, not music, that enacts human relations and preserves or overturns hierarchical distinctions. Music, like desire, becomes the sign for capitalist society's occult mechanism.

In the absurdity of Collier's doctoring we are inclined to overlook the fact that many scholars of the day advocated music for both palliative care and the remedy of disease and physical injury.[127] Further, music's curative properties were often cited in order to demonstrate the utility and social worth of music generally. Scholars like Marpurg disseminated claims about miraculous healing music in an attempt to elevate music from its aesthetically subordinate position.[128] However, Bicknell's handling of the theme in the 1770s shows the extent to which musical healing had become a mobile discourse. It could be parodied in order to rib quack doctors, gullible patients, and over-ambitious musicians. Especially in the case of tarantism, which was increasingly suspected of being a sham, it could be mocked in order to drive a wedge between music and mammon. In Bicknell, curative music also figures at the intersection between medicine and science in order to advance an idea about the shortcomings of music's scholarly apparatus.

Informing the reader about his musical precocity, Collier describes how, as a child, he would pinch the tails of the parson's pigs and listen to the notes the litter produced, a scale that ranged "from the f sharp whine of the least of the family, quite down to the b flat grunt of the old boar himself."[129] Even more inventive was an experiment conducted on puppies. Strings tied to the ears of six greyhounds were pulled with such "art and judgment" that the effect was comparable to the best viola da gamba playing. Cats suspended by their tails were then bobbed on the noses of two suckling pigs that were tied by their hind legs to the floor. If the performers seemed "somewhat embarrassed in their manner," the whole effect, says Collier, was still "quite original and truly theatric."[130]

It is possible that Bicknell intended such stories to be read as an indictment of animal cruelty. The first anticruelty legislation had been passed as early as 1760, and middle- and upper-class Britons were increasingly uneasy about blood sports like cock throwing and bear baiting. Bicknell's friend Thomas Day was a known critic of animal cruelty and refused to kill even a spider because of the precedent this might set. We find similar sentiments expressed in journals like the *Gentleman's Magazine* dating from the late 1740s and in Hogarth's series, *The Four Stages of Cruelty* (1750–1751). Burney himself referred to animal cruelty as the enemy of civilized society and criticized the Viennese for staging the kinds of "barbarous spectacle" that had long since been outlawed in England.[131]

At the same time there existed a countervailing discourse that considered animals and their suffering funny, evidenced by the popular tradition of animal concerts.[132] Perhaps the most peculiar instance of music-making animals was the *Katzenklavier* (cat clavichord), a "musical instrument" that in its earliest instantiation seems to have been meant ironically but that gained scholarly credibility during the seventeenth and eighteenth centuries, due to the work of scholars such as Athanasius Kircher, Caspar Schott, and Michael Valentini.[133] The contraption they described comprised variously sized cats arranged in a box with their tails affixed to a keyboard. When the keys were depressed, spiking the cats' tails, the animals mewed, each producing a different tone (figure 3.9). The effect of this caterwauling was said by some to be hilarious, but by others, like the pioneering psychologist Johann Christian Reil, who suggested it in 1803 as a cure for catatonia, to be quite electrifying.[134] Although doubt has been raised as to whether the cat clavichord ever in fact existed, references to actual cat clavichord performances (including ones in Prague in 1773) suggest that the instrument may indeed have had a literal, not just a parodic, source.[135]

Bicknell's cat joke was reminiscent of a supposed report to the Royal Society by one Mrs. Mary Midnight. Its author, Christopher Smart, is best known for an ode to his cat, Jeoffry, but in the parody he published in the *Midwife, or, Old Woman's Magazine* (1750), cats figure less kindly.[136] Smart has Mrs. Midnight propose a series of improvements to the cat clavichord, namely, performing the cat-organ at the "time of their Amours," when cats are at their most musical, and using "gelded" cats because "the best Voices are improved by Castration." She also adds a piece of music to the repertoire, "Mrs. Midnight's Maggot. A new Country-Dance for the *Cat-Organ*" (figure 3.10) and claims that her recent experiments convincingly prove that castrated English cats perform every bit as "delicately, piercingly and comprehensively" as foreign ones. The Royal Society was to conclude from this, she averred, that, if English citizens only shared the same advantages as Italians, they would "shine with an equal Lustre," and the nation would be saved umpteen thousand pounds.[137]

Smart's parody of the popular tradition of the animal concert anticipates Bicknell's appropriation of rough music and folk song a quarter of a century later. Both music commentators critique high culture via the low, mounting

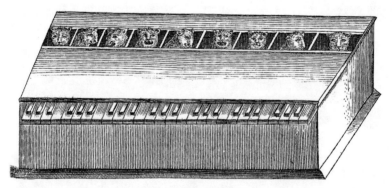

FIGURE 3.9. "Katzenklavier," in Michael Bernhard Valentini, *Museum Museorum,* Tom. 3, Tab. 34, fig. 2. By permission of the University of Michigan Special Collections Library.

The MIDWIFE.   103

Mrs. MIDNIGHT's MAGGOT.
A new Country-Dance for the *Cat-Organ.*

Caſt off one Couple. — The Man hands round
three at Bottom, and theWoman the ſame atTop.—
Caſt off the third Couple and turn. — Lead up to
the Top. — Caſt off Right and Left quite round.

FIGURE 3.10. Christopher Smart (1722–1771), "Mrs. Midnight's Maggot. A New Country-Dance for the Cat-Organ," in *The Midwife, or, Old Woman's Magazine* (1750), 103. By permission of the British Library.

an attack on the English preoccupation with castrati (i.e., Italian opera) and criticizing the economics of opera and the status of national culture in mid- to late-century England. But Smart and Bicknell share another feature as well: Their arguments are framed in extramusical terms. Specifically, they both invoke scientific method (observation and experiment) and scientific institutions (the laboratory, scholarly reports, and the Royal Society) in order to lend credibility to what are essentially aesthetic-economic arguments. We can read this kind of scientism in two directions. First, it parodied eighteenth-century scientific institutions, which pursued a sometimes rather indiscriminate interest in oddities, curiosities, and new phenomena. Smart's musical experiments, like Bicknell's, seemed to suggest that the current preoccupation with empiricism needed to be tempered by a more discerning scholarly approach to the selection of scientific objects. Second, this scientism pointed to the growing intent to professionalize music scholarship. The fact that a musical phenomenon like the cat clavichord had to be framed with a quasi-scientific apparatus reinforced the fact that, as a field of study, music had yet to acquire adequate critical and interpretive methods or a set of legitimizing institutions. Professional music scholars like Burney and his German counterparts might have insisted that music journalism, compositional analysis, travel writing, and historiography were sufficient to the task of explaining music, but this confidence did not necessarily extend to the educated layperson. Music—whether low or high, strange or familiar—was still seen as a rather opaque, even laughable, object of knowledge.

Thus we find that, in contradistinction to Baroque cat-clavichord accounts that proclaimed the mere sight of the instrument itself to be hilarious enough to "heal the melancholy vapors," in both Smart and Bicknell the joke does not come at the expense of the hapless animals.[138] Laughter's locus has shifted from the incongruous sight of squealing piglets, puppies, and cats to the recondite interests and perverse experiments of music investigators like Mrs. Midnight, Collier, and their real-world counterparts like Burney and Reil. By the latter part of the eighteenth century, the laugh stems not from the sight and sound of impaled animals but from the scholar and performer who is lunatic enough to consider the instrument aesthetically pleasing, economically significant, or medically useful. Laughter still heals, but in Bicknell's text the cat clavichordist appears specifically in order to cure the readers of their attachment to travel writing and their Orphic investment in music's capacity to cure.

Similar to the way in which a popular tradition like rough music was adopted in the eighteenth century for middle-class amusement, the animal concert was also reconfigured by its literary appropriation. Too little is known about the practice of early modern animal concerts to say much about their original social function beyond what I have already said—they intended to cure melancholy with laughter. Whether there was also a socially critical edge to this laughter, I do not know. By the mid- to late eighteenth century, however, when Smart and Bicknell appropriated the theme, the object of that laughter had been cleaved from the political in order to be resituated squarely within the realm of the aesthetic. In the space created by laughing at tormented and castrated cats, middle-class Englishness attempted to make itself heard.

THE CASTRATO, OR, ORPHEUS DISMEMBERED

Late eighteenth-century Britain was widely perceived to be in a state of dissipation.[139] Bicknell shared the views of an anonymous author in the *Gentleman's Magazine* (1768) who complained about travelers importing "the vanity and luxury of France, and blend[ing] the follies of other nations with their own."[140] Bicknell rejected the corrosive effects of foreign extravagance on Britain and became an outspoken opponent of soft living and luxury culture. Thus, *Musical Travels* mocks the middle-class Burney for fawning to his noble and royal sponsors (and subverting English music in the process) and lampoons aristocrats like Sandwich and the Duke of Württemberg for their dissolute, music-loving lifestyles. Censuring consumerism and advocating a kind of sober Methodism instead, the parody finds many ways to reiterate the theme. Its most ubiquitous expression, however, comes via a critique of the castrato.

Collier's first act when setting out to investigate English music is to dub himself "Collioni" (Italian for testicles). As the name change suggests, the protagonist is spurred on by the search for castrati—a play on Burney's apparent preoccupation with this brand of "vocal manufacture." Collioni is ultimately rewarded in his quest when he is caught in flagrante delicto with a barber's wife and is castrated by the irate husband. Instead of being unmanned by the experience, Collioni celebrates. Not only has he acquired new and superior vocal powers, but he has also successfully imitated the great master: Doctor Burney, we learn, was himself a *musico* (i.e., castrato) in disguise.

We have already seen that wits like Christopher Smart and Andrew Marvel played on scholarly and popular opinion by construing Italian musicians as a threat to musical life and to the economic well-being of the nation at large. In serious as well as parodic treatments, the figure of the castrato channels this disapproval. Yet the intensity and bitterness of this hostility surprises even today. An anonymous and today rather opaque satire, *The Remarkable Trial of the Queen of Quavers* (1777–1778), for example, is excoriating in its handling of the subject. Ian Woodfield points out that the impetus for this 150-page work was a war of letters between the managers of the King's Theatre, Frances Brooke, Mary Ann Yates and Richard Yates, and the famous actor and playwright David Garrick.[141] With Mary Ann Yates in the eponymous role, the satire tells the story of the Queen of Quavers, who has been brought to trial for spreading the "Quavering Itch," an affliction that causes outbreaks of irrationality and poor taste, and, above all, a liking for Italian opera. As a result of this pandemic, "seven exotic animals *yclep'd* [called] castrati" have been imported from the Continent:

Such filthy lumps of mortality as the wilds of Africa never produced!—They have the look of a crocodile, the grin of an ape, the legs of a peacock, the paunch of a cow . . . to crown the whole, if you sit but a few moments in their company, you will be sure of having your nostrils perfumed in a strange manner; for they have continually about them the odoriferous effluvia of onion and garlick, so that you would swear, that they always carry their dinner in their pockets . . . Indeed it is not possible to conceive a more nauseous and odious creature than a Castrato.[142]

Elsewhere the castrato is described as a monster and an "outlaw of nature," neither man nor woman, "but something betwixt the human species and the brute creation, like a monkey."[143] To this menagerie of invective is added the pig. The Grand Inquest makes the case that Italian opera is now regarded as "the quintessence of *bon ton* . . . and the first element of fashionable dissipation." The inquisitor adds that Italian opera can be performed only with the assistance of castrati because such music abounds in shrill notes, "as high as the upper stories of the tower of Babel, which no animal but a pig is able to reach." While England possesses a ready supply of cheap domestic "pigs," Italian swine are typically bought "in a poke" (i.e., indiscriminately) and at outrageous expense.[144] The satire belabors the porcine metaphor, adding numerous further examples of castrati who have swindled domestic "pigs" out of a livelihood. The satire concludes with the Queen of Quavers and her retinue being found guilty and sentenced to death, but, thanks to the merciful (and mercantile) intercession of the ruler, their sentence is commuted. The offending court will either be transported to "A-merry-key," where they will stage Italian opera, or, if this should prove impracticable, be taxed to the tune of the national debt.[145] Whereas in Burney's "Sketch for a Plan" the foreign singer had been held responsible for England's economic ruin, here the castrato was turned into a means of redressing it.

Not for the first or last time in history, the foreigner becomes a target for the forces that spell change. In many of the sources discussed so far—the anonymous *Remarkable Trial of the Queen of Quavers,* Smart's "Letter from Mrs. Midnight to the Royal Society," Marvel's *Essay on the Unfortunate Charms and Powers of Music,* Bicknell's *Musical Travels,* and Burney and Giardini's "Sketch of a Plan for a Public Music-School"—the foreign castrato becomes a whipping boy in conflicts over class, gender, nation, and religion. As Katherine Bergeron, George L. Mosse, and Elisabeth Krimmer argue, during the late eighteenth century the body was often construed as a site for negotiating new relationships between the natural and the artificial, and the bourgeois and the aristocratic, with the result that masculinity assumed an important role in constituting bourgeois identity.[146] The castrato thus becomes a means of prioritizing indigenous masculinity over imported effeminacy and "authentic" domestic middle-class culture over aristocratic imports. The texts cited here bear out these critical insights. Bicknell's *Musical Travels* uses the figure of the castrato to rail against aristocratic privilege and a system of patronage that sacrificed domestic interests for cosmopolitan feudal ones. As I pointed out above, this was also on Burney's agenda when he addressed the board of the Foundling Hospital. The rhetoric in "Sketch of a Plan for a Public Music-School" construes the foreign *musico* as both an economic threat and an artistic one: National interests—cultural, commercial, social, and political—could all be better served by promoting domestic musical education. The fact that there was no distinctly native form of high musical culture did not inhibit Burney, Bicknell, and others from asserting its necessary existence.[147]

Making a parallel point to Krimmer, who argues of her German sources that privileging middle-class masculinity and naturalizing the body came at the price of social justice, I maintain that it is also intense xenophobia that purchases the shift from high to low culture and from the cosmopolitan to the national.[148] In the English castrato parodies, Italians but also volubly Germans, French, Turks, Africans, Jews, and Catholics are all targets of invective. Yet the fact that there is no strict cleavage along either religious lines or longitudinal and latitudinal axes suggests that the discourse followed an indiscriminate, incoherent trajectory. Paradoxically, in the move toward a national culture, it seems that the specific identity of the foreign was less significant than foreignness itself. Anti-Italianism thus had less to do with antipathy toward Italians or Catholicism than with excluding or opposing generic difference in order to assert some form of indigenous identity. Compared with the mid- to late nineteenth century, when the figure of the rapacious, effeminate foreigner would be ever more rigidly codified in anti-Semitic or anti-Islamic terms, during our period the very flexibility of the category gave it its oppositional force. Further, debates about Italian opera show the extent to which the category of the foreign national was substitutive for domestic social class. To some extent, then, we can see the reaction against Italian opera as substitutive for revolutionary sentiments. Whereas the French would take their own aristocrats to the guillotine, in England this course of action would be assimilated culturally in the form of satirizing foreign aristocratic culture. Politically, however, it would be held at bay.

I have argued that the proliferation of music parodies during the last decades of the century was culturally, perhaps also socially, constitutive. Burlesquing figures like the musical traveler, scholar, aristocrat, amateur, and castrato, these parodies mobilized xenophobia to advocate particular forms of autochthonous cultural identity—ones that were more Little Theatre on the Haymarket than King's Theatre, more middlebrow than highbrow, and more peas pudding than truffle. Yet, the grim laughter that musical parody produced was also symptomatic of something else. In the anonymous

Remarkable Trial of the Queen of Quavers (1777–1778), the reader learns that, from Roman times on, "the most fatal national calamities were always announced by prodigies and monstrous appearances."[149] The author spells out the fact that the castrato signifies this "monstrous appearance," and the Lisbon earthquake, an event still within living memory in the 1770s, signifies "national calamities." The author's choice of cataclysm is unsurprising. The 1755 earthquake was the greatest natural catastrophe the European world had hitherto known, and it exerted a profound effect on writers and philosophers. However, whereas the seismic cataclysm in, say, Heinrich von Kleist's *Das Erdbeben in Chili* (The Earthquake in Chile, 1807) stood for religious and political upheaval, in *Remarkable Trial* the earthquake was configured in aesthetic terms. We learn that the city was razed and its population decimated because of a misjudgment in musical taste: The Portuguese king kept seven castrati at court. The historical fact is that castrati like Gaetano Guadagni had narrowly escaped the earthquake in Lisbon, while his colleague Gioachino Conti Gizziello was said to have been so rattled by the upheaval that he underwent a religious experience and retired to a monastery.[150] In *Remarkable Trial* the individual plight of the castrati comes to signify much more: They are omens that speak to the future. The author predicts that, given the continued propensity for this kind of music, a calamity of comparable magnitude will soon befall Britain's "tottering Empire."[151]

By definition, parody pushes its themes to extremes of credulity, and I do not mean to suggest that the castrato had a uniformly negative connotation. We know from accounts by memoirists and travelers like Casanova and Patrick Brydone, for example, that castrati also exerted powerful erotic appeal.[152] Some, as I have said, even attributed to castrati like Farinelli the power to cure mental afflictions. However, when the author of *Remarkable Trial* links the monstrous *musico* to the instability of the empire, we can see the author's elephantine claims as symptomatic of music's changing valence. Where serious music had once been construed as a force for good—socializing, improving, educating, emboldening, and healing—now we find uncertainty about its effects and purpose. Where it had once signified order and restraint, it now spelled the hypertrophy of the castrato's chest—deformity, abnormality, and indeterminacy. It thus does not surprise that a whole range of social, political, cultural, and philosophical issues coalesced in the figure of the "outlaw" singer who was neither one nor the other. Unease about the castrato's singing signaled unease about music's capacity to structure the world in predictable ways—either literally, through its physiological and psychological effects, or intellectually, as a system of quasi-rational explanation. Knowledge about music had once, to some significant degree, conveyed knowledge about the world: The action of music on disease had told its practitioners something about the body; its harmonic relationships seemed to explain the planetary gyre. Travel had held out the key to the origins of historical development. Now, music seemed to have lost much of its explanatory potential. Whatever security—call it intellectual or metaphysical—music had once conferred, its orderly progress and prognosticative character were now seriously in question. The castrato's incomplete, malformed body remained only as a frightening reminder of the vulnerability of the domestic and imperial body at the end of the ancien régime.

Conclusion

As I have argued throughout the book, Orphic discourse is a discourse of alterity that attaches significance to the role of music in mediating relations between selves and others. In fact, the Orpheus myth compels us to take seriously culture's privileged responsibility vis-à-vis difference. It tells us that society is constituted (and its integrity maintained or defended) via culture's capacity to mediate the divide between what belongs and what does not. Animal/human, natural/artificial, inanimate/animate, and human/ divine distinctions collapse at the moment when the trees, rocks, rivers, and beasts stop what they are doing to join Orpheus's circle. In the act of listening, difference is overcome. Translated into a type of social form, we find a model characterized by permeability toward outsiders. Membership might come at the price of assimilation, but the reward is the potentially rich one of inclusion and sociability.

British society in the latter part of the century was troubled by the problem of alterity. On the one hand, foreign peoples and their productions held tremendous arm's-length fascination kindled in the 1760s and 1770s by the intense engagement with the non-European world, the vogue for Celtic and Continental travel, and the fraught place of the American colonies in the public imagination. On the other hand, there was deep unease about the importation of foreignness. The influential Germany traveler and writer John Moore stressed that the English gentleman, even when free of prejudice and full of admiration for the talents and ingenuity of his neighbors, "did not think this kind of *grafting* at all admissible."[153] Questions thus remained as to whether this difference should, or even could, be proximated. Could it be, so to speak, invited into the fold to find a new home within the domestic order? Could it be made similar? Music scholars, travel writers, playwrights, and educated middle- and upper-class cultural consumers would make these questions their own and set about trying to delineate the proper place of the allochthonous in relation to a consolidating idea of Englishness.

Thus we come to the cultural crisis that this chapter maps out—one that can be traced back to the first decades of the eighteenth century but grew by an order of magnitude toward its end. The crisis saw serious English music defined mostly by interrogative and litotes—in other words, by that which it was not.[154] With this crisis came the fear that high culture, in particular opera, was so infused by foreign influence that it had lost its capacity to signify. With it came irritation over the fact that travelers were enchanted by the exotic to such an extent that they had lost the capacity for discernment or veracity, and with it also came dismay over the fact that culture lacked a science adequate to the task of interpreting the unfamiliar.[155] The stakes of this cultural predicament were easily spelled out: An Orpheus drowned out by the other stood in danger of losing the ability to unlock the portals of Orcas, to swing the gate of inclusion and exclusion, and to uphold communal limits. If the Orphic myth were to be believed, then the failure of domestic culture to manage its margins signaled the immanent breakdown of society itself. Thus, we find dire prognostications of economic ruin, imperial collapse, political turmoil, moral turpitude, and sexual perversion. Perhaps as never before, music would become a foil for the most pressing social and political concerns of the day.[156]

I should point out the rather obvious fact that this crisis was not sparked by the literal influx of foreigners into Britain: This was no eighteenth-century anticipation of postcolonial migration and an ensuing backlash against multiculturalism. If I had to pinpoint specific underlying factors for this critical state of affairs, I would say that it was impelled by a changing political landscape that reconfigured Britain's relations with its overseas possessions, its old Continental adversaries, and its marginalized domestic subjects. Jonathan Lamb argues that eighteenth-century British exploration did not mark a period of celebratory self-confidence, as is generally assumed, but rather one of deep-seated insecurities about the rights and responsibilities of the modern self in an emerging market economy.[157] I believe we see a similar crisis of confidence at play in late-century debates that deal with music. Changing class relations that emphasized vertical national distinctions over lateral cosmopolitan ones, the loss of the American colonies, the regency crisis in the late 1780s, abolitionism, and Jacobinism are among the broader issues that are played out in these musical turf wars.

This cultural juncture put Orphic discourse with its two critical terms— music and alterity—at the center of public and scholarly debate. Ranged on the one side of the barricade were those like Burney or Herder, who took an affirmative Orphic position and privileged the role of culture in constituting an idea of national belonging. For both scholars, the margins could be studied with an eye and an ear for what could be appropriated at home. Thus, in the most literal examples, we find Burney attempting to import Italian and German pedagogical methods into Britain and Herder collecting folk songs. The singing of sailors working the capstan, wheat threshers in the fields, women at their spinning wheels and cradles—these were among the kinds of songs worth documenting. The songs resonated not just because of their rough and lively charm—Herder was, in any event, more interested in texts than tunes—but also because of what they represented. Music was supposed to be the best indicator of a people's mind-set because these dignified folk songs, ballads, and epics provided a window on the collective character.[158] With this motto in mind, the musical Linnaeus set off from his Baltic home to collect and categorize the voices of the people in song—*Alte Volkslieder* (1774) and *Volkslieder* (1778–1779). In the process he contributed forcefully to the concept of national music.[159] For Herder, as for Burney, the significance of this "move to the margins" was the ability to fold the relative into a general historical sweep and ground the idea of national culture in the universal.[160]

Ranged on the other side of the barricade was the anti-Orpheus, a self-reflexive gesture found in risible travel writing, plays, poetry, and literature that mocked music, questioned its indexical value, parodied its capacity to act in extramusical ways, and questioned the traveler's authority over the cultural margins. Paul Gilroy argues in his work on the black Atlantic that the low other became a defining feature of modernity.[161] However, the eighteenth-century battle between Orpheus and anti-Orpheus over control of the margins prompts us to reexamine the rules of engagement. Orphic discourse was predicated on the idea that whatever was excluded could be assimilated if it relinquished both its difference and its right to signify. Anti-Orpheus, on the other hand, seized on various forms of low culture—a third term—as the permanent sign of difference and used these to upset existing cultural hierarchies.[162] This insight confirms a suspicion about anti-Orphic discourse that we have held all along. Although parody's foregrounding of the low, popular, and non-European seemed to give these excluded positions new voice and agency, its laughter in fact upheld the existing order. The choice between Orpheus and anti-Orpheus was thus a rather narrow one: Either way, music acted at the margins for the making of the national imaginary. The voices of the slave, colonial subject, and indigenous traveler had found a new audience, but at what cost to them?

CHAPTER FOUR | Conclusion

A S ANY TRAVEL writer knows, the worse the journey, the better the
story. Burney grasped this perfectly. His travelogue was framed as a
tour that took him from the center of the world to the terra incognita of the
German states. Along the way, there were bone-rattling carriages and bed-
buggy inns, moments of danger and encounters most strange. We recognize
the emphasis on extremity and affect as among the travelogue's most important rhetorical tropes. At the same time, this was not just an authorial
conceit, for traveling was viscerally felt. Life expectancy in the 1770s was
comparatively short, and at forty-six Burney was already on the wrong side of
middle age. Perhaps a soft bed and familiar food were not yet among life's
necessities, but they had begun to outweigh the attractions of floating about
on a leaky raft.

People often assume that traveling left its mark on the man but not on his
thought. Kerry Grant argues, for instance, that Burney's aesthetic preferences
were established before he departed for the Continent and that he returned, as
he left, committed to Italian music.[1] Here Grant follows some of Burney's
contemporaries—Ebeling, Reichardt, Forkel, and Schubart—who charged
the Englishman with neither valuing what he heard nor hearing what he
ought to have heard. The critics have a point. In Burney's final tally, composers like Gluck and C. P. E. Bach received mixed reviews; J. S. Bach was a
"learned" composer (not a good thing); Haydn warranted only passing
mention; and Mozart was reported to have bloomed too early.[2] These were
not entirely eccentric views, but they also did not show great aesthetic

foresight: Hasse—one of the intended "heroes" of Burney's music history—is not played much anymore; Johann Sebastian is the lynchpin in the German triumvirate of Bach, Beethoven, and Brahms, and it is difficult to think of late eighteenth-century Vienna without acknowledging the achievements of Viennese classicism.[3]

Burney's aesthetic judgments (or misjudgments) do not, however, strike me as the most salient aspect of his work, nor was the experience of traveling incidental to his intellectual project. The Continental journeys allowed him to listen to music, collect source material, and interview music makers of various stripes. Conducting this kind of research for a general history of music was, as he rightly claimed, unprecedented in both scope and intention, and it would be a model for universal histories to come.[4] He came to write about (and befriend) some of the leading representatives of the British, French, and German Enlightenments—Rousseau, Voltaire, Diderot, d'Holbach, Johnson, Goldsmith, Garrick, Cook, Banks, Piozzi, Baretti, Herschel, Reynolds, Klopstock, Nicolai, Sulzer, and others. He also knew some of Europe's power brokers, including George III, Pitt the Younger, Burke, Sandwich, Friedrich II, Marischal, and numerous representatives of high society in England and abroad.[5] Of particular relevance to us are Burney's prominent musical acquaintances, who were probably unrivaled in his day. Yet Burney's interests ranged down as well as up the social ladder. He was curious about "low" music and music that seemed characteristic of its time and place—the music making of the urban poor, peasants, soldiers, sailors, travelers, foreign correspondents, and non-European peoples. This kind of socially and anthropologically inflected study of music marked the beginnings of an approach that was taken up by future music ethnologists and music sociologists. Burney thus remains an influential observer of late eighteenth-century musical life, and it is in this sense that he appears in this book—our surrogate reader of the transnational musical scene in the late eighteenth century.

Although Burney's travelogues were published a quarter century before the portentous writings of E. T. A. Hoffmann, Heinrich von Kleist, Ludwig Tieck, and Wilhelm Wackenroder, his interests disqualify him (in contrast to, say, Forkel) from being seen as a harbinger of Romantic music discourse. Wackenroder has Joseph Berglinger, a character in his novella, proclaim: "How strange and singular is art! Is then its mysterious power for me alone— is it to all other men mere sensual pleasure and agreeable amusement?"[6] Consequently, Wackenroder's artistic genius becomes the frustrated mediator between the metaphysical and an indifferent society. Burney, in contrast, believed that "agreeable amusement" and "all other men" were precisely what were important: Music might be called frivolous and idle, but it was a universal human activity with a social purpose. Among its many "humane" uses were encouraging alms giving, subsidizing the support of the indigent, and ameliorating physical pain and disease (Burney suggested childbirth and venereal disease as two examples). Music was integral to divine worship, military discipline, and the theater; it promoted family life and polite society; it "alleviated labor," kept people "out of mischief," and blunted "the edge of care," he said.[7] Compared with Romanticism's exalted views on music, these were quiet claims, but they are claims that I like for their modest practicality and lack of elitism. More importantly, Burney's approach is one that we can work with today because it invites interrogation and critique. It is possible to probe, as I hope I have, not only the emancipatory character of music's uses in society but also its misuses and limitations.

Contrasting Romantic writers with their predecessor runs the risk of inscribing the long-standing dichotomies between the poetic metaphysicist and the rational empiricist. While my sympathies lie more with the latter than the former, my intention is not to pit the Enlightenment against Romanticism. I have taken pains to show that important continuities existed between late eighteenth- and early nineteenth-century aesthetic discourses; this in itself questions one of the standard narratives about the history of Western music. The early nineteenth century is often said to have revolutionized European thinking about music by putting an end to ethical and utilitarian conceptions.[8] According to this line of thought, the year 1800 marks the zero hour: The artistic work had been judged in terms of its uses and effects; now its meaning and purpose came to be located in the work and in subjective responses to the work.[9] Karl Philipp Moritz articulated this as the process of contemplating an artistic work that was "whole unto itself" and gave pleasure *"for the sake of itself."*[10]

Yet whether we date the beginnings of aesthetic autonomy to the turn of the nineteenth century or to earlier decades, it is clear that Orphic discourse was not superseded but was incorporated into the new aesthetics.[11] Forkel acknowledged in 1779 that classical claims about music's wondrous properties might be incorrect or at least exaggerated. At the same time, he believed that, by taking a more sober approach, scholars harmed the musical cause.[12] In his *Ideen zu einer Ästhetik der Tonkunst* (1806), Schubart took wondrous feats in the past as a sign that the ancient investment in music was worth emulating in the present.[13] E. T. A. Hoffmann likewise spoke in the language of Orpheus in his influential review of Beethoven's fifth symphony (1813), in which he claimed that Orpheus's lyre opened "the portals of Orcus" onto an "unknown realm, a world that has nothing in common with the external sensual world that surrounds him, a world in which he leaves behind him all definite feelings to surrender himself to an inexpressible longing."[14] These examples suggest that earlier and later architects of aesthetic autonomy reveled in claims about music's agency. Even if this agency was taken out of the level of the prosaic and causal—music that charmed mice and cured tarantism, for instance—music's ethical capacity became a rhetorical basis upon which to promote music above the other arts, valorize serious music, and prioritize German music over other national styles.[15]

Musicians and scholars like Ebeling, Reichardt, Forkel, Schubart, and Hiller called for a reevaluation of German music, and by the early decades of the nineteenth century this revolution would indeed have taken place. The reasons for this tend to be attributed to factors such as the professionalization of music, the emergence of a concert-going middle class, the rise of instrumental music, and philosophical idealism—factors that contributed to Austro-German music's role within what has been described as the "historical process of [German] self-comprehension and self-critique."[16] For scholars like Sanna Pederson, Mary Sue Morrow, and David Gramit, on the other hand, this process is not construed in the same nationally hermetic terms: The reevaluation of German (instrumental) music is instead shown to have involved privileging the German while simultaneously disavowing the foreign.[17] My study of Anglo-German music discourse offers various examples that corroborate this position and sets out some of the costs involved in stressing "German" musical characteristics. I further show that creating "German music" and, by extension, the German "cultural nation," was, from its earliest instantiations, a transnational enterprise that enlisted external observers.

Good and proper forms of musical knowledge would henceforth be centered on the musical composition and a related set of musical criteria. This aesthetics did not only involve, so to speak, attaining a higher position by stepping on other kinds of music. Here my findings branch out from the work of recent scholars to show something about the relationship between utilitarian and autonomous conceptions of culture. I argue that the inception of work-immanent criteria of value—criteria that would come to dominate the study of serious music—took place via a critique of the nature of musical knowledge making. By examining the Burney reception, I show how the long-standing practice of measuring music's uses and effects was now found wanting.

Ebeling, Reichardt, and Forkel objected to the Englishman's protosociological approach and what they saw as a tendency to judge the music along with the people. (In fact, Burney upheld a distinction between the improvability of serious European music and the more or less static character of popular and non-European musical forms, something that was wholly in line with the German view.) Ebeling, Reichardt, and Forkel's critique centered specifically on the epistemology of travel—the status of eye- and ear-witnessing, the credibility of the informant, and the contingent character of travel observations.[18] They objected to the kind of approach that we find also in a traveler like Klockenbring, who impugned "the fineness of the nation's ear" based on his observations of the "mob."[19] Because music was supposed to agitate the nerves, Klockenbring concluded that the capacity for musical discernment depended on "a very fine [physical] organization."[20] Ebeling, Reichardt, and Forkel cast doubt on the legitimacy of grounding aesthetic judgments in these kinds of physiological explanations (at least vis-à-vis Europeans). They did not delineate a clear alternative to the travel-based methodology, but their critique highlighted the need for an alternative approach. It would be up to Schiller, Kant, and others to spell out what some of the alternatives might be—fact disambiguated from value, art as an alternative to political and social concerns, and music reborn as an autonomous entity.[21]

My study of eighteenth-century musical travel thus suggests that there were two distinct responses to Bernard le Bovier de Fontenelle's famous question about the meaning of instrumental music. As Mary Sue Morrow points out, music scholars realized that the question "Sonata, what do you want of me?" had no answer: Instrumental music did not in fact "want" anything of the listener; it had no extramusical purpose because its value was inherent to itself.[22] This would be the intellectual step that liberated instrumental music from the charge of inferiority and upon which future claims about German musical superiority could be founded. At the same time, we find the notion of aesthetic autonomy construed as the special preserve of middle-class Europeans. The protomusic sociologist, Burney, was among those who later gave voice to this opinion when he claimed that there could be "no Chinese Fontenelle" because of Chinese music's exclusively utilitarian character.[23] I leave it to others to judge whether this claim has any literal truth. Important, however, is the fact that such a statement was not value neutral. This kind of categorical distinction created an ontological divide between Europeans and others, even while it promised a universally valid form of cultural expression.

My argument could perhaps be made with regard to other musical vernaculars, but I have focused on the less familiar example of Polynesian music, which first entered European discourse in the latter part of the eighteenth century. The voyagers who heard this music thought some of it monotonous and dull; elsewhere they found it pleasing and interesting. What especially surprised and puzzled metropolitan scholars was Polynesian part singing, a discovery that conflicted with their belief that polyphony was an exclusively European invention and historically quite recent. Such observations posed interpretative difficulties for these scholars. Instead of adapting their explanations to fit the new observations, they tried to reconcile the firsthand observations to existing interpretive categories. Eighteenth-century Polynesian music thus made little concrete impression on serious Western music—it was not really subject to musical borrowing as were a number of other non-European musical vernaculars.[24] On the other hand, we could say that Polynesian music left its ghostly trace. Scholarly ideas about the development and progress of music were worked out in oppositional terms: As I have suggested, by disavowing or downplaying certain characteristics of Polynesian music, scholars could uphold the singularity of Western music.

Cross-cultural musical encounters proved the inventiveness, variability, and appeal of some indigenous music; they also, on occasion, highlighted the flaws in explanations of musical development. What was transmitted in the scholarly reception was, however, another story. The encounter with the Pacific and its nineteenth-century reception suggests that the positions of Orpheus and his listeners became entrenched. Instead of Orpheus becoming a voluntary and attentive listener, the relationship between the performing Orpheus and his listeners would be fixed according to a set of hierarchically ordered subject positions.[25] This meant that if Mozart's Moorish character Monastatos had his own form of musical agency, no one heard it. In *Die Zauberflöte* (1791), Tamino, Pamina, and even the bird-catcher Papageno could be ennobled by music, but Monastatos and the slaves remained its unwitting subjects.[26] While aesthetic autonomy seemed to sound the death knell for musical utility, this was not in fact the case. Orpheus lived on as a paean to serious Western music, and his beastly listeners lived on, too, as music's involuntary respondents—Thracians permanently excluded from the enchanted circle and denied their own capacity for musical signification (figure 4.1).

This raises thorny issues for the present study of music.[27] For ethnomusicology and music sociology, the problems are not qualitatively different from the ones Burney faced some two hundred and fifty years ago—how to view culture as a product of society and as socially constitutive without, however, simplifying the indexical relationship between culture and its producers. For

FIGURE 4.1 *Orpheus's Beastly Listeners.* Paphos, Cyprus, 1989.
Photographer: Guillermo Aldana. By permission of the Getty
Conservation Institute.

approaches that center on national traditions and autonomous conceptions of
the artistic work, on the other hand, the specter of exclusion threatens the idea
of sufficiency and boundedness. If there is a need to reconcile these two approaches, it is not just because of the threats posed to Orpheus by his willful
deafness—loss, grief, and physical and social disintegration. Let us consider
instead the benefits that come from listening broadly and listening well.

Introduction

1. See Mead, *Grand Tour,* 335–43; and Riesbeck, *Briefe.*

2. For a biographical sketch, see Wagstaff, "Burney, Charles." The definitive biography of Burney remains Lonsdale's *Dr. Charles Burney,* which is the source of much of my background information on Burney.

3. For an account of Burney's inclusion in Barry's painting, see Scholes, *Great Dr. Burney,* vol. 2, 14–17; and Pressly, "A Chapel of Natural and Revealed Religion."

4. Grand tourists were sometimes reproved for indulging the eye and the tongue at the expense of the ear. See, for example, Samuel Sharp, "Letters from Italy (1767)," in *Music and Culture,* ed. Fubini, 209–10.

5. I take up Burton's point about the possibility of merging centers and peripheries, as well as nations and empires, rather than conceiving of these as "a teleological, imperialized sequence." See Burton, ed. *After the Imperial Turn,* 11. For a study that focuses on the larger set of interests served by the revival of early music in nineteenth-century France, see Ellis, *Interpreting the Musical Past,* xvi–xx.

6. For an anthology of primary sources, see Barker, ed., *Greek Musical Writings,* vol. 1.

7. There is extensive scholarly literature on Orpheus in opera and other vocal music. See, for example, Kerman, *Opera as Drama;* Sternfeld, *Birth of Opera;* and Harris, *Handel as Orpheus,* which provides a study of Handel's cantatas against the background of his social context and his sexuality. See also Puff, "Orpheus after Eurydice," 71–95.

8. Recent studies that emphasize music's agency include Robinson, *Deeper than Reason,* 397–98; Gioia, *Healing Songs* and his *Work Songs;* and DeNora, *Music in Everyday Life.*

9. Compare this with Horace, who describes the role of Orpheus's art as one that is constitutive of society—law giving and "religious as much as social." Horace, *Poetic Art,* 35.

10. Ovid, *Metamorphoses,* 195–99; 216–18.

11. For a study that follows Paul Gilroy's notion of the "Black Atlantic," see Middleton, "Musical Belongings," 60.

12. On not choosing between the hybrid and the authentic, see Aravamudan, *Tropicopolitans,* 12–14; on transitional belonging, see Konuk, *Mimesis in Istanbul.*

Chapter One

1. Apollonius Rhodius, *Argonautic expedition,* 62; see also Pindar, *Odes of Pindar,* 217ff.

2. See Apollodorus, *Library,* vol. 1, 18n1; and Smith, ed., *Dictionary of Greek and Roman Antiquities,* 59–60.

3. For a comparison of classical ideas with Aborigines "singing the country" that the Dreamtime ancestors sang into being, see Chatwin, *Songlines;* and for a less exoticizing account, see Watson, Chambers, and the Yolngu community at Yirrkala, *Singing the Land,* 43–50.

4. In *General History of the Science and Practice of Music,* vol. 1, xxiii, Hawkins, for instance, favors ancient music over modern music and dismisses non-European music; he makes it clear that these music histories were not genuinely universal in scope.

5. On Orpheus as historian, see Hell, "Angel's Enigmatic Eyes," 361–92.

6. I owe the phrase and the question to Applegate and Potter, "Germans as the 'People of Music'" 1, 3. For a critique of studies that overstate the case for music and German nationalism, see Applegate, "How German Is It?" 274–96.

7. See, for example, Rumph, "A Kingdom Not of This World," 50–67.

8. Goehr, *Imaginary Museum of Musical Works,* 122; see also Hosler, *Changing Aesthetic Views of Instrumental Music;* and Neubauer, *Emancipation of Music from Language,* for echoes of this idea.

9. I would not go so far, however, as to call this a musical *Sonderweg,* or special path of development, as Sponheuer suggests in "Reconstructing Ideal Types of the 'German' in Music," 42.

10. Burney's contemporaries took stock of both his views and his critical reception. In a tour of the German states in the late 1780s, Hester Lynch Piozzi, for instance, hedged her bets by describing German contrapuntal music as "complicated excellence." See Piozzi, *Observations and Reflections,* vol. 2, 529.

11. For Herder's contribution to the idea of nationhood, see Bohlman, "Landscape—Region—Nation—Reich," 105–27.

12. See, in particular, Burney, *Letters of Dr. Charles Burney;* and Burney, *Memoirs of Dr. Charles Burney,* both of which contain material Burney authored but not letters addressed to him.

13. For important bibliographical sources and information about Ebeling, see Stewart, *Literary Contributions of Christoph Daniel Ebeling.*

14. See, for example, Ebeling, ed., *Neue Sammlung von Reisebeschreibungen.*

15. Ebeling, "Versuch einer auserlesenen musikalischen Bibliothek"; and Burney, *Carl Burney's der Musik Doctors Tagebuch.*

16. Ebeling altered Virgil's Tiber to Thames (vi, 86–87), which Stewart quotes as "Tamesia." See Ebeling, letter to Charles Burney, June 20, 1773, in Stewart, "Christoph Daniel Ebeling," 50; and Virgil, *Aeneid,* ed. Knight, 149.

17. See Hannsjoachim W. Koch, *History of Prussia,* 135–36; and Dutt, *Economic History of India,* vol. 1, *Under Early British Rule,* 28–36; and on Germany's designs on Poland, see Kopp, "Contesting Borders."

18. Stewart, "Christoph Daniel Ebeling," 50–53.

19. Goldsmith, "Traveller," 269.

20. Kant, "Perpetual Peace," 105–106.

21. O'Brien, *Narratives of Enlightenment*, 1–2; see also Scrivener, *Cosmopolitan Ideal*, 1–5.

22. On dual allegiances, see McKillop, "Local Attachment and Cosmopolitanism," 196–200; and Walker, *German Hometowns*, 1–33.

23. On Hamburg's cultural progressiveness, cosmopolitanism, and republican political constitution, see Hohendahl, ed., *Patriotism, Cosmopolitanism, and National Culture*, 9–16.

24. Johann Esaias Nilson's engraving, "Die Lage des Königreichs Pohlen im Jahr 1773," shows Catherine II, Joseph II, Friedrich II, and a Russian diplomat reaching over a map of Poland to claim their respective regions. The diplomat points to an angel that ratifies the partition. See Schneider, *Die Macht der Karten*, 85.

25. For a study that deals with eighteenth-century claims about German colonial superiority, see Zantop, *Colonial Fantasies;* and on the Prussian policy of "internal colonization," see Hess, *Germans, Jews, and the Claims of Modernity*, 1–2, 27–28.

26. On the intersections between eighteenth-century German cosmopolitanism and colonial imaginaries, see Noyes, "Goethe on Cosmopolitanism and Colonialism."

27. On music as an element of late nineteenth- and early twentieth-century German colonial discourse, see Agnew, "Colonialist Beginnings of Comparative Musicology."

28. Burney, "Letter to Christoph Daniel Ebeling, November 1771," *Letters*, 101–107.

29. Stewart, "Christoph Daniel Ebeling," 45–47.

30. See Malinowski, *Argonauts of the Western Pacific*, 4–15; Lévi-Strauss, *Tristes Tropiques;* and John Austin's notion of infelicities applied to the study of exoticism in Mason, *Infelicities*, 6–10.

31. For an approach that investigates not what happened but "the stories told about [the] event—who told them, how they were told, and what their tellers were up to in telling them," see Brewer, *Sentimental Murder*, 1, 4.

32. On Burney's German reception as a question of "national pride," see Hust, "Introduction," 15–17; and Klemm, "Foreword," 12. On the lasting impact of the German reception on Burney's reputation, see Grant, *Dr. Burney as Critic and Historian*, 80.

33. See, for example, Ashcroft, Griffiths, and Tiffin, *Empire Writes Back;* Dening, *Islands and Beaches;* Salmond, *Two Worlds;* and Pratt, *Imperial Eyes*, 10, in which Pratt signals the possibility of applying a postcolonial framework to the study of intra-European travel—a point that is taken up in Calaresu, "Looking for Virgil's Tomb," 152.

34. Said, *Orientalism*, 12.

35. For a critique of postcolonial theory on the grounds that it overlooks complicity in the colonial project, see Cooper, "Conflict and Connection."

36. For further discussions of cross-cultural and colonial collaboration, see Thomas, *Colonialism's Culture*, 15–16; and Liebersohn, *Travelers' World*, 139–42. For discussions of cross-identification, see McClintock, *Imperial Leather*, 104–11; Aravamudan, *Tropicopolitans*, 19; Gikandi, *Maps of Englishness*, xiii–xiv; and Steinmetz, " 'Devil's Handwriting.' "

37. On postcolonialism as a "tool kit" and for a review of recent critiques, see Duara, "Postcolonial History," 417.

38. On the notion of Kulturnation, see Seeba, "'Germany—A Literary Concept,'" 356–57; and for an approach that focuses exclusively on the German context and the role of music in the making of the nineteenth-century Kulturnation, see Applegate, *Bach in Berlin.*

39. Treue, *Illustrierte Kulturgeschichte des Alltags,* 169; cited in Klemm, "Tagebuch einer musikalischen Reise," 5; and on the popularity of travel writing in eighteenth-century Britain, see Batten Jr., *Pleasurable Instruction,* 1; Turner, *British Travel Writers in Europe,* 10–11; and Kaufman, *Libraries and Their Users,* 31–32.

40. See Holcroft, *Travels from Hamburg;* and Gary Kelly, "Holcroft, Thomas (1745–1809)."

41. For overviews of the grand tour, see Black, *British and the Grand Tour;* and Stoye, *English Travellers Abroad, 1604–1667,* 27–29; on the grand tour establishing a "commonality of [elite] experience" based on humanistic learning, an established itinerary, and shared social networks, see Calaresu, "Looking for Virgil's Tomb," 140–41; and Gossman, *Medievalism and the Ideologies of the Enlightenment,* 23, where patrician travel is characterized as a form of cultural consolidation.

42. Boswell, *Boswell on the Grand Tour,* 166–69.

43. On Burney's "chief ambition and achievement . . . to be accepted as a 'man of letters' rather than as a 'mere musician,'" see Lonsdale, *Dr. Charles Burney,* viii; and on Burney's recognition that his readership increased thanks to his literary digressions, see Burney, *Dr. Burney's Musical Tours in Europe,* vol. 1, xxx.

44. On the low social status of professional musicians and the importance of literary accomplishments, see Ehrlich, *Music Profession in Britain,* 6–7, 42–44, who points out that both Burney's literary accomplishments and the patronage of Fulke Grenville "escorted him [Burney] into higher society."

45. Mozart's poor treatment is described in a letter to his father, June 9, 1781, cited in Gay, *Mozart: A Life,* 63.

46. For further examples, see Woodfield, *Salomon and the Burneys;* and Elias, *Mozart: Portrait of a Genius,* 10–27.

47. Parke, *Musical Memoirs,* vol. 1, 239.

48. Mozart to his father, March 17, 1781, in Bauers, Deutsch, and Eibl, eds., *Mozart: Briefe und Aufzeichnungen;* quoted in Gay, *Mozart: A Life,* 60.

49. Lonsdale, *Dr. Charles Burney,* viii.

50. The introduction to Burney's German travelogue shows that he had studied Nugent closely. He invoked Homer and Herodotus to legitimize his travel project and quoted Nugent almost verbatim on Asclepiades, who made the tour of the world on the back of a cow, while living on its milk. See Nugent, "Grand Tour," 15; and Burney, *Dr. Burney's Musical Tours,* vol. 2, xi.

51. For a critique of the grand tour, see Hurd's "Dialogues on the Uses of Foreign Travel," 18–20, in which Locke ironically refuted travel's capacity to promote cosmopolitanism and remove prejudice.

52. See the entries for the period April–May 1772 in Fanny Burney, *Early Journals and Letters of Fanny Burney,* vol. 2, 216–22.

53. Lonsdale, *Dr. Charles Burney,* 128–29; see also Wagstaff, "Burney, Charles."

54. In 1786 Fanny secured the position of the Queen's second keeper of the robes. For an account, see Lonsdale, *Dr. Charles Burney,* 322ff.

55. Nugent, "Grand Tour," 15.

56. Boswell, *Life of Johnson,* 742.

57. Although Bourdieu allows for changes in status, it is debatable whether he thought social positions could be fundamentally renegotiated. See Bourdieu, *Distinction: A Social Critique of the Judgment of Taste,* 273–78, 291; on the transformation of symbolic and cultural capital into economic capital, see Bourdieu, *Soziale Ungleichheiten,* 195–96; and for a discussion of Bourdieusian "symbolic profits," see Fowler, *Pierre Bourdieu and Cultural Theory,* 20.

58. For a psychoanalytically inflected understanding of Bourdieusian thought applied to a transnational context, see Steinmetz, " 'Devil's Handwriting,' " in which Steinmetz argues that colonial relations were shaped by colonizers' "fantasies of upward mobility or defense against social decline," 53. On the neglect of the psychic dimension in postcolonial studies and the social sciences, see his "Precoloniality and Colonial Subjectivity," 138.

59. Baretti, *Journey from London to Genoa,* vol. 2, 3.

60. See, for example, Schlözer, *Vorlesungen über Land- und Seereisen,* 5. For comparisons of domestic and foreign travel, see Peitsch, *Georg Forsters Ansichten,* 589n60.

61. Friedrich Nicolai, *Beschreibung einer Reise;* and Schlözer, *Vorlesungen über Land- und Seereisen,* 5. Emphasis added.

62. Staël-Holstein, *Germany,* vol. 1, 32.

63. Jahn, *Deutsches Volkstum,* 303–304.

64. For a debunking of the political *Sonderweg* thesis, see Blackbourn and Eley, *Mythen deutscher Geschichtsschreibung.*

65. See, for example, Veit, "Goethe's Fantasies about the Orient," 173–74, which follows the assertion about "better" German Orientalists made by Said, *Orientalism,* 19; see also Berman, *Enlightenment or Empire,* 10, 26, which contrasts the empathetic, "philosophical" Georg Forster with the calculating, "geometric" James Cook; and Osterhammel, "Distanzerfahrung," 11.

66. On the privileging of the "German wanderer," see Peitsch, "Round-trips from the Inside to the Outside," 26–27; and for a critique of the compensation argument, see Peitsch, " 'Noch war die halbe Oberfläche,' " 157–74.

67. For other work on this, see my "Red Feathers, White Paper, Blueprint."

68. Nugent, "Grand Tour," 15.

69. For a specifically German definition, see Zunkel, "Ehre/Reputation," vol. 2, 1–63.

70. Adam Smith, *Theory of Moral Sentiments,* 50–51.

71. See, for example, Millar's argument in *Origin of the Distinction of Ranks,* which extended to individuals, as well as to "nations."

72. Simmel, *Sociology of Georg Simmel,* 402–408.

73. See, for example, New, "Realism, Deconstruction, and the Feminist Standpoint," 349–72; and Lloyd S. Kramer, *Threshold of a New World,* 10; and on its critique, namely, that standpoint theory upholds binary oppositions between center and periphery, see Kaplan, *Questions of Travel,* 173.

74. Burney, *German Tour,* xi; and on the status of autopsy in travel writing, see my "Dissecting the Cannibal," 50–60.

75. Montagu, *Turkish Embassy Letters,* 10, 36, 72, 164–65.

76. For an analysis of the religious dimensions in this painting, see Koerner, *Caspar David Friedrich,* 194.

77. See Smollett, *Travels through France and Italy;* and Baretti, *Account of the Manners and Customs of Italy.*

78. Burney, *Dr. Burney's Musical Tours,* vol. 2, 72.

79. Goethe quoted in Stanzel, " 'Deutschland: Aber wo liegt es?' " 195.

80. Hust, "Introduction," 13; and, on French travelers' impressions of the German states and the subsequent process of "cultural transfer," see Wehinger, " 'Wir müssen bestrebt sein, eine Brücke zu schlagen,' " 235.

81. Robson-Scott describes the late eighteenth-century German enthusiasm for British political and social institutions and German travelers' "Anglomania" in *German Travellers in England, 1400–1800,* 136–37, 61; for a countervailing view, see Justus Möser's 1763–1764 travelogue, in which Möser describes Englishmen as "slaves of freedom"; quoted in Maurer, ed., *O Britannien, von deiner Freiheit einen Hut voll,* 192; and on the German reception of British travel writing, see Peitsch, "Georg Forster als Vermittler," 107–31.

82. On Hanover as "an outpost of English civilization," see Shackleton, *Montesquieu,* 117; quoted in Maurer, *Aufklärung und Anglophilie in Deutschland,* 44.

83. Moore, *View of society and manners,* vol. 1, 290; further references to Britain in the German intellectual imagination may be found in Maurer, *Aufklärung und Anglophilie in Deutschland,* 257; and Guthke, *Goethes Weimar,* which deals with the work of London correspondent and China traveler Johann Christian Hüttner.

84. See Habermas, *Strukturwandel der Öffentlichkeit;* and Lisa Aldis Fishman, "Critical Text as Cultural Nexus," 8.

85. See Anon., *Catalogue of the Miscellaneous Library of the Late Charles Burney.*

86. The point about Britain's gravitational pull (with specific reference to J. C. Bach and Abel) is made in Grant, *Dr. Burney as Critic and Historian,* 93; for exhaustive treatments of Handel and the British context, see Harris, *Handel as Orpheus;* and Burrows and Dunhill, *Music and Theatre in Handel's World.*

87. This inward-looking tendency was not peculiar to professional musicians. Frank Felsenstein points out in the preface to Smollett, *Travels through France and Italy,* xviii, that late eighteenth-century British travel books were often explicit in their "insular prejudice," with subtitles that refer to France as the "natural enemy."

88. "Burney (welcher, wie ich nun sehe, bey Claviersachen 12 Exemplare brauchen konnte aber bey deutschen Stücken nicht, weil vielleicht in ganz England nur ein Paar verständige Componisten sind, welche noch darzu kein Deutsch verstehen wollen u. können) kriegt 2 Exemplare." Letter from C. P. E. Bach to Breitkopf (Sept. 21, 1787) in Suchalla, ed., *Briefe von Carl Philipp Emanuel Bach,* 220.

89. The claim that Britain's empire had little impact on metropolitan society has been made by Marshall in "No Fatal Impact?" This appears in a study that takes the contrary view, see Wilson, *Island Race,* 212n68.

90. For a notable exception, see Trumpener, *Bardic Nationalism.*

91. The *Oxford English Dictionary* defines the umstroke as an old word for the edge or circumference of a map—its "utmost line," where towns stand, so to speak, "on tiptoes" and "are not in their exact position." The term is used in MacLean, "Strolling in Syria with William Biddulph," 435.

92. For an example of a highly detailed map of the German states, see Blair, *Chronology and history of the world.*

93. Burney, "Letter to Christoph Daniel Ebeling, 15 July 1773," in *Letters,* 130.

94. See Winichakul, *Siam Mapped;* and Anderson, *Imagined Communities,* 163–86.

95. Keyssler's travelogue was first published under the title *Neueste Reise durch Teutschland, Böhmen, Ungarn, die Schweitz, Italien und Lothringen;* for his biography, see *Allgemeine deutsche Biographie (ADB),* elektronische version, ed. Historische Kommission bei der Bayerischen Akademie der Wissenschaften und der Bayerischen Staatsbibliothek, Jan. 2003, vol. 15, 702–703; and on Mozart's use of Keyssler's account as a guide, see Angermüller with Geffray and von Glasner-Ostenwall, *Mozarts Reisen in Italien.*

96. Smollett, *Travels through France and Italy,* 239–40.

97. Cited in Cox, *Reference Guide to the Literature of Travel,* vol. 1, 144.

98. Keyssler, *Travels through Germany,* v. On utility as a rhetorical convention of the eighteenth-century travel account, see Golden, "Travel Writing," 214.

99. On the use of the mediating figure in landscape painting (e.g., Philipp Hackert's painting *Eruption of Vesuvius*), see Joppien and Smith, *Art of Captain Cook's Voyages,* vol. 3, 35–36; see also the illustrations using a mediating spectator in Humboldt, *Ansichten der Kordilleren,* and Charles Willson Peale's painting *The Artist in His Museum* (1822).

100. For a discussion of this image in relation to curiosity and the legitimization of natural history, see Thomas, "Objects of Knowledge," in *In Oceania,* 112–14; and his *Cook,* 148.

101. Rousseau and Porter, "Introduction: Approaching Enlightenment Exoticism," 4.

102. Montagu, *Turkish Embassy Letters,* 44.

103. According to Pliny, *Natural History,* ed. Rackham, vol. 7, 521, human sacrifice and cannibalism occurred in "parts beyond the Alps," and the tribe with eyes in their shoulders lived west of another tribe in India. As Montagu makes clear, Pliny's bestiary remained a persistent trope in travel writing into the eighteenth century.

104. On the comparative neglect of Germany as a travel destination, see Mead, *Grand Tour,* 335–43; and on the growing number of travelers to the German states at the end of the century, see Black, *British and the Grand Tour,* 12–13.

105. For generalizations about poor traveling conditions in the German states, see Black, *British and the Grand Tour,* 38–40; and Letts, "Germany and the Rhineland," 119–36. For a contradictory view held by the founder of the Moravian Church in England, see Burney, "Letter to James Hutton, 17 July 1773," in *Letters,* 131–34.

106. Tacitus, *Treatise on the situation, manners, and inhabitants of Germany,* 5.

107. Cox, *Reference Guide to the Literature of Travel,* vol. 1, 157.

108. "Hier ist es nicht wie in Frankreich und den meisten anderen Ländern, wo man in den Hauptstädten sozusagen die Nation in einer Nuß beisammen hat." Riesbeck, *Briefe,* 12–13.

109. "Hier ist keine Stadt, die dem ganzen Volk einen Ton gibt. Es ist in fast unzählige, größere und kleinere Horden zerteilt, die durch Regierungsform, Religion und andere Dinge unendlich weit voneinander unterschieden sind und kein anderes Band unter sich haben als die gemeinschaftliche Sprache." Ibid., 13.

110. Seume, *Spaziergang,* ix.

111. Riesbeck, *Briefe,* 12–13.

112. "Ich habe von Anfang an mehr versprochen, als eine bloße Reisebeschreibung. Diese sollte, meinem Plane gemäß, der Faden seyn, worauf ich Beobachtungen, Gedanken, Vorschläge aller Art, die mir für unser deutsches Vaterland nützlich schienen, reihen wollte." Nicolai, *Beschreibung einer Reise,* vol. 11, xxvi; quoted in Martens, "Ein Bürger auf Reisen," 100; see also Seume, *Spaziergang,* vii.

113. According to Schlemmer, Nicolai's purpose in traveling through Germany was to effect an "intellectual unification and to help forge a 'cultural nation.'" Nicolai, *Unter Bayern und Schwaben,* 17.

114. Riesbeck, *Briefe,* 330.

115. Ibid., 331–35.

116. "Selbst die Zerteilung, die ihm im äußeren Gebrauch seiner Kräfte so nachteilig ist, beförderte den inneren Anbau." Ibid., 332.

117. "Wenn sich Deutschland ganz geltend machen könnte; wenn es unter einem Regenten vereint wäre . . . wenn alle Teile genau in einen Körper verbunden wären . . . so würde das Reich noch viel schnellere Schritte zu seiner Kultur machen können. Aber dann könnte Deutschland auch ganz Europa Gesetze vorschreiben." Ibid., 334.

118. "Das Gefühl der Schwäche der kleineren Völkerschaften Deutschlands dämpft den Nationalstolz. Auch bloß deswegen, weil Deutschland seine Kräfte nicht vereint gebrauchen und seine Stärke andere Nationen fühlen lassen kann, werden seine Einwohner von anderen Völkern verachtet, die nichts voraushaben als eine festere Verbindung unter sich oder eine lächerliche Eitelkeit." Ibid., 335.

119. "Man denke sich dieses Reich in der Lage . . . wo es eine Seemacht bilden könnte, wozu es die günstigste Lage und alle Bedürfnisse in Überfluß hat; wo es die Kolonisten, die es so häufig für fremde Staaten liefert, für sich selbst benutzte." Ibid., 334.

120. "Der Deutsche ist der Mann für die Welt. Er baut sich unter jedem Himmel an und besiegt alle Hindernisse der Natur. Sein Fleiß ist unüberwindlich." Ibid., 335.

121. "Welches europäische Reich könnte sich mit den Deutschen messen?" Ibid., 334–35.

122. On the inclusion of J. S. Bach, Mozart, and Beethoven on one of the NASA probes that were sent into space in 1977, see Applegate and Potter, "Germans as the 'People of Music,'" 1.

123. Advertising campaign for a journey (Salzburg-Vienna-Prague) on the "Mozart Train." Online s.v. "Mozart Train," http://www.compacttours.com/mozart/en/index.htm (accessed June 16, 2006).

124. Anderson, *Imagined Communities,* 36–44; for a critique and the need to examine "musical elaborations of nationalism," see Askew, *Performing the Nation,* 9–13; Alter and Koepnick, "Introduction," *Sound Matters,* 19; on the necessity of incorporating music into Anderson's argument, see Applegate, *Bach in Berlin,* 9, 92–93, in which Applegate traces a process of cultural "consolidation" via the nineteenth-century reception of J. S. Bach; and on music and the construction of place, see Stokes, ed., *Ethnicity, Identity, and Music.*

125. For other research that links cultural production to geographical mapping, see Moretti, *Atlas of the European Novel,* 5, which establishes the "place-bound" character of the nineteenth-century European novel; Russell A. Berman, *Rise of the Modern German Novel,* 1–2, which links social geography and literary forms; and Bohlman, "Music,

Modernity, and the Foreign," 138–39, on the capacity of song to both mark and erase boundaries.

126. See Angermüller, *Mozarts Reisen in Europa;* and on the EU cultural routes, see http://www.coe.int/T/E/Cultural_Co-operation/Heritage/European_Cultural_Routes/; and http://www.mozartways.com/content.php?m_id=1182&id=1182&newsdetail=50&ch_id=0&ch2_id= (accessed Sept. 9, 2007).

127. On music's agency in overcoming the confessional divisions within the German states, see Steinberg, *Listening to Reason,* 14–15.

128. On the literary-musical connections between Hamburg and Berlin, see Grant, *Dr. Burney as Critic and Historian,* 85.

129. Burney, *Dr. Burney's Musical Tours,* vol. 2, 54–57; see also Rosselli, "Mingotti."

130. On another musician with a peripatetic career, see Michael Kelly, *Reminiscences of Michael Kelly.*

131. Beutler and Guts-Muths, *Allgemeines Sachregister,* vol. 1, 92.

132. Burney, *Dr. Burney's Musical Tours,* vol. 2, 37.

133. Stewart, "Christoph Daniel Ebeling," 48.

134. Ibid., 48–50.

135. While the purpose of apodemics was to facilitate travel practice and systematize the traveler's modes of inquiry, there were significant differences between types of apodemic. Compare, for example, Gray, *Traveller's companion,* vii; and Beaglehole, ed., *Journals of Captain James Cook,* vol. 1, cclxxix–cclxxxiv.

136. On the apodemic as "the precursor to sociological and ethnological methodology," see Stagl, "Der 'Patriotic Traveller,'" 219–21.

137. Stagl, *Apodemiken,* vol. 2, 9.

138. Ships "bound for discoveries" were issued with official instructions. For an early example, see Anon., "Directions for Seamen Bound on Far Voyages," 140–43; and on the ethnographic stipulations in the Admiralty's instructions, see Beaglehole, ed., *Journals of Captain James Cook,* vol. 1, cclxxix–cclxxxiv.

139. Anon., *Völkertafel,* Steiermark, ca. 1730–1740, Vienna, Austrian Ethnology Museum, depicted as the frontispiece in Stanzel, ed., *Europäischer Völkerspiegel.*

140. As Pederson points out in "Long-term Winning and Losing Strategies," the professional acceptance of cultural views on music was slow in coming.

141. Burney, *Dr. Burney's Musical Tours,* vol. 2, xi.

142. Ibid., 1–5.

143. Ibid., 12–13.

144. Ibid., 13–14.

145. Ibid., 24.

146. Ibid., 23.

147. Ibid., 26–28.

148. Ibid., 28–29.

149. Ibid., 33.

150. Ibid., 31.

151. Ibid., 35–36.

152. Ibid., vol. 1, 259.

153. Ibid., vol. 2, 36; and cf. Burney, *Carl Burney's der Musik Doctors Tagebuch* vol. 1, 77.

154. Burney, *Dr. Burney's Musical Tours,* vol. 2, 37–38.

155. Burney, "Letter to Christoph Daniel Ebeling, 15 July 1773," *Letters,* 129.

156. Louis Devisme, letter to Burney, Nov. 30, 1772, Osborn Collection, Yale University; see Oldman, "Charles Burney and Louis De Visme," 93–97. As Ribeiro points out, Burney seems to have elicited the comment in the first place; for a discussion, see Burney, *Letters,* 128n3.

157. Burney, "Letter to Christoph Daniel Ebeling, 15 July 1773," *Letters,* 128.

158. Burney, *Dr. Burney's Musical Tours,* vol. 2, 49–50, 53–54.

159. Ibid., 51.

160. Ibid., 63–70.

161. Ibid., 71.

162. Ibid., 71. Original emphasis.

163. Ibid., 72–78, 84, 112–13.

164. Ibid., 78. Original emphasis.

165. Ibid., 88, 111, 124n3.

166. Ibid., 101–104; and see Burney, *Memoirs of the Life and Writings of the Abate Metastasio.*

167. For Metastasio's views on the opera, see Burney, *Dr. Burney's Musical Tours,* vol. 2, 103–104.

168. Ibid., 81–82.

169. For a discussion of Burney's views on Hasse, see Grant, *Dr. Burney as Critic and Historian,* 73.

170. Burney, *Dr. Burney's Musical Tours,* vol. 2, 91–92. On Calzibigi's contribution to the reform operas, see Howard, *Gluck.*

171. Burney, *Dr. Burney's Musical Tours,* vol. 2, 93, 100, 120. Original emphasis.

172. Ibid., 96, 109, 116.

173. Ibid., 106, 116.

174. Ibid., 132–38.

175. Ibid., 131.

176. Ibid., 138.

177. Ibid., 138.

178. Ibid., 140–41.

179. Ibid., 149.

180. John Osborn, "Letter to Burney, 20 January 1773," Osborn Collection, Yale University.

181. Burney, *Dr. Burney's Musical Tours,* vol. 2, 151–52.

182. On Hiller's contribution to creating a folk idiom and the notion of a unified German nation, see Joubert, "Songs to Shape a German Nation," 213–30.

183. Burney, *Dr. Burney's Musical Tours,* vol. 2, 156–57.

184. Ibid., 161, 174–77.

185. Ibid., 207.

186. Ibid., 164. Original emphasis.

187. Ibid., 169.

188. Ibid., 171.

189. Ibid.

190. Ibid., 172.

191. Ibid.

192. Marischal's story was incorporated into Burney's article on Putaveri, which added a postscript to the effect that the Italian experiment had been performed on another occasion. See Charles Burney, "Putaveri," in Rees, ed. *Cyclopaedia,* vol. 29.

193. Burney, *Dr. Burney's Musical Tours,* vol. 2, 178–79.

194. Ibid., 180.

195. Ibid., 180–83; see also 207 for a description of Quantz's compositions as "common and insipid."

196. Ibid., 200.

197. Ibid., 201–203.

198. Ibid., 208, 215.

199. For a work that takes this up, see Harris, *Handel as Orpheus.*

200. Burney, *Dr. Burney's Musical Tours,* vol. 2, 214.

201. Ibid., 217–19.

202. Ibid., 213.

203. Ibid., 229.

204. Ibid., 230.

205. Ibid., 238. His sources were letters from Devisme (Nov. 30, 1772) and a Hamburg physician, J. Mumssen (Oct. 16, 1772), Osborn Collection, Yale University; cited in Lonsdale, *Dr. Charles Burney,* 119, 124.

206. Burney, *Dr. Burney's Musical Tours,* vol. 2, 235–36.

207. Ibid., 207.

208. Ibid., 243.

209. Young, *A six weeks tour.* For another example of a specialized travelogue, see Howard, *State of the Prisons.*

210. Young, *farmer's letters,* 303.

211. Young's apodemic included an itinerary, as well as instructions that stipulated the mode of observation ("slow" and comparative), what to collect (e.g., grains) and observe (e.g., roads, poor laws and their enforcement, agricultural machinery and methods, crops, climate, soil), and the method of documentation ("minute and exact"). Ibid., 309ff.

212. Ibid., 317.

213. Charles Burney, "Letter to Baron d'Holbach, 2 June 1772," in *Letters,* 114. For confirmation of this, see Towner, *Historical Geography of Recreation and Tourism,* 103, which shows that European travelers from the seventeenth to the mid-nineteenth century were consistently engrossed in art, architecture, and antiquities and increasingly interested in landscape. Their attraction to music, however, was not significant enough to have warranted its own category.

214. On this reception, see Lonsdale, *Dr. Charles Burney,* 128.

215. The Anglophone reception has not been uniform in its appraisal of Burney. Some have objected to his prioritization of music; others, like the music historian John Hawkins, thought Burney insufficiently "scientific." This polarization is also evident in contemporary scholarship. See, for example, Ford, "Review of 'Memoirs of Dr. Charles Burney,'" 285–87.

216. [Bewley, William], "Article VIII," 458.

217. D'Arblay, *Memoirs of Doctor Burney,* vol. 2, 78–79; see also Burney, *Early Journals,* vol. 1, 222; Boswell, *Boswell's Life of Johnson,* vol. 4, 186.

218. Boswell, *Boswell for the Defence,* 51; quoted in Lonsdale, *Dr. Charles Burney,* 129; see Paumgartner, ed., *Dr. Charles Burney's musikalische Reise,* ix, who takes Johnson's remark as an endorsement of Burney.

219. Hust, "Introduction," *Charles Burney: Tagebuch einer musikalischen Reise,* 13.

220. For an account of this episode, see Grant, *Dr. Burney as Critic and Historian,* 80, 82.

221. A discussion of Bode's editorializing appears in Peitsch, "Englische Reisebeschreibungen," 1–50.

222. Burney, *Carl Burney's der Musik Doctors Tagebuch,* vol. 2, 83n; vol. 3, 20n.

223. Ibid., vol. 2, 76–83; vol. 3, 80.

224. Ibid., vol. 3, 71–73, 91–92.

225. "In musikalischen Materien möchte der Uebersetzer gerne den Herrn Doktor Burney im Texte sagen lassen, was im Original stehet; obgleich vieles Fremdes, zu Zweck nicht Gehöriges, billig für den deutschen Leser ganz ausgelassen wird. Dergleichen Urtheile aber, wie dieses, welches, man nehme es auch noch so glimpflich, wenigstens ohne genugsame Ueberlegung hingeschrieben ist, möchte der Uebersetzer, so unbekannt er in der gelehrten und musikalischen Welt ist, und gerne bleiben wird, um Vieles nicht auf seiner Rechnung haben." Ibid., vol. 3, 30.

226. "Diese Mannigfaltigkeit der Instrumente . . . hält ein manches sehr musikalisches Genie zurück, etwas Vortreffliches auf einem Instrumente zu leisten." Ibid., vol. 3, 119.

227. "Sollte diese Anmerkung jemandem ein harter Vorwurf scheinen, den bitte ich, zu bedenken, dass sie bey einer Gelegenheit gemacht wird, da einer ganzen Nation, über eine Kunst, in der sie allen andern Nationen die achtungswürdigsten Meister geliefert hat, mit vier Worten [Patience, Profundity, Prolixity, and Pedantry] und eben so cavallierement ihr Urtheil gesprochen wird, als ob ein junger Herr von seinem Schneider urtheilte der ihm ein Kleid nicht zu Danke gemacht hätte." Ibid., vol. 3, 280n.

228. "Ich werde meine Leser mit allen magern Namen und Titulatur-Verzeichnissen und allen bereits bekannten Dingen, so viel als möglich verschonen, und ihnen durch die treue Darstellung alles Merkwürdigen, so ich selbst gehört und gesehen habe, den gegenwärtigen Zustand der Musik in jenen Ländern bekannt zu machen suchen. Man wird nicht selten die treueste Beschreibung gegen alle Erwartung und bisherige Meinung finden." Reichardt, "Johann Friedrich Reichardts musikalische Reisen," (1786): 1083–84; see also ibid., (1787), 1270–71.

229. Personal communication with Oliver Weiner, June 29, 2005.

230. According to Reichardt, the intimate letter (his addressee was an old friend) was the most suitable venue for critiquing Burney's work because the letter allowed frank opinions to be expressed, whereas the journal review was constrained by the need to avoid the appearance of partiality. Reichardt, "Briefe eines aufmerksamen Reisenden, die Musik betreffend (1774)," in *Briefe, die Musik betreffend,* 30.

231. Reichardt phrased this as "seinen Endzweck während der Reise beständig vor Augen [haben] und diesem alles andere aufopfern." Ibid.

232. Ibid., 31.

233. Ibid.

234. "Mit den schlechten Leuten." Ibid.

235. Ibid., 32.

236. "Wir fragen daher z. B. was sich von einer allgemeinen Geschichte der Musik erwarten lasse, deren Verfasser im Stande ist, bey der Aussuchung seiner Materialien, herumreisende gemeine Musikanten, oder eigentlich sogenannte Schenkenvirtuosen (Bierfiedler) so wichtig zu finden, dass er uns öfters ganze Seiten lang von ihnen erzählt, ihren Geschmack, ihren Vortrag, ihre Stücke, und alles was sie angeht, aufs genaueste beurtheilt? Ist dieses etwas anderes, als wenn der Geschichtschreiber der Malerkunst die Geschicklichkeit der Tüncher oder gemeinen Häuserbeklecker in große Betrachtung ziehen, und daraus auf den Zustand der Kunst in einem Lande schließen wollte?" Forkel, "Recensionen theoretischer Werke," 119.

237. On the need to travel in Germany with someone of high rank because it facilitated one's reception and obviated the need for introductory letters, see Moore, *View of society and manners,* vol. 1, 309. For a rather approving view of the "scrupulous precision" with which "the distinction of ranks" was observed in Germany, see travel anthologist Wyndham, *Travels through Europe,* vol. 2, 27, who observed this with regard to concert etiquette. Instead of subscribers' taking their seats in the order in which they arrived, the first rows were reserved for "ladies of quality."

238. Burney, *Dr. Burney's Musical Tours,* vol. 1, xxv–xxvi.

239. Poovey, *History of the Modern Fact,* 249.

240. M'Nicol, *Remarks on Dr. Samuel Johnson's Journey,* 109; cited in Trumpener, *Bardic Nationalism,* 317n72. Johnson's quote runs as follows: "My inquiries about brogues, gave me an early specimen of Highland information.... Many of my subsequent inquiries upon more interesting topicks [*sic*] ended in the like uncertainty.... The Highlander gives to every question an answer so prompt and peremptory, that skepticism is itself dared into silence, and the mind sinks before the bold reporter in unresisting credulity; but, if a second question be ventured, it breaks the enchantment; for it is immediately discovered, that what was told so confidently was told at hazard, and that such fearlessness of assertion was either the sport of negligence, or the refuge of ignorance." Johnson, *Journey to the Western Isles,* 111–12.

241. In her discussion of Johnson's method, Trumpener arrives at the opposite conclusion from Poovey, who stresses Johnson's willingness to "change his mind about some of the assumptions he had set out with"; see note 240; and Poovey, *History of the Modern Fact,* 256.

242. Burney, *Dr. Burney's Musical Tours,* vol. 2, 13–14.

243. Viviès argues that Johnson's project was characterized by epistemological instability because the oral culture of the Highlanders reminded the traveler of the fragility of testimony, which led Johnson to conclude that "The inhabitants...are not very scrupulous adherents to truth." Viviès, *English Travel Narratives,* 44–45.

244. Burney, *Dr. Burney's Musical Tours,* vol. 2, 23, 54.

245. Compare this with Scholes's prejudicial reading of Reichardt: "Poor pedantic Reichardt; thy race is not extinct in thy country to-day!" Scholes, *Great Dr. Burney,* vol. 1, 252.

246. Stephan, "'Ich bin ja auch nicht...begierig,'" 225–27.

247. For a rather positive account of this meeting, see Burney, *Dr. Burney's Musical Tours,* vol. 2, 39–40.

248. The word *welsch* referred to Italy, France, and the Rhaeto-Romance–speaking region of Switzerland, often with a pejorative connotation. On the word's Reformation

associations with foreignness and the "Italian sin" of sodomy, see Puff, *Sodomy in Reformation Germany and Switzerland*, 118. Ebeling had accused Burney of being "Welsh" and the "un[gra]tefull offspring of ancient Germany!" in his letter of 1773; this was a possible source for Schubart's later remark. In his reply to Ebeling, Burney said that Ebeling had "set [his] *Welsh Blood* up a little." See Schubart, *Leben und Gesinnungen*, 135–36; Gordon M. Stewart, "Christoph Daniel Ebeling," 50; and Burney, "Letter to Christoph Daniel Ebeling," 130.

249. See, for example, Klemm, "Tagebuch einer musikalischen Reise," 12; and Hust, "Introduction," 7, 17, who stresses that the German *Stolz* (pride) was hurt. Hust also points out, however, that Burney's views on southern Germany and Austria were not wholly negative, a point largely overlooked in middle and northern Germany. For reception that does not emphasize the national dimension, see Reichardt, "Briefe," 11, in which Siegmund-Schultze claims that the rivalry between Burney and Reichardt was due to their competing claims on Handel.

250. The notion of the Holy Roman Empire as a "perplexity" was an eighteenth-century British term; quoted in Geyken, "Gentlemen in Brandenburg," 19.

251. Riesbeck, *Briefe*, 13.

Chapter Two

1. On Rousseau's praise of German military music invoked for nationalist ends, see Kandler, *Deutsche Armeemärsche*, 3.

2. On the king's "Marsch in Es" (1741), also called "Prussian Army March," see Thouret, *Katalog der Musiksammlung*, 320.

3. Burney, *General History of Music*, vol. 1, 157.

4. Descartes, *Passions of the Soul*, 56.

5. On Cook's artifact trade, see Agnew, "Exchange Strategies on Cook's Second Voyage"; see also Kaeppler, "Artificial Curiosities."

6. Burney met the Polynesian Mai when he was brought to London by Captain Furneaux. Mai sang for the Burney family on several occasions and was also taken to hear a performance of Handel's *Jephtha* in London. See Fanny Burney, *Early Journals and Letters*, 194–95; and a report in the *Philosophical Transactions* 65 (1775): 28–29, quoted in McCormick, *Omai: Pacific Envoy*, 160.

7. Evidence of Burney's ethnomusicological interests are to be found in his correspondence about non-Western music with people like Hüttner, Marischal, Sandwich, Raper, Lind, Bruce, and Rousseau. This correspondence is included in Burney, *Letters of Dr. Charles Burney*.

8. In Altenburg, *Versuch einer Anleitung*, 25, the author, himself a war veteran, claimed that the army would have been defeated had it not been for the aid of the trumpet. On music's educational properties, see H. L. R., "Eine kleine Abhandlung," 1239.

9. Marpurg, "Ob und was für Harmonie die Alten gehabt," 276.

10. Anon., "Ueber die Gewalt der Musik," 681–86.

11. See, for example, the charge that Junker uncritically recycled classical stories and did not differentiate half-truths from the whole truth about music. Eschenburg, "Review of 'Ueber den Werth der Tonkunst,'" 442–43.

12. Sulzer, "Foreword," in *Allgemeine Theorie der schönen Künste*, 14; Junker, *Ueber den Werth der Tonkunst*, 94–95; and H. L. R., "Eine kleine Abhandlung," 1241.

13. "Glaubt ihr, daß Orpheus! Der große, um die Menschheit ewig verdiente Orpheus! Der Dichter, in dessen schlechten Überbleibseln die ganze Seele der Natur lebet, daß er ursprünglich etwas anders, als der edelste Schamane gewesen sei, den Thracien, das damals auch Nordische Tartarei war, sehen konnte? Und so ferner. Wollt ihr den Griechischen Tyrtäus kennen lernen: siehe da ein Kriegesfest und Kriegsgesang und singender Führer der Nordamerikaner!" Herder, "Lieder fremder Völker," in *Volkslieder, Übertragungen, Dichtungen*, 63.

14. For discussions of music's effects on the savage and the savage state, see Van der Zande, "Orpheus in Berlin," 175–208; Hoyt, "On the Primitives of Music Theory," 197–212; and Riley, "Civilising the Savage," 1–22. On the argument that late eighteenth-century scholars promoted German music by highlighting its effects on non-Europeans and minimizing the significance of other musical vernaculars, see Gramit, *Cultivating Music*, 27–62; and Morrow, *German Music Criticism*, 46.

15. The Cook voyages (1768–1771, 1772–1775, 1776–1780), the Bering Second Kamchatka Expedition (1733–1743), and the Macartney embassy to China (1793–1794) are cases in point.

16. On the significance of exploratory travel (and particularly the Pacific) for Enlightenment thought, see Outram, *Enlightenment;* and for a discussion of such cultural practices, see Barnouw, "*Eräugnis:* Georg Forster on the Difficulties of Diversity," 327; and Berg, *Zwischen den Welten*, 110.

17. Anon., "Etwas von der Kriegsschaubühne," 243.

18. The term is in DeNora, *Music in Everyday Life*, 7.

19. Homer, *Odyssey*, 131–35, and Ovid, *Metamorphoses*, 216.

20. See Hoare, *Tactless Philosopher.*

21. See, for example, Segalan and Agamben, *Tote Stimmen.*

22. Harrison, *Time, Place, and Music,* stresses the disciplinary value of this travel material; see also Meyers, "Ethnomusicology."

23. Qureshi argues that music scholars have tended to assume that "the inherent value of music is use value," not exchange value. Qureshi, "Focus on Ethnic Music," 343, quoted in Blum, "Conclusion: Music in an Age of Cultural Confrontation," 251.

24. Bohlman points out that ethnomusicological investigation and the study and promotion of serious music were interconnected activities in the eighteenth and nineteenth centuries. Bohlman, "European Discovery," 162–63; see also Born and Hesmondhalgh, eds., *Western Music and Its Others,* 1–12; Erlmann, *Music, Modernity, and the Global Imagination,* 8; Gramit, *Cultivating Music,* 28; Morrow, who argues that attempting to create a Germanic musical culture involved the "positing of a superior Germanic Chosen in opposition to an inferior musical 'Other,'" *German Music Criticism in the Late Eighteenth Century,* 46; Shelemay, "Crossing Boundaries," 19–20; and Tomlinson, *Singing of the New World.*

25. See Fonton, *Essai sur la musique orientale;* Amiot, *Mémoire sur la musique;* and Laborde, *Essai sur la musique ancienne et moderne.*

26. During the first decade of the twentieth century, major scientific expeditions were conducted in the Pacific by Emil Stephan, Richard Thurnwald, and Augustin Krämer, who returned with significant amounts of phonographic material. For a discussion, see Agnew, "Colonialist Beginnings of Comparative Musicology."

27. In conducting this research I drew on the bibliography in Lütteken, ed., *Die Musik in den Zeitschriften des 18. Jahrhunderts.*

28. Kaden, " 'Die New welt, der landschaften und Insulen,' " 253.

29. Bohlman, "European Discovery," 147–48; Kaden, " 'Die New welt, der landschaften und Insulen,' " 253–60; and Krader, "Ethnomusicology," 276.

30. On Orpheus's capacity for creating harmony and conformity ("Where Orpheus plays, the world is at peace"), see Leppert, *Sight of Sound,* 34; and Detienne, who sees Orpheus as having a "centripetal power": His music summons all living things to him and animates and subdues them. This primal voice, says Detienne, is "willing to give up the idea of a world that is ordered, separate, and characterized by fragmentation and division—that is to say, the world of others." Detienne, *Writing of Orpheus,* 134.

31. We are reminded here of Horkheimer and Adorno's insight that the Enlightenment took all its subject matter from myths in order to destroy them. Horkheimer and Adorno, *Dialektik der Aufklärung,* 18.

32. See Seipel, ed., *Für Aug' und Ohr.*

33. Leppert, *Sight of Sound,* 8–9.

34. "Nichts ist leichter: denn diese Völker haben einen Geschmack, u. es würde nicht viel Zeit vonnöthen seyn, sie zu bereden, ihre barbarischen Concerte, die auch die härtesten Ohren zerreissen, abzuschaffen, u. dafür unserer Musik u. Instrumente zu bedienen." Mizler added, "Aus dieser Nachricht von der barbarischen Musik im Königreiche Juda in Africa kann man sich anmerken, dass das Wachsthum der Musik mit dem Wachsthume der übrigen Wissenschaften unzertrennlich zusammenhängt." Mizler [von Kolof], "Nachricht von der barbarischen Musik," 577.

35. Anon., "Etwas von den Negern," 636.

36. Forkel, "Nachrichten von dem Zustand der Musik," 229–30.

37. Anon., "Ueber die Gewalt der Musik," 686.

38. Steller, *Steller's History of Kamchatka,* translator's preface, xiii.

39. Pallas, "Herrn D. Pallas Nachricht," 550.

40. [Georg Wilhelm Steller], [Sitten, Gebräuche, und Lebensrat der Kamtschadalen]." 245. On Steller's earlier travelogue, see his *Steller's History of Kamchatka,* 250–52.

41. In an 1814 article published in the *Allgemeine Musikalische Zeitung,* Michaelis drew on Steller's travelogue to point out that the Kamtschatkans' music was not monotonous like that of other "rough" peoples; they knew how to express a wide range of emotions and use "middle voices." Although Michaelis was explicitly interested in the effect of this music on European listeners, he neglected to mention the musical satirizing originally reported by Steller. Michaelis, "Ueber die Musik," 514.

42. Besides Steller (and later Pallas), the other German participants of the expedition included botanist Johann Georg Gmelin and historian Gerhard Friedrich Müller. See Gmelin's *Expedition ins unbekannte Sibirien.*

43. See Woodfield, *English Musicians in the Age of Exploration.*

44. See Austin, *How to Do Things with Words;* Dening, *Performances;* and DeNora, *Music in Everyday Life.* The notion of the performative has been comparatively neglected by musicologists, but for a different view, see Bohlman, "Stimmen der Lieder in Völkern."

45. Grewendorf, "How Performatives Don't Work," 26; and DeNora, *Music in Everyday Life,* 8.

46. Austin, *How to Do Things with Words,* 8–9.

47. See Diamond, *Guns, Germs, and Steel.*

48. Todorov, *Conquest of America,* 98–123; Sahlins, *Historical Metaphors and Mythical Realities.* For a critique of this and subsequent work by Sahlins, see Obeyesekere, *Apotheosis of Captain Cook.*

49. See, for example, Dening, *Mr. Bligh's Bad Language,* 198–201; and his *Performances,* 128ff; see also Seed, *Ceremonies of Possession,* 2–14, 35–36, and, on the use of music in possession ceremonies, 47ff.

50. Douglas, "Hints offered to the consideration of Captain Cooke," 515.

51. Agnew, "Bagpipes in the Eighteenth-century Pacific," 21–22.

52. Burke describes performative events as being "framed" and thus distinguished from everyday activities. Burke, "Performing History," 45.

53. This is evident from accounts of the Cook voyages, which show that, although voyagers were instructed to elicit indigenous consent, formal possession was contingent on narrating the event for a European public. Cook was officially instructed to deposit "traces" and "proper marks and inscriptions," including specially minted medals, of his act of territorial appropriation. See Zimmermann's account of the third voyage: *Heinrich Zimmermanns von Wißloch in der Pfalz Reise,* 37–38.

54. On his aims for the music history and the quest for the origins of harmony, see Burney, "Letter to Samuel Crisp, [late March 1775]," in Burney, *Letters,* 181; and Burney, *Dr. Burney's Musical Tours,* vol. 2, 13.

55. Captains James Cook (1728–1779) and Tobias Furneaux (1735–1781) sailed from Plymouth on July 13, 1772. Furneaux's ship, *Adventure,* with James Burney now appointed second lieutenant, returned on July 14, 1774. The ships had been separated in a storm, and Cook's *Resolution* did not return for another year. See Beaglehole, ed., *Journals of Captain James Cook,* vol. 2, xlix–cxiii.

56. Charles Burney, letter to Lord Sandwich, Feb. 11, 1784.

57. According to King, who had discussed the matter with Burney, the fact that the "separate parties sung together in different notes . . . overthrew [Burney's] whole system." James King, letter to Lord Sandwich, Woodstock, Jan. 30, 1784.

58. Manwaring, *My Friend the Admiral,* 48–50.

59. In the introduction to the German travelogue, Burney acknowledged his debt to Sandwich, whom he had first met in 1771. Sandwich (and others) had written to ministers and consuls at northern European courts and recommended Burney and his project. See Burney, *Letters,* 115; Burney, *German Tour,* xii; and Lonsdale, *Dr. Charles Burney,* 111–12.

60. At Sandwich's instigation, Burney sent information solicited from James and his daughter Susanna, who was married to another Pacific voyager, Molesworth Phillips. Sandwich and King (Cook was now dead) consulted Burney about Polynesian music while overseeing the publication of the official account of the third voyage. Their correspondence is among the Papers of John Montagu Sandwich, 1771–1784, MS 7218/30–36, National Library of Australia. Burney and Sandwich also hosted Mai, popularly known as Omai, the islander brought to England by Furneaux in 1774 and subsequently returned to Polynesia by Cook. For a discussion, see McCormick, *Omai: Pacific Envoy,* 94–134; and Clark, *Omai.*

61. Joseph Banks, naturalist on Cook's first voyage, may also have played a role. He had listened to Polynesian music during his visit, was himself musical, and planned to take his own group of musicians to Polynesia when he returned there with Cook. After

quarrelling with Cook, Banks withdrew from the second voyage and was replaced by the Forsters.

62. See, for example, accounts of music in earlier Pacific voyaging by Behrens, *Reise durch die Süd-Länder,* 88; and Bougainville, *Voyage round the World,* 225, quoted in Whaples, "Exoticism in Dramatic Music," 389–90.

63. Marine drummer, joined at Plymouth. See Beaglehole, ed., *Journals of Captain James Cook,* vol. 1, 598.

64. Roger, *Command of the Ocean,* 503–505.

65. Between January and May 1772, the Admiralty Secretary corresponded with the Plymouth and Chatham marine divisions about finding suitable musicians. The Chatham division was unable to supply a bagpiper but suggested that a drummer and violinist, Philip Brotherson, could be instructed on the fife and "use his utmost Diligence in perfecting himself on the said instrument," according to two letters from Admiralty Secretary to Colonel Smith, Chatham, dated Jan. 25, 1772; and a letter from Admiralty Secretary to Colonel Bell, Plymouth, dated Jan. 25, 1772. For a fuller discussion of this, see Agnew, " 'Scots Orpheus' in the South Seas," and *Music Afloat.*

66. Letter from Admiralty Secretary to Captain Cook, Long Reach, dated May 9, 1772 (ADM 2/1166). The *Resolution*'s monthly book lists the marines Phil. Brotherson, drummer, and Archibald McVicar as its musicians (ADM 36/7672, Public Record Office, Kew, London).

67. Sahlins proposes that in gift economies the relationship between social forms and appropriate acts is reversible: It is not just social forms that give rise to certain kinds of acts but customary kinds of acts that generate social forms. "The cultural form (or social morphology) can be produced the other way round: the act creating an appropriate relation, performatively, just as in certain famous speech acts: 'I now pronounce you man and wife.' " Sahlins, *Islands of History,* xi.

68. Beaglehole, ed., *Journals of Captain James Cook,* vol. 1, clxvii–clxx.

69. Ibid., vol. 2, 116–18.

70. See Sahlins's tripartite economic model in *Stone Age Economics,* 193–94; and for a lengthier discussion of these cross-cultural exchanges, see Agnew, "Exchange Strategies on Cook's Second Voyage," 1–33.

71. See, for example, Georg Forster's enthusiastic appraisal of Tahitians who gave something "as a friend and without any lucrative view." Forster, *Voyage round the World,* vol. 1, 184.

72. Ibid., 171; and see Sparrman, *Voyage round the World,* 55–56.

73. Forster, *Voyage round the World,* vol. 1, 181.

74. Beaglehole, ed., *Journals of Captain James Cook,* vol. 2, 208.

75. Forster, *Voyage round the World,* vol. 1, 195.

76. Ibid., 207.

77. On the instrument's associations, see Cocks, Baines, and Cannon, "Bagpipes," 100; and Baines, "Bagpipes," 116; and on the more positive view that emerged in relation to the invention of a Highland tradition, see Trevor-Roper, "Highland Tradition of Scotland," 18.

78. See Pennant, *Tour in Scotland and Voyage to the Hebrides,* 166; and Pennant, *Tour in Scotland 1769,* 167–68. Pennant was interested in the origins and diffusion of the bagpipes and wrote to Charles Burney for information (Burney, *Letters,* 158n11).

79. Macpherson, *Works of Ossian,* vol. 1, 6; and Tytler, "Ueber die alten Schottischen Balladen," 188.

80. Rochlitz, "Fragen eines Layen," 126.

81. Agnew, "Bagpipes in the Eighteenth-century Pacific," 21.

82. In her discussion of pre-Christian performance practices in the Society Islands, Stillman concludes that the combination of vocal and flute melodies did not constitute polyphony. Stillman, "Himene Tahiti," 360; see also McLean, *Weavers of Song.*

83. Ovid, *Metamorphoses,* 220–21. Burney drew on the Midas story for a parody of his rival in music history, John Hawkins. See "Trial of Midas the Second."

84. Burney, *General History,* vol. 1, 267.

85. Forster, *Voyage round the World,* vol. 1, 162, 171.

86. Ibid., 232–33.

87. This would not stop Sandwich from complaining that the junior Burney had transcribed too little, nor from changing his evaluation: James had a "good ear" became James had a "tolerable" knowledge of music. Montagu, Earl of Sandwich, Rough draft.

88. Forster, *Voyage round the World,* vol. 1, 233.

89. Ibid., 162.

90. Ibid., 232.

91. Beaglehole, ed., *Journals of Captain James Cook,* vol. 1, 285.

92. "Aki, mate aue Tupaia!" Forster, *Voyage round the World,* vol. 2, 616, 828n16.

93. Ibid., 615.

94. Forster senior also compared Tahitian music unfavorably with that of other Pacific Islanders. Forster, *Observations Made during a Voyage,* 468.

95. See Beaglehole, ed., Endeavour *Journal of Joseph Banks,* vol. 1, 350; vol. 2, 30.

96. Beaglehole, ed., *Journals of Captain James Cook,* vol. 1, clxxxvii–clxxxviii.

97. Jean Jacques Rousseau in Grassineau, *Musical Dictionary,* 21.

98. Forkel, for example, claimed that the transcription put the matter "beyond doubt." [Forkel], "Etwas von der Musik," 318. In a discussion of eighteenth-century transcriptions of non-Western music, Radano argues that transcriptions homogenized foreign aural productions and divorced them from the bodies of their performers and listeners, thereby performing a "colonialist function." See Radano, *Lying Up a Nation,* 190.

99. This is not to make value judgments about the superiority of Maori over Ta- hitian music but merely to report the perception that polyphonic music was perceived as more complex and hence more advanced than monophonic music.

100. See, for example, [King], "Merkwürdige Vorfälle," 171–72.

101. Beaglehole, ed., *Journals of Captain James Cook,* vol. 3, part 1, 109.

102. William Anderson, "Journal of a Voyage," vol. 3, part 2, 897–99; vol. 3, part 1, 109.

103. Ibid., vol. 3, part 1, 109.

104. Ibid., 110.

105. On music and dance in Tonga during the early contact period, see Ferdon, *Early Tonga as the Explorers Saw It,* 192–204.

106. Anderson was among the observers who recognized that the Tongans were displaying their own "ne plus ultra" (Anderson, "Journal of a Voyage," 897). For an- other account of this episode, see Samwell, "Some Account of a Voyage," vol. 3, part 2, 1016–21.

107. Zug, ed., *Last Voyage of Captain Cook*, 22–23.

108. According to a beachcomber, William Mariner, who later spent four years in Tonga, the chiefs had planned to kill Cook and his men during one of these night dances, but Finau called the plot off when the chiefs could not agree on the precise timing for the murder. See Thomas, *Cook: Extraordinary Voyages*, 317–18; Martin, *Account of the Natives;* and Salmond, *Trial of the Cannibal Dog*, 332–33.

109. [Klockenbring], "Nachlese zu dem Auszuge," 1614.

110. [Ellis], "Cooks dritte und letzte Entdeckungsreise," 969–70.

111. [Klockenbring], "Nachlese zu dem Auszuge," 1608.

112. "Obgleich die Neuseeländer ungemein viel härter, kriegerischer und heftiger von Leidenschaften sind, als die Bewohner der näher nach dem Aequator zu, unter mildern Himmelsstrichen belegenen Inseln: so übertrifft doch ihre Musik an Mannigfaltigkeit und Sanftheit der Töne, die Musik auf Taheite und Anamoka gar sehr." Klockenbring, "Etwas über die Musik," 93.

113. Ibid., 91.

114. Ibid., 91–92.

115. Ibid., 92.

116. Ibid., 95–96.

117. "Bey diesem allen aber, würde es nun ein wahres Wunderwerk seyn, auf Neuseeland Proben einer Nationalmusik zu finden, die gerade aus den Händen der Natur, und noch nicht in die Hände der Kunst gekommen, deren Intervallensystem aber dennoch mit dem, welches erst nach dem dreyzehnten Jahrhundert, als die altgriechischen Moden aussser Gebrauch zu kommen anfiengen, in Europa allmählich eingeführt wurde, so genau zusammen treffen sollte, als es hier in Noten Gesetzt worden, indem in den obigen Proben, das Verhältniß der Töne gegen einander, unserm neuern, gerade gleich ist." Ibid., 96–97.

118. Ibid.

119. Ibid., 97–98.

120. "Höchst wunderbar wäre es noch außer diesem, wenn bey dem noch so sehr uncultivirten Neuseeländer, eben dieselbe Tonmaaße, wie sie bey uns dermalen nach den genauesten Messungen des Monochords, so weit sie dem Ohre perceptibel sind, angetroffen werden sollte; und, wie wir gleich sehen werden, bey dem weit gebildetern und feinern Taheitier, ganz und gar nicht." Ibid., 98–99.

121. "[D]ass uns ihre Musik und ihnen die unsrige unverständlich, beschwerlich, und ohne alle Wirkung ist." Ibid., 96.

122. "Hier ist die Musik, der Natur noch eben so am nächsten, als es die Sitten und Lebensart der Nation sind; und deswegen kann sie auf uns eben so wenig einen besonders angenehmen Eindruck machen, als es uns im Ganzen genommen und im Ernst behagen würde, alle unser bisgen Kenntniß im Lethe zu ertränken, und alle unsere vielen Bedürfnisse mit der taheitischen Genügsamkeit zu vertauschen. Auch physicalisch kann jene Musik auf uns keinen Eindruck machen. Unser Ohr ist an jene Tonverhältnisse nicht gewöhnt, und zu stumpf sie bis zur Empfindung, zu unterscheiden. Forster und Cook berichten an mehreren Orten, wie unglaublich fein und scharf alle Sinne dieser nur noch wenig gebildeten Nation sind; und dass wir aufgeklärten Europäer dagegen als halb blind und taub angesehen werden können." Ibid., 100.

123. Pauw, *Philosophical Dissertations on the Greeks*, vol. 2, 82–83.

124. Klockenbring, "Etwas über die Musik," 103.

125. Forster, *Voyage round the World,* vol. 1, 168; Diderot, "Supplement to Bougainville's 'Voyage,' " 187; and Churchill, *Gotham: A Poem,* 4.

126. [Klockenbring], "Nachlese zu dem Auszuge," 1601–1602.

127. Anon., "Aufsätze, verschiedenen Inhalts," 86.

128. [Forkel], "Etwas von der Musik," 316; and B., "Article VII. Review of *A Voyage,*" 465–66.

129. This point would be made by an unidentified redactor of a travelogue by the assistant surgeon on Cook's third voyage, William Ellis ("Cooks dritte und letzte Entdeckungsreise," 965–66).

130. "Wir müssen noch als seine zwote musikalische Seltenheit anführen, was dem Hrn. Forster bey seinem dritten Besuch in Neu-Seeland aufgestoßen ist. Es muß seltsam scheinen, dass Harmonie, oder mehrstimmige Musik, die, wie man jetzt allgemein glaubt, und aus guten Gründen glauben kann, nicht einmal den erfinderischen und feinen Griechen bekannt gewesen ist, bey gewissen von der übrigen Welt ganz abgesonderten Barbaren gefunden werden sollte." [Forkel], "Etwas von der Musik," 317–18. This is close to what appeared in the *Monthly Review:* "It may seem strange that *harmony,* or music in parts, which is now generally acknowledged not to have been known even to the ingenious and refined Greeks, should be found in familiar use with certain barbarians, secluded from the rest of the world in the bosom of the Southern Ocean." B., "Article VII. Review of *A Voyage,*" 465–66.

131. "Es ist wahr, der Neu-Seeländische Contrapunkt besteht bloß aus einer immerwährenden Folge von untermischten großen und kleinen Terzen. Aber auch schon dieses wenige zeigt gewissermaßen eine Verfeinerung der Musik an, und um so viel mehr, wenn wir es als ein Produkt eines Haufens von hungrigen und elenden Cannibalen ansehen." [Forkel], "Etwas von der Musik," 319; see also the *Monthly Review* article by B., "Article VII. Review of *A Voyage,*" 466.

132. "Hr. Forster halt dafür, es sey Pathos und Ausdruck in den Worten und in der Musik dieses kleinen Stücks. Dem sey inzwischen wie ihm wolle, und wenn gleich unsere Ohren, welche diese unsere antarctische Componisten auf die zwo letzten Noten ihres Tupayischen Trauerliedes zu legen vermeynt haben, nicht für ächte Grazie anerkennen, oder gar nicht für geschickt halten sollten, schmerzvolle Leidenschaften glücklich auszudrücken; so ist es doch eine Grazie, oder musikalische Verfeinerung, die selbst bey uns von Sängern und Instrumentisten seit kurzem eingeführt worden ist. Mit wie viel Recht oder Unrecht, müssen wir hier unentschieden lassen." [Forkel], "Etwas von der Musik," 319–20; and see B., "Article VII. Review of *A Voyage,*" 466.

133. Koch, "Kurzer Abriß der Geschichte der Tonkunst," 122, 127.

134. Ibid., 130–31.

135. Ibid., 126, 129, 133. Koch did not include musical examples from any other contemporaneous peoples but cited travelogues and missionary reports for further reference.

136. Ibid., 129, 132.

137. Burney, for instance, adopted a similar historiographical approach to the study of ancient Egyptian music by drawing on James Bruce's Abyssinian travelogue as a source of evidence for the reconstruction of the musical past.

138. Koch, "Kurzer Abriß der Geschichte der Tonkunst," 132.

139. Heinrich Christoph Koch, *Musikalisches Lexikon,* 1466.

140. Burney, letter to Lord Sandwich, Feb. 11, 1784.

141. Ibid.

142. Montagu, Earl of Sandwich, Rough draft; see also McLean, *Weavers of Song,* 142.

143. Anon., "Article 5. Account of a Musical Instrument," 29; and see Steele, "Account of a Musical Instrument," 67–71; and Steele's "Remarks on a Larger System of Reed Pipes," 72–78.

144. Burney, letter to Lord Sandwich, Feb. 11, 1784.

145. Cook and King, *Voyage to the Pacific Ocean,* vol. 3, 144.

146. Montagu, Earl of Sandwich, Rough draft. Strikethrough in original; emphasis added.

147. Ibid.

148. Forster, *Voyage round the World,* vol. 2, 616.

149. "Der Rhythmus, das einzige musikalische Urelement in der Natur, ist auch das erste, so im Menschen erwacht, im Kinde, im Wilden am frühsten sich entwickelt. Wenn die Südsee-Insulaner mit Metallstücken und Holzstäben rhythmisch klappern und dazu ein unfaßliches Geheul ausstoßen, so ist das *natürliche* Musik, denn es ist eben *keine Musik.* Was wir aber einen Tiroler Bauer singen hören, zu welchem anscheinend keine Spur von Kunst gedrungen, ist durchaus *künstliche* Musik." Hanslick, *Vom musikalisch-Schönen,* 86–87. I am grateful to Sanna Pederson for pointing out this reference.

150. "Jedenfalls ist es interessant, diesem mächtigen Factor der Tonkunst selbst hier schon zu begegnen." He adds, "dieses in Terzen erklingende Zapfenstreichstückchen sind in ihrer Art eine Merkwürdigkeit, weil die Naturmenschen wie im Traume gefunden haben, was der ganzen antiken Welt—und bis in's 10. Jahrhundert auch der christlichen verborgen blieb—Harmonie des Gesanges: wenn auch nur gleichsam die ersten Keime davon." Ambros, "Die Musik bei den Naturvölkern," 545.

151. It was the very "accidental" character of the discovery that Sandwich queried: Polyphony could be attained only "by dint of study and knowledge of the system and theory upon which musical composition is founded." Cook and King, *Voyage to the Pacific Ocean,* 143.

152. Rousseau, quoted in the entry on "Harmonie" in Sulzer, *Allgemeine Theorie der schönen Künste;* and for more recent views that polyphony is an exclusively European invention ("eine europäische Sonderentwicklung"), see Krickeberg, "Einflüsse außer-europäischer Musik auf Europa," 447–49.

153. Homer, *Odyssey,* 135.

154. Ibid., 131–32.

155. The difficulty in reconciling apparently contradictory indices is evident in Forster, *Voyage round the World,* vol. 1, 438–39n28. For a further discussion, see Thomas, "Liberty and License: New Zealand Societies in Cook Voyage Anthropology," in *In Oceania,* 71–92.

156. Diffusionism was a key component of comparative musicology and lived on in the *Kulturkreislehre* (theory of cultural circles) that stamped much German ethnological thinking until after the Second World War. For discussion of diffusionism in relation to ethnomusicology, see Agnew, "Colonialist Beginnings of Comparative Musicology."

157. In his redaction of Niebuhr's travelogue, Forkel claimed that "Das Schreyen der egyptischen Tänzerinnen wird auch kein Europäer schön finden. Hingegen gefällt unsere

Musik den Türken und Arabern eben so wenig." [Forkel], "Auszug aus Carsten Niebuhrs Reisebeschreibung," 307.

158. Boethius, *Fundamentals of Music,* 3.

159. For a more affirmative reading of this material, see Irving, "Pacific in the Minds and Music," 205–29.

160. Burney, *General History,* vol. 1, 160.

161. Ibid., 163.

162. Michaelis, "Ueber die Musik," 509–30. My argument here owes a debt to Gramit, *Cultivating Music,* 38–41.

163. "So könnte das weniger Hinreissende, weniger Gewaltsame, in dem Wesen der Kunst liegen? Vielleicht auch in dem Wesen menschlicher Kultur? Wird vielleicht der Gebildete überhaupt weniger ganz hingerissen—theils schon aus physischen, von selbst einleuchtenden Ursachen, mehr aber, weil bey allem, was in ihm vorgeht—weil ganz besonders durch die Kunst, alle Theile seines Wesens beschäftiget werden, und nicht, wie bey dem Ungebildeten, blos Sinnlichkeit?" See Rochlitz, "Fragen eines Layen," 124, 146–47.

164. Schmidt, "An die Bewohner der Pelew-Inseln," 178–82.

Chapter Three

1. Ovid, *Metamorphoses,* 199, 216.

2. Marcus Wood, "Satire," 689.

3. "Che farò" was popular enough to be published in Domenico Corri, *A Select collection.* Burney, who seemed to share a high opinion of the "simple and ballad-like air," commented on its delivery by the castrato Gaetano Guadagni. Burney, *General History of Music,* vol. 2, 877. For further examples of the aria's reception, see Hanslick, *Vom musikalisch-Schönen,* 38–40; and Howard, *Gluck,* 57–61.

4. Jeremy Barlow suggests that there was something peculiarly English about the burlesquing of music, see his *The Enraged Musician,* 105.

5. See Barlow, *Enraged Musician,* which draws attention to many little-known sources.

6. Boswell, *Life of Johnson,* 874.

7. As I have pointed out in previous chapters, this is not an entirely unanimous view. See, for example, Morrow, *German Music Criticism.*

8. James Thompson, *Models of Value,* 3.

9. On the composition of the socially exclusive King's Theatre audience, see Petty, *Italian Opera in London 1760–1800,* 49–50; and Price, Milhous, and Hume, *Italian Opera in Late Eighteenth-century London,* vol. 1, 12; see also Moody, *Illegitimate Theatre in London, 1770–1840,* 10–33; and on the London playhouses and their audiences, see Fiske, *English Theatre Music,* 252–59.

10. On the King's Theatre as an important destination for those "bidding for a place in polite society," see Cowgill, " 'Wise Men from the East,' " 42.

11. On theaters and concert rooms as public sphere, see Weber, "Musical Culture and the Capital City," 81–85; and on patronage, Woodfield, *Salomon and the Burneys.*

12. On travel as a mobile site of knowledge production with "multiple nodes," see Liebersohn, *Travelers' World,* 8.

13. Stallybrass and White, *Politics and Poetics of Transgression,* 2–5; see also Bakhtin, *Rabelais and His World,* 437; and Kristeva, *Powers of Horror.*

14. Eagleton, *Walter Benjamin,* 48; quoted in Stallybrass and White, *Politics and Poetics,* 13.

15. Babcock, *Reversible World,* 32; quoted in Stallybrass and White, *Politics and Poetics,* 20.

16. Compare this with the notion of "triangulation" in, for example, Sieg, "Ethnic Drag and National Identity," 303.

17. For a discussion of Western musical borrowing, see Born and Hesmondhalgh, "Introduction," in *Western Music and Its Others,* 8; also see the helpful discussions of exoticism in Ralph P. Locke, "Reflections on Orientalism," 49–73; and Whaples, "Early Exoticism Revisited."

18. See, for example, Kristeva, *Powers of Horror.*

19. Peter Pindar [John Wolcot], *Complimentary Epistle,* 12, 17. See also the dual parody of Samuel Johnson's account of Scotland and Arthur Young's account of Ireland, where the project of scientific travel fails utterly: Couper, *Tourifications of Malachi Meldrum,* vol. 1, 108–10. For a discussion of Couper, see Trumpener, *Bardic Nationalism,* 92–93.

20. Goodwin, "Richard Paul Jodrell."

21. D'Arblay, *Memoirs of Doctor Burney,* vol. 1, 300.

22. Other parodies of Bruce include Anon., *Sequel to the Adventures of Baron Munchausen.* Writing in the 1820s, Cradock thought that doubt about Bruce's tale had since "sunk into acquiescence of its truth." Cradock, *Literary and Miscellaneous Memoirs,* vol. 4, 192. For a more recent recuperation of the explorer, see Moorefield, "James Bruce," 493–514.

23. Jodrell, *Widow and No Widow,* 35–36.

24. Darnton, *Great Cat Massacre,* 78.

25. Beattie, "Essay on Laughter and Ludicrous Composition," 346.

26. Jodrell, *Widow and No Widow,* 38.

27. For a discussion of the pantomime, see McCalman, "Spectacles of Knowledge," 11. On the music, see Fiske, "Covent Garden Pantomime," 574–76; and Agnew, "The Pantomime, 'Omai.'" On Shield, see Troost, "William Shield."

28. Forster, *Voyage round the World,* 361–63.

29. Anon., "Short Account of the new Pantomime," 621.

30. See McLean, "Nafa," vol. 2, 738–39; see also Beaglehole, *Journals of Captain James Cook,* vol. 2, 804; and Whaples, "Exoticism in Dramatic Music," 407–10. See also O'Keeffe, "A Short Account of the New Pantomime."

31. *Philosophical Transactions* 65 (1775): 28–29; quoted in McCormick, *Omai: Pacific Envoy,* 160.

32. See Hunter, "*Alla Turca* Style," 48–49.

33. Barthes, "Reality Effect," 141–48.

34. O'Quinn argues that theatrical productions in the 1770s and 1780s "commented on but also orchestrated national reactions to the recalibration of imperial sovereignty in the late eighteenth century." *Omai* specifically "marks a signal transition in middle-class politics from the shaming of the aristocracy to the racialization of the lower orders," and the pantomime's ethnographic realism is what authorizes this "recalibration of racial and class fantasy." O'Quinn, *Staging Governance,* 1, 114. For an analysis of sex and race in the pantomime, see Wilson, *Island Race,* 63–68.

35. In *Mr. Bligh's Bad Language,* 274, Dening points out that the British were engaged in a struggle with the Spanish over Gibraltar and would have had reason to boo Don Struttolando for that reason.

36. For a comparison of Spanish and British encounter practices, see Agnew, "Exchange Strategies on Cook's Second Voyage," 163–96; see also Archer, "Spanish Reaction to Cook's Third Voyage," 99–119.

37. For a discussion of these possession ceremonies, see Dening, *Mr. Bligh's Bad Language,* 200.

38. This would support David Mayer's argument about the imperialist thrust of the early nineteenth-century pantomime, an argument made in *Harlequin in His Element,* 139. O'Quinn argues, on the other hand, that the lower orders are racialized in the pantomime (see note 34, this chapter).

39. See Beer, "Travelling the Other Way."

40. On Giardini's English career, see McVeigh, "Felice Giardini."

41. Charles Burney, "Letter to Thomas Twining, 13 July 1774," in *Letters of Dr. Charles* Burney, vol. 1, 170.

42. Charles Burney, "Sketch of a Plan for a Public Music-School" (1774), in Osborn Collection, Yale University. One of the two existing copies of Burney's "Sketch" appears in Kassler, "Burney's Sketch," 228.

43. On the Royal Academy of Music, see Rainbow and Kemp, "London. Educational Institutions: Conservatories."

44. Anon., "Historical Chronicle, September 27," 490. In "Dr. Burney, 'Joel Collier' and Sabrina," in Wellek and Ribeiro, eds., *Evidence in Literary Scholarship,* 288n18, Roger Lonsdale cites the case in relation to Bicknell's parody and draws an implicit comparison with Burney and Giardini, who had proposed to pay themselves as directors of the music school. Kassler disagrees, pointing out that their salaries were commensurate with their responsibilities and workload. See "Burney's Sketch," 234n37.

45. Arnold, "Conservatories: The Role of the Conservatory." On music at the Foundling Hospital, see Nichols and Wray, *History of the Foundling Hospital,* 233–46; and on music's declining role in eighteenth-century philanthropy and the underlying economic and social reasons for this decline, see McVeigh, "Music and Lock Hospital," 235–37.

46. Charles Burney, *Dr. Burney's Musical Tours,* vol. 1, 112.

47. For a discussion of the discourse on genius, nature, and cultivation, see Kerstin Barndt, "'Mein Dasein ward unvermerkt,'" 169.

48. Burney, *Dr. Burney's Musical Tours,* vol. 2, 131.

49. Charles Burney, "Account of an Infant Musician," 186; see also d'Arblay, *Memoirs of Doctor Burney,* vol. 2, 206.

50. Burney, "Letter to Felice de Giardini, 21 June 1772," in *Letters,* 116.

51. Burney, *Dr. Burney's Musical Tours,* vol. 2, 52–54, 150–52.

52. Nugent, *Grand Tour,* vol. 2; cited in Burney, *Dr. Burney's Musical Tours,* vol. 2, 134.

53. Howard, *Gluck,* 4.

54. Wolf, "Johann Wenzel Anton [. . .] Stamitz."

55. Burney, *Dr. Burney's Musical Tours,* vol. 2, 132–33.

56. Ibid., 131. Original emphasis.

57. This statement did not cohere with Burney's secondhand dismissal of Mozart in the German travelogue. Burney, "Account of an Infant Musician," 203–206.

58. This point has been made in relation to, for example, John Peter Salomon, the German music impresario in London, in, for example, Kassler, "Burney's Sketch," 219n20, and Woodfield, *Salomon and the Burneys,* 4.

59. Grant, *Dr. Burney as Critic and Historian of Music,* 93.

60. Burney, *General History of Music,* vol. 2, 201, 456, 963.

61. Burney, "Sketch of a Plan for a Public Music-School"; quoted in Kassler, "Burney's Sketch," 228.

62. Burney made the point in reference to the Spartans, who encouraged "Music and Poetry in *other countries,* by being at the expense of tempting such strangers as had cultivated those arts with the most success, to come and practice them in their *own.*" Burney, *General History of Music,* vol. 2, 305nq.

63. D'Arblay, *Memoirs of Doctor Burney,* vol. 1, 234.

64. Burney, "Sketch"; quoted in Kassler, "Burney's Sketch," 217.

65. Ibid., 229.

66. Ibid.

67. Ibid.

68. Baretti, *Account of the Manners and Customs of Italy,* vol. 1, 146–47.

69. For a bibliography of early eighteenth-century sources, see Cervantes, "Tuneful Monsters."

70. André points out in *Voicing Gender,* 27–30, that castration resulted in hypogonadism, which elongated the limbs and inhibited the development of certain secondary sex characteristics and that this is exaggerated in the depiction of Farinelli, Cuzzoni, Senesino, and Berenstadt. For an account of Senesino and Cuzzoni, see Burney, *Dr. Burney's Musical Tours,* vol. 2, 188, 192–93.

71. Marvel, "An Essay upon the Unfortunate Charms"; quoted in Petty, *Italian Opera in London,* 4.

72. Wilkes, *General View of the Stage,* 69–70; quoted in Petty, *Italian Opera in London,* 5. According to Mollie Sands in "Music as a Profession," 91, English musicians were generally better paid than those on the Continent, and this was pointed out by German music critic Mattheson as early as 1713.

73. On the salaries of opera singers, see Petty, *Italian Opera in London,* 8–10; and on the disparity between the social standing of musicians and their pecuniary rewards, see Sands, "Music as a Profession," 90–92.

74. Plato, *Republic,* 410a–412b; 423d–425a; in Barker, ed., *Greek Musical Writings,* vol. 1, 136–40.

75. Anon., "Some Account of the Life and Writings of Dr. Charles Burney," 164.

76. D'Arblay, *Memoirs of Doctor Burney,* vol. 2, 237.

77. Burney, "Sketch of a Plan for a Public Music-School," in Kassler, "Burney's Sketch," 229.

78. Besides being an important abolitionist and author of *Sandford and Merton,* an influential pedagogical novel (1783, 1786, 1789), Thomas Day (1748–1789) collaborated with Bicknell and worked for the revolutionary cause. See Rowland, "Thomas Day."

79. *Public Advertiser,* Aug. 18, 1774. The work was attributed to Joseph [Joel] Collier.

80. Cradock, *Literary and Miscellaneous Memoirs*, 168; cited in Lonsdale, *Dr. Charles Burney*, 155; see also Twining's letter to Burney, Sept. 17, 1774.

81. Sandwich had been satirized in a poem by Charles Churchill, "The Candidate" (1764). For references to scandal surrounding Sandwich, see Brewer, *Sentimental Murder.*

82. On this earlier fracas, see Price, Milhous, and Hume, *Impresario's Ten Commandments.* Charles Burney was critical of Giardini and described him as wanting in "benevolence and rectitude of heart" in "Felice Giardini." Burney made no mention of the Foundling Hospital here, although in his *Memoirs of Dr. Charles Burney*, 196–97, Burney blamed Giardini personally for the failure of the plan.

83. Collyer [John Bicknell], "Scientific Account of the Musical Festival," 183–93; and Collyer [John Bicknell], "Musical Sketches," 109–14. These articles, published in Hamburg, have received no mention in the critical literature on Burney and Bicknell, and the source of their first appearance in Britain is unclear.

84. According to Smith, Bicknell's literary estate conclusively proved authorship of the parody. John Thomas Smith, *Nollekens and His Times*, vol. 1, 196–97.

85. The final (1818) edition is abridged, and the parody has been adapted to a new subject, the piano teacher, John Bernard Logier (1777–1846). See Lonsdale, "Dr. Burney, 'Joel Collier,' and Sabrina," 291. Lonsdale has supplied many of the bibliographical references dealt with in my discussion of Bicknell and the parody.

86. For references to Bicknell, see Anon., "Obituary for John Bicknell," 296; Boswell, *Life of Johnson*, 224; and Anon., "Biographical Anecdotes of George Steevens, Esq.," 180. Publishing in 1828, Cradock said that the "real author had been announced," without, however, specifying the name. Cradock, *Literary and Miscellaneous Memoirs*, vol. 4, 168.

87. Jodrell, *Widow and No Widow*, ix.

88. Anon., "Review of Joel Collier's Musical Travels," 499–500.

89. Twining, letter to Charles Burney, Sept. 17, 1774; quoted in Burney, *Letters of Dr. Charles Burney*, vol. 1, 189n4.

90. Bewley, "Review of Joel Collier's Musical Travels," 242. For a fuller treatment of the reception, see Lonsdale, "Dr. Burney, 'Joel Collier' and Sabrina," 281–84.

91. See, for example, a 1774 letter from the imperial ambassador to Berlin, Gottfried van Swieten, to James Harris Jr., which requested the purchase of books and scores, including works by Burney and "the amusing" Bicknell. Burrows and Dunhill, *Music and Theatre in Handel's World*, 769.

92. [Bicknell], *Musical Travels through England*, 3.

93. Ibid.

94. Charles Burney, *Essay towards a History of the Principal Comets.*

95. [Bicknell], *Musical Travels through England*, 5.

96. For an explanation of celestial harmony, see Lippman, *History of Western Musical Aesthetics*, 5–8.

97. [Bicknell], *Musical Travels through England*, 5.

98. Borsay, "Concert Topography and Provincial Towns," 19–20, 33.

99. [Bicknell], *Musical Travels through England*, 22.

100. On this wind-string instrument, see Rycroft, "Gora."

101. [Bicknell], *Musical Travels through England*, 23.

102. Ibid., 24.

103. Their poem "The Dying Negro" was a response to the Mansfield judgment of 1772, which outlawed the forcible removal of slaves from Britain but not the slave trade itself. Slavery would not be outlawed until 1807 with the Abolition of the Slave Trade Act.

104. Odell, "Charivari."

105. Ingram, "Ridings, Rough Music, and Mocking Rhymes," 168–69.

106. Thompson, "Rough Music," 478. My analysis is indebted to Thompson, Ingram, and Barlow's chapter on rough music in *The Enraged Musician.*

107. Although the skimmington was an "extralegal" custom, during the early modern period, it seems to have been practiced with quasi-official sanction. Ingram thus concludes that the practice represented "no great challenge to the existing political, social and moral structure." Ingram, "Ridings, Rough Music, and Mocking Rhymes," 192.

108. For a discussion of Cecilian odes in Restoration England, see Mellers, "Heroism of Henry Purcell," 33; and on Neoplatonist ideas in the famous painting of the saint, see Mossakowski, "Raphael's 'St. Cecilia,' " 1–26.

109. See, for example, Handel's 1736 setting of Dryden's "Ode for St. Cecilia's Day." Thornton's inversion is taken up again in a parodic poem by Churchill. Charles Churchill, "Gotham: A Poem," 7–8. McKillop cites a number of similar odes and points out that rough and burlesque music were combined with literary satire. McKillop, "Bonnell Thornton's Burlesque Ode," 322.

110. Thornton, "Ode," 8.

111. Bicknell may have been aware of Burney's setting of Thornton's "Ode" to music, which was performed at Ranelagh some time around 1758. For Burney's account of the event and evidence as to its dating, see Burney, *Memoirs,* 130–31.

112. [Bicknell], *Musical Travels through England,* 35.

113. On the cross-class audience for late eighteenth-century ballads, see Perry, "Anna Gordon Brown's Ballads."

114. [Chesterfield and Waller], *Case of the Hanover Forces,* 13.

115. [Bicknell], *Musical Travels through England,* 9.

116. Sterne, *Life and Opinions of Tristram Shandy,* 365.

117. Reichardt, "Fingerzeige," 46; and Forkel, "Recensionen theoretischer Werke," 119.

118. Bicknell was certainly regarded as an opportunist by reviewers like Bewley. See Bewley, "Review of Joel Collier's Musical Travels," 242. There is, on the other hand, some indication that Bicknell intended his parody as a serious piece of criticism. Later editions of *Musical Travels* included a biting, if veiled, response to Bewley and a defense of the critic's responsibility. [Bicknell], *Musical Travels through England,* 31.

119. William Wordsworth, cited in Wood, "Satire," 690.

120. [Bicknell], *Musical Travels through England,* 16.

121. Ibid., 10. Bicknell particularly disapproved of Handel. He also authored journal articles under the pseudonym of Joel Collier, in which Handel (and Burney's initiative to revive Handel) are lampooned. See [Bicknell], "Musical Sketches" and "Scientific Account of the Musical Festival."

122. See, for example, Burney's investigation of tarantism in Italy, which showed that "not only the cure but the malady itself" was a fraud. Burney, *Dr. Burney's Musical Tours,* vol. 1, 255. The castrato Farinelli was reputed to have cured the melancholy Philip

V, king of Spain, by singing Hasse arias. See Burney, *General History of Music,* vol. 2, 815; and Burney, "Farinelli."

123. [Bicknell], *Musical Travels through England,* 11.

124. Ibid.

125. See, for example, the doubts raised by Samuel Johnson's physician, Richard Brocklesby, in *Reflections on Antient and Modern Musick,* 58–59.

126. For examples of paid sexual transactions, see Giacomo Casanova, *History of My Life,* vol. 2, 6–10.

127. For an account, see Gouk, ed. *Musical Healing in Cultural Contexts.*

128. See, for example, Kästner, "Betrachtungen über die alte und neue Musik, 16–37; and Marpurg, "Historie von einem durch Musik geheilten Tonkünstler," 396.

129. [Bicknell], *Musical Travels through England,* 7.

130. Ibid., 18.

131. See Rowland, "Thomas Day." According to Horace Walpole, the first legislation that prohibited animal cruelty passed sometime around 1760. Burney, *German Tour,* 112–13n1.

132. Anglo-German composer J. C. Pepusch apparently imitated these animal performances with a highly successful Pig Concert in Berlin, in which bassoons played the pig parts. Lichtenberg, *World of Hogarth,* 101.

133. As far as I am aware, the earliest depiction of the instrument was in Johann Theodor de Bry's *Emblemata Saecularia* (1596). For references to the instrument, see Richards, "Rhapsodies on a Cat-Piano," 700–36. References to several additional sources, including Athanasius Kircher, *Musurgia Universalis* (1650), and Gaspar Schott, *Magiae universalis Naturae et Artis* (1658), are to be found in Hankins, "Ocular Harpsichord of Louis-Betrand Castel." To this can be added Valentini, *Museum Museorum,* vol. 1, 505; and Christopher Smart's parody discussed later in this chapter.

134. Reil, *Rhapsodieen über die Anwendung,* 205.

135. Richards, "Rhapsodies on a Cat-Piano," 721n50. Lonsdale, on the other hand, mentions the tradition of the eighteenth-century animal concert, and Storck describes its use in 1753 processional celebrations for Saint Germain. Storck, *Musik und Musiker,* 223.

136. Smart, *Jubilate Agno,* 115–19.

137. Smart, "Letter from Mrs. Mary Midnight," 98–103. The final issue of the journal came out in 1753, but the journal was also adapted for the Haymarket Theatre and was said by Hester Piozzi to have been "wondrous droll." See Williamson, "Christopher Smart"; and on Smart's friendship with Burney, see Devlin, *Poor Kit Smart,* 116.

138. [Wiedemann], "[Anmerkungen zur Dichtung Fido]," 15.

139. "The present state of dissipation in the fashionable world." Anon., *Euterpe,* 5; see also Weber, "Musical Culture and the Capital City," 85.

140. Anon., *Gentleman's Magazine* 38 (1768): 217.

141. Woodfield has made sense of an otherwise highly topical satire. He points out that Frances Brooke was angry with Garrick for having declined one of her plays. In retaliation she published an anti-Garrick satire, *The Excursion* (1777). The response was Anon., "A Téte-à-Téte [*sic*] between the King of Quavers and the Heroine of Romance," and the pro-Garrick satire discussed earlier in this chapter. In Woodfield's view, the latter was directed at the opera managers rather than Italian opera per se. Woodfield, *Opera and*

Drama, 17, 166–81. Woodfield's argument does not, however, preclude the satire from being seen as *also* attacking Italian opera.

142. Anon., *Remarkable Trial,* 7–8.

143. Ibid., 9.

144. Ibid., 11.

145. Ibid., 147–48.

146. See Bergeron, "Castrato as History," 167–84; Mosse, *Image of Man,* 17; and Krimmer, "'Eviva il Coltello'?" 1553–59.

147. See, for example, Anon., *Euterpe,* 12.

148. Based on her analysis of two German examples—Heinse's *Hildegard von Hohenthal* (1795–1796) and Schiller's "Kastraten und Männer" (1782)—Krimmer claims that "the delegitimization of class hierarchy depended on the law-giving power of nature and on the potency of bourgeois masculinity," from which she concludes that, if this is so, then "social justice came at a price." Krimmer, "Eviva il Coltello," 1554.

149. Anon., *Remarkable Trial,* 8–9.

150. Cited in Burney, *General History of Music,* vol. 2, 800ni, 875.

151. Anon., *Remarkable Trial,* 10.

152. That Casanova's Bellino is ultimately revealed to be a woman—a castrato *en travesti*—does not change the fact that his ambiguous presentation only exaggerates his sexual appeal. Casanova, *History of My Life,* vol. 2, 31. Brydone tells of an actor playing the part of a cruel tyrant who was so moved by Farinelli's performance that he broke character and became utterly meek. This is taken as a sign of the bewitching powers of music. Brydone, *Tour through Sicily and Malta,* 361. For a discussion of the castrato's positive reception, see Heriot, *Castrati in Opera;* see also Cervantes, who draws attention to the fact that far more scholarly attention has been paid to sources that criticize castrati than to those that praise them. Cervantes, "Tuneful Monsters," 11.

153. Moore, *View of society and manners,* vol. 1, 290. Emphasis added.

154. See, for instance, Avison's interrogation of Handel and English music in *Reply to the Author,* 45; quoted in Weber, "Intellectual Origins of Musical Canon," 503. I am indebted to Jonathan Lamb for his insights into litotes.

155. Hence the complaint that opera was nothing more than "unmeaning and extravagant," an "aukward succession of unnatural sounds—*signifying nothing.*" Anon., *Euterpe,* 9–10.

156. At least not until Alan Bloom turned MTV into a vehicle for the moral and sexual corruption of contemporary youth in *The Closing of the American Mind,* 74–75; quoted in Leppert, "Music 'Pushed to the Edge of Existence,'" 96–97.

157. Lamb, *Preserving the Self,* 4–5.

158. Folk songs were supposed to reveal the people's mindset (*Denkart des Volks*). Herder, *Volkslieder, Übertragungen, Dichtungen,* vol. 3, 17, 24. Plutarch (or pseudo-Plutarch) was said to have believed that "the manners of any people are best denoted by the prevailing state of the Music of their country." Plutarch, "On Music," quoted in Anon., *Euterpe,* 2.

159. Gaier points out that the second collection did not categorize the songs according to origin (e.g., a Peruvian rain song appears between two songs from the *Edda*). Only later did Herder synthesize the anthropological with the national. This is not evident from the ethnologically informed collection *Stimmen der Völker in Liedern* (the

"Vulgata," 1807), which was compiled after his death by Caroline and Johannes von Müller. Herder, *Volkslieder, Übertragungen, Dichtungen,* 852.

160. For an account that emphasizes Herder's contribution to the invention of "world music," see Bohlman, *World Music,* 39.

161. Gilroy, *Black Atlantic,* ix–xi. There is an interesting adaptation of Gilroy's thesis in Middleton, "Musical Belongings," 60.

162. Compare this with the process of "transculturation" and the appropriation of the Chinese garden for the imagining of class in midcentury Britain in Batchelor, "Concealing the Bounds."

Chapter Four

1. Grant, *Dr. Burney as Critic and Historian,* 65, 93–94.

2. Burney, *Dr. Burney's Musical Tours,* vol. 2, 81, 100, 124, 219, 238. See also Burney, *General History of Music,* vol. 2, 96, 942–43, 958–60.

3. On Hasse, see Burney, *Dr. Burney's Musical Tours,* vol. 2, 83; and Burney's letter to Count Firmian, June 22, 1772, in Burney, *Letters of Dr. Charles Burney,* vol. 1, 119.

4. Burney, *Dr. Burney's Musical Tours in Europe,* vol. 1, xxvii.

5. For a partial list of these friends and acquaintances, see Scholes, *Great Dr. Burney,* xvi–xx.

6. Wackenroder, "Remarkable Musical Life," 1069.

7. Burney, *Dr. Burney's Musical Tours,* vol. 1, xxvi.

8. For an account of the shift in late eighteenth-century aesthetics from "passive effect (*Wirkung*) to what Wackenroder and Herder would characterize as reverent contemplation (*Andacht*)," see Bonds, "Idealism and the Aesthetics of Instrumental Music," 393.

9. Goehr, *Imaginary Museum of Musical Works,* 122; on the aesthetic break at the end of the eighteenth century, see also Hess, *Reconstituting the Body Politic,* 13–14.

10. The artistic work was described as "*in sich Vollendetes, das also in sich ein Ganze ausmacht, und mir um sein selbst willen* Vergnügen gewährt." Moritz, "Versuch einer Vereinigung," 3. Original emphasis.

11. On the view that "absolute music is an extramusical idea," see Chua, *Absolute Music,* 6. I share Matthew Riley's rejection of an epistemic break in his *Musical Listening in the German Enlightenment,* 3.

12. Forkel, "Recensionen theoretischer Werke," 131–35, 160.

13. Schubart, *Ideen zu einer Ästhetik der Tonkunst,* 45.

14. Hoffmann, "Beethoven's Instrumental Music (1813)," 1193.

15. For a catalogue of "prosaic" examples, see Bodmer, "Von denen Verwunderungs-würdigen Würkungen der Music," 69–70. Bonds rightly points out that idealist aesthetics did not attempt cause-and-effect explanations of the relationship between the work and the listener. Bonds, "Idealism and the Aesthetics of Instrumental Music," 407.

16. See, for example, Dahlhaus, *Die Idee der absoluten Musik,* 14–15; Puri, "Review," 495; and Bonds, "Idealism and the Aesthetics of Instrumental Music," 420.

17. Pederson, "A. B. Marx," 89; Gramit, *Cultivating Music,* 27–62; and Morrow, *German Music Criticism,* 46.

18. On Ebeling's insistence on the need to corroborate reports by travelers and indigenous informants, see also Doll, "American History," 482.

19. "Das was ich von der Musik der Holländer gehört habe, macht mir eben keine großen Begriffe von der Feinheit des Ohrs der Nation." Klockenbring adds that he is not referring to the taste of refined people, "sondern von der Musik der Nation, des großen Haufens." Klockenbring, "Schluß der Anmerkungen über Holland," col. 1481.

20. "Wenn das wahr ist, daß die Musik durch die Erschütterung der Nerven, auf die Seele würkt, und daß die Empfindung ihrer feinsten Schönheiten, eine sehr feine Organisation voraussetzt, so könnte man allenfalls aus diesen Sätzen beweisen, daß der Charakter der Holländer nicht musikalisch sey." Ibid., col. 1482.

21. Kant, *Critique of Judgment*, 5–6; and Schiller, *On the Aesthetic Education*, 9.

22. "Sonate, que me veux tu?" Morrow, *German Music Criticism*, 4–5.

23. Burney, "Chinese Music."

24. Polynesian music and dance forms did impact popular Western forms. On the subsequent dissemination of Polynesian music, see Barbara B. Smith, "Polynesia: Music."

25. For an account of late eighteenth- and early nineteenth-century performance discourse as the "merging" of the performer with the composer and the "collapsing of apparently intractable dualisms," including performer and listener, see Hunter, " 'To Play as if from the Soul of the Composer,' " 371–72.

26. For a reading of this under the perspective of "universal hegemony through rationalistic 'German' harmony," see Vazsonyi, "Hegemony through Harmony," 33–48.

27. On the polarization between musicology and ethnomusicology and the need to overcome this, see Wong, "Ethnomusicology and Difference."

Periodical Sources

Allgemeine Deutsche Bibliothek [Universal German Library]

Allgemeine Musikalische Zeitung [Universal Musical Journal]

Allgemeines Sachregister über die wichtigsten deutschen Zeit- und Wochenschriften [General Subject Index of the Most Important German Journals and Weeklies]

Der Arzt [The Doctor]

Berlinische Musikalische Zeitung [Berlin Musical Journal]

Bibliothek für Denker und Männer von Geschmak [Library for Thinkers and Men of Taste]

Bragur. Ein Litterarisches Magazin der Deutschen und Nordischen Vorzeit [Bragur. A Literary Magazine of the German and Northern Antiquity]

Chronologen. Ein periodisches Werk. [Chronologers. A Periodical Work]

Critica Musica

Deutsche Monatsschrift [German Monthly]

Deutschland [Germany]

The English Lyceum

The European Magazine

Freymüthige Nachrichten von neuen Büchern und anderen zur Gelahrtheit gehörigen Sachen [Candid Reports about New Books and Other Matters pertaining to Learnedness]

Gelehrte Beyträge zu den Braunschweigischen Anzeigen [Scholarly Contributions to the Braunschweig Announcements]

The Gentleman's Magazine and Historical Chronicle

Hamburgisches Magazin [Hamburg Magazine]

Hannoverisches Magazin [Hanoverian Magazine]

Historisch-kritische Beyträge zur Aufnahme der Musik [Historico-critical Contributions on the Reception of Music]

Historisch-poetische Gefangenschafften [Historico-poetic Captivities]

Journal der Tonkunst [Journal of the Tonal Arts]
Kritische Briefe über die Tonkunst [Critical Letters about the Tonal Arts]
The London Magazine
London Museum of Politics, Miscellanies, and Literature
Magazin der Musik [Magazine of Music]
The Midwife
The Monthly Review, or Literary Journal
Musikalisch-kritische Bibliothek [Music-critical Library]
Musikalische Bibliothek [Musical Library]
Musikalischer Almanach für Deutschland [Musical Almanack for Germany]
Musicalisches Kunstmagazin [Musical Art Magazine]
Neu-eröffnete musikalische Bibliothek [Newly Established Musical Library]
Neue Bibliothek der schönen Wissenschaften [New Library of the Fine Arts]
Studien für Tonkünstler und Musikfreunde [Studies for Musicians and Friends of Music]
Der Teutsche Merkur [The German Mercury]
Town and Country Magazine
Unterhaltungen [Conversations]
Der Wißbegierige, eine Wochenschrift [The Inquirer, a Weekly]
Wöchentliche Nachrichten und Anmerkungen die Musik betreffend [Weekly News and Notes concerning Music]

Archival Sources

RECORDS OF THE ADMIRALTY, NAVAL FORCES,
ROYAL MARINES, COAST GUARD, AND RELATED BODIES.
PUBLIC RECORD OFFICE, KEW

Admiralty Secretary to Colonel Bell, Plymouth, dated January 25, 1772. ADM 2/1166, Public Record Office, Kew.
Admiralty Secretary to Captain Cook, Long Reach, dated May 9, 1772. ADM 2/1166, ADM 36/7672, Public Record Office, Kew.
Admiralty Secretary to Colonel Smith, Chatham, dated January 25, 1772. ADM 2/1166, Public Record Office, Kew.

PAPERS OF JOHN MONTAGU SANDWICH, 1771–1784,
NATIONAL LIBRARY OF AUSTRALIA, CANBERRA

Burney, Charles. Letter to Lord Sandwich, February 11, 1784, with enclosure by Susanna Phillips. Papers of John Montagu Sandwich, 1771–1784. MS 7218/32, National Library of Australia, Canberra.
King, James. Letter to Lord Sandwich, Woodstock, January 30, 1784. Papers of John Montagu Sandwich, 1771–1784, MS 7218, Item 30, National Library of Australia, Canberra.
Montagu, John, Earl of Sandwich. Rough draft by Sandwich of footnote referring to opinions of Lieutenant Burney and Lieutenant Phillips on singing of South Sea Islanders. Papers of John Montagu Sandwich, 1771–1784, MS 7218/36, National Library of Australia, Canberra.

BRITISH LIBRARY, LONDON

Twining, Thomas. Letter to Charles Burney, September 17, 1774. BL Add. MS 39933, folios 114–51, 1774.

Published Sources

Adorno, Theodor W. *Aesthetic Theory,* edited by Gretel Adorno and Rolf Tiedemann, translated by Robert Hullot-Kentor. Minneapolis: University of Minnesota Press, 1997.

———. *Einleitung in die Musiksoziologie.* Frankfurt am Main: Suhrkamp, 1962.

———. *Essays on Music,* edited by Richard Leppert, translated by Susan H. Gillespie. Berkeley: University of California Press, 2002.

Agnew, Vanessa. "The Bagpipes in the Eighteenth-century Pacific." *Piping Today* 11 (2004): 153–54.

———. "The Colonialist Beginnings of Comparative Musicology." In *Germany's Colonial Pasts: An Anthology in Memory of Susanne Zantop,* edited by Eric Ames, Marcia Klotz, and Lora Wildenthal, 41–60. Lincoln: University of Nebraska Press, 2005.

———. "Dissecting the Cannibal: Comparing the Function of the Autopsy Principle in the Diaries and Narratives of Cook's Second Voyage." In *Marginal Forms/Marginal Voices: Diaries in European History and Literature,* edited by Rachel Langford and Russell West, 50–60. Amsterdam: Rodopi, 1999.

———. "Exchange Strategies on Cook's Second Voyage." In *Cross-cultural Encounters and Constructions of Knowledge in the 18th and 19th Century: Non-European and European Travel Exploration in Comparative Perspective,* edited by Philippe Despoix, Justus Fetscher, and Michael Lackner, 163–96. Kassel: Kassel University Press, 2004.

———. *Music Afloat.* Radio program, 30 min. Prod. Clare Csonka. BBC Radio 4, 2000.

———. "The Pantomime 'Omai, or a Trip round the World.'" Forster Collection. Pitt Rivers Museum, University of Oxford, 2003. http://projects.prm.ox.ac.uk/forster/pathways.html (accessed January 30, 2006).

———. Red Feathers, White Paper, Blueprint: Exchange and Informal Empire in Georg Forster's "Voyage round the World." PhD diss., University of Wales, 1998.

———. "'Scots Orpheus' in the South Seas, or, the Use of Music on Cook's Second Voyage." *Journal for Maritime Research* (May 2001): 1–25.

Altenburg, Johann Ernst. *Versuch einer Anleitung zur heroisch-musikalischen Trompeter- und Paukenkunst.* Halle: Johann Christian Hendel, 1795. Reprint, edited by Frieder Zschoch. Leipzig: VEB Deutscher Verlag für Musik, 1972.

Alter, Nora M., and Lutz Koepnick, eds. *Sound Matters: Essays on the Acoustics of Modern German Culture.* New York: Berghahn, 2004.

Ambros, A. W. "Die Musik bei den Naturvölkern." In *Geschichte der Musik,* edited by B. von Sokolowsky. Leipzig: F. E. C. Leuckart, 1887.

Amiot, Joseph-Marie. *Mémoire sur la musique des Chinois.* Paris: Nyon, 1779. Reprint, Geneva: Minkoff, 1973.

Anderson, Benedict. *Imagined Communities: Reflections on the Origin and Spread of Nationalism.* London: Verso, 1991.

Anderson, William. "A Journal of a Voyage Made in His Majestys Sloop Resolution." In *The Journals of Captain James Cook on His Voyages of Discovery: The Voyage of the Resolution and Discovery 1776–1780,* edited by J. C. Beaglehole. Cambridge, UK: Published for the Hakluyt Society at the University Press, 1967.

André, Naomi. *Voicing Gender: Castrati, Travesti, and the Second Woman in Early-Nineteenth-century Italian Opera.* Bloomington: University of Indiana Press, 2006.

Angermüller, Rudolph. *Mozarts Reisen in Europa 1762–1791.* Bad Honnef: K. H. Bock, 2004.

———, with Geneviève Geffray and Vera von Glasner-Ostenwall. *Mozarts Reisen in Italien.* Salzburg: Internationale Stiftung Mozarteum, 2004.

Anon. "Article 5. Account of a Musical Instrument, which was brought by Captain Fourneaux, from the Isle of Amsterdam, in the South Seas, to London, in the Year 1774, and given to the Royal Society. By Joshua Steel, Esq. Article 6. Remarks on a larger System of Reed Pipes, from the Isle of Amsterdam, with some Observations on the Nose Flute of Otaheite. By the same." *Monthly Review, or Literary Journal* 54 (1775): 28–29.

———. "Aufsätze, verschiedenen Inhalts, von Friedrich Arnold Klockenbring. III. Etwas über die Musik in den neuerlich entdeckten Südländern." *Neue Bibliothek der schönen Wissenschaften* 36, no. 1 (1788): 79–94.

———. "Biographical Anecdotes of George Steevens, Esq." *Gentleman's Magazine and Historical Chronicle* (1800): 178–80.

———. *A Catalogue of the Miscellaneous Library of the Late Charles Burney . . . which will be sold by auction, by Leigh and Sotheby . . . on Thursday, the 9th of June, 1814.* London: Leigh and Sotheby, 1814.

———. "Directions for Seamen Bound on Far Voyages." *Philosophical Transactions of the Royal Society of London* 1 (1665–1666): 140–41.

———. "Diverses observations de physique générale." In *Histoire de l'Académie royale des sciences,* 1707. Reprint, Paris, 1730.

———. "Etwas von den Negern." *Der Wißbegierige* 41 (1784): 636–39.

———. "Etwas von der Kriegsschaubühne aus Irokesen-Lieder." *Chronologen* 6 (1780): 239–46.

———. *Euterpe; or, Remarks on the Use and Abuse of Music, as a Part of Modern Education.* London: J. Dodsley, Pall-Mall; sold by T. Shrimpton, York-Buildings; S. Hazard, King's-Mead-Square; and all the other Booksellers in Bath [1780?].

———. "Historical Chronicle, September 27." *Gentleman's Magazine and Historical Chronicle* 44 (1774): 490.

———. "Obituary for John Bicknell." *European Magazine* 11 (1787): 296.

———. *The Remarkable Trial of the Queen of Quavers and her Associates, for Sorcery, Witchcraft, and Enchantment, at the Assizes Held in the Moon, for the County of Gelding, before the R. Hon. Sir Francis Lash, Lord Chief Baron of the Lunar Exchequer.* London: J. Bew, 1777–1778.

———. "Review of Joel Collier's Musical Travels through England." *London Magazine* 43 (1774): 499–500.

———. *A Sequel to the Adventures of Baron Munchausen. Humbly dedicated to Mr. Bruce, the Abyssinian traveller.* 2 vols. London: Printed for H. D. Symonds and J. Owen, 1792.

————. "A Short Account of the new Pantomime called OMAI, or a Trip Round the World performed at the Theatre Royal in Covent Garden. With Recitatives, Airs, Duets, Trios, & Choruses, & a Description of the Procession. The Pantomime & the whole of the Scenery designed & invented by Mr. de Loutherbourg. The words written by Mr. O'Keefe; and the Music composed by Mr. Shield. 8vo. 6d Cadell 1785." *Monthly Review* 3 (1786): 621.

————. "Some Account of the Life and Writings of Dr. Charles Burney." *European Magazine, and London Review; for March 1785* (1785): 163–64.

————. "Tagebuch von Kapitain Cooks neuester Reise um die Welt und die südliche Hemisphäre, nebst dem Tagebuche von Lieutnant Fourneaux Reise um die Welt. Angehängt ist C. D. Ebelings Geschichte der Entdeckungen in der Südsee, und Geographie des fünften Welttheils. Erster Theil. Leipzig. 1776. 8." *Allgemeine deutsche Bibliothek* (1777): 281.

————. "A Téte-à-Téte [*sic*] between the King of Quavers and the Heroine of Romance." *Town and Country Magazine* (September 1777): 460–63.

————. "Ueber die Gewalt der Musik." *Gelehrte Beyträge zu den Braunschweigischen Anzeigen* 13, no. 85 (October, 30, 1773): Columns [681]–86; 13, no. 86 (November, 11, 1773): [689]–94.

Apollodorus. *The Library.* Translated by James George Frazer. Vol. 1. Cambridge, Mass.: Harvard University Press, 1921.

Applegate, Celia. *Bach in Berlin: Nation and Culture in Mendelssohn's Revival of the St. Matthew Passion.* Ithaca, N.Y.: Cornell University Press, 2005.

————. "How German Is It? Nationalism and the Idea of Serious Music in the Early Nineteenth Century." *19-Century Music* 21, no. 3 (Spring 1998): 274–96.

————. "Saving Music: Enduring Experiences of Culture." *History and Memory* 17, no. 1/2 (2005): 217–37.

————, and Pamela Potter. "Germans as the 'People of Music': Genealogy of an Identity." In *Music and German National Identity,* edited by Celia Applegate and Pamela Potter, 1–35. Chicago: University of Chicago Press, 2002.

Apollonius Rhodius. *The Argonautic expedition. Translated from the Greek of Apollonius Rhodius, into English verse, with critical, historical, and explanatory remarks, and prefatory essays, with a large appendix.* Translated by Edward Burnaby Greene. London: Printed for Thomas Payne and Son; and Robert Faulder, 1780.

Aravamudan, Srinivas. *Tropicopolitans: Colonialism and Agency, 1688–1804.* Durham, N.C.: Duke University Press, 1999.

Archer, Christian I. "The Spanish Reaction to Cook's Third Voyage." In *Captain James Cook and His Times,* edited by Robin Fisher and Hugh Johnston, 99–119. Seattle: University of Washington Press, 1979.

Arnold, Denis. "Conservatories: The Role of the Conservatory. Up to 1790." In *New Grove Online,* edited by L. Macy. http://www.grovemusic.com.proxy.lib.umich.edu, s.v. "Conservatories" (accessed March 5, 2007).

Ashcroft, Bill, Gareth Griffiths, and Helen Tiffin. *The Empire Writes Back: Theory and Practice in Post-colonial Literatures.* London: Routledge, 1989.

————, eds. *The Post-colonial Studies Reader.* London: Routledge, 1995.

Askew, Kelly. *Performing the Nation: Swahili Music and Cultural Politics in Tanzania.* Chicago: Chicago University Press, 2002.

Austin, John L. *How to Do Things with Words,* edited by J. O. Urmson and Marina Sbisà. 2d ed. Cambridge, Mass.: Harvard University Press, 1975.

Avison, Charles. *A Reply to the Author of Remarks on the Essay on Musical Expression.* London: C. Davis, 1753.

B., "Article VII. Review of *A Voyage round the World, in his Britannic Majesty's Sloop, Resolution, commanded by Capt. James Cook, during the Years 1772, 3, 4, and 5.* By George Forster, F. R. S. Member of the Royal Academy of Madrid, and of the Society for promoting Natural Knowledge at Berlin, 2 Vols . . . 1777." *Monthly Review, or Literary Journal* 56 (1777): 465–66.

Babcock, Barbara A. *The Reversible World: Symbolic Inversion in Art and Society.* Ithaca, N.Y.: Cornell University Press, 1978.

Bähr, Andreas. "Einleitung: Aufklärung und die Tötung des Körpers." In *Grenzen der Aufklärung: Körperkonstruktionen und die Tötung des Körpers im Übergang zur Moderne,* edited by Andreas Bähr. Hanover: Wehrhahn, 2005.

Baines, Anthony C. *Bagpipes Occasional Papers on Technology 9,* edited by T. K. Penniman and B. M. Blackwood. Oxford, UK: Pitt Rivers Museum, Oxford University Press, 1960.

Bakhtin, M. M. *Rabelais and His World,* translated by Héléne Iswolsky. Bloomington: Indiana University Press, 1984.

Baretti, Giuseppe [Joseph]. *An Account of the Manners and Customs of Italy; with Observations on the Mistakes of some Travellers with Regard to that Country.* 2 vols. London: T. Davis, L. Davis, and C. Reymers, 1768.

———. *A Journey from London to Genoa, through England, Portugal, Spain, and France.* London: Printed for T. Davies and L. Davis, 1770. Reprint, New York: Praeger, 1970.

Barker, Andrew, ed. *Greek Musical Writings.* Vol. 1, *The Musician and His Art.* New York: Cambridge University Press, 1984.

Barlow, Jeremy. *The Enraged Musician: Hogarth's Musical Imagery.* Burlington, Vt.: Ashgate, 2005.

Barndt, Kerstin. " 'Mein Dasein ward unvermerkt das allgemeine Gespräch': Anna Louisa Karsch im Spiegel zeitgenössicher Populärphilosophie." In *Anna Louisa Karsch (1722–1791): Von schlesischer Kunst und Berliner 'Natur': Ergebnisse des Symposions zum 200. Todestag der Dichterin,* edited by Anke Bennholdt-Thomsen and Anita Runge, 162–76. Göttingen: Wallstein, 1992.

Barnouw, Dagmar. "*Eräugnis:* Georg Forster on the Difficulties of Diversity." In *Impure Reason: Dialectic of Enlightenment in Germany,* edited by W. Daniel Wilson and Robert C. Holub, 322–43. Detroit: Wayne State University Press, 1993.

Barthes, Roland. "The Reality Effect." In *The Rustle of Language,* translated by Richard Howard. Berkeley: University of California Press, 1989.

Batchelor, Robert. "Concealing the Bounds: Imagining the British Nation through China." In *The Global Eighteenth Century,* edited by Felicity A. Nussbaum, 79–92. Baltimore: Johns Hopkins University Press, 2003.

Batten, Charles L., Jr. *Pleasurable Instruction: Form and Convention in Eighteenth-century Travel Literature.* Berkeley: University of California Press, 1978.

Bauers, Wilhelm A., Otto Erich Deutsch, and Joseph Heinz Eibl, eds. *Mozart: Briefe und Aufzeichnungen.* 7 vols. Kassel: Bärenreiter, 1962–1975.

Beaglehole, J. C., ed. *The* Endeavour *Journal of Joseph Banks 1768–1771.* Vols. 1–2. Sydney: Trustees of the Public Library of New South Wales in Association with Angus and Robertson, 1962.

———, ed. *The Journals of Captain James Cook on His Voyages of Discovery.* Vol. 1, *The Voyage of the* Endeavour *1768–1771.* Vol. 2, *The Voyage of the* Resolution *and* Adventure *1772–1775.* Vol. 3, parts 1 and 2, *The Voyage of the* Resolution *and* Discovery *1776–1780.* Cambridge, UK: Published for the Hakluyt Society at the University Press, 1955–1967.

Beattie, James. "An Essay on Laughter and Ludicrous Composition Written in the Year 1764." In *Essays on the nature and immutable opposition to sophistry and scepticism; on poetry and music, as they affect the mind; on laughter and ludicrous composition; and, on the utility of classical learning.* Dublin: C. Jenkin, 1778.

Beer, Gillian. "Travelling the Other Way." In *Cultures of Natural History,* edited by N. Jardine, J. A. Secord, and E. C. Spary, 322–37. New York: Cambridge University Press, 1996.

Behrens, Carl Friedrich. *Reise durch die Süd-Länder und um die Welt {mit Jac. Roggeveen, im J. 1721}.* Frankfurt: n.p., 1737.

Bent, Ian, ed. *Music Theory in the Age of Romanticism.* New York: Cambridge University Press, 1996.

Berg, Eberhard. *Zwischen den Welten: Über die Anthropologie der Aufklärung und ihr Verhältnis zu Entdeckungs-Reise und Welt-Erfahrung mit besonderem Blick auf das Werk Georg Forsters.* Berlin: Reimer, 1982.

Bergeron, Katherine. "The Castrato as History." *Cambridge Opera Journal* 8, no. 2 (1996): 167–84.

Berman, Nina. "K. u. K. Colonialism: Hofmannsthal in North Africa." *New German Critique* 75 (Autumn 1998): 3–27.

Berman, Russell A. *Enlightenment or Empire: Colonial Discourse in German Culture.* Lincoln: University of Nebraska Press, 1998.

———. *The Rise of the Modern German Novel: Crisis and Charisma.* Cambridge, Mass.: Harvard University Press, 1986.

Beutler, Johann Heinrich Christoph, and Johann Christoph Friedrich Guts-Muths. *Allgemeines Sachregister über die wichtigsten deutschen Zeit- und Wochenschriften: Voran als Einleitung ein raisonnirendes litterarisches Verzeichniss aller in diesem Jahrhundert bis jetzt erschienenen periodischen Blätter, nach Dezennien gearabeitet und mit einem Namenverzeichniss aller dabei befindlichen Mitarbeiter.* 2 vols. Leipzig: In der Weigandschen Buchhandlung, 1790. Reprint, Hildesheim: Georg Olms, 1976.

[Bewley, William]. "Article VIII. Review of the present State of Music in Germany, the Netherlands, and United Provinces: or, the Journal of a Tour through those Countries, undertaken to collect Materials for a General History of Music. By Charles Burney, Mus. D. 2 vols. 8vo. 10s. Becket. 1773." *Monthly Review* 48 (1773): 457–69; 49 (1773): 212–24.

———. "Review of Joel Collier's Musical Travels through England." *Monthly Review* 101 (1774): 242.

[Bicknell, John]. *Musical Travels through England: By the Late Joel Collier, Licentiate in Music.* London: G. Kearsley, 1785.

Bitterli, Urs. *Die "Wilden" und die "Zivilisierten": Grundzüge einer Geistes- und Kultur-geschichte der europäisch-überseeischen Begegnung.* Munich: C. H. Beck, 1976.

Black, Jeremy. *The British and the Grand Tour.* London: Croom Helm, 1985.

———. "Tourism and Cultural Challenge: The Changing Scene of the Eighteenth Century." In *All before Them, 1660–1780,* edited by John McVeagh, 185–202. London: Ashfield, 1989.

Blackbourn, David, and Geoff Eley, *Mythen deutscher Geschichtsschreibung: Die gescheiterte bürgerliche Revolution von 1848.* Frankfurt am Main: Ullstein, 1980.

Blair, John. *The chronology and history of the world from the creation to the year of Christ, 1768, illustrated in LVI tables; of which IV are introductory and include the centurys prior to the 1st. Olympiad, and each of the remaining LII contain in one expanded view, 50 years or half a century.* London: n.p., 1768.

Bloom, Allan. *The Closing of the American Mind: How Higher Education Has Failed De-mocracy and Impoverished the Souls of Today's Students.* New York: Simon and Schuster, 1987.

Blum, Stephen. "Conclusion: Music in an Age of Cultural Confrontation." In *Music Cultures in Contact: Convergences and Collisions,* edited by Margaret J. Kartomi and Stephen Blum, 250–77. Basel: Gordon and Breach, 1994.

———, Philip V. Bohlman, and Daniel M. Neuman, eds. *Ethnomusicology and Modern Music History.* Urbana: University of Illinois Press, 1991.

Bödeker, Hans Erich. "Reisebeschreibungen im historischen Diskurs der Aufklärung." In *Aufklärung und Geschichte: Studien zur deutschen Geschichtswissenschaft im 18. Jahrhun-dert,* edited by Hans Erich Bödeker et al., 276–98. Göttingen: Vandenhoeck und Ruprecht, 1986.

Bodmer, Johann Jakob. "Von denen Verwunderungs-würdigen Würkungen der Music." *Freymüthige Nachrichten von neuen Büchern und anderen zur Gelahrtheit gehörigen Sachen* (1750): 69–70.

Boethius, Anicius Manlius Severinus. *Fundamentals of Music,* edited by Claude V. Palisca, translated by Calvin M. Bower. New Haven, Conn.: Yale University Press, 1989.

Bohlman, Philip V. "The European Discovery of Music in the Islamic World and the 'Non-Western' in 19th-Century Music History." *Journal of Musicology* 5 (1987): 147–63.

———. "Landscape–Region–Nation–Reich: German Folk Song in the Nexus of Na-tional Identity." In *Music and German National Identity,* edited by Cecilia Applegate and Pamela Potter, 105–27. Chicago: University of Chicago Press, 2002.

———. "Music, Modernity, and the Foreign in the New Germany." *Modernism/modernity* 1, no. 1 (January 1994): 121–52.

———. "Stimmen der Lieder in Völkern—'Musikalische Einheiten' in der Einheit der Nation." Lecture, Musikwissenschaftliches Seminar, Humboldt-Universität zu Ber-lin, June 23, 2005.

———. *World Music: A Very Short Introduction.* Oxford, UK: Oxford University Press, 2002.

Bonds, Mark Evans. "Idealism and the Aesthetics of Instrumental Music at the Turn of the Nineteenth Century." *Journal of the American Musicological Society,* vol. 50, no.2/3 (Summer/Autumn 1997): 387–420.

Born, Georgina, and David Hesmondhalgh, eds. *Western Music and Its Others: Difference, Representation, and Appropriation in Music.* Berkeley: University of California Press, 2000.

Borsay, Peter. "Concert Topography and Provincial Towns in Eighteenth-century England." In *Concert Life in Eighteenth-century Britain,* edited by Susan Wollenberg and Simon McVeigh, 19–33. Burlington, Vt.: Ashgate, 2004.

Boswell, James. *Boswell for the Defence, 1769–1774,* edited by William K. Wimsatt Jr., and Frederick A. Pottle. New York: McGraw-Hill, 1959.

—————. *Boswell on the Grand Tour: Germany and Switzerland, 1764,* edited by F. A. Pottle. London: Heinemann, 1953.

—————. *Boswell's Life of Johnson,* edited by G. B. Hill and revised by L. F. Powell. 6 vols. Oxford, UK: Clarendon, 1934–1950.

—————. *Life of Johnson.* Oxford, UK: Oxford Standard Authors, 1965.

Bougainville, Louis de. *A Voyage round the World,* translated by John Reinhold Forster. London: Printed for J. Nourse [etc.], 1772. Reprint, Amsterdam: N. Israel [1967].

Bourdieu, Pierre. *Distinction: A Social Critique of the Judgment of Taste,* translated by Richard Nice. Cambridge, Mass.: Harvard University Press, 1984.

—————. *The Logic of Practice,* translated by Richard Nice. Cambridge, UK: Polity, 1990.

—————. *Soziale Ungleichheiten,* edited by Reinhard Kreckel. Göttingen: Otto Schwartz, 1983.

Bowman, Wayne D. *Philosophical Perspectives on Music.* New York: Oxford University Press, 1998.

Brewer, John. *A Sentimental Murder: Love and Madness in the Eighteenth Century.* New York: Farrar, Straus, and Giroux, 2004.

Brocklesby, Richard. *Reflections on Antient and Modern Musick, with the Application to the Cure of Diseases.* London: M. Cooper, 1749.

Browne, Richard. *A Mechanical Essay on Singing, Musick, and Dancing: Containing Their Uses and Abuses.* London: J. Pemberton, 1727.

Brunschwig, Henri. *Enlightenment and Romanticism in Eighteenth-century Prussia,* translated by Frank Jellinek. Chicago: University of Chicago Press, 1974.

Brydone, Patrick. *A Tour through Sicily and Malta, in a Series of Letters to William Beckford of Somerly in Suffolk.* 2 vols. London: J. Johnson, 1792.

Buelow, George J. "Athanasius Kircher." In *Grove Music Online,* edited by L. Macy. http://www.grovemusic.com, s.v. "Athanasius Kircher" (accessed April 30, 2007).

Burke, Peter. "Performing History: The Importance of Occasions." *Rethinking History* 9, no. 1 (2005): 35–52.

Burkert, Walter. *Greek Religion,* translated by John Raffan. Cambridge, Mass.: Harvard University Press, 1985.

Burney, Charles. "Account of an Infant Musician [William Crotch]." *Philosophical Transactions of the Royal Society of London* 69 (1779): 183–206.

—————. *Carl Burney's der Musik Doctors Tagebuch einer Musikalischen Reise durch Frankreich und Italien welche er unternommen hat um zu einer allgemeinen Geschichte der Musik Materialien zu sammeln. Aus dem Englischen übersetzt von C. D. Ebeling. Aufsehern der Handlungsakademie zu Hamburg.* Hamburg: Bey Bode, 1772.

—————. *Carl Burney's der Musik Doctors Tagebuch seiner Musikalischen Reisen.* Vol. 2. *Durch Flandern, die Niederlande und am Rhein bis Wien. Aus dem Englischen übersetzt.* Hamburg: Bey Bode, 1773.

————. *Carl Burney's der Musik Doctors Tagebuch seiner Musikalischen Reisen.* Vol. 3. *Durch Böhmen, Sachsen, Brandenburg, Hamburg und Holland. Aus dem Englischen übersetzt. Mit einigen Zusätzen und Anmerkungen zu zweiten und dritten Bande.* Hamburg: Bey Bode, 1773.

————. "Chinese Music." In *The Cyclopaedia; or, Universal Dictionary of Arts, Sciences, and Literature,* vol. 7, edited by Abraham Rees. London: Printed for Longman, Hurst, Rees, Orme, and Brown, 1819.

[————]. "Doktor Burney's Versuch über die musikalische Kritik. Aus dem Englischen übersetzt von Herrn Hofrath Eschenburg." In *Musikalisches Wochenblatt* 1, no. 10 (1791): 73–75; [1], no. 11 (1791): 81–82.

————. *Dr. Burney's Musical Tours in Europe: An Eighteenth-century Musical Tour in France and Italy,* edited by Percy Alfred Scholes. 2 vols. New York: Oxford University Press, 1959.

————. *An Essay towards a History of the Principal Comets that have appeared since the Year 1742. Including a particular Detail of the Return of the famous Comet of 1682 in 1759, according to the Calculation and Prediction of Dr. Halley. Compiled from Observations of the most eminent Astronomers of this Century. With Remarks and Reflections upon the Present Comet. To which is prefixed, by way of Introduction, a Letter upon Comets. Addressed to a Lady, by the late M. de Maupertuis.* London: T. Becket and P. A. de Hondt, 1769.

————. "Farinelli." In *The Cyclopaedia; or, Universal Dictionary of Arts, Sciences, and Literature,* vol. 14, edited by Abraham Rees. London: Longman, Hurst, Rees, Orme, and Brown, 1802–1820.

————. "Felice Giardini." In *The Cyclopædia; or, Universal Dictionary of Arts, Sciences, and Literature,* vol. 16, edited by Abraham Rees. London: Longman, Hurst, Rees, Orme, and Brown, 1802–1820.

————. *A General History of Music from the Earliest Ages to the Present Period (1789),* edited by Frank Mercer. 2 vols. New York: Dover, 1957.

————. *The Letters of Dr. Charles Burney, 1751–1784,* edited by Alvaro Ribeiro. Vol. 1. Oxford, UK: Clarendon, 1991.

————. *Memoirs of Dr. Charles Burney, 1726-1769,* edited by Slava Klima, Garry Bowers, and Kerry S. Grant. Lincoln: University of Nebraska Press, 1988.

————. *Memoirs of the Life and Writings of the Abate Metastasio: In which are incorporated, Translations of his Principal Letters.* London: G. G. and J. Robinson, 1796.

————. *Music, Men, and Manners in France and Italy 1770,* edited by H. Edmund Poole. London: Folio Society, 1969.

————. *The Present State of Music in France and Italy: or, the Journal of a Tour through those countries, undertaken to collect Materials for a general history of music.* London: T. Becket, 1771.

————. *The Present State of Music in Germany, the Netherlands, and United Provinces: or, the Journal of a Tour through those Countries, undertaken to collect Materials for a General History of Music.* London: T. Becket, 1773.

————. "Putaveri." In *The Cyclopædia; or, Universal Dictionary of Arts, Sciences, and Literature,* vol. 29, edited by Abraham Rees. London: Printed for Longman, Hurst, Rees, Orme, and Brown, 1819.

————. *Tagebuch einer musikalischen Reise durch Frankreich und Italien, durch Flandern, die Niederlande und am Rhein bis Wien, durch Böhmen, Sachsen, Brandenburg, Hamburg und*

Holland 1770–1772, edited by Eberhardt Klemm, translated by Christoph Daniel Ebeling. Wilhelmshaven, Germany: Heinrichshofen, 1980.

———. *Tagebuch einer musikalischen Reise.* Edited by Christoph Hust. Kassel: Bärenreiter, 2003.

———. *Verses on the Arrival in England of the Great Musician Haydn.* London: T. Payne, 1791.

Burney, Fanny. *The Early Journals and Letters of Fanny Burney, 1774–1777,* edited by Lars E. Troide. Oxford, UK: Clarendon, 1990.

Burney, James. *Chronological History of the Voyages and Discoveries in the South Sea or Pacific Ocean.* London: Luke Hansard, 1817.

Burrows, Donald, and Rosemary Dunhill. *Music and Theatre in Handel's World: The Family Papers of James Harris, 1732–1780.* New York: Oxford University Press, 2001.

Burton, Antoinette M., ed. *After the Imperial Turn: Thinking with and through the Nation.* Durham, N.C.: Duke University Press, 2003.

Calaresu, Melissa. "Looking for Virgil's Tomb: The End of the Grand Tour and the Cosmopolitan Ideal in Europe." In *Voyages and Visions: Towards a Cultural History of Travel,* edited by Jas Elsner and Joan-Pau Rubiés, 138–61. London: Reaktion Books, 1999.

Casanova, Giacomo. *History of My Life,* translated by Willard R. Trask. Baltimore: Johns Hopkins University Press, 1966.

Casanova, Pascale. *The World Republic of Letters.* Cambridge, Mass.: Harvard University Press, 2005.

Cervantes, Xavier. "Tuneful Monsters: The Castrati and the London Operatic Public, 1667–1737." *Restoration and Eighteenth-century Theatre Research* 13, no. 1 (1998): 1–24.

Chakrabarty, Dipesh. *Provincializing Europe: Postcolonial Thought and Historical Distance.* Princeton, N.J.: Princeton University Press, 2001.

Chandler, James. *England in 1819: The Politics of Literary Culture and the Case of Romantic Historicism.* Chicago: University of Chicago Press, 1998.

Chatterjee, Partha. *The Nation and Its Fragments: Colonial and Postcolonial Histories.* Princeton, N.J.: Princeton University Press, 1994.

Chatwin, Bruce. *The Songlines.* London: Jonathan Cape, 1987.

Cheah, Pheng. *Spectral Nationality: Passages of Freedom from Kant to Postcolonial Literatures of Liberation.* New York: Columbia University Press, 2003.

———, and Bruce Robbins, eds. *Cosmopolitics: Thinking and Feeling beyond the Nation.* Minneapolis: University of Minnesota Press, 1998.

[Chesterfield, Philip Dormer Stanhope, Earl of, and Edmund Waller]. *The Case of the Hanover Forces, in the Pay of Great-Britain, Impartially and freely examined: With some Seasonable Reflexions on the Present Conjuncture of Affairs.* London: Printed for T. Cooper, 1743.

Chua, Daniel K. L. *Absolute Music and the Construction of Meaning.* New York: Cambridge University Press, 1999.

Churchill, Charles. *Gotham: A Poem.* London: Printed for the author and sold by W. Flexney, G. Kearsley, C. Henderson, J. Coote, J. Gardiner, and J. Almon, 1764.

Clark, Thomas Blake. *Omai. First Polynesian Ambassador to England. The true story of his voyage there in 1774 with Captain Cook; of how he was feted by Fanny Burney, approved by*

Samuel Johnson, entertained by Mrs. Thrale and Lord Sandwich and painted by Sir Joshua Reynolds. Honolulu: University of Hawaii Press, 1969.

Clifford, James. *Routes: Travel and Translation in the Late Twentieth Century.* Cambridge, Mass.: Harvard University Press, 1997.

Cocks, William A., Anthony C. Baines, and Roderick D. Cannon. "Bagpipes." In *The New Grove Dictionary of Music and Musicians,* edited by Stanley Sadie. New York: Grove, 2001.

Collyer, Joel [John Bicknell]. "Musical Sketches." In *The English Lyceum, or, Choice of Pieces in Prose and verse, selected from the best periodical papers, magazines, pamphlets and other British publications,* edited by Johannes Wilhelm von Archenholtz (1787): 109–14.

————. "Scientific Account of the Musical Festival." In *The English Lyceum, or, Choice of Pieces in Prose and verse, selected from the best periodical papers, magazines, pamphlets and other British publications,* edited by Johannes Wilhelm von Archenholtz. Vol. 1, no. 2 (1787): 183–93.

Cook, James, and James King. *A Voyage to the Pacific Ocean: Undertaken by the command of His Majesty, for making Discoveries in the Northern Hemisphere.* 4 vols. London: Printed by W. and A. Strahan for G. Nicol and T. Cadell, 1784.

Cooper, Frederick. "Conflict and Connection: Rethinking Colonial African History." *American Historical Review* 99, no. 5 (December 1994): 1516–45.

Corri, Domenico. *A Select collection of the most admired songs, duetts, &c.: from operas in the highest esteem, and from other works, in Italian, English, French, Scotch, Irish, &c., &c.* Edinburgh: Printed for John Corri [1779].

Cotsell, Michael, ed. *English Literature and the Wider World: Creditable Warriors 1830–1877.* London: Ashfield, 1990.

Couper, Robert. *The Tourifications of Malachi Meldrum, Esq., of Meldrum Hall.* 2 vols. Aberdeen, UK: J. Chelmers, 1803.

Cowart, Georgia J. "Sense and Sensibility in Eighteenth-century Musical Thought." *Acta Musicologica* 56 (July–December 1984): 251–66.

Cowgill, Rachel. "'Wise Men from the East': Mozart's Operas and Their Advocates in Early Nineteenth-Century London." In *Music and British Culture, 1785–1914: Essays in Honour of Cyril Ehrlich,* edited by Christina Bashford and Leanne Langley, 39–64. New York: Oxford University Press, 2000.

Cox, Edward Godfrey. *A Reference Guide to the Literature of Travel including Voyages, Geographical Descriptions, Adventures, Shipwrecks, and Expeditions.* Vol. 1, *The Old World, 1935.* Reprint, Mansfield Centre, Conn.: Martino, 1948.

Cradock, Joseph. *Literary and Miscellaneous Memoirs.* Vol. 4. London: J. B. Nichols, 1828.

Dahlhaus, Carl. *Esthetics of Music,* translated by William Austin. New York: Cambridge University Press, 1995.

————. *Die Idee der absoluten Musik.* Kassel: Bärenreiter, 1978.

d'Arblay, Frances. *Memoirs of Doctor Burney, arranged from his own manuscripts, from family papers, and from personal recollections.* 3 vols. London: Edward Moxon, 1832.

Darnton, Robert. *The Great Cat Massacre and Other Episodes in French Cultural History.* New York: Basic Books, 1984.

Daston, Loraine, and Katharine Park. *Wonder and the Order of Nature.* New York: Zone Books, 2001.

Davis, Natalie Zemon. *Trickster Travels: A Sixteenth-Century Muslim between Worlds.* New York: Hill and Wang, 2006.

Dening, Greg. *Islands and Beaches.* Melbourne: Melbourne University Press, 1980.

——. *Mr. Bligh's Bad Language: Passion, Power, and Theatre on the* Bounty. New York: Cambridge University Press, 1992.

——. *Performances.* Melbourne: Melbourne University Press, 1996.

DeNora, Tia. *Music in Everyday Life.* New York: Cambridge University Press, 2000.

Descartes, René. *The Passions of the Soul,* translated by Stephen H. Voss. Indianapolis: Hackett, 1989.

Detienne, Marcel. *The Writing of Orpheus: Greek Myth in Cultural Context,* translated by Janet Lloyd. Baltimore: John Hopkins University Press, 2003.

Devlin, Christopher. *Poor Kit Smart.* London: Rupert Hart-Davis, 1961.

Diamond, Jared. *Guns, Germs, and Steel: The Fates of Human Societies.* New York: Norton, 1997.

Diderot, Denis. "Supplement to Bougainville's 'Voyage.'" In *Rameau's Nephew and Other Works,* 177–228. New York: Macmillan, 1964.

Dolinski, Kurt. *Die Anfänge der musikalischen Fachpresse in Deutschland.* Berlin: H. Schmidts Buch- und Kunstdruckerei, 1940.

Doll, Eugene Edgar. "American History as Interpreted by German Historians from 1770 to 1815." *Transactions of the American Philosophical Society* 38, pt. 5 (1948): 421–526.

Douglas, John. "Hints offered to the consideration of Captain Cooke, Mr. Bankes, doctor Solander, and the other Gentlemen who go upon the Expedition on Board the *Endeavour.*" In *The Journals of Captain James Cook on His Voyages of Discovery.* Vol. 1, *The Voyage of the* Endeavour, *1768–1771,* edited by J. C. Beaglehole. Cambridge, UK: Published for the Hakluyt Society by Cambridge University Press, 1955.

Duara, Prasenjit. "Postcolonial History." In *A Companion to Western Historical Thought,* edited by Lloyd Kramer and Sara Maza, 417–31. Malden, Mass.: Blackwell, 2002.

Duckles, Vincent. "Johann Nicolaus Forkel: The Beginnings of Music Historiography." *Eighteenth-Century Studies* 1 (1967–1968): 277–90.

——, and Jann Pasler. "Musicology." In *Grove Music Online,* edited by L. Macy. http://www.grovemusic.com, s.v. "Musicology" (accessed January 30, 2007).

Dutt, Romesh. *The Economic History of India.* Vol. 1, *Under Early British Rule.* New Delhi: Publications Division, Ministry of Information and Broadcasting, Govt. of India, 1970.

Eagleton, Terry. *The Function of Criticism: From the Spectator to Post-structuralism.* London: Verso, 1984.

——. *Walter Benjamin: Towards a Revolutionary Criticism.* London: Verso, 1981.

Eastcott, Richard. *Sketches of the origin, progress and effects of music . . . By the Rev. Richard Eastcott.* Bath: Printed and sold by S. Hazard; sold likewise by Messrs. G. G. J. & J. Robinson, Cadell, Dilly, and Vernor and Hood, London, 1793.

Ebeling, Christoph Daniel, ed. *Neue Sammlung von Reisebeschreibungen.* 10 vols. Hamburg: Bey Carl Ernst Bohn, 1780–1790.

——. "Versuch einer auserlesenen musikalischen Bibliothek." *Unterhaltungen* 10, no. 4 (1770): 303–22; no. 6 (1770): 504–34.

——. "Vorrede." In Charles Burney, *Tagebuch einer musikalischen Reise,* edited by Christoph Hust. Vol. 1, 1772, 1773. Reprint, Kassel: Bärenreiter, 2003.

Ehrlich, Cyril. *The Music Profession in Britain since the Eighteenth Century: A Social History.* New York: Oxford University Press, 1985.

Elias, Norbert. *Mozart: Portrait of a Genius,* edited by Michael Schröter, translated by Edmund Jephcott. Berkeley: University of California Press, 1993.

————. *Über den Prozeß der Zivilisation: Soziogenetische und psychogenetische Untersuchungen.* Frankfurt am Main: Suhrkamp, 1990.

Ellis, Katharine. *Interpreting the Musical Past: Early Music in Nineteenth-Century France.* New York: Oxford University Press, 2005.

[Ellis, William]. "Cooks dritte und letzte Entdeckungsreise um die Welt, in den Jahren 1776 bis 1780." *Hannoverisches Magazin* 21, no. 61 (August 1, 1783): Columns 961–76.

Erlmann, Veit. *Music, Modernity, and the Global Imagination: South Africa and the West.* New York: Oxford University Press, 1999.

Eschenburg, Johann Joachim. "Review of 'Ueber den Werth der Tonkunst; von C[arl]. B. [*sic*] Junker. Bayreuth und Leipzig, bey Lübecks Erben 1786.' " *Allgemeine Deutsche Bibliothek* 74, no. 2, 1787: 442–43.

[Feijóo, Benito Jerónimo]. "Auszug aus einer spanischen Abhandlung des Don Feyjoo über den Einfluß der Musik auf das menschliche Herz." *Unterhaltungen* 1, no. 6 (1766): 526–33.

Ferdon, Edwin N. *Early Tonga as the Explorers Saw It, 1618–1810.* Tucson: University of Arizona Press, 1987.

Findlen, Paula. *Possessing Nature: Museums, Collecting, and Scientific Culture in Early Modern Italy.* Berkeley: University of California Press, 1994.

Fishman, Lisa Aldis. Critical Text as Cultural Nexus: The Journalistic Writings of J. N. Forkel, C. F. Cramer, and J. F. Reichardt. PhD diss., State University of New York, Stony Brook, 1997.

Fiske, Roger. "A Covent Garden Pantomime." *Musical Times* 8 (1963).

————. *English Theatre Music in the Eighteenth Century,* 2d ed. New York: Oxford University Press, 1986.

Fonton, Charles. *Essai sur la musique orientale comparée à la musique européenne.* Reprint of autograph facsimile, Frankfurt am Main: Institute for the History of Arab-Islamic Science, 1999.

Ford, Robert. "Review of 'Memoirs of Dr. Charles Burney' by Charles Burney, edited from autograph fragments by Slava Klima, Garry Bowers, and Kerry S. Grant." *Journal of Musicological Research* 10, no. 3–4 (1991): 285–87.

Forkel, Johann Nicolaus. *Allgemeine Geschichte der Musik.* 2 vols. Leipzig: Schwickertschen Verlage, 1788–1801.

————. *Allgemeine Litteratur der Musik, oder Anleitung zur Kenntniss musikalischer Bücher, welche von den ältesten bis auf die neusten Zeiten bey den Griechen, Römern, und den meisten neuern europäischen Nationen sind geschrieben worden.* Leipzig: Schwickertschen Verlage, 1792. Reprint, Hildesheim: Georg Olms, 1962.

[————]. "Auszug aus Carsten Niebuhrs Reisebeschreibung von Arabien und andern umliegenden Ländern." *Musikalisch-kritische Bibliothek* 2 (1778): 306–16.

[————]. "Etwas von der Musik der um den Südpol herum wohnenden Völker, aus Cooks Reise um die Welt." *Musikalisch-kritische Bibliothek* 2 (1778): 316–20.

————. *Musikalisch-kritische Bibliothek* 1. Gotha: Ettinger, 1777–1779. Reprint, Hildesheim: Georg Olms, 1964.

[————]. "Nachrichten von dem Zustand der Musik bey den Egyptiern und Chinesern, aus den philosophischen Untersuchungen des Herrn von Paw." *Musikalisch-kritische Bibliothek* 1 (1778): 229–30.

————. "Recensionen theoretischer Werke. A general History of Music, from the earliest ages to the present period. To which is prefixed, a Dissertation on the Music of the ancients. By Charles Burney. Vol. 1." *Musikalisch-kritische Bibliothek* 3 (1779): 117–91.

————. "Review. Ueber die Musik und deren Wirkungen, mit Anmerkungen herausgegeben von Joh. Adam Hiller. Leipzig, 1781." *Musikalischer Almanach* 2 (1783 [1782]): 5–7.

————. *Ueber Johann Sebastian Bachs Leben, Kunst, und Kunstwerke,* edited by Claudia Maria Knispel. Berlin: Henschel, 2000.

[————]. "Verzeichniss jetztlebender musikalischer Schriftsteller in Deutschland." *Musikalischer Almanach* 1 (1782 [1781]): 40–51; 2 (1783 [1782]): 20–26; 3 (1784 [1783]): 39–53; 4 (1789 [1788]): 37–67.

————. "Von der Musik der Chineser." *Musikalischer Almanach für Deutschland auf das Jahr 1784* (1783): 233–74.

————. "Von der Theorie der Musik in so fern sie Liebhabern und Kennern nothwendig und nützlich ist (Eine Einladungschrift zu musikalischen Vorlesungen von Johann Nicolaus Forkel)." *Magazin der Musik* 1, no. 2 (1783): 855–912.

————. "Vorrede." In *Musikalisch-kritische Bibliothek* 1 (1778): [iii]–xxvi.

Forster, Antonia. *Index to Book Reviews in England, 1749–1774.* Carbondale, Ill.: Southern Illinois University, 1990.

————. *Index to Book Reviews in England, 1775–1800.* London: British Library, 1997.

Forster, Georg. *Georg Forsters Werke: Sämtliche Schriften, Tagebücher, Briefe: Briefe an Forster,* edited by Brigitte Leuschner, Siegfried Scheibe, Horst Fiedler, Klaus-Georg Popp, and Annerose Schneider. Vol. 18. Berlin: Akademie-Verlag, 1982.

————. "Noch etwas über die Menschengeschlechter." *Der Teutsche Merkur* 4 (1786): 57–86.

————. "A Reply to Mr. Wales's Remarks." London: B. White, J. Robson, and P. Elmsley, 1778.

————. *A Voyage round the World,* edited by Nicholas Thomas and Oliver Berghof. 2 vols. Honolulu: University of Hawaii Press, 2000.

————, and Georg Christoph Lichtenberg. *Cook der Entdecker: Schriften über James Cook.* Leipzig: Reclam, 1981.

Forster, Johann Reinhold. *Observations Made during a Voyage round the World.* London: G. Robinson, 1778.

Foucault, Michel. *Die Ordnung der Dinge: Eine Archäologie der Humanwissenschaften,* translated by Ulrich Köppen. Frankfurt am Main: Suhrkamp, 2003.

Fowler, Bridget. *Pierre Bourdieu and Cultural Theory: Critical Investigations.* London: Sage, 1997.

Friedson, Steven M. "Dancing the Disease: Music and Trance in Tumbuka Healing." In *Musical Healing in Cultural Contexts,* edited by Penelope Gouk, 67–85. Brookfield, Vt.: Ashgate, 2000.

Fubini, Enrico. *Geschichte der Musikästhetik: Von der Antike bis zur Gegenwart,* translated by Sabina Kienlechner. Stuttgart: J. B. Metzler, 1997.

————. *Music and Culture in Eighteenth-Century Europe: A Source Book,* edited by Bonnie J. Blackburn, translated by Wolfgang Freis, Lisa Gasbarrone, and Michael Louis Leone. Chicago: University of Chicago Press, 1994.

Gay, Peter. *The Enlightenment: An Interpretation.* New York: Knopf, 1966.

————. *Mozart: A Life.* New York: Penguin, 1999.

Geyken, Frauke. "Gentlemen in Brandenburg." In *Europäische Ansichten: Brandenburg-Preußen um 1800 in der Wahrnehmung europäischer Reisender und Zuwanderer,* edited by Iwan-Michelangelo D'Aprile, 19–33. Berlin: Berliner Wissenschafts-Verlag, 2004.

Gikandi, Simon. *Maps of Englishness: Writing Identity in the Culture of Colonialism.* New York: Columbia University Press, 1996.

Gilroy, Paul. *The Black Atlantic: Modernity and Double Consciousness.* Cambridge, Mass.: Harvard University Press, 1993.

Gioia, Ted. *Healing Songs.* Durham, N.C.: Duke University Press, 2006.

————. *Work Songs.* Durham, N.C.: Duke University Press, 2006.

Gmelin, Johann Georg. *Expedition ins unbekannte Sibirien,* edited by Dittmar Dahlmann. Sigmaringen: Jan Thorbecke, 1999.

Goehr, Lydia. *The Imaginary Museum of Musical Works: An Essay in the Philosophy of Music.* New York: Oxford University Press, 1992.

————. *The Quest for Voice: On Music, Politics, and the Limits of Philosophy.* Berkeley: University of California Press, 1998.

Goethe, Wolfgang von. *Goethes Gedanken über Musik,* edited by Hedwig Walwei-Wiegelmann. Frankfurt am Main: Insel, 1985.

Golden, Morris. "Travel Writing in the *Monthly Review* and *Critical Review,* 1756–1775." *Papers on Language and Literature* 13 (1977): 213–23.

Goldsmith, Oliver. "The Traveller." In *Selected Poems of Johnson and Goldsmith,* edited by A. Rudrum and P. Dixon. London: Edward Arnold, 1965.

Goodwin, Gordon. "Richard Paul Jodrell." In *Oxford Dictionary of National Biography,* revised by S. J. Skedd. New York: Oxford University Press, 2004.

Görner, Rüdiger. *Grenzen, Schwellen, Übergänge: Zur Poetik des Transitorischen.* Göttingen: Vandenhoeck und Ruprecht, 2001.

————. *Literarische Betrachtungen zur Musik.* Frankfurt am Main: Insel, 2001.

Gossman, Lionel. *Medievalism and the Ideologies of the Enlightenment: The World and Work of LaCurne de Sainte-Palaye.* Baltimore: Johns Hopkins University Press, 1968.

Gouk, Penelope. *Music, Science, and Natural Magic in Seventeenth-Century England.* New Haven, Conn.: Yale University Press, 1999.

————, ed. *Musical Healing in Cultural Contexts.* Brookfield, Vt.: Ashgate, 2000.

————, and Helen Hills, eds. *Representing Emotions: New Connections in the Histories of Art, Music, and Medicine.* Burlington, Vt.: Ashgate, 2005.

Gramit, David. *Cultivating Music: The Aspirations, Interests, and Limits of German Musical Culture, 1770–1848.* Berkeley: University of California Press, 2002.

Grant, Kerry S. *Dr. Burney as Critic and Historian of Music.* Ann Arbor: UMI Research Press, 1983.

Grassineau, James. *A Musical Dictionary: containing a full explanation of all the terms made use of in the historical, theoretical, and practical parts of music. To which is added an appendix, selected from the "Dictionnaire de Musique" of m. Rousseau.* London: J. Robson, 1769.

Gray, Thomas. *The traveller's companion, in a tour through England and Wales; containing a catalogue of the antiquities, houses, parks, in England and Wales, arranged and edited by the late Mr. Gray. To which are now added, considerable improvements and additions, by Thomas Northmore, Esq.* London: G. Kearsley, 1799.

Grewendorf, Günther. "How Performatives Don't Work." In *Speech Acts, Mind, and Social Reality: Discussions with John R. Searle,* edited by Günther Grewendorf and Georg Meggle. Dordrecht, the Netherlands: Kluwer, 2002.

Griep, Wolfgang, and Hans-Wolf Jäger, eds. *Reisen im 18. Jahrhundert: Neue Untersuchungen.* Heidelberg: Carl Winter, 1986.

Guthke, Karl S. *Goethes Weimar und "Die große Öffnung in die weite Welt."* Wiesbaden: Harrassowitz, 2001.

Guthrie, W. K. C. *Orpheus and Greek Religion: A Study of the Orphic Movement.* New York: Norton, 1967.

Habermas, Jürgen. *Strukturwandel der Öffentlichkeit: Untersuchungen zu einer Kategorie der bürgerlichen Gesellschaft.* Neuwied: H. Luchterhand, 1962.

Hankins, Thomas. "The Ocular Harpsichord of Louis-Betrand Castel; or, the Instrument That Wasn't." *Osiris,* 2d ser., no. 9 (1994): 141–43.

Hanslick, Eduard. *Vom musikalisch-Schönen: Ein Beitrag zur Revision der Ästhetik der Tonkunst.* Wiesbaden: Breitkopf and Härtel, 1989.

Harap, Louis. "Some Hellenic Ideas on Music and Character." *Musical Quarterly* 24, no. 2 (1938): 153–68.

Harris, Ellen T. *Handel as Orpheus: Voice and Desire in the Chamber Cantatas.* Cambridge, Mass.: Harvard University Press, 2001.

Harrison, Frank. *Time, Place, and Music: An Anthology of Ethnomusicological Observation c. 1550 to c. 1800.* Amsterdam: Frits Knuf, 1973.

Hawkesworth, John. *An Account of the Voyages . . . for Making Discoveries in the Southern Hemisphere.* London: Printed for W. Strahan and T. Cadell, 1773.

Hawkins, John. *A General History of the Science and Practice of Music.* 2 vols. London: Novello, Ewer, 1875.

Hegar, Elisabeth. *Die Anfänge der neueren Musikgeschichtsschreibung um 1770 bei Gerbert, Burney, und Hawkins.* Vol. 7, *Sammlung musikwissenschaftlicher Abhandlungen.* Baden-Baden: Valentin Koerner, 1974.

Hegel, Georg Wilhelm Friedrich. "Aesthetik." In *Music and Aesthetics in the Eighteenth and Early-nineteenth Centuries,* edited by Peter le Huray and James Day, 339–53. New York: Cambridge University Press, 1981.

Hell, Julia. "The Angel's Enigmatic Eyes, or the Gothic Beauty of Catastrophic History in W. G. Sebald's 'Air War and Literature.'" *Criticism* 46, no. 3 (2004): 361–92.

Herder, Johann Gottfried. *Volkslieder, Übertragungen, Dichtungen,* edited by Ulrich Gaier. Frankfurt am Main: Deutscher Klassiker Verlag, 1990.

Heriot, Angus. *The Castrati in Opera.* London: Secker and Warburg, 1956.

Hermand, Jost. *Konkretes Hören: Zum Inhalt der Instrumentalmusik.* Berlin: Argument, 1981.

Hess, Jonathan. *Germans, Jews, and the Claims of Modernity.* New Haven, Conn.: Yale University Press, 2002.

———. *Reconstituting the Body Politic: Enlightenment, Public Culture, and the Invention of Aesthetic Autonomy.* Detroit: Wayne State University Press, 1999.

Hiller, Johann Adam. *Mein Leben: Autobiographie, Briefe, und Nekrologe,* edited by Mark
  Lehmstedt. Leipzig: Lehmstedt, 2004.

———. *Ueber die Musik und deren Wirkungen, mit Anmerkungen.* Leipzig: Friedrich
  Gotthold Jacobäer, 1781.

———. *Wöchentliche Nachrichten und Anmerkungen die Musik betreffend.* Leipzig: Zeitungs-
  Expedition, 1768. Reprint, Hildesheim: Georg Olms, 1970.

Hoare, Michael E. *The Tactless Philosopher: Johann Reinhold Forster (1729–1798).* Melbourne: Hawthorn, 1976.

Hoffmann, E. T. A. "Beethovens Instrumentalmusik." In *Kreisleriana.* Stuttgart: Philipp
  Reclam, 2000.

———. "Beethoven's Instrumental Music (1813)." In *Source Readings in Music History,*
  edited by Oliver Strunk, revised and edited by Leo Treitler, 1193–98. New York:
  Norton, 1998.

———. *Der goldene Topf.* Stuttgart: Philipp Reclam, 1999.

Hohendahl, Peter Uwe, ed. *Patriotism, Cosmopolitanism, and National Culture: Public
  Culture in Hamburg 1700–1933.* Amsterdam: Rodopi, 2003.

Holcroft, Thomas. *Travels from Hamburg through Westphalia, Holland, and the Netherlands.*
  2 vols. London: Printed for R. Phillips, 1804.

Homer. *The Odyssey,* 2d ed., edited and translated by Albert Cook. New York: Norton,
  1993.

Horace. *The Poetic Art: A Translation of Horace's "Ars Poetica,"* translated by C. H. Sisson.
  Cheshire, UK: Carcanet Press, 1975.

Horden, Peregrine, ed. *Music as Medicine: The History of Music Therapy since Antiquity.*
  Brookfield, Vt.: Ashgate, 2000.

Horkheimer, Max, and Theodor W. Adorno. *Dialektik der Aufklärung.* Frankfurt am
  Main: Fischer, 1969.

Hosler, Bellamy. *Changing Aesthetic Views of Instrumental Music in 18th-Century Germany.*
  Ann Arbor: UMI Research Press, 1981.

Howard, John. *The State of the Prisons in England and Wales, with Preliminary Observations,
  and an Account of some Foreign Prisons and Hospitals,* 3d ed. Warrington, UK: Printed
  by William Eyres, and sold by T. Cadell, J. Johnson, and C. Dilly, in London, 1784.

Howard, Patricia. *Gluck: An Eighteenth-Century Portrait in Letters and Documents.* New
  York: Oxford University Press, 1995.

Hoyt, Peter A. "On the Primitives of Music Theory: The Savage and Subconscious as
  Sources of Analytical Authority." In *Music Theory and Natural Order from the Re-
  naissance to the Early Twentieth Century,* edited by Suzannah Clark and Alexander
  Rehding, 197–212. New York: Cambridge University Press, 2001.

Hulme, Peter. *Colonial Encounters: Europe and the Native Caribbean 1492–1797.* London:
  Methuen, 1986.

Humboldt, Alexander von. *Ansichten der Kordilleren und Monumente der eingeborenen Völker
  Amerikas,* edited by Oliver Lubrich and Ottmar Ette, translated by Claudia Kal-
  scheuer. Frankfurt am Main: Eichborn, 2004.

———. *Ansichten der Natur mit wissenschaftlichen Erläuterungen.* Tübingen: Cotta, 1808.

Hunter, Mary. "The *Alla Turca* Style in the Late Eighteenth Century: Race and
  Gender in the Symphony and the Seraglio." In *The Exotic in Western Music,* edited by
  Jonathan Bellman, 43–73. Boston: Northeastern University Press, 1998.

————. "'To Play as if from the Soul of the Composer': The Idea of the Performer in Early Romantic Aesthetics." *Journal of the American Musicological Society* 58, no. 2 (2005): 357–98.

Hurd, Richard. "Dialogues on the Uses of Foreign Travel; Considered as a Part of an English Gentleman's Education: Between Lord Shaftesbury and Mr. Locke (1775)." In *Travel Writing 1700–1830: An Anthology,* edited by Elizabeth A. Bohls and Ian Duncan, 18–19. New York: Oxford University Press, 2005.

Hust, Christoph. "Introduction." In *Charles Burney: Tagebuch einer musikalischen Reise,* edited by Christoph Hust, 7–17. Reprint, Kassel: Bärenreiter, 2003.

Ingram, Martin. "Ridings, Rough Music, and Mocking Rhymes in Early Modern England." In *Popular Culture in Seventeenth-Century England,* edited by Barry Reay, 166–97. London: Croom Helm, 1985.

Irving, David. "The Pacific in the Minds and Music of Enlightenment Europe." *Eighteenth-century Music* 2 (2005): 205–29.

Jahn, Friedrich Ludwig. *Deutsches Volkstum.* Berlin: Aufbau, 1991.

Jodrell, Richard Paul. *A Widow and No Widow: A Dramatic Piece of Three Acts. As it was performed at the Theatre-Royal in the Hay-Market, in the Year 1779.* Dublin: G. Bonham, 1780.

Johnson, Samuel. *A Journey to the Western Isles of Scotland.* London: Printed for W. Strahan and T. Cadell, 1775.

Joppien, Rüdiger, and Bernard Smith. *The Art of Captain Cook's Voyages.* Vol. 3, *The Voyage of the* Resolution *and* Discovery *1776–1780.* New Haven, Conn.: Yale University Press, in association with the Australian Academy of the Humanities, 1988.

Joubert, Estelle. "Songs to Shape a German Nation: Hiller's Comic Operas and the Public Sphere." *Eighteenth-century Music* 3 (2006): 213–30.

Junker, Carl Ludwig. *Ueber den Werth der Tonkunst.* Bayreuth und Leipzig: Joh. Andreas Lübecks sel. Erben, 1786.

Kaden, Christian. "'Die New welt, der landschaften und Insulen.' Reiseberichte als historische Quellen der Musikethnologie?" *Historische Volksmusikforschung: Studiengruppe zur Erforschung historischer Volkmusikquellen im ICTM: Beiträge der 10. Arbeitstagung in Göttingen 1991* (1994): 253–60.

Kaeppler, Adrienne L. *"Artificial Curiosities": An Exposition of Native Manufactures Collected on the Three Pacific Voyages of Captain James Cook, R. N.* Bernice P. Bishop Museum Special Publication 65. Honolulu: Bishop Museum Press, 1978.

Kandler, Georg. *Deutsche Armeemärsche: Ein Beitrag zur Geschichte des Instrumentariums, des Repertoires, der Funktion, des Personals, und des Widerhalls der deutschen Militärmusik.* Bad Godesberg: Hohwacht, 1962.

Kant, Immanuel. *Critique of Judgment,* translated by James Creed Meredith. Oxford, UK: Clarendon, 1986.

————. "Perpetual Peace: A Philosophical Sketch." In *Kant: Political Writings,* edited by H. S. Reiss, 93–130. New York: Cambridge University Press, 1991.

————. "Vergleichung des ästhetischen Werts der schönen Künste untereinander." In *Schriften zur Ästhetik und Naturphilosophie,* edited by Manfred Frank and Véronique Zanetti. Frankfurt am Main: Deutscher Klassiker, 1996.

Kaplan, Caren. *Questions of Travel: Postmodern Discourses of Displacement.* Durham, N.C.: Duke University Press, 1996.

Kästner, Abraham Gotthelf. "Betrachtungen über die alte und neue Musik, mit der-
selben Anwendung zur Heilung der Krankheiten nebst einem Versuche die Frage
aufzulösen: Worinn der Unterschied der alten und neuen Musik bestanden hat." In
Friedrich Wilhelm Marpurg, *Historisch-kritische Beyträge zur Aufnahme der Musik.* Vol.
2, part 1. Berlin: Gottlieb August Lange, 1756. Reprint, Hildesheim: Georg Olms,
1970.

Kassler, Jamie Croy. "Burney's Sketch of a Plan for a Public Music-School." *Musical
Quarterly* 58, no. 2 (1972): 210–234.

Kaufman, Paul. *Libraries and Their Users: Collected Papers in Library History.* London:
Library Association, 1969.

Kaufman Shelemay, Kay. "Crossing Boundaries in Music and Musical Scholarship: A
Perspective from Ethnomusicology." *Musical Quarterly* 80, no. 1 (Spring 1996): 13–30.

Kelly, Gary. "Holcroft, Thomas (1745–1809)." In *Oxford Dictionary of National Biography.* New York: Oxford University Press, 2004. http://www.oxforddnb.com, s.v.
"Thomas Holcroft" (accessed May 21, 2006).

Kelly, Michael. *Reminiscences of Michael Kelly, of the King's Theatre, and Theatre Royal Drury
Lane, Including a Period of Nearly Half a Century; with Original Anecdotes of Many
Distinguished Persons, Political, Literary, and Musical.* Reprint edited by Roger Fiske.
New York: Oxford University Press, 1975.

Kerman, Joseph. *Opera as Drama.* Berkeley: University of California Press, 1988.

Keysler [*sic*], Johann Georg. *Neueste Reise durch Teutschland, Böhmen, Ungarn, die Schweitz,
Italien, und Lothringen.* Hanover: N. Försters Erben, 1740.

Keyssler, Johann Georg. *Travels through Germany, Bohemia, Hungary, Switzerland, Italy,
and Lorrain. Giving a true and just description of the present state of those countries. Carefully
translated from the second edition of the German.* 4 vols. London: Printed for A. Linde and
T. Field, 1756–1757.

[King, James]. "Merkwürdige Vorfälle auf Capit. Cook's letzter Reise (Fortsetzung)."
Gelehrte Beyträge zu den Braunschweigischen Anzeigen 25, no. 20 (1785): Columns
165–72.

Kircher, Athanasius. *Philosophischer Extract und Auszug aus des Welt-berühmten Teutschen
Jesuitens Athanasii Kircheri von Fulda Musurgia Universali, in Sechs Bücher verfasset . . . ;
Ausgezogen und verfertiget . . . von Andrea Hirschen.* Schwäbisch Hall: Hans Reinh. Lai-
digen, 1662. Facsimile, edited by Wolfgang Godhan. Kassel: Bärenreiter, 1988.

Kivy, Peter. *Osmin's Rage: Philosophical Reflections on Opera, Drama, and Text.* Princeton,
N.J.: Princeton University Press, 1988.

Kleist, Heinrich von. *Das Erdbeben in Chili und andere Erzählungen,* ed. Joanna Rudolph.
Berlin: Verlag Neues Leben, 1980.

Klemm, Eberhardt. "Foreword." In *Tagebuch einer musikalischen Reise durch Frankreich und
Italien, durch Flandern, die Niederlande und am Rhein bis Wien. 1770–1772 von Charles
Burney.* Reprint, Wilhelmshaven: Heinrichshofen, 1980.

Klockenbring, Friedrich Arnold. "Etwas über die Musik in den neuerlich entdeckten
Südländern." In *Aufsätze, verschiedenen Inhalts.* Hanover: Im Verlage der Schmidtschen
Buchhandlung, 1787.

[———]. "Nachlese zu dem Auszuge aus Cooks Reise um die Welt; aus Georg Forsters
Beschreibung eben dieser Reise." *Hannoverisches Magazin* 15, no. 101 (December 19,
1777): Columns 1601–16; 15, no. 102 (December 22, 1777): Columns 1617–32.

————. "Schluß der Anmerkungen über Holland," *Hannoverisches Magazin* 93 (November 20, 1769): Columns 1473–84.

Klotz, Sebastian. *Kombinatorik und die Verbindungskünste der Zeichen in der Musik zwischen 1630 und 1780.* Berlin: Akademie Verlag, 2006.

Koch, Hannsjoachim W. *A History of Prussia.* London: Longman, 1978.

Koch, Heinrich Christoph. "Kurzer Abriß der Geschichte der Tonkunst bey den Völkern der Vorzeit." *Journal der Tonkunst* (1795): 122–33.

————. *Musikalisches Lexikon.* Frankfurt am Main: August Hermann dem Jüngern, 1802. Reprint, edited by Nicole Schwindt. Kassel: Bärenreiter, 2001.

Koerner, Joseph Leo. *Caspar David Friedrich and the Subject of Landscape.* New Haven, Conn.: Yale University Press, 1990.

Konuk, Kader. *Mimesis in Istanbul: Erich Auerbach in Turkish Exile.* Book manuscript.

Kopp, Kristin Leigh. Contesting Borders: German Colonial Discourse and the Polish Eastern Territories. PhD diss., University of California, Berkeley, 2001.

Koshar, Rudy. *German Travel Cultures.* Oxford, UK: Berg, 2000.

Krader, Barbara. "Ethnomusicology." In *The New Grove Dictionary of Music and Musicians,* edited by Stanley Sadie. London: Macmillan, 1980.

Kramer, Cheryce. "Music as Cause and Cure of Illness in Nineteenth-century Europe." In *Music as Medicine: The History of Music Therapy since Antiquity,* edited by Peregrine Horden, 338–52. Brookfield, Vt.: Ashgate, 2000.

Kramer, Lloyd S. *Threshold of a New World: Intellectuals and the Exile Experience in Paris, 1830–1840.* Ithaca, N.Y.: Cornell University Press, 1988.

Krickeberg, Dieter. "Einflüsse außereuropäischer Musik auf Europa." In *Focus Behaim Globus.* Nuremberg: Verlag des Germanischen Nationalmuseums, 1992.

Krimmer, Elisabeth. "'Eviva il Coltello'? The Castrato Singer in Eighteenth-century Literature and Culture." *Publications of the Modern Language Association of America* 120, no. 5 (2005): 1543–59.

Kristeva, Julia. *Powers of Horror: An Essay on Abjection,* translated by Leon S. Roudiez. New York: Columbia University Press, 1982.

Kümmel, Werner Friedrich. *Musik und Medizin: Ihre Wechselbeziehung in Theorie und Praxis von 800 bis 1800.* Freiburg: Karl Alber, 1977.

[Labat, Jean-Baptiste]. "Nachricht von der barbarischen Musik der Einwohner im Königreich Juda in Africa, nebst der Abbildung ihrer musikalischen Instrumente." *Musikalische Bibliothek, oder Gründliche Nachricht nebst unpartheyischem Urtheil von alten und neuen musikalischen Schriften und Büchern, worinn alles, Was aus der Mathematik, Philosophie, und den schönen Wissenschafften zur Verbesserung und Erläuterung* 3, no. 3 (1747): 572–77.

Laborde, Jean Benjamin de. *Essai sur la musique ancienne et moderne.* Vol. 1. Paris: Eugene Onfroy, 1780. Reprint of first edition. New York: AMS, 1978.

Lamb, Jonathan. *Preserving the Self in the South Seas, 1680–1840.* Chicago: University of Chicago Press, 2001.

le Huray, Peter, and James Day, eds. *Music and Aesthetics in the Eighteenth and Early-nineteenth Centuries.* New York: Cambridge University Press, 1981.

Leppert, Richard. *Music and Image: Domesticity, Ideology, and Socio-cultural Formation in Eighteenth-century England.* New York: Cambridge University Press, 1988.

————. "Music 'Pushed to the Edge of Existence' (Adorno, Listening, and the Question of Hope)." *Cultural Critique* 60 (Spring 2005): 96–97.

————. *The Sight of Sound: Music, Representation, and the History of the Body.* Berkeley: University of California Press, 1993.

Lessing, Gotthold Ephraim. *Werke und Briefe,* edited by Wilfried Barner et al. 12 vols. Frankfurt am Main: Deutscher Klassiker Verlag, 1985–.

Letts, Malcolm. "The Fifth Stage: Germany and the Rhineland." In *Grand Tour: A Journey in the Tracks of the Age of Aristocracy,* edited by R. S. Lambert, 119–36. London: Faber and Faber, 1935.

Lévi-Strauss, Claude. *Tristes Tropiques,* translated by John Weightman and Doreen Weightman. Harmondsworth, UK: Penguin, 1973.

Lichtenberg, Georg Christoph. *The World of Hogarth: Lichtenberg's Commentaries on Hogarth's Engravings,* translated by Innes Herdan and Gustav Herdan. Boston: Houghton Mifflin, 1966.

Liebersohn, Harry. *Aristocratic Encounters: European Travelers and North American Indians.* New York: Cambridge University Press, 1998.

————. *The Travelers' World: Europe to the Pacific.* Cambridge, Mass.: Harvard University Press, 2006.

Lippman, Edward. *A History of Western Musical Aesthetics.* Lincoln: University of Nebraska Press, 1992.

Locke, John. *Two Treatises of Government,* edited by Mark Goldie. London: Everyman, 1993.

Locke, Ralph P. "Exoticism." *Grove Music Online,* edited by L. Macy. http://www.grovemusic.com, s.v. "Exoticism" (accessed July 18, 2005).

————. "Reflections on Orientalism in Opera and Musical Theatre." *Opera Quarterly* 10, no. 1 (1993): 49–73.

Lonsdale, Roger. *Dr. Charles Burney: A Literary Biography.* Oxford, UK: Clarendon, 1965.

Lütteken, Laurenz, ed. *Die Musik in den Zeitschriften des 18. Jahrhunderts: Eine Bibliographie.* Kassel: Bärenreiter, 2004.

MacLean, Gerald. "Strolling in Syria with William Biddulph." *Criticism* 46, no. 3, (Summer 2004): 415–39.

Macpherson, James. *The works of Ossian, the son of Fingal. In two volumes. Translated from the Galic [sic] language by James Macpherson,* 3d ed., 2 vols. London: Printed for T. Becket and P. A. Dehondt, 1765.

Malinowski, Bronisław. *Argonauts of the Western Pacific.* New York: Dutton, 1961.

Manwaring, George Ernest. *My Friend the Admiral: The Life, Letters, and Journals of Rear-Admiral James Burney, F. R. S., the Companion of Captain Cook and Friend of Charles Lamb.* London: Routledge, 1931.

Marpurg, Friedrich Wilhelm. "Historie von einem durch Musik geheilten Tonkünstler." In *Kritische Briefe über die Tonkunst.* Berlin: Friedrich Wilhelm Birnstiel, 1760. Reprint, Hildesheim: Georg Olms, 1974.

————. *Historisch-kritische Beyträge zur Aufnahme der Musik.* Vol. 2. Berlin: Gottlieb August Lange, 1756. Reprint, Hildesheim: Georg Olms, 1970.

————. "Ob und was für Harmonie die Alten gehabt, und zu welcher Zeit dieselbe zur Vollkommenheit gebracht worden." *Historisch-kritische Beyträge zur Aufnahme der Musik* 2, no. 4 (1756).

Marshall, Peter. "No Fatal Impact? The Elusive History of Imperial Britain." *Times Literary Supplement* (March 12, 1993): 8–10.

Martens, Wolfgang. "Ein Bürger auf Reisen." In *Friedrich Nicolai 1733–1811: Essays zum 250. Geburtstag,* edited by Bernhard Fabian. Berlin: Nicolaische Verlagsbuchhandlung, 1983.

Martin, John. *An Account of the Natives of the Tonga Islands in the South Pacific Ocean with an Original Grammar and Vocabulary of Their Language.* 2 vols. London: John Murray, 1817.

Marvel, Andrew. "An Essay upon the Unfortunate Charms and Power of Music." *London Museum of Politics, Miscellanies, and Literature* 1 (1770): 41–43.

Mason, Peter. *Infelicities: Representations of the Exotic.* Baltimore: Johns Hopkins University Press, 1998.

Mattheson, Johann. *Critica Musica.* Vol. 1. Hamburg: Auf Unkosten des Autors, 1722. Reprint, edited by Sven Hiemke. Laaber: Laaber Verlag, 2003.

———. *Der vollkommene Capellmeister.* Hamburg: Christian Herold, 1739. Reprint, edited by Friederike Ramm. Kassel: Bärenreiter, 1999.

Maurer, Michael. *Aufklärung und Anglophilie in Deutschland.* Göttingen: Vandenhoeck and Ruprecht, 1987.

———, ed. *"O Britannien, von deiner Freiheit einen Hut voll": Deutsche Reiseberichte des 18. Jahrhunderts.* Munich: C. H. Beck, 1992.

Mayer, David. *Harlequin in His Element: The English Pantomime 1806–1836.* Cambridge, Mass.: Harvard University Press, 1969.

McCalman, Iain. "Spectacles of Knowledge: OMAI as Ethnographic Travelogue." In *Cook and Omai: The Cult of the South Seas.* Canberra: National Library of Australia, in association with the Humanities Research Centre, Australian National University, 2001.

McClintock, Anne. *Imperial Leather: Race, Gender, and Sexuality in the Colonial Contest.* New York: Routledge, 1995.

McCormick, E. H. *Omai: Pacific Envoy.* Auckland: Auckland University Press, 1977.

McKillop, Alan Dugald. "Bonnell Thornton's Burlesque Ode." *Notes and Queries* 194 (1949): 321–24.

———. "Local Attachment and Cosmopolitanism: The Eighteenth-century Pattern." In *From Sensibility to Romanticism: Essays Presented to Frederick A. Pottle,* edited by Frederick W. Hilles and Harold Bloom, 191–218. New York: Oxford University Press, 1965.

McLean, Mervyn. "Nafa." In *The New Grove Dictionary of Musical Instruments,* vol. 2, ed. Stanley Sadie, 738–39. London: Macmillan, 1984.

———. *Weavers of Song: Polynesian Music and Dance.* Auckland: Auckland University Press, 1999.

McVeagh, John, ed. *All before Them, 1660–1780.* London: Ashfield, 1990.

McVeigh, Simon. "Felice Giardini: A Violinist in Late Eighteenth-century London." *Music and Letters* 64 (1983): 162–72.

———. "Music and Lock Hospital in the 18th Century." *Musical Times* 129, no. 1743 (1988): 39–40, 235–37.

Mead, William Edward. *The Grand Tour in the Eighteenth Century.* Boston: Houghton Mifflin, 1914.

Mellers, Wilfrid. "The Heroism of Henry Purcell: Music and Politics in Restoration England." In *Music and the Politics of Culture,* edited by Christopher Norris, 20–40. London: Lawrence and Wishart, 1989.

Meyers, Helen. "Ethnomusicology: Pre-1945, Background." *Grove Music Online,* edited by L. Macy. http://www.grovemusic.com, s.v. "Ethnomusicology" (accessed July 18, 2005).

Michaelis, Christian Friedrich. "Ueber die Musik einiger wilden und halb cultivierten Völker." *Allgemeine Musikalische Zeitung* 31 (1814): 509–30.

Middleton, Richard. "Musical Belongings: Western Music and Its Low-Other." In *Western Music and Its Others: Difference, Representation, and Appropriation in Music,* edited by Georgina Born and David Hesmondhalgh, 59–85. Berkeley: University of California Press, 2000.

Millar, John. *The Origin of the Distinction of Ranks.* London: Thoemmes, 1990.

Mizler [von Kolof], Lorenz Christoph. "Horologium Musicum." In *Neu-eröffnete musikalische Bibliothek,* vol. 1. Leipzig: Im Verlag des Verfassers und bey Brauns Erben, 1739; fac. ed., Hilversum: Frits Knuf, 1966, 61–62.

———. "Nachricht von der barbarischen Musik der Einwohner im Königreich Juda in Africa, nebst der Abbildung ihrer musikalischen Instrumente." In *Neu-eröffnete musikalische Bibliothek,* vol. 3. Leipzig: Im Mizlerishen Bücher-Verlag, 1747; fac. ed., Hilversum: Frits Knuf, 1966, 573–75.

———. "Physicalischer Tractat von den Wirkungen der Musik in den belebten Körper. Herausgegeben von D. Joh. Wilh. Albrecht, Leipzig 1734." *Musikalische Bibliothek, oder gründliche Nachricht nebst unpartheyischem Urtheil von alten und neuen musikalischen Schriften und Büchern . . .* (1754).

M'Nicol, Donald. *Remarks on Dr. Samuel Johnson's Journey to the Hebrides, in which are contained, Observations in the Antiquities, Language, Genius, and Manners of the Highlanders of Scotland.* London: T. Cadell, 1779.

Montagu, Mary Wortley. *The Turkish Embassy Letters,* edited by Anita Desai. London: Virago, 1994.

Moody, Jane. *Illegitimate Theatre in London, 1770–1840.* New York: Cambridge University Press, 2000.

Moore, John. *A view of society and manners in France, Switzerland, and Germany: with anecdotes relating to some eminent characters. By a gentleman, who resided several years in those countries.* London: Printed for W. Strahan and T. Cadell, 1781.

Moorefield, A. A. "James Bruce: Ethnomusicologist or Abyssinian Lyre?" *Journal of the American Musicological Society* 28 (1975): 493–514.

Moretti, Franco. *Atlas of the European Novel, 1800–1900.* London: Verso, 1998.

Moritz, Karl Philipp. "Versuch einer Vereinigung aller schönen Künste und Wissenschaften unter dem Begriff des in sich selbst Vollendeten." *Schriften zur Ästhetik und Poetik,* edited by Hans Joachim Schrimpf. Tübingen: Max Niemeyer, 1962.

Morrow, Mary Sue. *German Music Criticism in the Late Eighteenth Century: Aesthetic Issues in Instrumental Music.* New York: Cambridge University Press, 1997.

Mossakowski, Stanisław. "Raphael's 'St. Cecilia.' An Iconographical Study." *Zeitschrift für Kunstgeschichte* 31, no. 1 (1968): 1–26.

Mosse, George L. *The Image of Man: The Creation of Modern Masculinity.* New York: Oxford University Press, 1996.

Moyle, Richard. *Tongan Music.* Auckland: Auckland University Press, 1987.

Neubauer, John. *The Emancipation of Music from Language: Departure from Mimesis in Eighteenth-century Aesthetics.* New Haven, Conn.: Yale University Press, 1986.

New, Caroline. "Realism, Deconstruction, and the Feminist Standpoint." *Journal for the Theory of Social Behaviour* 28, no. 4 (1998): 349–72.

Nichols, Reginald H., and F. A. Wray. *History of the Foundling Hospital.* London: Oxford University Press, 1935.

Nicolai, Ernst Anton. *Die Verbindung der Musik mit der Arzneygelahrtheit.* Halle: Hemmerde, 1745.

Nicolai, Friedrich. *Beschreibung einer Reise durch Deutschland und die Schweiz im Jahre 1781: Nebst Bemerkungen über Gelehrsamkeit, Industrie, Religion, und Sitten.* 12 vols. Berlin: n.p., 1783–1796.

———. *Unter Bayern und Schwaben: Meine Reise im deutschen Süden 1781,* edited by Ulrich Schlemmer. Stuttgart: Erdmann, 1989.

Noyes, John K., *Colonial Space: Spatiality in the Discourse of German South West Africa, 1884–1915.* Philadelphia: Harwood, 1992.

———. "Goethe on Cosmopolitanism and Colonialism: *Bildung* and the Dialectic of Critical Mobility." *Eighteenth-century Studies* 39, no. 4 (Summer 2006): 443–62.

Nugent, Thomas. "The Grand Tour. Containing an Exact Description of Most of the Cities, Towns, and Remarkable Places of Europe. Together with a Distinct Account of the Post-Roads and Stages (1756)." In *Travel Writing 1700–1830: An Anthology,* edited by Elizabeth A. Bohls and Ian Duncan, 14–17. New York: Oxford University Press, 2005.

———. *The Grand Tour; or, a Journey through the Netherlands, Germany, Italy, and France.* London: Printed for D. Browne, A. Millar, G. Hawkins, W. Johnston, and P. Davey and B. Law, 1756.

Nussbaum, Felicity A. *The Limits of the Human: Fictions of Anomaly, Race, and Gender in the Long Eighteenth Century.* New York: Cambridge University Press, 2003.

Obeyesekere, Gananath. *The Apotheosis of Captain Cook: European Mythmaking in the Pacific.* Princeton, N.J.: Princeton University Press, 1997.

O'Brien, Karen. *Narratives of Enlightenment: Cosmopolitan History from Voltaire to Gibbon.* New York: Cambridge University Press, 1997.

Odell, Jay Scott. "Charivari." *Grove Music Online,* edited by L. Macy. http://www.grovemusic.com, s.v. "Charivari" (accessed March 3, 2006).

O'Keeffe, John. "A Short Account of the New Pantomime called Omai, or, a Trip round the World." In *The Plays of John O'Keeffe,* vol. 2, edited by Frederick M. Link, 1–24. New York: Garland, 1981.

Oldman, C. B. "Charles Burney and Louis De Visme." *Music Review* 27 (1966): 93–97.

O'Quinn, Daniel. *Staging Governance: Theatrical Imperialism in London, 1770–1800.* Baltimore: Johns Hopkins University Press, 2005.

Osterhammel, Jürgen. "Distanzerfahrung: Darstellungsweisen des Fremden im 18. Jahrhundert." In *Der europäische Beobachter außereuropäischer Kulturen: Zur Problematik der Wirklichkeitswahrnehmung,* ed. Hans-Joachim König et al. *Zeitschrift für historische Forschung* 7 (1989): 9–42.

Outram, Dorinda. *The Enlightenment,* 2d ed. New York: Cambridge University Press, 2005.

Ovid. *The Metamorphoses,* translated by David R. Slavitt. Baltimore: Johns Hopkins University Press, 1994.

Pallas, [Peter Simon]. "Herrn D. Pallas Nachricht von den russischen Entdeckungen in dem Meere zwischen Asia und Amerika." *Gelehrte Beyträge zu den Braunschweigischen Anzeigen* 26, no. 67 (1786): 547–52.

Parke, William Thomas. *Musical Memoirs.* 2 vols. London: H. Colburn and R. Bentley, 1830.

Pauly, Reinhard G. *Music in the Classic Period,* 2d ed. Englewood Cliffs, N.J.: Prentice-Hall, 1973.

Paumgartner, Bernhard, ed. *Dr. Charles Burney's musikalische Reise durch das alte Österreich.* Vienna: Hollinek, 1948.

Pauw, Cornelius de. *Philosophical Dissertations on the Greeks.* Vol. 2. London: R. Faulder, 1793.

Pederson, Sanna. "A. B. Marx, Berlin Concert Life, and German National Identity," *19th-Century Music* 18, no. 2 (1994): 87–107.

————. Enlightened and Romantic German Music Criticism, 1800–1850. PhD diss., University of Pennsylvania, 1995.

————. Long-term Winning and Losing Strategies for Writing about Music in a Modern World: The Case of Wilhelm Heinrich Riehl (1823–1897). Presentation at German Studies Association Conference, Pittsburgh, September 30, 2006.

Peitsch, Helmut. "Englische Reisebeschreibungen in der *Neuen Bibliothek der schönen Wissenschaften und der freyen Künste.*" *Internationales Archiv für Sozialgeschichte der deutschen Literatur* 31 (2006): 1–50.

————. "Georg Forster als Vermittler englischer Reisebeschreibungen." *Georg-Forster-Studien* 9 (2004): 107–31.

————. *Georg Forsters Ansichten vom Niederrhein: Zum Problem des Übergangs vom bürgerlichen Humanismus zum revolutionären Demokratismus.* Frankfurt am Main: Peter Lang, 1978.

————. " 'Noch war die halbe Oberfläche der Erdkugel von tiefer Nacht bedeckt': Georg Forster über die Bedeutung der Reisen der europäischen 'Seemächte' für das deutsche 'Publikum.' " *Das Europa der Aufklärung und die außereuropäische koloniale Welt,* edited by Hans-Jürgen Lüsebrink, 157–74. Göttingen: Wallstein, 2006.

————. "Round-trips from the Inside to the Outside: The Changing Places of Georg Forster's Travelogues in the German Literary Canon from 1797 to 1989." *Carleton Germanic Papers* (Ottowa) 24 (1996): 17–31.

Pennant, Thomas. *A Tour in Scotland 1769.* Chester, UK: John Monk, 1771.

————. *A Tour in Scotland and Voyage to the Hebrides.* Chester, UK: John Monk, 1772.

Pepys, Samuel. *The Diary of Samuel Pepys,* edited by Henry B. Wheatley. Vol. 2. London: George Bell, 1893.

Perry, Ruth. "Anna Gordon Brown's Ballads." Presentation at Gender and Popular Culture Conference, University of Michigan, October 21–22, 2005.

Petty, Frederick Curtis. *Italian Opera in London 1760–1800.* Ann Arbor: UMI Research, 1980.

Pfau, Thomas. *Romantic Moods: Paranoia, Trauma, and Melancholy, 1790–1840.* Baltimore: Johns Hopkins University Press, 2005.

Pindar. *The Odes of Pindar,* translated by John Sandys. Cambridge, Mass.: Harvard University Press, 1937.

Pindar, Peter [John Wolcot]. *A Complimentary Epistle to James Bruce, Esq. the Abyssinian Traveler.* London: H. D. Symonds, 1792.

Piozzi, Hester Lynch. *Observations and Reflections made in the course of a Journey through France, Italy, and Germany.* 2 vols. Dublin: H. Chamberlaine, L. White, P. Byrne, P. Wogan, Grubier, and M'Allister, 1789.

Pliny. *Natural History,* edited by H. Rackham. Cambridge, Mass.: Harvard University Press, 1989.

Pocock, J. G. A. "European Perceptions of World History in the Age of Encounter." In *Voyages and Beaches: Pacific Encounters, 1769–1840,* edited by Alex Calder, Jonathan Lamb, and Bridget Orr, 25–44. Honolulu: University of Hawaii Press, 1999.

Poovey, Mary. *A History of the Modern Fact: Problems of Knowledge in the Sciences of Wealth and Society.* Chicago: Chicago University Press, 1998.

Porta, John Baptista Porta [Giovanni Battista della Porta]. *Natural Magick.* London: Thomas Young and Samuel Speed, 1658. Reprint, edited by Derek J. Price, New York: Basic Books, 1957.

Porter, Roy. *Flesh in the Age of Reason.* New York: Norton, 2005.

Powers, Harold S., and Frans Wiering. "Modes." *Grove Music Online,* edited by L. Macy. http://www.grovemusic.com, s.v. "Modes" (accessed February 16, 2005).

Pratt, Mary Louise. *Imperial Eyes: Travel Writing and Transculturation.* London: Routledge, 1992.

Pressly, William L. "A Chapel of Natural and Revealed Religion: James Barry's Series for the Society's Great Room Reinterpreted." *Royal Society for the Encouragement of Arts, Manufactures, and Commerce Journal* 132, no. 5336 (July 1984): 543–46.

Price, Curtis Alexander, Judith Milhous, and Robert D. Hume. *Italian Opera in Late Eighteenth-century London.* Vol. 1, *The King's Theatre, Haymarket 1778–1791.* New York: Oxford University Press, 1995.

———. *The Impresario's Ten Commandments: Continental Recruitment for Italian Opera in London 1763–1764.* London: Royal Musical Association, 1992.

Puff, Helmut. *Sodomy in Reformation Germany and Switzerland, 1400–1600.* Chicago: University of Chicago Press, 2003.

———. "Orpheus after Eurydice (according to Albrecht Duerer)." In *Dead Lovers: Erotic Bonds and the Study of Premodern Europe,* edited by Basil Dufallo and Peggy McCracken, 71–95. Ann Arbor: University of Michigan Press, 2006.

Puri, Michael James. "Review: *Programming the Absolute: Nineteenth-century German Music and the Hermeneutics of the Moment,* by Berthold Hoeckner. Princeton, NJ and Oxford: Princeton University Press, 2002." *Journal of the American Musicological Society* 59, no. 2 (Summer 2006): 495.

Qureshi, Regula Burckhardt. "Focus on Ethnic Music." In *Ethnomusicology in Canada,* edited by Robert Witmer, 339–44. Toronto: Institute for Canadian Music, 1990.

R., H. L. "Eine kleine Abhandlung über die Musik, von deren Nutzen und Wirkung." *Hannoverisches Magazin* 24, no. 78 (1786): 1237–48.

Radano, Ronald. *Lying Up a Nation: Race and Black Music.* Chicago: University of Chicago Press, 2003.

Rainbow, Bernarr, and Anthony Kemp. "London. Educational Institutions: Conservatories." *Grove Music Online,* edited by L. Macy. http://www.grovemusic.com, s.v. "London" (accessed January 30, 2006).

Rees, Abraham, ed. *The Cyclopaedia; or, Universal Dictionary of Arts, Sciences, and Literature.*
Vol. 7. London: Printed for Longman, Hurst, Rees, Orme, and Brown, 1819.

Reichardt, Johann Friedrich. *Briefe, die Musik betreffend: Berichte, Rezensionen, Essays,*
edited by Grita Herre and Walther Siegmund-Schultze. Leipzig: Reclam, 1976.

————. "Fingerzeige für den denkenden und forschenden deutschen Tonkünstler."
Musikalisches Kunstmagazin 1, no. 1 (1782): 46–48; 1, no. 2 (1782): 101–102.

————. "Johann Friedrich Reichardts musikalische Reisen in England, Frankreich, und
Deutschland." *Magazin der Musik* 2, no. 2 (1786): 1083–84; (1787): 1270–71.

Reil, Johann Christian. *Rhapsodieen über die Anwendung der psychischen Curmethode auf
Geisterzerrüttungen.* Halle: Curt, 1803.

Richards, Robert J. "Rhapsodies on a Cat-piano, or Johann Christian Reil and the Foun-
dations of Romantic Psychiatry." *Critical Inquiry* 24, no. 3 (Spring 1998): 700–36.

Richter, Simon. *Laocoön's Body and the Aesthetics of Pain: Winckelmann, Lessing, Herder,
Moritz, Goethe.* Detroit: Wayne State University Press, 1992.

Riesbeck, Johann Kaspar. *Briefe eines reisenden Franzosen über Deutschland an seinen Bruder
zu Paris,* edited by Wolfgang Gerlach. Stuttgart: Steingrüben, 1967.

Riley, Matthew. "Civilising the Savage: Johann Georg Sulzer and the 'Aesthetic Force' of
Music." *Journal of the Royal Musical Association* 127, no. 1 (2002): 1–22.

————. "Johann Nikolaus Forkel on the Listening Practices of 'Kenner' and
'Liebhaber.'" *Music and Letters* 84, no. 3 (2003): 414–33.

————. *Musical Listening in the German Enlightenment: Attention, Wonder, and Astonishment.* Burlington, Vt.: Ashgate, 2004.

Rishton, Timothy J. "Plagiarism, Fiddles, and Tarantulas." *Musical Times* 125, no. 1696
(June 1984): 325–27.

Roberts, W. W. "The Trial of Midas the Second." *Bulletin of the John Rylands Library* 17
(1933): 322–32; reprinted in *Music and Letters* 14 (1933): 303–12.

Robinson, Jenefer. *Deeper than Reason: Emotion and Its Role in Literature, Music, and Art.*
New York: Oxford University Press, 2005.

Robson-Scott, W. D. *German Travellers in England, 1400–1800.* Oxford, UK: Basil
Blackwell, 1953.

Rochlitz, Friedrich. "Fragen eines Layen über mancherley Gegenstände welche Musik
und Musiker angehen." *Allgemeine Musikalische Zeitung* 3 (1800): 121–27, 146–47.

Roger, N. A. M. *The Command of the Ocean: A Naval History of Britain, 1649–1815.*
London: Penguin, 2004.

Rosselli, John. "Mingotti [nee Valentini], Regina [Caterina]." *Grove Music Online,* edited
by L. Macy. http://www.grovemusic.com, s.v. "Regina Mignotti" (accessed March
15, 2007).

Rouget, Gilbert. *Music and Trance: A Theory of the Relations between Music and Possession.*
Chicago: University of Chicago Press, 1980.

Rousseau, G. S., and Roy Porter, eds. *Exoticism in the Enlightenment.* Manchester, UK:
Manchester University Press, 1990.

Rowland, Peter. "Thomas Day (1748–1789)." In *Oxford Dictionary of National Biography.*
New York: Oxford University Press, 2004.

Rumph, Stephen. "A Kingdom Not of This World: The Political Context of E. T. A.
Hoffmann's Beethoven Criticism." *19th-Century Music* 19, no. 1 (Summer 1995):
50–67.

Rycroft, David K. "Gora." *Grove Music Online,* edited by L. Macy. http://www
.grovemusic.com, s.v. "Gora" (accessed February 10, 2006).

Sahlins, Marshall. *Historical Metaphors and Mythical Realities: Structure in the Early History
of the Sandwich Islands Kingdom.* Ann Arbor: University of Michigan Press, 1981.

———. *The Islands of History.* Chicago: Chicago University Press, 1985.

———. *Stone Age Economics.* London: Tavistock, 1972.

Said, Edward. *Orientalism.* New York: Vintage, 1979.

Salmond, Anne. *The Trial of the Cannibal Dog: The Remarkable Story of Captain Cook's
Encounters in the South Seas.* New Haven, Conn.: Yale University Press, 2003.

———. *Two Worlds: First Meetings between Maori and Europeans, 1642–1772.* Auckland:
Viking, 1991.

Samwell, David. "Some Account of a Voyage to South Seas in 1776–1777–1778.
Written by David Samwell, Surgeon of the *Discovery.*" In *The Journals of Captain James
Cook on His Voyages of Discovery: The Voyage of the* Resolution *and* Discovery *1776–
1780,* edited by J. C. Beaglehole. Cambridge, UK: Published for the Hakluyt Society
at the University Press, 1967.

Sands, Mollie. "Music as a Profession in Eighteenth-century England." *Music and Letters*
24 (1943): 90–92.

Sarjala, Jukka. *Music, Morals, and the Body: An Academic Issue in Turku, 1653–1808.*
Helsinki: Suomalaisen Kirjallisuuden Seura-Finnish Literature Society, 2000.

Scheibe, Johann Adolph. *Der critische Musicus* 2 (May 14, 1737). Hamburg: Wierings
Erben, 1737–1740.

———. *Der critische Musikus.* Leipzig: Bernhard Christoph Breitkopf, 1745. Reprint,
Hildesheim: Georg Olms, 1970.

Scherpe, Klaus. "Die Ordnung der Dinge als Exzess. Überlegungen zu einer Poetik der
Beschreibungen in ethnographischen Texten." *Zeitschrift für Germanistik* 2 (1999):
13–44.

Schiebeler, Daniel, Johann Joachim Eschenburg, Albrecht Wittenberg, and Christoph
Daniel Ebeling, eds. *Unterhaltungen.* Hamburg: Michael Christian Bock, 1766.

Schiller, Friedrich von. *On the Aesthetic Education of Man in a Series of Letters,* edited and
translated by Elizabeth M. Wilkinson and L. A. Willoughby. Oxford, UK: Oxford
University Press, 1967.

Schlözer, August Ludwig. *Vorlesungen über Land- und Seereisen, nach dem Kollegheft des stud.
jur. E. F. Haupt (Wintersemester 1795/96),* edited by Wilhelm Ebel. Göttingen:
Musterschmidt, 1962.

Schmidt, Friedrich Wilhelm August. "An die Bewohner der Pelew-Inseln im Südmeer.
(Etwas für Emigranten) und Antwort der Insulaner (Überbracht durch Cap. Wilson)." *Deutsche Monatsschrift* 2 (1794): 178–82.

Schneider, Ute. *Die Macht der Karten: Eine Geschichte der Kartographie vom Mittelalter bis
heute.* Darmstadt: Primus, 2004.

Scholes, Percy Alfred. *The Great Dr. Burney: His Life, His Travels, His Works, His Family,
and His Friends.* 2 vols. New York: Oxford University Press, 1948.

Schubart, Christian Friedrich Daniel. *Briefe,* edited by U. Wertheim and H. Böhm.
Munich: C. H. Beck, 1984.

———. *Deutsche Chronik: Jahrgang 1774–1777.* Augsburg: Conrad Heinrich Stage,
1774–1777. Reprint, Heidelberg: L. Schneider, 1975.

————. *Ideen zu einer Ästhetik der Tonkunst.* Vienna: J. V. Degen, 1806.

————. *Leben und Gesinnungen, von ihm selbst im Kerker aufgesetzt.* Leipzig: VEB Deutscher Verlag für Musik, 1980.

Scrivener, Michael. *The Cosmopolitan Ideal in the Age of Revolution and Reaction, 1776–1832.* London: Pickering and Chatto, 2007.

Seeba, Hinrich C. " 'Germany—A Literary Concept': The Myth of National Literature." *German Studies Review* 17, no. 2 (1994): 353–69.

Seed, Patricia. *Ceremonies of Possession in Europe's Conquest of the New World, 1492–1640.* New York: Cambridge University Press, 1995.

Segalan, Victor, and Giorgio Agamben. *Tote Stimmen: Maori-Musik. Mit einem Essay Ursprung und Vergessen,* edited and translated by Maria Zinfert. Berlin: Merve, 2006.

Seipel, Wilfried, ed. *Für Aug' und Ohr: Musik in Kunst- und Wunderkammern.* Milan: Skira; Vienna: Kunsthistorisches Museum, 1999.

Seume, Johann Gottfried. *Spaziergang nach Syrakus im Jahre 1802,* edited by Albert Meier. Munich: Deutscher Taschenbuch, 1991.

Shackleton, Robert. *Montesquieu: A Critical Biography.* [London]: Oxford University Press, 1961.

Sharp, Samuel. *Letters from Italy describing the customs and manners of that country, in the years 1765, and 1766.* London: Printed by R. Cave and sold by W. Nicol, 1766.

Sieg, Katrin. "Ethnic Drag and National Identity: Multicultural Crises, Crossings, and Interventions." In *The Imperialist Imagination: German Colonialism and Its Legacy,* edited by Sara Lennox, Sara Friedrichsmeyer, and Susanne Zantop, 295–319. Ann Arbor: University of Michigan Press, 1998.

Simmel, Georg. *The Sociology of Georg Simmel,* translated by Kurt Wolff. New York: Free Press, 1950.

Smart, Christopher. *Jubilate Agno,* edited by W. H. Bond. Westport, Conn.: Greenwood, 1969.

————. "A Letter from Mrs. Mary Midnight to the Royal Society, containing some new and curious Improvements upon the Cat Organ." *Midwife* 1 (1750): 98–103.

Smith, Adam. *The Theory of Moral Sentiments,* edited by D. D. Raphael and A. L. Macfie. New York: Oxford University Press, 1976. Reprint, Indianapolis: Liberty Fund, 1982.

Smith, Barbara B. "Polynesia: Music." *Grove Music Online,* edited by L. Macy. http://www.grovemusic.com, s.v. "Polynesia" (accessed May 21, 2007).

Smith, John Thomas. *Nollekens and His Times: Comprehending a Life of That Celebrated Sculptor and Memoirs of Several Contemporary Artists.* Vol. 1. London: Henry Colburn, 1828.

Smith, William, ed. *Dictionary of Greek and Roman Antiquities: Illustrated by numerous engravings on wood.* Boston: C. Little and J. Brown [London, printed], 1870.

Smollett, Tobias. *Travels through France and Italy,* edited by Frank Felsenstein. New York: Oxford University Press, 1979.

Sörlin, Sverker. "National and International Aspects of Cross-boundary Science: Scientific Travel in the Eighteenth Century." In *Denationalizing Science: The Contexts of International Scientific Practice,* edited by Terry Shinn Elisabeth Crawford and Sverker Sörlin, 43–72. Dordrecht, the Netherlands: Kluwer, 1993.

Sparrman, Anders. *A Voyage round the World with Captain James Cook in H.M.S.* Resolution, translated by Huldine Beamish and Averil Mackenzie-Grieve. London: Robert Hale, 1953.

Sponheuer, Bernd. "Reconstructing Ideal Types of the 'German' in Music." In *Music and German National Identity,* edited by Celia Applegate and Pamela Potter, 59–77. Chicago: University of Chicago Press, 2002.

Staël-Holstein, Anne Louise de. *Germany,* edited by O. W. Wight. 2 vols. Boston: Houghton Mifflin, 1887.

Stagl, Justin. *Apodemiken: Eine räsonnierte Bibliographie der reisetheoretischen Literatur des 16., 17., und 18. Jahrhunderts,* edited by M. Rassem and J. Stagl. Vol. 2, *Quellen und Abhandlungen zur Geschichte der Staatsbeschreibung und Statistik: QASS.* Paderborn: Ferdinand Schöningh, 1983.

―――. "Der 'Patriotic Traveller' des Grafen Leopold Berchtold und das Ende der Apodemik." In *Sehen und Beschreiben: Europäische Reise im 18. und frühen 19. Jahrhundert,* edited by Wolfgang Griep, 213–25. Heide: Eutiner Landesbibliothek und Westholsteinische Verlagsanstalt Boyens, 1991.

Stallybrass, Peter, and Alon White. *The Politics and Poetics of Transgression.* Ithaca, N.Y.: Cornell University Press, 1986.

Stanzel, Franz K. " 'Deutschland: Aber wo liegt es?' " In *Europäischer Völkerspiegel: Imagologisch-ethnographische Studien zu den Völkertafeln des frühen 18. Jahrhunderts,* edited by Franz K. Stanzel with Ingomar Weiler and Waldemar Zacharasiewicz, 195–209. Heidelberg: Universitätsverlag Winter, 1999.

―――, ed., with Ingomar Weiler and Waldemar Zacharasiewicz. *Europäischer Völkerspiegel: Imagologisch-ethnographische Studien zu den Völkertafeln des frühen 18. Jahrhunderts.* Heidelberg: Universitätsverlag Winter, 1999.

Stauffer, George B., ed. *The Forkel-Hoffmeister and Kühnel Correspondence: A Document of the Early Nineteenth-century Bach Revival.* New York: C. F. Peters, 1990.

Steele, Joshua. "Account of a Musical Instrument, Which was brought by Captain *Fourneaux* from the Isle of *Amsterdam* in the *South Seas* to *London* in the Year 1774, and Given to the Royal Society." *Philosophical Transactions of the Royal Society* 65 (1775): 67–71.

―――. "Remarks on a Larger System of Reed Pipes from the Isle of *Amsterdam,* with some Observations on the Nose Flute of *Otaheite.*" *Philosophical Transactions of the Royal Society* 65 (1775): 72–78.

Steinberg, Michael P. *Listening to Reason: Culture, Subjectivity, and Nineteenth-century Music.* Princeton, N.J.: Princeton University Press, 2004.

Steinmetz, George. " 'The Devil's Handwriting': Precolonial Discourse, Ethnographic Acuity, and Cross-identification in German Colonialism." *Comparative Studies in Society and History* 45 (2003): 41–95.

―――. "Precoloniality and Colonial Subjectivity: Ethnographic Discourse and Native Policy in German Overseas Imperialism, 1780s–1914." *Political Power and Social Theory* 15 (2002): 135–228.

[Steller, Georg Wilhelm]. [Sitten, Gebräuche, und Lebensart der Kamtschadalen, besonders des Frauenzimmers im Kamtschatka. Aus Herrn Stellers Beschreibung dieses Landes gezogen] Beschluß des vorigen. *Die Akademie der Grazien* 3, no. 68 (1775): [241]–56.

————. *Steller's History of Kamchatka: Collected Information concerning the History of Kam-chatk, Its Peoples, Their Manners, Names, Lifestyle, and Various Customary Practices*, edited by Marvin W. Falk, translated by Margritt Engel and Karen Willmore. Fairbanks: University of Alaska Press, 2003.

Stephan, Inge. "'Ich bin ja auch nicht . . . begierig, an meinem eigenen Körper Wir-kungen der Revolution zu erleben': Kritische Anmerkungen zum Revolutionstour-ismus, am Beispiel der 'Vertrauten Briefe über Frankreich' (1792–1793) von Johann Friedrich Reichardt." In *Reisen im 18. Jahrhundert: Neue Untersuchungen,* edited by Wolfgang Griep and Hans-Wolf Jäger, 224–40. Heidelberg: Universitätsverlag Winter, 1986.

Sterne, Laurence. *The Life and Opinions of Tristram Shandy,* edited by Graham Petrie. Harmondsworth, UK: Penguin, 1967.

Sternfeld, Frederick W. *The Birth of Opera.* New York: Oxford University Press, 1993.

————. "Orpheus, Ovid, and Opera." *Journal of the Royal Musical Association* 113, no. 2 (1988): 172–202.

Stewart, Gordon M. "Christoph Daniel Ebeling, Hamburger Pädagoge und Litera-turkritiker, und seine Briefe an Charles Burney." *Zeitschrift des Vereins für hamburgische Geschichte* 61 (1975): 33–58.

————. *The Literary Contributions of Christoph Daniel Ebeling.* Amsterdam: Rodopi, 1974.

Stewart, Susan A. *On Longing: Narratives of the Miniature, the Gigantic, the Souvenir, the Collection.* Durham, N.C.: Duke University Press, 1993.

Stillman, Amy Ku'uleialoha. Himene Tahiti: Ethnoscientific and Ethnohistorical Per-spectives on Choral Singing and Protestant Hymnody in the Society Islands, French Polynesia. PhD diss., Harvard University, 1991.

Stokes, Martin, ed. *Ethnicity, Identity, and Music: The Musical Construction of Place.* Pro-vidence, R.I.: Berg, 1997.

Storck, Karl. *Musik und Musiker in Karikatur und Satire: Eine Kulturgeschichte der Musik aus dem Zerrspiegel von Dr. Karl Storck.* Oldenburg: Gerhard Stalling, 1910. Reprint, Laaber: Laaber Verlag, 1998.

Stoye, John Walter. *English Travellers Abroad, 1604–1667.* London: Jonathan Cape, 1952.

Strunk, Oliver, ed. *Source Readings in Music History,* revised and edited by Leo Treitler. New York: Norton, 1998.

Suchalla, Ernst, ed. *Briefe von Carl Philipp Emanuel Bach an Johann Gottlob Immanuel Breitkopf und Johann Nikolaus Forkel.* Tutzing: Hans Schneider, 1985.

Sulzer, Johann Georg. *Allgemeine Theorie der schönen Künste, in einzeln, nach alphabetischer Ordnung der Kunstwörter auf einander folgenden, Artikeln.* Leipzig: Weidemanns Erben und Reich, 1771–1774. Reprint, Hildesheim: Georg Olms, 1969.

Süskind, Patrick. *On Love and Death,* translated by Anthea Bell. New York: Overlook/Rookery, 2006.

Sykes, J. B., ed. *The Concise Oxford Dictionary of Current English.* New York: Oxford University Press, 1982.

Tacitus, Cornelius. *A treatise on the situation, manners, and inhabitants of Germany; and the life of Agricola,* translated by John Aikin. Warrington, UK: Printed by W. Eyres for J. Johnson, 1777.

Thomas, Nicholas. *Colonialism's Culture: Anthropology, Travel, and Government.* Princeton, N.J.: Princeton University Press, 1994.

———. *Cook: The Extraordinary Voyages of Captain James Cook.* New York: Walker, 2003.

———. *In Oceania.* Durham, N.C.: Duke University Press, 1997.

Thompson, E. P. "Rough Music." In *Customs in Common.* New York: New Press/Norton, 1991.

Thompson, James. *Models of Value: Eighteenth-century Political Economy and the Novel.* Durham, N.C.: Duke University Press, 1996.

Thornton, Bonnell. *An ode on Saint Cæcilia's Day, Adapted to the Ancient British Musick. As it was performed on the Twenty-second of November.* London: Printed for J. and J. Rivington, and C. Corbet, 1749.

Thouret, Georg. *Katalog der Musiksammlung auf der Königlichen Hausbibliothek im Schlosse zu Berlin.* Leipzig: Breitkopf and Härtel, 1895.

Todorov, Tzvetan. *The Conquest of America: The Question of the Other,* translated by Richard Howard. New York: Harper Perennial, 1992.

Tomlinson, Gary. *Metaphysical Song: An Essay on Opera.* Princeton, N.J.: Princeton University Press, 1999.

———. *Music in Renaissance Magic: Toward a Historiography of Others.* Chicago: Chicago University Press, 1993.

———. *The Singing of the New World: Indigenous Voice in the Era of European Contact.* New York: Cambridge University Press, 2007.

Towner, John. *An Historical Geography of Recreation and Tourism in the Western World 1540–1940.* New York: Wiley, 1996.

Trevor-Roper, Hugh. "The Highland Tradition of Scotland." In *The Invention of Tradition,* edited by Eric Hobsbawm and Terence Ranger, 15–42. New York: Cambridge University Press, 1983.

Treue, Wilhelm. *Illustrierte Kulturgeschichte des Alltags.* Munich: R. Oldenbourg, 1952.

Troost, Linda. "William Shield." In *The New Grove Dictionary of Music and Musicians,* edited by Stanley Sadie and John Tyrell. London: Macmillan, 2002.

Trumpener, Katie. *Bardic Nationalism: The Romantic Novel and the British Empire.* Princeton, N.J.: Princeton University Press, 1997.

Turner, Katherine. *British Travel Writers in Europe 1750–1800.* Burlington, Vt.: Ashgate, 2001.

Twining, Thomas. *Recreations and Studies of a Country Clergyman of the Eighteenth Century, being selections from the correspondence of the Rev. Thomas Twining.* London: J. Murray, 1882.

Tytler, William. "Ueber die alten Schottischen Balladen und Lieder und die Schottische Musik überhaupt." *Bragur: Ein Litterarisches Magazin der Deutschen und Nordischen Vorzeit* 3 (1794): 120–201.

Unzer, Johann August. *Erste Gründe einer Physiologie der eigentlichen thierischen Natur thierischer Körper.* Leipzig: Weidmanns Erben und Reich, 1771.

———. "Von der Musik." *Der Arzt: Eine medicinische Wochenschrift* (1761): 161–76.

Valentini, Michael Bernhard. *Museum Museorum, oder Vollständige Schau-Bühne aller Materialien und Specereyen nebst deren natürlichen Beschreibung, Selection, Nutzen und Gebrauch.* Frankfurt am Main: Johann D. Zunner and J. A. Jungen, 1714.

Van der Zande, Johan. "Orpheus in Berlin: A Reappraisal of Johann Georg Sulzer's Theory of the Polite Arts." *Central European History* 56 (1995): 175–208.

van Orden, Kate. *Music, Discipline, and Arms in Early Modern France.* Chicago: University of Chicago Press, 2005.

Vazsonyi, Nicholas. "Hegemony through Harmony: German Identity, Music, and Enlightenment around 1800." In *Sound Matters: Essays on the Acoustics of Modern German Culture,* edited by Nora M. Alter and Lutz Koepnick, 33–48. New York: Berghahn, 2004.

Veit, Walter. "Goethe's Fantasies about the Orient." *Eighteenth-century Life: Exoticism and the Culture of Exploration* 26, no. 3 (2002): 164–80.

Vickers, Brian. "Analogy versus Identity: The Rejection of Occult Symbolism, 1580–1680." In *Occult and Scientific Mentalities in the Renaissance,* 95–163. New York: Cambridge University Press, 1984.

Vila, Anne C. *Enlightenment and Pathology: Sensibility in the Literature and Medicine of Eighteenth-century France.* Baltimore: Johns Hopkins University Press, 1998.

Virgil. *The Aeneid,* edited by W. F. Jackson Knight. Harmondsworth, UK: Penguin, 1956.

Viviès, Jean. *English Travel Narratives in the Eighteenth Century: Exploring Genres,* translated by Claire Davison. Burlington, Vt.: Ashgate, 2002.

Wackenroder, Wilhelm Heinrich. "Das merkwürdige musikalische Leben des Tonkünstlers Joseph Berglinger." In *Herzensergießungen eines kunstliebenden Klosterbruders.* Stuttgart: Philipp Reclam, 1979.

Wade, Bonnie C. *Thinking Musically: Experiencing Music, Expressing Culture.* New York: Oxford University Press, 2004.

Wagstaff, John. "Burney, Charles (1726–1814)." In *Oxford Dictionary of National Biography.* New York: Oxford University Press, 2004.

Walker, Mack. *German Hometowns: Community, State, and General Estate 1648–1871.* Ithaca, N.Y.: Cornell University Press, 1998.

Watson, Helen, David Wade Chambers, and the Yolngu community at Yirrkala. *Singing the Land, Signing the Land.* Geelong, Victoria, Australia: Deakin University Press, 1989.

Weber, Friedrich August. "Über den Einfluss des Singens auf die Gesundheit." *Allgemeine musikalische Zeitung* 6 (1803/1804): Columns 813–22.

———. "Von dem Einflusse der Musik auf den menschlichen Körper." *Allgemeine musikalische Zeitung* 4 (1801/1802): Columns 77–89, 93–99, 561–69, 609–17.

Weber, William. "The Intellectual Origins of Musical Canon in Eighteenth-century England." *Journal of the American Musicological Society* 47, no. 3 (1994): 488–520.

———. "Musical Culture and the Capital City: The Epoch of the *beau monde* in London, 1700–1870." In *Concert Life in Eighteenth-century Britain,* edited by Susan Wollenberg and Simon McVeigh, 71–92. Burlington, Vt.: Ashgate, 2004.

Wehinger, Brunhilde. " 'Wir müssen bestrebt sein, eine Brücke zu schlagen.' Madame de Staël unterwegs in Deutschland." In *Europäische Ansichten: Brandenburg-Preußen um 1800 in der Wahrnehmung europäischer Reisender und Zuwanderer,* edited by Iwan-Michelangelo D'Aprile, 231–50. Berlin: Berliner Wissenschafts-Verlag, 2004.

Wellek, René, and Alvaro Ribeiro, eds. *Evidence in Literary Scholarship: Essays in Memory of James Marshal Osborn.* New York: Oxford University Press, 1979.

Whaples, Miriam K. "Early Exoticism Revisited." In *The Exotic in Western Music,* edited by Jonathan Bellman, 3–25. Boston: Northeastern University Press, 1998.

———. Exoticism in Dramatic Music, 1600–1800. PhD diss., Indiana University, 1958.

[Wiedemann, Michael]. "[Anmerkungen zur Dichtung Fido, oder der unbesorgte Musicant]." *Historisch-poetische Gefangenschafften* (1689): 114–20.

Wilkes, Thomas. *A General View of the Stage.* London: J. Coote, 1762.

Williamson, Karina. "Christopher Smart." In *Oxford Dictionary of National Biography.* New York: Oxford University Press, 2004.

Wilson, Kathleen. *The Island Race: Englishness, Empire, and Gender in the Eighteenth Century.* New York: Routledge, 2003.

Winichakul, Thongchai. *Siam Mapped: A History of the Geo-body of a Nation.* Honolulu: Hawaii University Press, 1994.

Wolf, Eugene K. "Johann Wenzel Anton [Jan Waczlaw (Václav) Antonin (Antonín)] Stamitz." *Grove Music Online,* edited by L. Macy. http://www.grovemusic.com, s.v. "Stamitz" (accessed January 16, 2006).

Wong, Deborah. "Ethnomusicology and Difference." *Ethnomusicology* 50, no. 2 (Spring/Summer 2006): 259–79.

Wood, Marcus. "Satire." In *An Oxford Companion to the Romantic Age: British Culture 1776–1832,* edited by Iain McCalman, Jon Mee, Gillian Russell, and Clara Tuite, 689–91. New York: Oxford University Press, 1999.

Woodfield, Ian. *English Musicians in the Age of Exploration.* Stuyvesant, N.Y.: Pendragon 1995.

———. *Opera and Drama in Eighteenth-century London: The King's Theatre, Garrick, and the Business of Performance.* New York: Cambridge University Press, 2001.

———. *Salomon and the Burneys: Private Patronage and a Public Career.* Burlington, Vt.: Ashgate, 2003.

Wyndham, Neville. *Travels through Europe. Containing a geographical, historical, and topographical description of all the empires, kingdoms. Drawn from unerring sources of information. The whole digested into one uniform narrative. Interspersed with the editor's observations and improvements.* 4 vols. London: Printed for H. D. Symonds, [1790?].

Young, Arthur. *The farmer's letters to the people of England: Containing the sentiments of a practical husbandman, on various subjects of the utmost importance: Particularly the exportation of corn, emigrations to the colonies, &c. &c. &c. To which is added, Sylvæ: or, Occasional tracts on husbandry and rural öeconomics.* London: Printed for W. Nicholl, 1767.

———. *A six weeks tour, through the southern counties of England and Wales. Describing, particularly, I. The present state of agriculture and manufactures. II. The different methods of cultivating the soil. III. The success attending some late experiments on various grasses, &c. In several letters to a friend. By the author of the Farmer's letters.* London: W. Nicoll, 1768.

Z., A. "Ein Brief an den Herausgeber des Gentleman's Magazine. Aus dem Stück für den Monat Februar 1754, translated by C. D." *Hamburgisches Magazin* 14 (1755): 91–93.

Zantop, Susanne. *Colonial Fantasies: Conquest, Family, and Nation in Precolonial Germany, 1770–1870.* Durham, N.C.: Duke University Press, 1997.

Zimmermann, Heinrich. *Heinrich Zimmermanns von Wißloch in der Pfalz, Reise um die Welt, mit Captain Cook.* Amsterdam: N. Israel, 1973.

Zug, James, ed. *The Last Voyage of Captain Cook: The Collected Writings of John Ledyard.* Washington, D.C.: National Geographic, 2005.

Zunkel, Friedrich. "Ehre/Reputation." In *Geschichtliche Grundbegriffe: Historisches Lexikon zur politisch-sozialen Sprache in Deutschland,* vol. 2, ed. Otto Brunner, Werner Conze, and Reinhart Koselleck. Stuttgart: Klett, 1972.

Note: page numbers followed by *f* refer to figures; those followed by "n" indicate endnotes.

amateur musicians (*continued*)
Burney critiqued for considering, 66–67
See also dilettantism
The Ambassadors (Holbein), 80
Ambros, August Wilhelm, 115–116, 198n150
Amiot, Joseph-Marie, 79, 83
Amsterdam, 59–60
ancient vs. modern music, 64, 119
Anderson, Benedict, 34, 42, 183n94
Anderson, William, 195n106
André, Naomi, 202n70
Angermüller, Rudolph et al., 183n95, 185n126
animal
concerts, 157–159, 160, 205n132, 205n135
cruelty, 157
as term of invective, 162
See also listeners and listening
anthropologists, 20, 78
anti-Orphic discourse
overview, 121–127
alterity, problem of, 165–167
castrati and, 159, 160–165
curative music and scientism, 155–160
Jodrell's *A Widow and No Widow*, 128–130
margins, 127, 148–155
in O'Keeffe and Shield's *Omai*, 130–135, 131f, 132f, 134f, 135f, 200n34
parodies as culturally constitutive, 163–164
travel parody, role of, 127–128
See also Musical Travels thro' England (Bicknell)
anti-Semitism, 132, 163
antiquity, legacy for Enlightenment, 7, 14, 35–37, 76, 83, 94, 108, 111–112, 121–122, 150
Antwerp, 48–50
Aotourou (Putaveri), 58, 187n192
apodemics (travel instructions)
overview, 46–48
Royal Society guidelines for navigators, 88
variation in, 185n135
by Young, 62, 187n211
Apollo, 95
Applegate, Celia, 14, 178n6, 180n38, 184n122, 184n124
Aravamudan, Srinivas, 178n12, 179n36
Archer, Christian I., 201n36

Argonaut, Orpheus as, 11–14, 61
Argonauts of the Western Pacific (Malinowski), 20
Arnold, Denis, 201n45
Asclepiades, 180n50
Ashcroft, Bill, 21, 179n33
Askew, Kelly, 184n124
astronomy, 146–147
audiences
for cross-cultural exchange of music, 89
metropolitan, 125
See also listeners and listening
Augustan age of music, 58
Austin, John, 179n30, 192n44, 192n46
Austria, 41
authenticity vs. hybridity, 10, 114, 130, 153, 165
autoethnography, 21
autopsy. *See* eye- and earwitnessing
Aztecs, 87

Babcock, Barbara A., 126
Bach, Carl Philipp Emanuel, 16, 20, 33, 59, 169
Bach, Johann Christian, 3, 45
Bach, Johann Sebastian, 41, 56–57, 169, 170, 184n124
bagpipes, 88, 93–95, 107, 129
Bakhtin, M. M., 126, 199n13
ballad, 153, 167
Banks, Joseph, 37–38, 38f, 98, 193n61
Baretti, Giuseppe, 25, 31, 142
Barlow, J., 143f
Barlow, Jeremy, 199n4, 204n106
Barndt, Kerstin, 201n47
Barnouw, Dagmar, 191n16
Baroque view of music, 119
Barrington, Daines, 144
Barry, James, 5f
Barthes, Roland, 131–132
Bartolozzi, Francisco, 96f
Batchelor, Robert, 207n162
Batten, Charles L., Jr., 180n39
Beaglehole, J. C., 185n135
Beattie, James, 129
Beckford, Alexander, 145
beer fiddlers (*Schenkenvirtuosen*), 67, 154
Beer, Gillian, 201n39
Beethoven, Ludwig van, 41, 170, 171
Belgium, 48–50

German regional-national tension
  Burney on music and, 60
  Burney vs. Ebeling on, 17–19, 34, 70
  "national pride" and, 70–71
  Riesbeck on empire and, 40–41
German states and Germany
  British perceptions of, 3, 32–33, 154
  characterization of German music, 53,
    58, 60, 140, 172
  confessional divisions, 44, 163
  critiques of Polynesian music, 104–112
  ethnomusicology in, 79
  music education in, 54, 138–140
  perception of Britain, 31
  political and cultural fragmentation,
    40–42, 154
  reputation of, 15, 39, 172
  rise to musical prominence, 14–15, 172
  South Pacific power relations and,
    103–104
  spatial decentering and, 153
  symbolic capital of travel and, 26–27, 29
  as traveling nation, 27
  travels within, 39–41
  as *umstroke* (periphery), 31–34, 39
  See also cultural nation; nationalism;
    imperial discourse
gesture, 31, 37
Geyken, Frauke, 190n250
Giardini, Felice de, 136–137, 139, 141, 143,
    145, 162, 201n44, 203n82
gift giving
  goodwill and, 93–94
  music and, 94, 194n67
  trade goods, 94
Gikandi, Simon, 179n36
Gilroy, Paul, 167, 207n161
Gioia, Ted, 179n8
Giziello, Gioachino Conti, 164
Gluck, Christoph Willibald Ritter von, 6,
    46, 54–55, 121–122, 139, 169
Gmelin, Johann Georg, 192n42
Goethe, Johann Wolfgang von, 31, 182n79
Goehr, Lydia, 178n8, 207n9
Golden, Morris, 183n98
Goldsmith, Oliver, 18, 62
goodwill, 93–94, 103
gora (musical instrument), 149
Gossman, Lionel, 180n41
Göttingen, 26, 31

Gouk, Penelope, 205n127
Gramit, David, 78, 172, 191n24, 199n162
grand tour
  Boswell on, 23, 29
  commonality of elite experience through,
    180n41
  Germany as peripheral to, 31, 33
  insufficient interest in music, 177n4
  Keyssler's frontispiece and, 37
  motivations for, 23–25
  Nugent on, 25, 139
  Young, criticism of, 62
Grant, Kerry, 140, 169, 182n86, 185n128,
    188n220, 202n59
Graun, Carl Heinrich, 57, 58, 59, 60, 64
Graun, Johann Gottlieb, 58
Gray, Thomas, 46
Great Britain. *See* Britain
Grenville, Fulke, 180n44
Grétry, André-Ernest-Modeste, 48, 51, 56
Grewendorf, Günther, 192n45
Griffiths, Gareth, 21
Grundlage einer Ehrenpforte (Mattheson), 20
Guadagni, Gaetano, 52, 164, 199n3
Guthke, Karl S., 182n83
"gypsies," Bohemian, 53

Habermas, Jürgen, 182n84
haka, 87, 97
Hamburg, 16, 31, 44, 59, 140, 179n23
Hamilton, William, 25
Handel, George Frederic, 32, 59, 136, 143*f*,
    204n121
Hankins, Thomas, 205n133
Hannoverisches Magazin, 103, 105, 108, 109*f*,
    110
Hanover, 31
Hanoverian dynasty, 32, 154
Hanslick, Eduard, 115, 122, 198n149
Harmondshalgh, Desmond, 78
harmony. *See* counterpoint; polyphony
harmony of the spheres, 147, 165
Harris, Ellen T., 182n86, 187n199
Harrison, Frank, 191n22
Harrison, John, 92
Hasse, Faustina, 55
Hasse, Johann Adolf, 54–55, 56, 59, 60, 69,
    153, 170
Hawkesworth, John, 25
Hawkins, John, 14, 178n4

Noyes, John K., 179n26
Nugent, Thomas, 24, 25, 27, 139, 180n50

Obeyesekere, Gananath, 193n48
O'Brien, Karen, 179n21
observation
    Burney and, 61
    German critiques of Polynesian
        ethnomusicology, 106, 108–112
    Monthly Review author on, 114
"Ode on Saint Cæcilia's Day" (Thornton),
    152, 204n109, 204n111
Odell, Jay Scott, 204n104
Odysseus, 76, 77f, 116, 156
O'Keeffe, John, 130–135
Omai. *See* Mai
Omai or, a Trip round the World (O'Keeffe and
    Shield), 130–135, 131f, 132f, 134f,
    135f, 200n34, 201n35
ontological relationship of travel and
    music, 12
opera
    Bicknell on, 148, 151, 155
    Burney on Germany and, 46, 48, 57
    class and, 163, 166
    comparison between French and Italian,
        58
    Duke of Württemberg's enthusiasm for,
        46, 51–52
    by Gluck, 6, 55
    Italian opera in Britain, 141–142, 159,
        166
    in Jodrell's *A Widow and No Widow*, 128,
        130
    Marischal on, 57–58
    in *Remarkable Trial of the Queen of Quavers*,
        162
    satires of Italian opera, 123*See also* castrati
O'Quinn, Daniel, 200n34, 201n38
orchestral music in Mannheim, 51, 67, 139
Orfeo ed Euridice (Gluck), 55, 122, 122f
Orphée charmant les animaux (Anon.), 8f
*Orpheus, oder die wunderbare Beständigkeit der
    Liebe* (Telemann), 59
Orpheus among the Thracians (Orpheus Pain-
    ter), 12f
Orpheus before Pluto and Persephone (Perrier),
    13f
Orpheus's Beastly Listeners (mosaic at Paphos),
    175

Orphic discourse and Orpheus
    aesthetic autonomy and, 72, 174
    Argonaut, Orpheus as, 11–14, 72
    British cultural crisis and, 166–167
    Burney and, 14, 72, 143
    cross-cultural encounters and, 80–81,
        85, 119
    as ethical paradigm, 9–10
    female, 152
    German vs. British framing of, 72
    Handel as Orpheus, 59
    as harmonizing force, 192n30
    Herder on, 75
    Horace on, 177n9
    margins and, 10, 116, 148, 165–166
    Marpurg on, 75
    music as socially constitutive vs.
        destructive, 7, 8f, 9–10, 108, 148,
        156, 165, 170–171, 174–175
    myth of Orpheus, 7–9, 11–12, 121
    Neoplatonism and, 6–7, 143
    as paradigm for ethnomusicological and
        music sociological approaches, 72, 170
    Polynesian polyphony and, 99, 116
    power of music in, 6, 9, 20, 73, 81, 116
    as promotion of serious music, 9, 72, 75,
        171–172
    Romanticism and, 171–172
    as self-reflexive gesture for music
        scholarship, 9
    South Pacific power relations and, 104,
        116
    tested by travel, 10, 75, 78, 86, 94, 99,
        108, 119, 140
    violence and, 9–10, 16, 73, 94, 99,
        103–104, 116–117, 118f, 119
    as vulnerable listener, 117, 118f, 119, 174
    See also agential power of music;
        anti-Orphic discourse; Neoplatonism;
        performative use of music
Ossian (Macpherson), 94
Osterhammel, Jürgen, 181n65
Other and otherness. *See* alterity
Outram, Dorinda, 191n16
Ovid, 9, 121, 148

paean, 72, 81, 144, 152
Palatinate, 50–51
Pallas, Peter Simon, 83–84
pan-European relations, deemphasis of, 33

pan-generic approach, 124, 125
panpipes, 95, 112. *See also* instruments, musical
pantomime, 131, 200n34, 201n38. *See also Omai or, a Trip round the World* (O'Keeffe and Shield)
Paride ed Elena (Gluck), 55
Parke, William, 24
parody. *See* anti-Orphic discourse
patrons, Burney's pandering to, 53
Paumgartner, Bernhard, 188n218
Pauw, Cornelius de, 107–108
peasants, 53, 67, 115
Pederson, Sanna, 172, 185n140, 207n17
Peitsch, Helmut, 181n60, 182n81, 188n221
Pennant, Thomas, 94, 194n78
pentatonicism, 88
Pepusch, J. C., 205n132
performative use of music
    Burke on, 193n52
    cross-cultural encounter and hermeneutics, 86–89
    Polynesian polyphony and, 116
    starting mechanism and, 92
    theorization of, 86–87
    Tongan contest and power relations, 99–104
    See also agential power of music; Orphic discourse
performers, 3, 7
Peri, Jacopo, 6
periphery. *See* margins; terra incognita
Perrier, François, 13*f*
Perry, Ruth, 204n113
Petty, Frederick Curtis, 199n9, 202n72
Philip V, 204n122
Phillips, Molesworth, 113, 193n60
Phillips, Susanna (née Burney), 91, 113, 193n60
Philosophical Transactions, 114, 131
Pindar, Peter. *See* Wolcot, John
Piozzi, Hester Lynch, 178n10, 205n137
plagiarism and parody, 155
Plato, 58, 147
Pliny, 39, 183n103
Plutarch, 206n158
Pococke, Richard, 34
Poland, 19, 41, 179n24
Polynesians and Polynesian music
    Admiralty's musician marines and, 90–92

Banks and, 193n61
Burney and Sandwich on, 90, 113–115, 193n57, 193n60
elements associated with, 130–131
ethnographic collections, 3, 37–38*f*, 74
European interest in, 6, 37–38, 76–78, 104–105
German critiques, 104–112
Hanslick on, 115
hierarchical ordering of, 105, 107
impact on Western music, 173–174, 208n24
Koch on, 112
later commentators, 115–116
polyphony, 97–99, 110, 113, 114–115, 116–117, 130–131, 173–174, 195n82
universal history and, 112
See also Cook's second voyage (1772–1775); exoticization and the exotic; Maori and Maori music; Tahitians and Tahitian music; Tongans and Tongan music
polyphony
    "accidental," 198n151
    Ambros on, 115–116
    Bach and, 56–57
    of Bohemian peasants, 53–54
    Burney's quest for origins of, 50, 79, 89–90
    Polynesian, 97–99, 110, 113, 114–115, 116–117, 130–131, 173–174, 195n82
poor scholars *(Singschüler),* 50, 52, 56, 69, 139
Poovey, Mary, 68, 189n239, 189n241
Porter, Roy, 183n101
Potsdam, 57–59, 64, 73
Potter, Pamela, 14, 178n6, 184n122
power of music. *See* agential power of music; Neoplatonism; Orpheus and Orphic discourse; performative use of music
Prague, 3, 41, 55–56, 139
Pratt, Mary Louise, 21, 179n33
Price, Curtis Alexander, 199n9, 203n82
prodigies, 138, 140
professionalization, 9, 45, 63, 68, 104, 105, 111, 154, 159
Protestantism in Saxony, 56
provincial towns and cities in Bicknell's *Musical Travels,* 149–151
Prussia, 19, 73–74

Puff, Helmut, 179n7, 190n248
Putaveri (Aotourou), 58, 187n192
Pythagoras, 147

Quantz, Johann Joachim, 46, 57, 58, 59, 64
Qureshi, Regula Burckhardt, 191n23

race
   music and, 119
   in O'Keeffe and Shield's *Omai,* 134, 200n34
Radano, Ronald, 195n98
Rainbow, Bernarr, 201n43
Reichardt, Johann Friedrich, 65–69, 169, 172–173, 188n230, 189n245, 190n249
Reil, Johann Christian, 158
Reisecolleg ("Travel College") course, Göttingen University, 26
relativism
   aesthetic judgment and, 83
   Bicknell on, 150–151
   Jodrell on, 129
   Klockenbring and, 106
The Remarkable Trial of the Queen of Quavers (Anon.), 161–162, 164
Reynolds, Joshua, 25
Rhineland, 50–51
Ribeiro, Alvaro, 186n156, 201n44
Richards, Robert J., 205n135
Riesbeck, Johann Kaspar, 39–41, 44, 71
Riley, Matthew, 191n14, 207n11
Ring, Pieter de, 80–81, 82f
Robinson, Jenefer, 179n8
Robson-Scott, W. D., 182n81
Rochlitz, Friedrich, 94, 119
Roger, N. A. M., 194n64
Romanticism, 170, 171
Rosselli, John, 185n129
Rossiter, Thomas, 90
rough music (charivari; *Katzenmusik; skimmington*), 151–152, 158
Rousseau, Jean-Jacques, 28, 73, 98–99, 140
Rousseau, G. S., 183n101
Royal Society, 46, 88, 158
Rowland, Peter, 205n131
Rumph, Stephen, 178n7
Russia, 19, 41, 85
Russian Academy of Sciences, 83

Sacchini, Antonio Maria Gasparo, 51
Sackbut, Fustian. *See* Thornton, Bonnell
Sahlins, Marshall, 87, 92, 193n48, 194n67, 194n70
Said, Edward, 22, 179n34, 181n65
Saint Cæcilia, 152
Salieri, Antonio, 56
Salmond, Anne, 21, 179n33, 196n108
Salomon, John Peter, 202n58
Sands, Mollie, 202n72
Sandwich, John Montagu, fourth Earl of
   Bicknell's *Musical Travels* and, 144–145, 154, 161
   Burney's acknowledgment of, 193n59
   Churchill's satire of, 203n81
   friendship with Burney, 90
   on James Burney, 195n87
   Polynesian music and, 193n60
   on polyphony, 114–115, 198n151
Sanssouci, 58
satirical music in Kamchatka, 84–86. *See also* anti-Orphic discourse
Saxony, 56
Scheibe, Johann Adolph, 20
Schenkenvirtuosen (beer fiddlers), 67, 154
Schiller, Friedrich von, 173
Schlemmer, Ulrich, 184n113
Schlözer, August Ludwig, 26, 71
Schmeling, Gertrud Elisabeth, 57
Schneider, Ute, 179n24
Scholes, Percy Alfred, 189n245
Schopenhauer, Arthur, 143
Schott, Caspar, 157
Schubart, Christian Daniel Friedrich, 14, 46, 70, 169, 171
Schwetzingen, 51
Siegmund-Schultze, Walther, 190n249
sciences, Burney on German state of, 60
scientism, 147, 159–160
Scottish music, 88, 93–95, 107. *See also* Highlanders
Scrivener, Michael, 179n21
Seeba, Hinrich C., 180n38
Seed, Patricia, 193n49
Segalan, Victor, 78, 191n21
Seipel, Wilfried, 192n32
semiotics, cross-cultural, 87–88
Senesino [Bernardi, Francesco], 143f
Seume, Johann Gottfried, 40, 71

Winichakul, Thongchai, 34, 183n94

Williamson, Karina, 205n137

Wilson, Kathleen, 182n89

Wöchentliche Nachrichten und Anmerkungen die Musik betreffend (Hiller), 20, 45

Wolcot, John, 127

Wood, Marcus, 199n2

Woodfield, Ian, 86, 161, 180n46, 192n43, 199n11, 205n141, 205n141

Wong, Deborah, 208n27

Wordsworth, William, 16, 155

Wray, F. A., 201n45

Württemberg, 50–51, 64

Württemberg, Duke of, 46, 52, 161

Wyndham, Neville, 189n237

xenophobia, 142, 162, 163

Yates, Mary Ann, 161

Yates, Richard, 161

Young, Arthur, 62, 66, 187n211

Zantop, Susanne, 179n25

Zémire et Azor (Grétry), 51

Zum ewigen Frieden (Kant), 18

Zunkel, Friedrich, 181n69